ORGANIZING KNOWLEDGE

An Introduction to Managing Access to Information

Third Edition

Jennifer Rowley and John Farrow

ASHGATE

First edition published in 1987, second edition 1992, by Ashgate Publishing Limited.

The edition published by
Gower Publishing Limited

Reprinted 2002, 2004, 2005 by
Ashgate Publishing Limited
Gower House
Croft Road
Aldershot
Hampshire GU11 3HR
England

Ashgate Publishing Limited
Suite 420
101 Cherry Street
Burlington, VT 05401-4405
USA

Ashgate website:http://www.ashgate.com

British Library Cataloguing in Publication Data

Rowley, J. E. (Jennifer E), 1950–
   Organizing knowledge : an introduction to managing access
   to information. – 3rd ed.
   1. Information storage and retrieval systems – Management
   I. Title   II. Farrow, John
   025.5′24

ISBN 0 566 08047 8

Printed in Great Britain by MPG Books Ltd, Bodmin, Cornwall

Contents

List of figures

Introduction

The opportunity to revise this text represented an opportunity to reconceptualize the way in which we think about the structures for the organization of knowledge. The first and second editions of this text were written at a time when although the significance of electronic databases was increasing, many of the applications of such databases were in relation to bibliographic, directory or factual databases and databanks. Today much more information, and many more documents are delivered in electronic form, and the Internet has had a significant effect on information and document delivery. Some have seen this evolution in relation to technology as being defined by the unit that is processed:

- Data – early computer systems managed data, in the form of structured records.
- Information – the next generation of systems concerned themselves with information, or using one definition of information, useful data, and there was an increase in user focus and the interpretation and presentation of data.
- Knowledge – the latest systems are concerned with knowledge, described in simple terms as information with structure and context.

It is important to remember that this gradual development of the application of information systems, in the direction of knowledge or knowledge-based systems, is only restricted to the application of computer systems and electronic databases. There have always been, and always will be, data, information and knowledge. Until recently, knowledge has resided in individuals' memories and understandings, and in printed documents. Authors, editors, referees, reviewers, abstractors, indexers and searchers have always contributed to the structuring of knowledge. We explore these issues further in Chapter 1.

Similarly, there has long been recognition that knowledge, both in the form of documents and in relation to the contents of documents, needs to be structured or organized. Some of the most seminal thinking in this field was conducted around one hundred years ago. Such structuring is at the heart of processes associated with:

- Understanding and cognition – we learn by comparing concepts with one another and understanding relationships between ideas. New concepts are integrated with reference to concepts that we already hold in our memory. Authors and others who create knowledge representations organize information at the micro level in order to help others to understand and learn.
- Finding information or knowledge – as the quantity of knowledge has grown, so it has become increasingly important to develop tools for finding information and knowledge within a store or collection of information.

This book is primarily concerned with the tools that have been developed and used for finding knowledge, but in electronic environments these two processes are sometimes, but not always, intimately interlinked.

The transition to more databases and documents in electronic form has been accompanied by another significant trend, the increased use of networking to provide access to information resources and knowledge. This has been largely through the Internet and the World Wide Web (WWW), but networking within organizations through intranets and other networks has also been important. Ultimately this means that users have potential access to a wide range of information, but the challenge of location and selection of appropriate information becomes all the more significant. Tools such as search engines have been developed to assist users in this process. User experience of access to information is currently in a hybrid environment, which embraces both electronic and printed documents. These printed documents may be located in libraries or other collections, or may be acquired through bookshops and book suppliers. Organizations, also, still make use of print for reports, minutes of meetings and other applications.

The principles that underlie the structuring of knowledge in these various environments are common, although there are occasions on which the use of divergent terminology for the same concept but in different application areas may hinder transparency. This book seeks to identify and explain these principles, and the way in which they might be applied in different environments. The challenge facing the authors has been to strike an appropriate balance between extracting principles from their application in specific contexts in order that the reader can understand the key issues in the organization of knowledge, and giving a clear practical exposition which allows the reader to be able to apply principles in their different areas of application.

One factor that has not changed is the underlying choice in the organization of knowledge, in terms of where the responsibility for organization lies. Broadly there are three contributors to this process: creator, knowledge/information intermediary and user.

Creators, such as authors and publishers, have a responsibility to structure the documents which they create, but are generally not in a position to contribute to the organization of knowledge from a variety of different sources. Organization of knowledge must be managed by the users themselves, with or without the assistance of an information intermediary or knowledge agent. The information intermediary may create tools for the organization of knowledge. The fundamental dilemma that underlies many of the debates on the organization of knowledge is how many resources should be devoted to the creation of these tools in advance of, but in anticipation of, need and how much should be devoted to supporting the user at the point of need, or educating the user and designing user-friendly systems so that the user can navigate rather less structured knowledge mazes. This issue is revisited in a number of contexts later in the book.

The book is structured into four parts, and chapters are grouped into these parts. The first part, 'Information Basics', comprises two chapters which explore the nature of information and knowledge, and the various different ways in which they can be incorporated into documents. An understanding of the nature of information and knowledge is essential in understanding why, when and how structure might be imposed upon knowledge. The variety of different types of documents, and some of the common components of such documents, such as abstracts, titles and contents pages, are important in understanding the nature of documents and some of their inherent structure.

Part II focuses on the different ways in which documents can be described. These descriptions are used as the basis for records in bibliographic databases. Both the contents of records and record formats are described.

Part III focuses on the range of tools that can be applied in order to achieve access to information resources and knowledge bases. An understanding of the different types of users, the processes of indexing and searching, and the constraints and opportunities presented by different types of human computer interfaces is important in setting the context. There is a wide range of different types of indexing and searching languages, including alphabetical indexing languages and classification and systematic order. In addition, author names are important in catalogue and other databases; an introduction to the key rules in this area in the Anglo-American Cataloguing Rules is given.

Part IV is concerned with the systems contexts through which knowledge can be organized and accessed. Although there are many similarities between the different systems contexts, it is important to explore the unique features of say, compact disc read-only memory (CD-ROM), online search services, online public access catalogues (OPACs), and the Internet. And, finally, although the organization of knowledge is increasingly through a plethora of different computer-based tools, there remains a wide range of applications in which it is important to be able to organize printed documents, and to create and use printed indexes. These are briefly explored in Chapter 12.

Each chapter commences with an introduction which gives a clear view of the key issues covered within the chapter. Chapter coverage is revisited at the end of each chapter, in the chapter summary. Throughout the text key points are illustrated with the use of a range of different figures. Checklists are offered in places where a summary of features or factors can most effectively be summarized in such a form.

AUDIENCE

In common with the earlier editions of this book, this edition is written for undergraduate and postgraduate students of information management and library studies. It is intended to be an introductory textbook.

These students need to understand the searching process for two reasons. The first is that as information intermediaries and designers of information systems they themselves need to be exemplary searchers of information. Success in searching will not be achieved solely through the identification of an appropriate source, but also depends on skills in extracting the information from that source. The second reason is that they are likely to act as trainers in assisting others in effective information retrieval. Information retrieval, despite the plethora of information available to us, is not simple and requires considerable skill if the best information or document for the purpose is to be extracted.

ACKNOWLEDGEMENTS

It would be impossible to list all of those to whom the authors show some debt in the creation of this book. The ideas gathered here have been drawn from many authors, and represent a melding of the traditional contributors to the debates around cataloguing and classification, and the more recent enthusiasts who are members of the Internet generation. The authors would like to acknowledge all the publishers, authors and systems suppliers who have permitted them to make use of extracts from their works. These are individually acknowledged at the point at which they are included in this work. The honing of the ideas in this book has been undertaken with innumerable cohorts of students; their questions and difficulties in understanding have driven us to seek to think more clearly about the concepts in the area described as the Organization of Knowledge.

List of acronyms and abbreviations

Note: This is a list of the more common abbreviations and acronyms used in the text. It is not an exhaustive list.

AAAF	Anglo-American Authority File
AACR	Anglo-American Cataloguing Rules
ABN	Australian Bibliographic Network
ALA	American Library Association
ANSI	American National Standards Institute
ASCII	American Standard Code for Information Interchange
ASSIA	*Applied Social Sciences Index and Abstracts*
BC	(Bliss) Bibliographic Classification
BC2	(Bliss) Bibliographic Classification, 2nd edn
BIDS	Bath Information and Data Services
BL	British Library
BLAISE	British Library Automated Information Service
BLCMP	Birmingham Libraries Co-operative Mechanization Project
BNB	*British National Bibliography*
BT	broader term
BT (G)	broader term (generic}
BT (P)	broader term (partitive)
BTI	*British Technology Index*
CC	Colon Classification
CCF	Common Communications Format
CD	compact disc
CD-ROM	compact disc read-only memory
CIP	Cataloguing in Publication
CONSER	Conversion of Serials project

DBMS	database management system
DDC	Dewey Decimal Classification
DOS	disc operating system
DTD	document type definition
DVD	digital versatile disc
DVI	digital video interactive
EARL	Electronic Access to Resources in Libraries
EDD	Electronic data delivery
EIS	executive information systems
ERIC	Educational Resources Information Center
FID	Fédération Internationale d'Information et de Documentation
FTP	file transfer protocol
GUI	graphical user interface
HTML	Hypertext Markup Language
HTTP	hypertext transfer protocol
IFLA	International Federation of Library Association
IIB	Institut International de la Bibliographie
IP	Internet Protocol
ISBD	International Standard Bibliographic Description
ISBN	International Standard Book Number
ISDS	International Serials Data System
ISO	International Standards Organization
ISSN	International Standard Serial Number
IT	information technology
KWIC	keyword in context (index)
KWOC	keyword out of context (index)
LAN	local area network
LASER	London and South East Region
LC	Library of Congress
LCC	Library of Congress Classification
LCSH	Library of Congress Subject Headings
LMS	library management system
MARC	Machine-Readable Cataloguing
MeSH	Medical Subject Headings
MM-DBMS	multimedia database management system
NCSA	National Center for Supercomputer Applications
NSDC	National Serials Data Centre
NT	narrower term
NT (G)	narrower term (generic)
NT (P)	narrower term (partitive)

OCLC	Online Computer Library Center (originally Ohio College Online Computer Library Center)
OPAC	online public access catalogue
OSI	Open systems interconnection
PC	personal computer
PDF	portable document format
PIF Editor	Program information files editor
PRECIS	Preserved Context Index System
RLG	Research Libraries Group
RT	related term
SDI	Selective Dissemination of Information
SGM	Standard Generalized Markup Language
SISP	Strategic Information Systems Planning
SLIC	Selective Listing in Combination
SN	scope note
TCP/IP	transmission control protocol/Internet protocol
TT	top term
UDC	Universal Decimal Classification
UF	used for
UKMARC	United Kingdom MARC (format)
UNESCO	United Nations Educational, Scientific, and Cultural Organization
URL	Uniform Resource Locator
URN	Uniform Resource Number
USMARC	United States MARC (format)
VCR	video cassette recorder
WAN	wide area network
Web	World Wide Web
WWW	World Wide Web

Part I
Information Basics

1 Contexts for the organization of knowledge

INTRODUCTION

> Information is only valuable to the extent that it is structured. Because of a lack of structure in the creation, distribution and reception of information, the information often does not arrive where it is needed and, therefore, is useless.
>
> (Koniger and Janowitz, 1995, p. 6)

> In my 30-year professional career I can't remember a time when traditional LIS skills have been more vaunted by commmentators outside the profession. In an increasingly chaotic information world, the librarian as organiser, disseminator, selector, facilitator, and trainer is increasingly recognised.
>
> (Foster, 1999, p. 149)

This chapter emphasizes the significance of the organization of knowledge. It explores some of the contexts in which we organize knowledge, and considers the contribution of the organization of knowledge to the wider issue of knowledge management. At the end of this chapter you will:

- have considered the definition of knowledge and information
- appreciate some of the characteristics of knowledge that are important to its organization and use
- understand how the model of the 7 Rs of information management can be used to represent the processes associated with the creation and dissemination of knowledge and information
- appreciate the distinction between information processing, information management and knowledge management.

Information is all around us. Our senses collect and our brains filter and organize information every minute of the day. At a very fundamental level information colours our perceptions of the world around us, and thereby influences attitudes,

3

emotions and actions. Although the focus of this book is 'recorded knowledge' it is significant that the boundaries of 'recorded knowledge' are increasingly difficult to draw. For example, each product on the supermarket shelves carries 'recorded' information, concerning, say, its ingredients, its use, what it looks like and its value. At a more technologically sophisticated level, multimedia kiosks with information from *Gardening Which?* are made available in garden centres to support customers in the selection of garden products. Political parties and pressure groups seek to draw public attention to facts and figures that support their position or case. Planning documents are made available to facilitate local participation in decisions that affect the community. Television documentaries and historical dramas serve to enlighten us about the past and the present. Multimedia encyclopaedias include both text and information in other formats, such as sound and video. In all of these contexts, information shapes our perception of the society in which we live. Organizations collect data concerning the external market-place and internal processes and operations, which support the delivery of a quality product. Access to information is important in contributing to the quality of a manager's decision-making. The way in which decisions are communicated is an indicator of the culture of an organization, and is likely to impact on employee involvement, empowerment and motivation, which are recognized to be some of the foundations for quality management. It is not difficult to subscribe to the view that:

> Information is not merely a necessary adjunct to personal, social and organizational functioning, a body of facts and knowledge to be applied to the solution of problems or to support actions. Rather it is a central and defining characteristic of all life forms, manifested in genetic transfer, in stimulus response mechanisms, in the communication of signals and messages and, in the case of humans, in the intelligent acquisition of understanding and wisdom.
>
> (Kaye, 1995, p. 37)

Martin describes information as the lifeblood of society:

> Without an uninterrupted flow of the vital resource, society as we know it would quickly run into difficulties, with business and industry, education, leisure, travel, and communications, national and international affairs all vulnerable to disruption. In more advanced societies this vulnerability is heightened by an increasing dependence on the enabling powers of information and communications technologies.
>
> (Martin, 1995, p. 18)

This chapter commences with a consideration of some definitions of the terms 'information' and 'knowledge'. These definitions are used to identify the way in which our common understanding of these and related terms are intertwined. This is followed by a summary of the differing perspectives on the nature of information. There is a range of characteristics of information and knowledge that need to be considered in any approach to the organization of knowledge. The

7 Rs of information management is a model that identifies the stages in the creation and processing of information, and is useful in identifying the stages in which knowledge is structured. The chapter concludes with a short review of the essence of information processing, information management and knowledge management. Chapter 2 follows this broad exploration of the contexts for the organization of knowledge by exploring the various ways in which recorded knowledge is formatted into documents.

DEFINING INFORMATION AND KNOWLEDGE

A preliminary examination of some dictionary definitions of the concepts of 'information' and 'knowledge' serves as a starting-point. The *Oxford English Dictionary* (as quoted in Rowley, 1992, p. 4) provides a useful general definition:

> Information is informing, telling, thing told, knowledge, items of knowledge, news.

This definition uses the related term 'knowledge' to define 'information', so, in addition to making the observation that the two concepts are closely related, it might be useful to refer to the *Oxford English Dictionary*'s definition of 'knowledge':

> Knowledge is knowing, familiarity gained by experience; person's range of information; a theoretical or practical understanding of; the sum of what is known.

> (Rowley, 1992, p. 4)

The central significance of information has led many authors to seek to define the concept of 'information', and to better understand how information is, and might be, processed and managed. These contributions offer a variety of different perspectives, which can be summarized as five distinct definitions:

- information as subjective knowledge
- information as useful data
- information as a resource
- information as a commodity
- information as a constitutive force in society.

It is helpful to explain each of these concepts.

CONCEPTS OF INFORMATION

Information as subjective knowledge

The concept of information as subjective knowledge is the concept that has attracted most attention, both from early thinkers in the library and information field and from the cognitive sciences.

The *subjective knowledge* held in the mind of the individual may be viewed as being translated into *objective knowledge* through public expression, via speech and writing. The information profession is primarily concerned with this objective knowledge. In particular, they are primarily interested in *recorded knowledge* as it appears in documents. More recent commentators in the field of knowledge management have distinguished between explicit knowledge and tacit knowledge. *Explicit knowledge* might be viewed as equivalent to objective knowledge and a proportion of this explicit knowledge will be recorded in documents of various types. *Tacit knowledge* is the knowledge that is in the mind of the individual, and may be implicitly shared, probably through actions and shared ways of doing things within an organization.

Information as useful data

Another perspective on information can be gained by examining its relationship to data. This perspective derives primarily from the information systems literature, which is, agreed that 'Information is data processed for a purpose' (Curtis, 1989, p. 3) or 'Information is data presented in a form that is meaningful to the recipient' (Senn, 1990, p. 8). Senn continues:

> It must tell the recipient something that was not previously known or could not be predicted. In other words it adds to knowledge but must be relevant for the situation in which it will be applied. The lack of knowledge – that is, the absence of information about a particular area of concern – is uncertainty.
>
> (Ibid., p. 58)

Data is then, information that has undergone some processing and the results of that processing have been communicated for a particular purpose. If information is to be defined in terms of data – what then is data? Lester (1992) offers a simple perspective that is in line with other writers on information systems. He says:

> In a business organization, many events take place in the course of a single working day. When the facts about such events are recorded, they become data, and we can thus say that data is the raw facts concerning occurrences or happenings in a business ... raw data ... is too voluminous. A system is needed which will transform raw data into meaningful information.
>
> Lester, 1992. p. 191)

Information and knowledge as a resource

Many professional groups in organizations take an objective and instrumental view of information and knowledge that might be described as *information and knowledge as a resource*. This perspective holds that information is an objective resource, which is attainable and usable and which accordingly can be managed like other factors of production such as energy, raw materials and labour. Some proponents of knowledge management argue that knowledge is a key resource in determining competitive advantage and marketplace success in the know-ledge-based society. They have sought to develop approaches to valuing *knowledge as an asset*, and to recording that asset on the balance sheet of a business. It is important to remember, however, that information is distinct from the more traditional factors of production such as labour and raw materials, in the following respects:

- The value of information is not readily quantifiable – value depends on content and use, and, indeed, it may be argued that information as it rests in an electronic database has no inherent value.
- Consumption of information – information is not lost when it is given to others. Information is not sacrificed when it is given or sold to others.
- Dynamics of information – information is a dynamic force for change in the systems within which it operates and must be viewed within an organization as a formative organizational entity, rather than as an accumulated stockpile of facts. Information should influence decisions, affect what an organization does and how it does it and, ultimately, these actions and decisions will influence the information that is available for the next decision-making cycle.

Information as a commodity

Intellectual property laws, such as those associated with copyright are the precursors to a range of national and international laws and policies relating to trade in information and its associated goods and services. This has led to another view of information, that of *information as a commodity*. The concept of information as a commodity is wider than that of information as a resource, as it incorporates the exchange of information among people and related activi-ties as well as its use. The notion of information as commodity is tied closely to the concept of value as it progresses through the various steps of creation, processing, storage and use.

Information as a constitutive force in society

Braman (1989) identifies the wider perspective of *information as a constitutive force in society*. Definitions of this type view information as not just being embedded within a social structure, but also as an agent in the creation of that structure. It may be argued that information policy decisions are inevitably coloured by the view of a society and are inextricably linked with culture and values.

CHARACTERISTICS OF INFORMATION OR KNOWLEDGE

The exploration of the definition of knowledge and information in the previous section illustrates that there are multiple perspectives on the nature of knowledge and information. Knowledge, for example, cannot be organized and arranged like tins on the supermarket shelves (although books, which are one form in which knowledge is presented and through which information is disseminated, can be arranged on library shelves). Any discussions about the way in which knowledge or information can be managed, or structured, need to take into account a number of the characteristics of knowledge. These include objectivity, explicitness, currency, relevance, structure, and systems. We discuss each of these characteristics in turn.

Objectivity

The debate associated with the objectivity of knowledge is relevant to all types of knowledge and all disciplines. All knowledge is a product of the society and cultural environment in which it is created. However, the issue of objectivity has been most hotly debated in the social sciences. Social science researchers and knowledge users have been acutely aware of the difficulties associated with creating a shared reality, which could be regarded as valid and transferable objective knowledge. Science and technology, on the other hand, often investigates problems and environments where experiments can be repeated under similar conditions to give consistent results and what can be identified as objective knowledge. Related to the issue of objectivity are those of reliability and accuracy. *Accuracy* means that data or information is correct. *Reliability* implies that the information is a true indicator of the variable that it is intended to measure. Users often judge reliability of information on the basis of the reputation of the source from which it has been drawn.

Accessibility

Accessibility is concerned with the availability of knowledge to potential users. The distinction between implicit or tacit knowledge and explicit knowledge is relevant here. Tacit knowledge is subjective knowledge, which is owned by the individual or team. Most explicit knowledge is stored in the printed and electronic archives of societies (libraries) and organizations, and is, in general likely to be more accessible than tacit knowledge. However, the storage and communication media and the form and style of communication are also important. Knowledge may be stored and communicated via people, print or electronic media. A real challenge for most individuals and organizations is the integration of information that is presented in different formats. Also the form and style of communication needs to be amenable. The user's subject knowledge, environmental context, language used and preferences all influence the success with which a message is received.

Relevance

Knowledge available to an individual must be appropriate to the task in hand. Knowledge available to an organization must be relevant, or pertinent, to its current direction, vision and activities. Knowledge is relevant when it meets the user's requirements, and can contribute to the completion of the task in which the user is engaged, whether that task is decision-making, problem-solving or learning. Relevance can be assessed in relation to many of the other characteristics listed in this section, such as currency and accuracy, but may specifically be judged in terms of level of detail and completeness. *Completeness* is normally judged in relation to a specific task or decision; all of the material information that is necessary to complete a specific task must be available. In addition the level of detail, or *granularity*, of the information must match that required by the task and the user. We return to the concept of relevance and define a more specialized use of the term in Chapter 13.

Currency

Currency and life span of knowledge are important for two reasons – some information may supersede other information; the most current information is required, and outdated information needs to be discarded. Each type of information has its own *life cycle*. At one end of the time-scale there is a core of relatively stable knowledge for each discipline, such as the way in which the heart functions or the process for the refining of steel. Other information is outdated within hours. Examples include the weather report and international exchange rates. There is a real challenge in being able to recognize the positioning on a time-scale of specific knowledge and to be able to manage that knowledge in accordance with its life cycle. Users need to be presented with information that is still current, and collections of knowledge need to be weeded of redundant and outdated material.

Structure and organization

All knowledge has a structure. At the individual cognitive level, the brain holds associations between specific concepts. Structure is important to understanding. This cognitive structure is reflected in the way in which individuals' structure information in their communications in the form of verbal utterances, text and graphical representations. Some disciplines have inherent structures; biology, for example, is organized in accordance with a structure that reflects the structure of living matter, and documents on biology can be organized in a way that is consistent with this structure. Newspapers, similarly group information into categories such as news, politics and sport. The two important features of this structure are:

- the way in which items are grouped into categories
- the relationships between these categories.

Systems

Structure is often imposed by systems, whether those systems are conceptual frameworks, communication systems or information systems. Knowledge will be communicated through information systems and stored in information systems. Such systems embrace people and hardware and software. The central theme of this book is the systems for the organization of knowledge. These systems need to be designed in order to achieve effective and efficient information retrieval. Such systems include printed indexes, card indexes, databases, OPACs, Web browsers and search engines.

THE 7 RS OF INFORMATION MANAGEMENT

Figure 1.1 is intended as a summary of the processes that contribute to information processing and the creation of knowledge. The significance of this model for this book is that knowledge or information is being organized, or structure is being imposed, during each of these processes. Information management as a discipline must be concerned with the management of all of these processes, although the professional group who describe themselves as information managers, or perhaps knowledge managers, are more involved with some of these processes than others. Some of these processes are performed by individuals, whilst others are performed by organizations, or, in some cases, information professionals on behalf of organizations. On the left-hand side of the model in Figure 1.1 are the processes that the individual performs in information management. On the right-hand side are processes performed by organizations. The completion of all these processes may be supported by systems, but this will more evidently be the case in respect of those processes that are organizationally based. The relationships between the processes on the left-hand side of Figure 1.1 and those on the right-hand side are many to many. In other words, an individual may interact with the information management processes of many organizations and, on the other hand, any one organization will draw on the contribution of many individuals in the management of its knowledge base. It is the nature of this many-to-many relationship that poses some of the most significant challenges to information management. Perhaps, in passing it may be worthwhile to comment that Figure 1.1 does not explicitly identify the role of those responsible for the systems that facilitate each of the processes. Importantly, however, Figure 1.1 does emphasize that information and knowledge management involves a series of stages in a cycle.

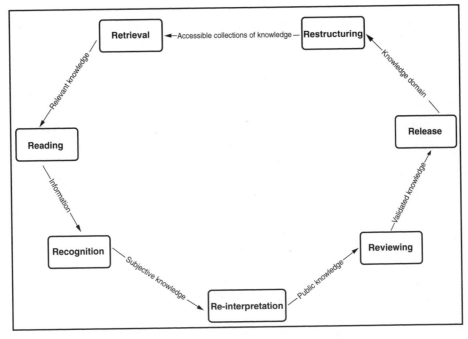

Figure 1.1 The 7 Rs of information management

Relevant knowledge	Reading	Information
Information	Recognition	Subjective knowledge
Subjective knowledge	Reinterpretation	Public knowledge
Public knowledge	Reviewing	Validated knowledge
Validated knowledge	Release	Knowledge domain
Knowledge domain	Restructuring	Resource bank
Resource bank	Retrieval	Relevant knowledge

Figure 1.2 Inputs and outputs in the 7 Rs of information management

Perhaps the best way to explain the processes that comprise the information management cycle in more detail is to examine the inputs and outputs from each of these processes. Figure 1.2 summarizes the inputs and outputs from each of the processes.

Starting with the Reading process, the cycle in Figure 1.1 works like this:

1. A person *Reads* a collection of relevant *knowledge* recorded in both electronic and printed documents. They may also absorb other inputs from the external environment, or real-world data, using a range of data collection methodologies.

2. Once read, the relevant knowledge becomes *information* which is absorbed into the cognitive framework of the individual. This statement implies a definition of information as subjective knowledge. Other definitions of information exist and may be attractive to some audiences. The use adopted here allows a clear differentiation between knowledge and information, and relates both of these concepts to one of the 7 Rs. This process of *Recognition* is concerned with matching the concepts in the user's cognitive framework with those in the document that is read. Recognizing is concerned with converting information into *subjective knowledge*.

3. *Reinterpretation* is concerned with the conversion of knowledge into a form that can be easily communicated, such as in a document. Although documents might be the primary concern of information managers, it is important to remember that public utterances can also be in verbal or graphical form. We describe this knowledge as *public knowledge*.

4. *Review*, or evaluation, is concerned with the conversion of public knowledge into *validated knowledge*. This process is conducted through the various channels that filter communications from individuals, at some stage in its process to the entry of validated knowledge. Typical activities concerned with validation include reviewing, refereeing, listing, and other processes for evaluating public knowledge.

5. *Release* or distribution is concerned with making public knowledge available within the community, organization or market-place that might find it to be of value. Once validated knowledge has been released, it enters the *knowledge domain* upon which individuals, organizations and communities can draw. Release for documents is typically in the form of publication, but other public announcements can also be made through, say, television, cinema, and other information media.

6. Organizations will interact with this knowledge domain, select items from it and collect or provide routes of access to a subject in the knowledge domain that they judge to be of specific interest in meeting their objectives. Processing that might be involved here might be data warehousing, indexing, and physical arrangement of printed documents. This may take place in libraries, document collections and document management systems. All such processes can be said to broadly fit into the category of *restructuring* of knowledge to meet a specific purpose. This *collection of knowledge* will be supplemented within organizations by information that emerges from the collection of *transaction-based data*, such as sales data, within the organization.

7. This accessible collection of knowledge will then be used by individuals as a *resource* from which they can *Retrieve* relevant knowledge. Users will approach this collection with individual objectives, and seek to differentiate between *relevant knowledge* and *rubbish* as defined by their specific objectives.

8. Relevant knowledge, once retrieved, must be *Read* before the knowledge recorded in documents of various types can be converted into information and the cycle can recommence.

The cycle in Figure 1.1 shows the stages in the order in which they are often encountered. However, the processes may occur in alternative orders. For example, Review may occur, before or after Release. If the stages are switched, then the inputs and outputs to the processes need to be adjusted accordingly. In addition, there are, of course, many subprocesses within each of the processes identified in this model. Restructuring is particularly concerned with the collection of knowledge in libraries, document collections and databases, and the structuring of these collections of knowledge. This is the primary focus of this book. Such collections are, however, of no value unless individuals use them to retrieve knowledge, and it is therefore also important to consider the Retrieval stage, which is concerned with information retrieval.

INFORMATION PROCESSING, INFORMATION MANAGEMENT AND KNOWLEDGE MANAGEMENT

There is a sense in which all members of knowledge-based society and the organizations within that society engage in information management and the organization of knowledge. Here we seek to differentiate between:

- information processing which is conducted by all members of a knowledge-based society
- information management which is concerned with managing information on behalf of others, within an organization or a community, and is primarily the domain of the professional information manager
- knowledge management which is concerned with creating organizations and societies in which subjective, tacit knowledge can be converted into objective knowledge and shared in the pursuit of communal or organizational objectives, and is the domain of politicians, chief executives and senior managers.

The structuring and organizing of information and knowledge is performed in all three of information processing, information management and knowledge management. The agents involved in the structuring and organization differ, and it is useful to recognize the basic differences between the roles of these different parties.

INFORMATION PROCESSING

Information processing is doing something to information to make it into something else. Curtis (1989), for example identifies the following as types of information processing:

- classification of data
- rearranging/sorting data
- summarizing/aggregating data
- performing calculations on data
- selection of data.

Information processing might then be viewed as an activity common to all information users. As a society or organization becomes increasingly knowledge based, the extent of individual involvement in these processes and the expertise required of individuals in their execution increases.

14

INFORMATION MANAGEMENT

Information management is concerned with the promotion of organizational (and possibly societal) effectiveness through the enhancement of the capabilities of the organization in coping with the demands of its internal and external environments in dynamic as well as stable conditions. Fairer-Wessels is more specific about the processes that this involves:

> Information management is viewed as the planning, organising, directing and controlling of information within an open system (i.e. organisation). Information management is viewed as using technology (e.g. computers, information systems, IT [information technology]) and techniques (e.g. information auditing/mapping) effectively and efficiently to manage information resources and assets from internal and external sources for meaningful dialogue and understanding to enhance pro-active decision making and problem solving to achieve aims and objectives on a personal, operational, organisational and strategic level of the organisation for competitive advantage and to improve the performance of the system and to raise the quality of life of the individual (by teaching him/her information skills, of which information management is one, to become a global citizen).
>
> (Fairer-Wessels, 1997, p. 99)

Information managers are professionals who act as agents on behalf of information processors to create and continuously improve systems, so that information processors are better able to meet their objectives. Information managers need to be able to understand and interpret these objectives in the context of the resources available to them. The structuring of knowledge is a key role for information managers, and there will be a continuing need for professionals who can perform this structuring on behalf of others, either through systems and knowledge design, or through support to searchers.

KNOWLEDGE MANAGEMENT

Knowledge management is concerned with the exploitation and development of the knowledge assets of an organization with a view to furthering the organization's objectives. The knowledge to be managed includes both explicit, documentary knowledge and tacit or subjective knowledge, which resides in the minds of employees. Knowledge management embraces all of the processes associated with the identification, sharing and creation of information. Successful knowledge management requires systems for the management of knowledge repositories, and to cultivate and facilitate the sharing of knowledge and organizational learning. Knowledge management projects focus on one or more of the following four objectives:

1. *To create knowledge repositories*, which store both knowledge and infor-

mation, often in documentary form. A common feature is 'added value' through categorization and pruning.

2. *To improve knowledge access*, or to provide access to knowledge or to facilitate its transfer among individuals; here the emphasis is on connectivity, access and transfer, and technologies such as videoconferencing systems, document scanning and sharing tools and telecommunications networks are central to this objective.

3. *To enhance the knowledge environment* so that the environment is conducive to more effective knowledge creation, transfer and use. This involves tackling organizational norms and values as they relate to knowledge.

4. *To manage knowledge as an asset*, and to recognize the value of knowledge to an organization. Assets, such as technologies that are sold under licence or have potential value, customer databases and detailed parts catalogues are typical of companies' intangible assets to which a value can be assigned.

SUMMARY

Information and knowledge are the lifeblood of organizations and society, but to be useful they need to be structured and organized. This chapter commences with a consideration of some definitions of the terms 'information' and 'knowledge'. These are used to identify the way in which our common understanding of these and related terms are intertwined. This is followed by a summary of the differing perspectives on the nature of information. The following characteristics of information and knowledge need to be considered in any approaches to the organization of knowledge: objectivity, accessibility, relevance, currency, structure and organization, and systems. The 7 Rs of information management is a model which identifies the stages in the creation and processing of information, and is useful in identifying the stages in which knowledge is structured. Information and knowledge may be structured and organized through information processing, information management and knowledge management.

REFERENCES AND FURTHER READING

Allee, V. (1997) 12 principles of knowledge management. *Training and Development*, **51** (11), November, 71–5.

Blackler, F. (1995) Knowledge, knowledge work and organisations: an overview and interpretation. *Organisation Studies*, **16** (6), 1021–46.

Braman, S. (1989) Defining information: an approach for policymakers. *Telecommunications Policy*, **13** (3), 233–42.

Brookes, B. C. (1974) Robert Fairthorne and the scope of information science. *Journal of Document-ation*, **30** (2), June, 139–52.

Buckland, M. (1991) Information as a thing. *Journal of the American Society for Information Science*, **42** (5), 351–60.

Butcher, D. R. and Rowley, J. E. (1998) The 7 R's of information management. *Managing Information*, **5** (2), March, 34–6.

Choo, C. W. (1996) The knowing organisation: how organisations use information to construct meaning, create knowledge and make decisions. *International Journal of Information Management*, **16** (5), 329–40.

Cronin, B. and Davenport, E. (1991) *Elements of Information Management*. Lanham, MD: Scarecrow Press.

Curtis, G. (1989) *Business Information Systems: Analysis, Design and Practice*. Wokingham: Addison-Wesley.

Davenport, T. H., DeLong, D. W. and Beers, M. C. (1998) Successful knowledge management projects. *Sloan Management Review*, **39** (2), Winter, 43–57.

Davenport, T. H. and Prusak, L. (1998) *Working Knowledge: Managing What your Organisation Knows*. Boston: Harvard Business School Press

Demarest, M. (1997) Understanding knowledge management. *Journal of Long Range Planning*, **30** (3), 374–84.

Eaton, J. J. and Bawden, D. (1991) What kind of resource is information? *International Journal of Information Management*, **11**, 156–65.

Fairer-Wessels, F. A. (1997) Information management education: towards a holistic perspective. *South African Journal of Library and Information Science*, **65** (2), 93–102.

Fairthorne, R. A. (1965) Use and mention in the information sciences. In *Proceedings of the Symposium for Information Sciences*, September. Washington: Spartan Press.

Foster, A. (1999) Knowledge management – not a dangerous thing. *Library Association Record*, **101** (3), 149.

Kaye, D. (1995) The nature of information. *Library Review*, **44** (8), 37–48.

Koniger, P. and Janowitz, K. (1995) Drowning in information, but thirsty for knowledge. *International Journal for Information Management*, **15** (1), 5–16.

Lester, G. (1992) *Business Information Systems*. London: Pitman.

Martin, W. J. (1995) *The Global Information Society*. Aldershot: Aslib/Gower.

Mullin, R. (1996) Knowledge management: a cultural revolution. *Journal of Business Strategy*, **17** (5), September–October, 56–60.

Nonaka, I. (1991) The knowledge creating company. *Harvard Business Review*, **69**, November–December, 96–104.

Nonaka, I. (1995) *The Knowledge Creating Company*. New York: Oxford University Press.

Nonaka, I. (1996) The knowledge creating company. In K. Starkey (ed.) *How Organisations Learn*, pp. 18–31. London: International Thomson.

Ruggles, R. (1997) *Knowledge Management Tools*. Boston: Oxford: Butterworth-Heinemann

Senn, J. A. (1990) *Information Systems in Management*, 4th edn. Belmont, CA: Wadsworth.

Skyrme, D. J. and Amidon, D. M. (1998) New measures of success. *Journal of Business Strategy*, **19** (1), 20–24.

Wilson, D. A. (1996) *Managing Knowledge*. Oxford and Boston: Institute of Management and Butterworth Heinemann.

2 Formatting and structuring knowledge

INTRODUCTION

Chapter 1 was concerned with the significance of knowledge management in general terms; here we turn specifically to the organization of knowledge. After reading this chapter you will:

- understand the uses of information
- be aware of the need to organize information
- have a plan of the principal fields within which information is organized
- be aware of the traditional tools for organizing information
- appreciate the different types of databases that might be important in the organization of knowledge
- be aware of the need for database structures
- learn how text is organized into documents
- understand the formats in which documents are presented
- be aware of intellectual relationships between documents
- understand the forms of markup and metadata that are applied to electronic and printed documents.

INFORMATION AND ITS USES

'Knowledge', said Samuel Johnson, 'is of two kinds. We know a subject ourselves, or we know where we can find information upon it.' Most of this chapter, and of this book, is concerned with Dr Johnson's second kind of knowledge. An information scientist today would define *knowledge* as the integration of new information into previously stored information to form a large and coherent view of a portion of reality – a definition which fits both human- and machine-held knowledge, and describes the knowledge bases used in expert systems. *Information* to an information scientist is a set of data matched to a particular information need. This again is valid, whether the information is stored in a computer system or in our brain. Most of the information that reaches the brain never gets beyond short-term memory: where to find the doorknob, whether the traffic lights have changed to green. Some might be useful enough to be committed to long-term memory: the price of a loaf; the time of the last bus home. We need information to enable us to make decisions, everyday decisions like when it is safe to cross the road, or decisions with far-reaching import-ance like whether to change our job or move house. This at its higher levels constitutes *wisdom*, a purely human attribute, where information, knowledge and value criteria combine over time to enable a person to make balanced judgements. At the opposite end of the scale we have *data*: literally, things given. Data are impersonal and not matched to an information need: a passenger on a bus may see the traffic lights change, but does not need to act on it. The data collected by a surveillance camera or hospital heart-monitoring machine may or may not be used subsequently.

Information informs our leisure activities: we read books, pursue hobbies, talk to friends, join clubs and societies, all the while picking up and exchanging information. Sometimes information becomes an end in itself, as with the obsessive collector or the earnest-faced members of a pub quiz team. We read newspapers and watch news and current affairs programmes to keep ourselves informed about the wider community. We use information in education – our own and our children's. With academics and other researchers, it can be said that the generation of information is their business. More generally though, information is everybody's professional stock-in-trade. Information is the know-ledge that we either know or have access to; professional skill is knowing how to apply that information. These may be the executive skills of the head of a business – or of a nation-state, or the persuasive skills of the barrister, or the diagnostic and remedial skills of the physician, or the practised manual dexterity of the surgeon, or plasterer or French polisher.

To sum up, then, these examples illustrate how our definition of information can include all the perspectives suggested in Chapter 1: as news, subjective knowledge, useful data, a resource, a commodity and a constitutive force in society. They also suggest some of the major purposes of information, namely:

- decision-making
- problem-solving
- communication and interpersonal relationships
- learning

- entertainment and leisure
- citizenship
- business and professional effectiveness.

KNOWLEDGE, INFORMATION AND DATA

The data that are the raw material of information may often be generated with a minimum of human participation, as with the transaction logging of the supermarket cashier or the video-recording of the surveillance camera. There are also established research techniques – such as observation, surveys, interviews – for collecting information. In everyday life, we obtain our information from a wide range of sources. For many, the mass media – television, radio, press – are their principal sources. In Western societies, whether or not a person reads the press, there are many other printed sources, such as advertisements, instructions and other ephemera, and books. Electronic sources are supplementing, and in some cases supplanting, traditional printed sources. People are also a major source of information. Informal networks – friends, colleagues, business or professional acquaintances – are often the first resort in gathering information. Internet discussion groups are a new development of informal networking. Networks can also be formal: people who share a common interest often form organizations, which may be consulted in their area of specialization. Indeed, organizations comprise a final category of information source. Organizations generate information primarily to serve the needs of the organization, whether it be a business, a government department, an academic institution, a professional body, a political party, etc. An organization's information is not personal to individuals acting in a private capacity, nor (with few exceptions) is it published for all to see.

Broadly, then, we can categorize our sources of information into *personal*, *published* and *organizational* sources. Personal information sources include personal observation and enquiry, and our use of informal networks. Published sources include the media, books, journals, directories, the World Wide Web, etc. Organizational sources include information relating to our employment and the information generated by public, private and voluntary organizations primarily for their own use. All these sources are *primary* sources of information. To back them up, a huge range of *secondary* sources has grown up; not information as such, but tools for organizing information. It is these that we must now consider.

TOOLS FOR ORGANIZING INFORMATION

What happens to information? The greater part by far of information stored in the brain is discarded after immediate use. The time of day is important only for planning some subsequent action; the phase of a set of traffic lights serves only the immediate purpose of crossing the road or proceeding across a junction. We do not record this information, or give it house room in our long-term memory. Some background information we do retain in long-term memory because we need to use it frequently: how to tell the time, or to proceed on green – this is part of our personal knowledge base. In between, there is information that we may possibly need to reuse at some future date or time, and this we record in personal information files. At their most basic, these files may be notes scribbled on the backs of envelopes, but most of us maintain more sophisticated databases: diaries, address books, lists of telephone numbers, sometimes commonplace books and Filofaxes and electronic personal organizers or, in the case of researchers, personal databases of documentary sources. Everybody needs to organize their own information sources. There is no single way of doing this – each of us structures our information to suit ourselves. Figure 2.1 shows one such construct.

All this is without doubt excellent advice; but once we move outside the area of personal and domestic information and into published and organizational information, the pattern changes. The information we use in our professional lives – indeed, in all contexts outside the home – has a corporate existence. Many others besides ourselves may need to access it. We will be accessing information that others have created or organized. The organization of infor- mation in professional, academic and research contexts is complex and highly formalized.

In this work we are concerned with the organization of knowledge and infor- mation retrieval in these specific contexts. In particular we are concerned with those techniques that are of interest to information professionals. These will include techniques and tools found and used in libraries, as well as other approaches used in the management of information in organizations. However, one important feature to note about such systems is that some of them do not, in fact, organize or retrieve information. Some are actually concerned with the organization and retrieval of documents or references to documents.

Conventionally, librarians have concentrated on documents and resources that have been generated elsewhere and bought in, whereas information managers have specialized in the records or files that an organization generates internally: letters, leaflets, personnel documents and a host of other items. Even this distinction is no longer clear-cut. What is clear, however, is that resources of all

Essential information for living includes practical information. Thus, in the future, this page will contain more gems like the following:

- **On Books, Finding:** *The Library of Congress Online Catalog* lets you search for over 4 million books, plus a lot of other fun stuff.
- **On Capital Punishment, Informed Opinions:** Don't assume you have one 'til you brief yourself courtesy of the *ACLU*.
- **On Dieting, Tricks:** Okay, so I'm not very qualified to give information on dieting, having never done much myself, but, I pass this along. Drinking two glasses of water a few minutes before meals is supposed to substantially curb your hunger, allowing you to eat enough, but less. Also, cutting table salt out of your diet will help your heart, and may help you lose weight.
- **On Giving, Charitable:** Give! Give 'til it hurts! But to whom? That is the question, ain't it? You not only want to put your money to a good cause, you also want to know it's being used for what you intended and used effectively. There is a solution! The *National Charities Information Bureau* has scrutinized 400 of the most popular charities in the U.S. according to its 'Standards in Philanthropy' guidelines. Check your favorite charities online and order one full report for free!
- **On Jars, Opening:** Among the techniques generally used has been to either abrade your hands, or to attempt to heat the metal lid, assuming it will expand 'til it's relatively loose on the jar. This pretty much sucks. I recommend turning the jar upside down, and striking it once, forcibly on the bottom with the heel of your hand. Voila! (It usually tends to open easily after this, so it makes you look pretty cool.)
- **On Inkstains, Removal:** . . . soak the offended garment in milk . . .
- **On Politics, Progressive:** So, I hear you clamoring for a major meta-link site for progressive politics and updates on every conceivable policy issue of the day. Baby, I'm there for ya. The *Electronic Policy Network* is wicked replete with a veritable plethora of progressive networking opportunities and links . . .
- **On Renewable Energy and Sustainable Technology, Centers for:** Look, this is pretty self-explanatory. *Solstice*, the web presence for **CREST**. (figure out the acronym yourself) . . .
- **On Travel, Cheap:** . . . Try *The Internet Guide to Hostelling*.

Lastly, a good way of staying informed is to CHECK THE NEWS, YOU CYBERJERK!, so click here to find the official account of what happened today (Note that these sight-bytes of infotainment do little other than make you aware of the 'issueness' of any item. For a deeper understanding, pursue the subject on your own.)

Figure 2.1   Found on the Web: one person's way of organizing everyday information
Source: www.geocities.com/Athens/5199/info.html

kinds, irrespective of their source, need organizing so that their contents can be retrieved when required. If we need our personal organizers and other devices to store and retrieve our personal, professional and domestic information, how much more true is this of libraries and organizations of all kinds?

FIELDS IN THE ORGANIZATION OF KNOWLEDGE

There are now four fields in the organization of knowledge which have had separate lines of development but are now moving closer together. All can profitably make use of the tools of the organization of knowledge. These fields are:

- *catalogues and bibliographies*, which are used by librarians to list the documents in a collection or within a specified field
- *indexing and abstracting services*, which are used by information scientists to identify the documents that are required to meet a specific subject request
- *records management systems*, which are the responsibility of records managers and archivists to maintain an orderly collection of records
- *networked resources*, and in particular the Internet and World Wide Web, whose organization is to all intents and purposes a free-for-all of competing search engines and directories.

These categories are intended to represent stereotypes, and as such describe extremes. All share some common goals; but to take the issue of standards, only in the cataloguing world are standards for the creation and categorization of records widely applied. Standards exist in abstracting and indexing services and in the museum, archives and records management world, but are less widely followed. In the heady world of the Internet, the problems have been identified and there are moves towards defining standards, but the whole ethos of the Internet is so anarchic that it would be a brave person who could predict the imposition of any kind of order.

APPROACHES TO RETRIEVAL: THE HUMAN PERSPECTIVE

In any of these environments, the objective of the organization of knowledge is the successful subsequent retrieval. Different people may wish to retrieve a document or unit of information for different reasons, and may therefore approach the retrieval process in different ways. A fundamental difference in searching strategy is between known-item searching and browsing.

- *Known-item searching* is performed by users when they know what they are looking for and usually possess some clue or characteristic by which they can identify the item, such as its author or all or part of its title.
- *Subject searching* is performed by users who do not have a specific item in mind. This approach does not provide positive identification: it can, in A. C. Foskett's phrase, only 'optimise our responses to requests for information on subjects' (Foskett, 1982, p. 8). We call it the subject approach, though in practice all manner of other considerations come into play, such as literary form, level of difficulty, the author's viewpoint, whether designed for continuous reading, among others. *Browsing* describes the situation when users have a less precise view of the information or documents that may be available

or are not sure whether their requirements can be met. It is often used for the activity of scanning through a number of documents in order to refine the user's requirements. *Surfing* is its Web equivalent – though this includes browsing with no purpose other than to revel in the sheer range and diversity of available resources.

There are a number of types of subject information need. A common one is for a specific item of information: the searcher knows what information is required, but is less certain where to look for it. Another very common situation is for one or more documents to be required, but less than the total available. Less frequently a comprehensive (exhaustive) search may be required when it is important not to overlook any significant piece of information. This kind of information need is often encountered in the early stages of research to avoid duplicating research that has already taken place. What is common to all these types of subject information need is that they are *retrospective*: the searcher is looking backwards over available resources. A quite different kind of subject need is for *current awareness*: the need for professionals, academics and keen amateurs to keep abreast of developments within their areas of interest.

Irrespective of the type of information need, there are from the point of view of the information professional two methods of conducting a search. The first kind of search is user-conducted: the documents or resources are set out in such a way that users can retrieve information for themselves. Information that is obtained in this way is said to be *heuristic*: users can modify their search requirements as they go along. The second kind uses an information professional as an intermediary to carry out the search on behalf of the end-user. If the user is present when the search is taking place, this kind of search may also be heuristic. If not, the search is *iterative*: if the search results do not adequately match the end-user's requirements, the search has to be started again from scratch.

APPROACHES TO RETRIEVAL: THE MACHINE PERSPECTIVE

Here we examine approaches to retrieval from the point of view of the way information is processed. Overwhelmingly, the commonest approach is by linking words. Words in a query are matched against words in documents. This approach is implicit throughout this book. But it is not the only approach. Other approaches include:

- *Citation indexing*. This makes use of the citations (references) appearing at the end of many documents, particularly research papers. Effectively, the author of a paper has established a link between the paper and those earlier documents that are cited at the end. A citation index makes a separate record

25

for each cited document. Documents in the citation index are linked to a separate file (source index) of their source documents. Searching begins with a document known to be relevant, and it is possible to check either which later documents have cited it or which earlier documents it cites. Searches can be recycled backwards and forwards to build up a file of promising-looking citations.

- *Hypertext links* are closely identified with the World Wide Web, even though their history goes back to the 1960s and they have many other applications. A hypertext link consists of an identifier – a highlighted word or phrase in a passage of text or a button to be clicked with the mouse – and a pointer that links to a related document or to another part of the same document. The user can choose whether or not to break the flow of a document by clicking a link. Souls who get carried away with this activity are said to be surfing the Web.

- *Information filtering* is one name given to techniques for pre-sorting large volumes of data in response to a given search in order to eliminate the least relevant. The search proper then takes place on a subset of the database. Another name for this is *data mining*.

- *Image and sound processing* is still in its infancy. Much research is taking place into techniques for directly retrieving images, video and sound, but most working systems still rely on the use of words.

THE TRADITIONAL TOOLS OF INFORMATION RETRIEVAL

Traditionally, the tools of information retrieval have been catalogues, bibliographies and printed indexes. These can be defined as follows:

- A *catalogue* is a list of the materials or items in a library, with entries representing the items arranged in either alphabetical order or some systematic order. Many catalogues today are held as computer databases, when they are known as *OPAC*s. Other catalogues are held as card catalogues, or in microform.

- A *bibliography* is a list of items, originally books, but a broader definition is widely accepted as not confined to one collection but restricted in some other way. A bibliography may list the materials published in one country, or in a given form, or between certain dates, or a combination of these or other factors. Bibliographies may be held in the same formats and arrangements as catalogues. Like catalogues, too, the entries in a bibliography represent items, and because the layout of an entry in a bibliography is very similar to that in a catalogue, *bibliographic* is used interchangeably to describe either.

- An *index* is an alphabetically arranged list of pointers guiding the user to entries in a catalogue or bibliography, or to specific places in the text of a document. The pointers, or index entries, are derived from the items contained in the collection.

- A *database* is a collection of similar records, with relationships between the records.
- A *file* is a collection of letters, documents or other resources dealing with one organization, person, area or subject. Files may hold paper documents or be computer based.

All the above are the traditional tools for organizing knowledge. Catalogues and bibliographies are databases. The whole concept of the database is central to the structuring of information, and will be discussed further in the next section.

DATABASES

Library and information managers have always compiled files of information, in the form of catalogues, and lists of borrowers. Early computer-based systems in many businesses held master files typically containing data relating to payroll, sales, purchase and inventory. Such applications comprise a series of related and similarly formatted records. External databases may be accessed through the online hosts or acquired on CD-ROM or through the Internet. The information manager may download sections of these databases, with appropriate licensing arrangements, to integrate into local databases. Since databases are central to the way in which data is stored and retrieved, it is important for the information manager to be aware of the types of database that are available, any standard record formats that are likely to be encountered and approaches to database structure.

Databases may be stored on magnetic or optical media such as discs, and accessed either locally or remotely. This may include access to an organization's database covering transactions and financial records or other databases that might be accessed remotely. Some of these databases will hold publicly accessible information, such as abstracting and indexing databases, full text of reports, encyclopaedias and directories, while others will be databases that are shared within an organization or group of organizations.

Databases that might be available to information users in the public arena and which might be access remotely via an online search service or, more locally, on CD-ROM can be categorized into either reference or source databases.

REFERENCE DATABASES

Reference databases refer or point the user to another source such as a document, an organization or an individual for additional information, or for the full text of a document. They include:

- *Bibliographic databases*, which include citations or bibliographic references, and sometimes abstracts of literature. They tell the user what has been written and in which source (e.g. journal title, conference proceedings) it can be located and, if they provide abstracts, will summarize the original document. Figure 2.2 shows part of a bibliographic database.
- *Catalogue databases*, which show the stock of a given library or library network. Typically, such databases list which monographs, journal titles and other items the library has in stock, but do not give much information on the contents of these documents. Catalogue databases are a special type of bibliographic database, but since their orientation is rather different from that of the other bibliographic databases, they are worth identifying as a

---

7 VEGETABLES, FRUIT AND BAKERY PRODUCTS

394 – Apples – Shelf life – *Effect of* **– Heat treatment**
Cell wall changes and partial prevention of fruit softening in prestorage heat treated 'Anna' apples. N. B. Shalom et al. *Journal of the Science of Food and Agriculture,* 72 (2) Oct 96, pp. 231–4. il.tables.refs.
Prestorage heat treatment at 38°C for 4 days retarded the softening of apples during storage at 0°C. Histological and chemical changes induced by the heat treatment are discussed.

395 – Apples – Shelf life – Testing
Monitoring post-harvest quality of *Granny Smith* apple under simulated shelf-life conditions: destructive, non-destructive and analytical measurements. K. Tu et al. *International Journal of Food Science and Technology,* 31 (3) Jun 96, pp. 267–76. il.refs. Destructive and non-destructive indicators correlated well. Of the non-destructive methods used, the acoustic impulse technique was superior to the random vibration test because of its efficiency and less variation. Testing for mealiness with tensile and compression tests was also undertaken.

396 – Bakery products – Manufacture – Equipment
Baking: product focus. *Food Processing,* 65 (9) Sep 96, pp. 13–15. il.

397 – Brassica – Glucosinolates – Anticancer properties
My best friend's a Brussels sprout. G. Vines. *New Scientist, 152* (2061/2) 21/28 Dec 96, pp. 46–9. il. Broccoli and Brussels sprouts contain sinigrin, a glucosinolate that has no nutritive value but may prevent cancers. Another glucosinolate is present in broccoli: called glucoraphanin, it breaks down into an isothiocyanate called sulphoraphane which works by neutralising cancer-causing substances. Research into how these chemicals work, including attempts to improve broccoli by breeding and by gene cloning, is described at the Institute of Food Research at Norwich, and elsewhere.

Figure 2.2 Bibliographic database (Abstracts in new technology and engineering)

While the illustration of records from a bibliographic database (Figure 2.2) was derived from its print version, our illustration of a catalogue database is from an Online Public Access Catalogue. COPAC is a *union catalogue* – one that includes the stock of more than one library system. This and Figures 2.4, 2.5 and 2.6 show the stages in a subject search.

unified access to the catalogues of some of the largest university research libraries in the UK and Ireland.

about COPAC
libraries
userguide
user info
other interfaces
...z39.50, telnet
other services
feedback

To Search COPAC select the COPAC button below.

✿ Search ▒COPAC▒

✿ **News:** Loading of the Warwick University catalogue has now started.
News: An Updated Version of the Web Interface has been released. This includes a change to the Download record format.
News: COPAC will soon be moving to a faster machine.

To use the **old** COPAC interface select one of the following links.

⏴ Author/Title Search
⏴ Periodical Search
⏴ Subject Search

COPAC is one of the MIDAS services, produced at Manchester Computing, University of Manchester.

COPAC is funded by ▦ and uses records supplied by CURL.

For Information and Advice contact the COPAC Helpdesk.

Figure 2.3 Catalogue database. 1: OPAC search screen

COPAC Help: The Search Menu

COPAC offers three search options. Each of these gives you a Search Form consisting of several fields into which you may type as much or as little information as you have available. You do not have to enter information into every field, in fact if you do so your search is more likely to fail.

⏎ The Author/Title Search

This option allows you to search using author names (editors, translators etc.) and/or document titles. For example you might wish to see what works are available by a particular author, or you might search for the details of a specific document using the editor and title. This option searches the entire database, including periodical materials.

⏎ The Periodical Search

This option limits your search to journals and other regularly published materials. If you fail to find what you are looking for it is possible that the material has not been identified as a periodical, so it is worth trying an Author/Title search as this will search all the records in the database, including periodicals.

⏎ The Subject Search

This option allows you to search for materials on a topic. A subject search retrieves records from the entire database, including periodical materials. It searches on both the subject details in the record and the document titles.

Note that many of the subjects included in the records use American spellings and terminology. For more comprehensive results it can be useful to repeat a search twice, once using US and once using UK English, eg 'behavior' vs 'behaviour'.

The COPAC Home Page gives access to a variety of background information, including details about the records available from COPAC, a copy of the online Userguide, and links to the contributing libraries' Web pages.

 For Information and Advice contact the COPAC Helpdesk. copac@mcc.ac.uk

Figure 2.4 Catalogue database. 2: Search menu (help screen)

separate category. Figures 2.3 to 2.6 show a search conducted on a catalogue database.

● *Referral databases*, which offer references to information or data such as the

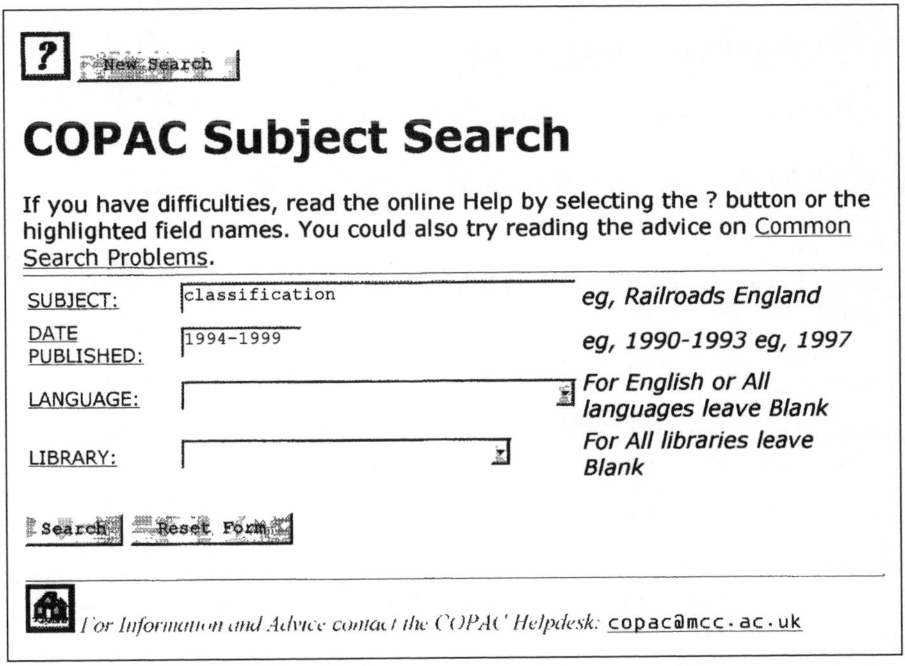

Figure 2.5 Catalogue database. 3: OPAC subject search

names and addresses of organizations, and other directory-type data. Records from a referral database are shown in Figure 2.7.

Source databases contain the original source data, and are one type of electronic document. After successful consultation of a source database the user should have the information that is required and should not need to seek information in an original source (as is the case with reference databases). Data are available in machine-readable form instead of, or as well as, printed form. Source databases can be grouped according to their content:

- numeric databases, which contain numerical data of various kinds, including statistics and survey data
- full-text databases of newspaper items, technical specifications and software
- text-numeric databases, which contain a mixture of textual and numeric data (such as company annual reports) and handbook data
- multimedia databases, which include information stored in a mixture of different types of media, including, for example, sound, video, pictures, text and animation. Figure 2.8 shows part of such a database.

Bibliographic databases contain a series of linked bibliographic records

31

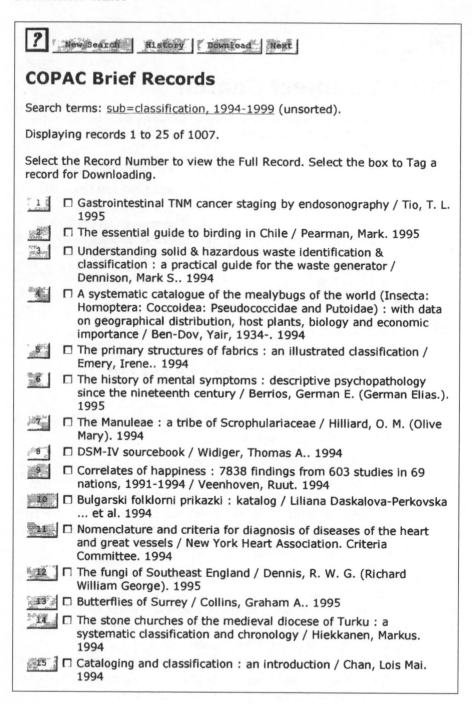

COPAC Brief Records

Search terms: sub=classification, 1994-1999 (unsorted).

Displaying records 1 to 25 of 1007.

Select the Record Number to view the Full Record. Select the box to Tag a record for Downloading.

1. ☐ Gastrointestinal TNM cancer staging by endosonography / Tio, T. L. 1995

2. ☐ The essential guide to birding in Chile / Pearman, Mark. 1995

3. ☐ Understanding solid & hazardous waste identification & classification : a practical guide for the waste generator / Dennison, Mark S.. 1994

4. ☐ A systematic catalogue of the mealybugs of the world (Insecta: Homoptera: Coccoidea: Pseudococcidae and Putoidae) : with data on geographical distribution, host plants, biology and economic importance / Ben-Dov, Yair, 1934-. 1994

5. ☐ The primary structures of fabrics : an illustrated classification / Emery, Irene.. 1994

6. ☐ The history of mental symptoms : descriptive psychopathology since the nineteenth century / Berrios, German E. (German Elias.). 1995

7. ☐ The Manuleae : a tribe of Scrophulariaceae / Hilliard, O. M. (Olive Mary). 1994

8. ☐ DSM-IV sourcebook / Widiger, Thomas A.. 1994

9. ☐ Correlates of happiness : 7838 findings from 603 studies in 69 nations, 1991-1994 / Veenhoven, Ruut. 1994

10. ☐ Bulgarski folklorni prikazki : katalog / Liliana Daskalova-Perkovska ... et al. 1994

11. ☐ Nomenclature and criteria for diagnosis of diseases of the heart and great vessels / New York Heart Association. Criteria Committee. 1994

12. ☐ The fungi of Southeast England / Dennis, R. W. G. (Richard William George). 1995

13. ☐ Butterflies of Surrey / Collins, Graham A.. 1995

14. ☐ The stone churches of the medieval diocese of Turku : a systematic classification and chronology / Hiekkanen, Markus. 1994

15. ☐ Cataloging and classification : an introduction / Chan, Lois Mai. 1994

Figure 2.6 Catalogue database. 4: Search results

[227]
Gaucher's Association
  25 West Cottages
  London NW6 1RS
Telephone: 0171 433 1121
World Wide Web: http://www.gaucher.org.uk
Contact: Mrs Susan Lewis (Secretary)
Objectives and Purposes: To provide information about Gaucher's Disease and to keep families and medical advisers up-to-date with the latest developments; to encourage the availability of treatment, including enzyme replacement therapy; to keep families in touch for support; and to compile a register of those affected by the disease
Stock and Subject Coverage: Material covering all matters relating to Gaucher's Disease
Availability: Telephone and written enquiries, from bona fide researchers only (photocopies of articles available, £1 each)
Hours: 10.00–17.00 (answerphone available out of hours)
Publications: Information pack; bi-annual newsletter

[228]
General Dental Council (GDC)
  37 Wimpole Street
  London W1M 8DQ
Telephone: 0171 486 2171
Fax: 0171 224 3294
Contact: The Registrar
Objectives and Purposes: To maintain and publish the Dentists Register and to promote high standards of dental education at all its stages and high standards of professional conduct among dentists. Also has responsibilities in relation to the training, enrolment and conduct of dental auxiliaries
Hours: 09.15–16.00
Publications: Dentists Register (annual); The Rolls of Dental Auxiliaries; GDC Gazette

Figure 2.7 Referral database
Source: Dale, 1997.

(described in Chapter 3). Even though a number of the large bibliographic databases have been available in machine-readable form for more than 20 years, the basic elements in the database still have their roots in the printed product, which was often an abstracting or indexing tool with which they are associated. These databases were often originally constructed to aid in the more efficient generation of a printed abstracting or indexing service, and a print product often still accounts for a significant component of the database producer's revenue. One of the benefits of maintaining records in a machine-readable format is the opportunity to generate a series of different products for different market-places from the one set of records. These products often include current awareness services, online search services, licensing for downloading sections of databases, printed abstracting and indexing services.

Source databases are electronic documents. Many such databases take advan-

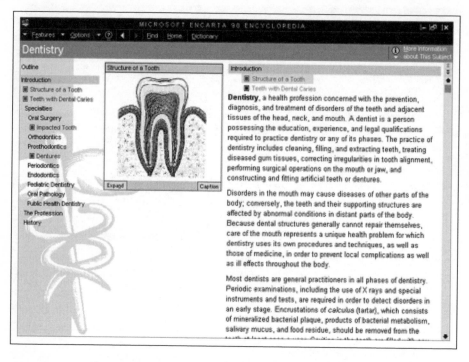

Figure 2.8 Multimedia source database (Encarta encyclopedia)

tage of the fact that they are not constrained by the same physical limitations as print, and are multimedia, embracing, in addition to text and numeric data, computer software, images, sound, maps and charts. These databases can be accessed online through the online search services, or on CD-ROM or via videotext and teletext or through the Internet.

Source databases are so varied in their nature and origins that it is difficult to make generalizations. Earlier in this chapter we divided source databases into numeric, full-text and text-numeric. We might also consider referral databases in this context. Although these are categorized as reference databases in the sense that they offer a pointer to further information, they are often also source databases in that they might contain the full text of a directory that could be regarded as a source document. Source databases, then, may include the full text of journal articles, newsletters, newswires, dictionaries, directories and other source materials. Many, although not all, source databases have a print equivalent. Some source databases do not contain the complete contents of the print equivalent, but only offer selected coverage.

DATABASE STRUCTURES: THE INVERTED FILE

The crudest way to search a database is to go through it record by record looking for the appropriate data element. As this is slow, alternative methods of locating specific records have been developed. The online search services and other applications that use document management systems have always used the *inverted file* approach described below. This is useful for searching complex text-based databases, where the searcher does not know the form in which the search key may have been entered in the database, and has, essentially, to guess the most appropriate form.

Transaction-processing systems, such as library management systems, travel bookings information systems, and sales and marketing information systems, may also use this approach to locate individual records within a database, but these also need a mechanism for linking a series of distinct databases together so that information can be drawn from more than one database for display on the screen or printing at one time. This requirement in transaction-processing systems has led to the development of strategies for optimizing database design.

The *inverted file* similar to an index. In the inverted file approach there may be two or three separate files. The two-file approach uses two files – the text or print file and the inverse or index file. The text file contains the actual records. The index file provides access to these records. The index file contains a record for each of the indexed terms from all of the records in the database, arranged in alphabetical order. Each term is accompanied by information on its frequency of occurrence in the database, the file in which it is to be located, the record in which it is entered, and possibly further location information such as the paragraph (or field) within which it is located. When a new record is added to the database, it is necessary to update the index file.

These files are used together in the search of a database. A user who is interested in performing a search on the word 'hedges', for instance, will enter the term at the keyboard, and the system will seek the term in the index file. If the term is not present in the index file, the system responds by indicating that there are no postings for that term. If the term is found, the user will be told how many postings, or occurrences, of the term there are in the database. To display the records, the text file location is used to locate records in the text file.

If three files are used, there is an intermediate file that allows search terms input at the keyboard to be checked quickly and the number of postings displayed on the screen. This is particularly useful with a complex search that may involve using the index file records for a number of search terms.

The above description is intended to offer a simple introduction to the basic concept of an inverted file. In practice, file structures may be more complicated, as the following examples indicate:

- If it is possible to search terms in proximity to other terms (e.g. terms within two words of each other), the index file must contain information about word positions within a field for each term.
- Inverted files are often created for a number of fields within a record. However, not all fields are usually indexed, because each index takes disc storage space; indexes are created for those fields that are commonly searched. Inverted files are often created for author names, title words, subject-indexing terms and author-title acronyms.
- Long full-text records need to be split into paragraphs and those paragraphs must be assigned identifiers before indexing can commence. Alternatively, the positions of individual words in the file can be used as identifiers.

DATABASE STRUCTURES: THE RELATIONAL MODEL

In the early days of computing, business and library systems worked with a series of individual master files covering, for example, in the case of libraries, borrowers and books in stock or, in the case of many businesses, payroll, sales, and inventory. It soon became apparent that programmes for, say, circulation control in a library needed to access two or more different files, and it was appropriate to start to examine the relationships between these files. This led to the introduction of the concept of a database, and the software to manage such databases, known as database management systems (DBMS). It then became necessary to examine the optimum way to structure data or to develop data models to support specific applications.

Relational databases use one type of database structure, which has been widely adopted in database systems. In relational systems, information is held in a set of relations or tables. Rows in the tables are equivalent to records, and columns in the tables are equivalent to fields. The data in the various relations are linked through a series of keys. Figure 2.9 shows a simple example of a relation known as catalogued–book. In this relation the International Standard Book Number (ISBN) is the primary key and may be used in other relations to identify a specific book. For example, if we maintain the relation order–book the ISBN acts as a link to the order–book relation. If we wish to complete an order form with details from the order file, data for each book can be extracted from the catalogue file and printed on the order slips alongside data from the order file.

(a) Catalogued–book relation occurrences

ISBN	Title	Author	Year
0–82112–462–3	Organic chemistry	A.J. Brown	1989
0–84131–460–7	Alchemy	R.M. Major	1987
0–69213–517–8	Expert systems	S. Estelle	1988
0–93112–462–1	Computer science	S. Estelle	1989
0–71143–526–6	Bibliography	J. Johns	1991

(b) Order–book relation occurrences

Order no.	ISBN	Quantity ordered
678	0–82112–462–3	1
678	0–84131–460–7	4
678	0–69213–517–8	20
679	0–93112–462–1	2
680	0–82112–462–3	3
681	0–71143–526–6	2

Figure 2.9 Two simple relations

MULTIMEDIA DATABASE STRUCTURES

Multimedia databases present new challenges for database structure. Multimedia DBMSs (MM-DBMSs) are being designed to manage such databases. As pictures, animation, sound, text and data tables have very different storage needs, MM-DBMS seek to use a range of technologies, such as relational technology for tables, text databases for documents and image storage devices for graphics and animation. A central problem is the handling of non-text items such as drawings and moving images. In time varying media, access by frame is provided by digital video interactive (DVI) standards. For more sophisticated access the images have to be indexed with keywords in a similar manner to text-based documents.

TEXT AND MULTIMEDIA

Historically, databases have been compiled from representations of documents, or document surrogates, rather than the documents themselves. It is only since the mid-1980s that it has become technically and economically feasible to store whole documents in an immediately accessible machine format, and the computer storage of graphics, sound and multimedia resources is more recent still. Many of the tools and techniques for organizing document representations have been adapted to whole documents. Others are new. The rapid growth of the Internet has produced a whole new generation of information specialists from a variety of backgrounds whose interest is in the retrieval of networked documents and other resources – whole documents and not representations of documents. We start therefore with a consideration of the formats of knowledge itself – documents and resources in their various guises – before looking at document representations in Chapter 3.

The rise of multimedia notwithstanding, text remains the basis of information. In the global society, it is worth pausing briefly to consider some of the implications of this statement. Most of the world's languages have no written codes. On the other hand, English has effectively replaced Latin as the lingua franca of international communication. The Latin alphabet used by the English language has variants and extensions when applied to other European languages. Many Asian languages, and a few European ones, use other alphabets, and transliteration standards are needed to represent one language in the script of another. Two major languages – Japanese and Chinese – have non-alphabetic writing systems: the one is syllabic, the other logographic, each symbol representing a complete word.

The study of written languages recognizes two basic components. A language has a *vocabulary* of words, and a *syntax*: a set of rules for stringing words together to make meaningful statements. *Semantics* is the name given to the study of meaning in language. We will meet these terms again in Chapter 5.

The word is the unit on which many retrieval systems operate, but what is a word? Is *folk-lore* one word, or two? (Some retrieval systems will make three words out of it: *folk, lore, folk-lore.*) Most of us recognize that many words are inflected – that is, they have different inflections (endings) according to their grammatical function – but many languages take this far beyond the simple *dog – dogs* or *bark – barks – barked – barking* of the English language. Retrieval systems can easily reconcile different word endings, but sometimes languages are agglutinative – they place prefixes on to words, or string several words together to make portmanteau words. Important in German and some other languages, in English this is a problem that needs to be systematically addressed mainly in chemical information retrieval systems.

It is important to be aware of the structure of text. We – not just information professionals, but any literate person – can become more effective in understanding the gist of a document by skimming it if we have some idea how text is structured, so we know where to look and where to skip. Computers can be made to mimic human processes and apply them to text analysis. Two important structural patterns are:

- *Problem–Solution*: at its simplest, a problem is stated and a solution proposed. A four-part variant is often found in research papers: Introduction (statement of the problem to be solved); Method; Results; discussion of Conclusions.

Another variant is: statement of problem; discussion of one or more inadequate responses; and, finally, a successful response.

- *General–Particular*: a generalization is made, and provided with one or more examples. There may be hierarchies of generalizations in that a sentence may function both as an example to a generalization and as a generalization which is itself exemplified. This hierarchical organization of text is explicit in report writing.

These structural patterns are often found in combination. Anyone used to skimming text to obtain its gist soon learns to look for cues that help to establish the subject-matter. These include elements such as section headings, or stock phrases like 'In this paper we . . .', 'This paper seeks to . . .', and so on. Additionally, the hierarchical organization of text teaches us that the more significant parts of a text are likely to be found near the beginning of the whole document, of individual sections and of paragraphs. Not only can we learn to do these things ourselves, we can also design our search systems to act in a similar way, for example, by giving greater weight to words found near the beginning of a document.

Multimedia pose problems not encountered with text. Many non-textual collections – images, video clips, mixed media – are now held online, ranging from the large-scale digitization projects of national libraries and art galleries to personal collections, now that flatbed scanners and digital cameras can be bought quite cheaply. The types of verbal and structural cues that text offers are simply not available. Images do not even have titles, so viewers have to rely on their own conceptual interpretations. The same image can be studied at different generic levels and from a range of disciplinary viewpoints. A set of pictures of Hardwick Hall ('more glass than wall') in Derbyshire might be of interest to historians, architects, art historians or to someone researching the history of windows; it is an example of Elizabethan architecture, and a source of the social history of the sixteenth-century English upper classes; the National Trust (its present owner) calls it 'a magnificent statement of the wealth and authority of its builder, Bess of Hardwick'; and its setting might be studied by landscape historians, or by a film or television producer looking for a setting for a costume drama. Faced with complexity of this order, the manual indexing of non-text media is inevitably subjective and slow. Researchers into the automatic indexing and retrieval of images by their content have an uphill struggle. Some success has been reported with systems operating on simple graphic shapes within limited domains, like engineering drawings, plant-leaf types or, operationally, fingerprints.

DOCUMENTS

A document is a record of knowledge, information or data, or a creative expression. A document's creator has recorded ideas, feelings, images, numbers or concepts in order to share them with others. Until recently, this would have been a sufficient definition. Documents were normally text based, but the definition could easily be extended to include the minority of documents which expressed themselves in some other way. Basically, stored data, in any form, constitute a document. Documents include, for example, broadcast messages and three-dimensional objects such as models and realia. This is not a new idea: the suggestion that everyday objects could be considered to be documents goes back to the early years of this century, if not earlier: did not Shakespeare find 'tongues in trees, books in the running brooks, Sermons in stones . . .'? (A study in the 1950s concluded that an antelope was a document if kept in a zoo as an object of study, but not when running wild.)

Documents are traditionally perceived by the unaided eye, less commonly by touch. Formats requiring optical apparatus – slides, microforms etc. – have been with us for a long time. Electronically readable formats have a shorter history but are revolutionizing our notions of a document. Libraries have conventionally been concerned with books. Most libraries have also collected conference proceedings, reports, microforms, serials, maps, videos, slides, filmstrips and computer software; some, specializing in such media, are often described as resource centres. Libraries have always been network conscious, with their well-established and efficient networks for interlending books. More recently, libraries have begun to make use of computer networks, sometimes for housekeeping tasks like acquisitions and cataloguing, but increasingly to obtain information electronically – references to documents, actual documents, factual information, images, software, interactive media. Some people are still happy to call these documents, but it is now more conventional to use the word *resources* for networked resources of all kinds. The term *virtual library* is also used of the range of networked resources.

A recent discussion by Schamber (1996) of the definition of a document has identified some characteristics of electronic documents. They are:

- easily manipulable, in that they can be cut-and-pasted, rotated, etc
- internally and externally linkable, through hyperlinks
- readily transformable, on to disc, print, etc.
- inherently searchable, by means of search software
- instantly transportable, via electronic networks
- infinitely replicable, in that copying does not degrade the quality of the original.

The growth of electronic documents has given rise to some alternative notions of a document. A document can be considered in any of the following ways:

- a homogeneous item: that is, a physical entity
- linked heterogeneous items, e.g. the H. W. Wilson Company's *Humanities Abstracts Full Text* database
- a contextual display of related items, e.g. the results of a search on such a database
- homogeneous items created by the user, e.g. a Web home page with its unstable set of links.

To reconcile these different perspectives, Schamber defines a document as:

a unit:
- consisting of dynamic, flexible, nonlinear content
- represented as a set of linked information items
- stored in one or more physical media or networked sites
- created and used by one or more individuals
- in the facilitation of some process or project.

(Schamber, 1996, p. 670)

In the context of networked resources, definitive lists of resource types and formats are being prepared by the Dublin Core (see below). There is a basic list consisting simply of these six types: text, image, data, software, sound and interactive. Greater detail is available if required. For example, image can be moving (animation, film), photograph, or graphic; sound is ambient, effect, music, narration or speech, and there are over 30 categories and subcategories of text.

While the formats of networked resources are still being formalized, the forms of presentation and arrangement of text-based documents are well established. Figure 2.10 is based on the categories found in a major classification scheme, the Bliss Bibliographic Classification (described in Chapter 8).

This is not a comprehensive listing, but simply serves to illustrate some of the more common formats. Each format has its own features and problems of indexing and retrieval. The contents of encyclopaedias and dictionaries, for example, are virtually self-indexing, and information professionals need do little more than identify them and indicate where they are located. The contents of periodicals, on the other hand, require massive and complex organization. Also, specialist areas of knowledge have their own specialized information formats. Figure 2.11 shows the formats recognized by the Educational Resources Information Center (ERIC).

Comprehensive works
Introductory works
Reference works: encyclopaedias, dictionaries
Partially comprehensive works: periodicals, newspapers, yearbooks, directories
Works for a particular class of reader: by subject interest, e.g. for nurses; sociological characteristics, e.g. for women; or by level of understanding, e.g. for children
Surveys, reports, reviews
Research reports
Forward-looking: proposals, recommendations, forecasts, feasibility studies
Critical studies
Notices, bulletins, announcements, manifestos, agendas, circulars
Composite works: essays, speeches, interviews, conference proceedings, anthologies, readings
Study aids: syllabuses, exercises, identification manuals, digests
Tabulated information: timetables, chronologies, almanacs, technical data, formulae
Numerical information: statistics, accounts
Imaginative literature
Personal observations
Case studies

Figure 2.10 Forms of presentation and arrangement in documents

BIBLIOGRAPHIC RELATIONSHIPS

Documents seldom exist in isolation from one another, but draw on one another in all kinds of ways. In literary studies this is known as intertextuality, and includes a range of pursuits from the tracking down of passing allusions, to full-blown parody. Information retrieval makes use of relationships between documents in a number of ways. It is clear that, if some kind of intellectual relationship exists between two documents, a user who is interested in one may well be interested in the other also. One way is through *citation indexes*. These are reverse indexes to the lists of cited works that appear at the end of research and other documents, and enable searchers to see which later documents have cited an earlier one. Another way concerns cataloguers in particular, who are engaged in a re-examination of what used to be known as the bibliographic unit problem. The problem is one of identifying the overt relationships between two or more documents. Recent research has identified seven categories of relationship:

- *Equivalence relationships* between exact copies of the same manifestation of a work. These include copies, issues, facsimiles, photocopies, and microforms.
- *Derivative relationships*, also called horizontal relationships, are between a bibliographic item and modifications based on the same item, including

42

<(http://ericir.syr.edu/Eric/pub__types.html>

010 Books

COLLECTED WORKS
020 General
021 Conference Proceedings
022 Serial
030 Creative Works (Literature, Drama, Fine Arts)

DISSERTATIONS/THESES
040 Undetermined
041 Doctoral
042 Masters Theses
043 Practicum Papers

GUIDES
050 General (use more specific code, if possible) Classroom Use
051 Instructional Materials (for Learner)
052 Teaching Guides (for Teacher)
055 Non-Classroom Use (for Administrative and Support Staff, and for Teachers, Parents, Clergy,
    Researchers, Counsellors, etc., in Non-classroom Situations)
060 Historical Materials
070 Information Analyses (State-of-the-Art Papers, Research Summaries, Reviews of the literature
    on a Topic)
071 ERIC Information Analysis Products (IAPs)
072 Book/Product Reviews
073 ERIC Digests (Selected) in Full Text
074 Non-ERIC Digests (Selected) in Full Text
080 Journal Articles
090 Legal/Legislative/Regulatory Materials
100 Audiovisual/Non-Print Materials
101 Computer Programs
102 Machine-readable Data Files (MRDFs)
110 Statistical Data (Numerical, Quantitative, etc.)
120 Viewpoints (Opinion Papers, Position Papers, Essays, etc.)

REFERENCE MATERIALS
130 General (use more specific code, if possible)
131 Bibliographies/Annotated Bibliographies
132 Directories/Catalogs
133 Geographic Materials/Maps
134 Vocabularies/Classifications/Dictionaries

REPORTS
140 General (use more specific code, if possible)
141 Descriptive (i.e., Project Descriptions)
142 Evaluative/Feasibility
143 Research/Technical
150 Speeches, Conference Papers
160 Tests, Evaluation Instruments

Figure 2.11 ERIC publication types

43

variations, versions, editions, revisions, translations, adaptations, and paraphrases.

- *Descriptive relationships*: the relationship between a work and a description, criticism, evaluation or review of that work. These include annotated editions, casebooks, commentaries, critiques, etc.
- *Whole-part relationships*, also called vertical or hierarchical relationships, are between a component part of a work and its whole, for example, a selection from an anthology, collection or series. This may even apply to the chapters of a book, as it is sometimes more convenient to regard an electronically stored book as a coordinated collection of documents rather than as a single document.
- *Accompanying relationships*, where two works augment each other, whether equally (as with supplements) or with one subordinate to the other (as with concordances and indexes).
- *Sequential relationships*, also called chronological relationships, where bibliographic items continue or precede one another, as with successive titles in a serial, sequels of a monograph, or parts of a series.
- *Shared characteristic relationships*, where items not otherwise related have, coincidentally, a common author, title, subject or other characteristic used as an access point. This relationship differs from the other six in that there is no intellectual relationship between the works.

Another approach argues that a document may exist at up to four levels:

- *Work*: an intellectual or artistic creation
- *Expression*: the intellectual or artistic realization of a work, e.g. a translation.
- *Manifestation*: the physical embodiment of a work: for example, an author's manuscript, or the copies in an edition of a book, or American Standard Code for Information Interchange (ASCII) and Postscript versions of a networked resource.
- *Item*: a single exemplar of a manifestation, for example a copy of a book.

This approach is of particular interest to cataloguers, who are finding a need for new structures that accommodate networked resources.

TEXT ANALYSIS

Computers are able to process very large quantities of text. With text analysis we can automate such processes as:

- extracting keywords
- preparing document representations, for example, by scanning title pages of

books to generate catalogue descriptions or by processing the text to generate an abstract

- determining various characteristics of a text, for example, its level of reading difficulty, its authorship, its chronological place within the canon of its author's works, or the attitudes or beliefs of its author
- translating the text into another language.

There are broadly two approaches to text analysis:

- *Statistical analysis* is based on counting the frequency of particular words in the text, together with a range of more sophisticated devices, including phrases, pairs of words or clusters of words in proximity to one another. Concept frequency is another such device, where the text is analysed to generate a thesaurus, or list of words that share some aspect of their meaning, or a semantic network of words that are to be found in association with one another.
- *Structural analysis*, or knowledge-based analysis, scans the text for words, phrases or sentences that are in significant positions within the text. For example, for indexing purposes, section headings and figure captions; for abstracting purposes and also for indexing, the first and final paragraphs of sections, the opening sentences of paragraphs, or the positions of such cue words and phrases as 'In this paper we', 'method', 'results show', 'in conclusion'. For abstracting, translation and other applications which generate sentences, the text is parsed – parsing is a word-by-word analysis of each sentence using an algorithm which gradually builds up an interpretation of the text.

Knowledge-based text processing systems – expert systems – use many forms of knowledge representation. One that is commonly found is *frames*, which are based on human mental processes. A frame is a receptacle for information about an entity or event. It contains slots to hold the attributes of the entity. As the text is parsed or the cues read, the slots are gradually filled in. A simple frame, which could be used for newspaper stories, is shown in Figure 2.12.

At present, text analysis seems to work best within fairly specific domains, for example news items or papers in medicine. New applications are constantly being developed. One is *data mining*: the processing of large numbers of documents for information that is of use to an organization.

Slot	Look for indicator
Type of disaster	look for indicator word such as *train wreck, earthquake*
Where	look for place name
When	look for time words: *yesterday, Friday* etc.
Number of dead	look for *killed* or *dead* and a number close by
Number of wounded	look for *wounded* or *injured* and a number close by
Amount of damage	look for £, $ or *dollar* adjacent to a number, especially when close to *damage* or *worth* or *destroyed*

Figure 2.12 Frame for understanding and summarizing disasters

TEXT MARKUP AND METADATA

Information workers in developed countries have become accustomed in recent years to being able to use computer-based search systems to search on the full text of documents. This is a very recent development, however, and the bulk of the world's recorded information is still to be found in documents having a print or hard-copy format that is not machine readable. The traditional way of organizing such documents has been by means of surrogate documents, consisting of records showing the principal elements – title, author etc. – which identify and characterize the documents for retrieval. These take the form of citations in bibliographies and indexes, and catalogue entries. These are discussed further in Chapter 3. Collectively they are known as bibliographic records.

The electronic retrieval of text has led to the development of yet another tradition: *metadata*. Metadata ('data about data') describes the additional elements needed to identify and characterize an electronic document. It always accompanies the document, and to that extent corresponds, very loosely, with the preliminaries (title page, etc.) of a printed book. Functionally it has much in common with bibliographic records.

Electronic text at its most basic uses the ASCII character set. This includes all the characters found on a keyboard plus a few others. Extended ASCII character sets (256 characters) also include the diacriticals found in many European languages. (Chinese logograms are a problem apart. One encoding system has 65 536 possible characters, enough for everyday use but not for advanced work.) ASCII does not include any of the elements which define the layout of text into paragraphs etc., or its actual appearance, as for example the use of bold type or different fonts. Word-processing and publishing software have used their own codes, and this has lessened the portability of documents between systems. Also, within an organization it is often necessary to store documents for retrieval

```
<memo> <to>
A.C. Stanhope
</to><from>
Earl of Chesterfield
</from><date>
12 October 1765
</date><subject>
Advice
</subject><text><para>
In matters of religion and matrimony I never give any advice; because I will not have anybody's
torments in this world or the next laid to my charge.
</para></text></memo>
```

Figure 2.13 A simple SGML document

and reuse. Often only parts of a document will be reused, and selective revision and reformatting may be applied. The application of *markup* to plain (ASCII) text enables electronic documents to be stored and reused efficiently.

Markup is of two kinds:

- *Procedural markup* originally denoted the handwritten instructions that would tell typesetters how to lay out text for printing. Word-processing and desktop publishing software use procedural markup in the same way. Procedural markup defines the final presentation of a document and, so, is specific to the application as, for example, when we instruct our word processor to change the font size or insert a page break.
- *Descriptive*, or *generic*, *markup* defines the headings, content lists, paragraphs and other elements which make up the structure of a document, without reference to its appearance on the page.

Standard Generalized Markup Language (SGML) is the international standard (International Standards Organization, ISO 8879:1986) for embedding descriptive markup within a document, and thus for describing the structure of a document. Standard Generalized Markup Language formally describes the role of each piece of text, using labels enclosed within <brackets> It is a descriptive, not a procedural, markup language. It separates document structure from appearance, and so allows documents to be created that are independent of any specific hardware or software, and thus are fully portable between different systems.

A document type definition (DTD) accompanies every SGML document. The DTD describes the structure of the document by means of a set of rules (for example, 'a chapter heading must be the first element after the start of a chapter') which help to ensure that the structure of the document is logical and consistent. Many publishers use SGML.

Hypertext Markup Language (HTML) is a subset of SGML – formally, it is an

47

```
<html>
<head>
<title>This is an example of HTML</title>
</head>
<body>
<hl>Here is an example of a link</hl>
<p>The Department of Information and Communications at Manchester Metropolitan University has
its own
<a>href='http://www.mmu.ac.uk/h-ss/dic/'>Home Page</a>.</p>
<p>In it you will find links to a wide range of useful sources.</p>
</body>
</html>
```

Figure 2.14 A simple HTML document

SGML document type definition – that has been specially developed for creating World Wide Web documents. As with SGML, an HTML document can be created using any text editor. There are also a number of HTML editors, some within word-processing packages, which insert the markup automatically.

Non-text resources (images, sound, video, multimedia) are especially reliant on markup, as systems which can automatically analyse sounds and images for retrieval are very much in their infancy.

METADATA

Metadata, data about data, is especially used in the context of data that refer to digital resources available across a network. Metadata differs from markup in being distinct from, rather than integrated with, the body of the resource: in the HTML example above, the metadata is included in the <head> section. So metadata is a form of document representation, but it is not a document surrogate in the way that a catalogue entry is. Metadata is linked directly to the resource, and so allows direct access to the resource.

Metadata also differs from bibliographic or cataloguing data in that the location information is held within the record in such a way as to allow direct document delivery from appropriate applications software; in other words, the records may contain detailed access information and network addresses. In addition, bibliographic records are designed for users to use both in judging relevance and making decisions about whether they wish to locate the original resource, and as a unique identifier of the resource so that a user can request the resource or document in a form that makes sense to the recipient of that request. These roles remain significant. Internet search engines (see Chapter 11) use metadata in the indexing processes that they employ to index Internet resources.

Metadata needs to be able to describe remote locations and document versions. It also needs to accommodate the lack of stability of the Internet, redundant data, different perspectives on the granularity (what is a document or a resource?) of the Internet, and variable locations on a variety of different networks.

The need for some kind of bibliographic control over networked resources has become acute with the burgeoning of the WWW. There are a number of metadata formats in existence, and the current situation is volatile. Among the various formats, the Dublin Metadata Core Element Set appears to be the strongest contender for general acceptance.

DUBLIN CORE

The Dublin Metadata Core Element Set, known simply as the Dublin Core, is a list of metadata elements originally developed at a workshop in 1995 organized by the Online Computer Library Center (OCLC, whose headquarters are in Dublin, Ohio) and the National Center for Supercomputer Applications (NCSA). The objective was to improve the indexing and bibliographic control of Internet documents by defining a set of data elements for metadata records of 'document like objects' – the scope was deliberately left open. The intention was to make the data element set as simple as possible, so that the developers of authoring and network publishing tools could incorporate templates for this information in their software. Authors and publishers of Internet documents could thus create their own metadata. This approach is akin to the practices of research publishing, where contributors to primary journals commonly supply their own abstracts, subject keywords, and affiliation details when submitting papers for publication. The Dublin Core does not prescribe any record structure and originally excluded details of access methods and constraints, though these have subsequently been added. All elements are optional, and repeatable, and can be extended as required. Controlled vocabularies are also being developed for certain of the data elements, as an aid to consistency.

The data elements are:

1. *Title*: the name given to the resource by the Creator or Publisher.
2. *Author or creator*: the person or organization primarily responsible for creating the intellectual content of the resource.
3. *Subject and keywords*: keywords or phrases that describe the subject or content of the resource. The use of controlled vocabularies and formal classification schemas is encouraged.
4. *Description*: a textual description of the content of the resource, including abstracts in the case of document-like objects or content descriptions in the case of visual resources.

5. *Publisher*: the entity responsible for making the resource available in its present form, such as a publishing house, a university department, or a corporate entity.

6. *Other contributor*: an editor, transcriber, illustrator or other person or organization who has made significant intellectual contributions to the resource, but secondary to that specified in a Creator element Label.

7. *Date*: the date the resource was made available in its present form. The recommended format is an eight-digit number in the form YYYY-MM-DD.

8 *Resource type*: the category of the resource, such as home page, novel, poem, working paper, technical report, essay, dictionary. A list of approved categories is under development.

9. *Format*: the data format of the resource, used to identify the software and possibly hardware that might be needed to display or operate the resource. A list of approved categories is under development.

10. *Resource identifier*: a string or number used to uniquely identify the resource. Examples for networked resources include Uniform Resource Locators (URLs) and Uniform Resource Numbers (URNs, when implemented). Other globally unique identifiers, such as ISBNs or other formal names would also be candidates for this element in the case of offline resources.

11. *Source*: a string or number used to uniquely identify the work from which this resource was derived, if applicable. For example, the ISBN for the physical book from which the portable document format (PDF) version of a novel has been derived.

12. *Language*: the language(s) of the intellectual content of the resource.

13. *Relation*: the relationship of this resource to other resources, for example, images in a document, chapters in a book or items in a collection. Formal specification of relation is currently under development.

14. *Coverage*: the spatial and/or temporal characteristics of the resource. Formal specification of coverage is currently under development.

15. *Rights management*: a link to a copyright notice, to a rights-management statement, or to a service that would provide information about terms of access to the resource. Formal specification of rights is currently under development.

TRADITIONAL FORMS OF METADATA USED BY INDEXERS

While the term metadata is applied to networked resources, we should not forget that traditional printed materials have always had what is in effect their own metadata, which for books is called the *preliminaries*: the parts of a book that precede (and follow) the actual text. The preliminaries are the principal source

Metadata elements of 'Photograph of the first public telegram in the world'. URL:
http://moriarty.bobst.nyu.edu/markup/Notebook/Morse/morse6.JPG

Metadata in File Header:
```
<HTML>
<HEAD>

<META NAME = 'DC.title'
CONTENT = 'Photograph of the first public telegram in the world'>

<META NAME = 'DC.creator' TYPE = 'Name.Personal' CONTENT = 'Hering, Daniel Webster, 1850–1938'>

<META NAME = 'DC.subject'
SHEME = 'LCSH'
CONTENT = 'Telegraph—History'>

<META NAME = 'DC.subject'
SHEME = 'LCSH'
CONTENT = 'New York University—History—19th century'>

<META NAME = 'DC.subject'
SHEME = 'AAT'
CONTENT = 'Photoprint'>

<META NAME = 'DC.description'
CONTENT = 'Photograph of the original message sent over ten miles of wire in the City University of
New York, January 24, 1838. The message was loaned to the University for exhibit on occasion of the
Columbian Exposition of 1893. The photo accompanies a biographical essay of Samuel Morse'>

<META NAME = 'DC.publisher'
CONTENT = 'New York University Libraries'>

<META NAME = 'DC.date'
CONTENT = '1997'>

<META NAME = 'DC.type'
CONTENT = 'photograph'>

<META NAME = 'DC.format'
CONTENT = 'JPEG image'>

<META NAME = 'DC.identifier'
CONTENT =
'http://moriarty.bobst.nyu.edu/markup/Notebook/Morse/morse6.JPG'>

<META NAME = 'DC.language'
SCHEME = 'Z39.53'
CONTENT = 'eng'>

<META NAME = 'DC.relation'
TYPE = 'Relation.IsMemberOf'
CONTENT = 'Hering, Daniel Webster, 1850–1938. Papers, 1889–1939'>

<LINK REL = SCHEMA.dc
HREF = 'http://purl.org/metadata/dublin__core__elements'>

</HEAD>
<BODY>
. . .
```

Figure 2.15 Dublin Core metadata

of information, both in preparing document representations and in providing the index terms used to access documents. They consist of the title, contents list, preface and introduction, and index, and the blurb on the dust jacket. Any or all of these may be of value in determining the subject.

Titles

Printed documents of all types have titles, almost always given by their authors. Indexes based on titles go back at least 150 years. A title is the author's own summarization, identifier and retrieval cue. Research papers can usually be relied on to have informative titles, and editors of most primary journals issue guidelines to authors on the content of titles.

For subject searching, titles summarize the content of a document at its most basic level. Many indexes are based on keywords in titles, so it is important that titles so indexed should adequately reflect the subject content of the document. Less frequently, and mostly in the case of books, an author may feel that it is more important that the title should attract attention: *Women, Fire and Dangerous Things* (a study of the mental processes of categorization) and *How to Hold up a Bank* (a civil engineering manual) are two examples among many. Having decided on an oblique title, the author may make amends by means of an explicit subtitle (*What Categories Reveal about the Mind*). A few bibliographic search services provide title enrichment – the addition of a few extra keywords, or even a short annotation – to supplement titles that are perceived to be inadequate. This, however, requires the service of a human indexer with the knowledge to perceive and remedy the inadequacy; which in turn affects the cost and currency of the service.

It is virtually unknown for a published text not to have a title that has been assigned at or before publication. Non-textual media (e.g. graphic and cartographic material) may well not be furnished with titles, and similarly unpublished text – many untitled documents find their way on to the WWW.

Contents pages

Contents pages are usually to be found within books and journals. Their main purpose is to guide the reader through the book or journal, once it has been selected. The Institute for Scientific Information publishes a range of *Current contents* indexes, consisting of reproductions of the contents pages of issues of journals with very basic title keyword indexes to the papers listed on them, and used for current awareness. Some have suggested ways in which the contents pages of books may be used as an extra subject approach in catalogues and indexes. By scanning tables of contents into the bibliographic record, chapter and section headings become available as additional keywords for searching.

Preface and introduction

Where both occur, the precise demarcation line can vary. For the cataloguer, the preface and introduction often provide the author's own succinct statement of what a book is attempting to achieve.

Back-of-book indexes

Back-of-book indexes provide even more detailed subject information than contents pages, and experimental work has been carried out in using the computer to compile consolidated indexes to a range of books. As with indexes based on contents pages, no commercial systems are yet available.

Publisher's blurbs

Publisher's blurbs, if found, are the most eye-catching kind of additional subject information, but should be approached with caution. Their function is to sell the item, not to provide objective information. To that extent they may either represent the subject content as appealing to an implausibly wide range of interest groups or, conversely, focus on an aspect of the content that the publisher hopes will catch the attention. They have, however, been found adequate for the subject indexing of fiction.

In practice, indexers examine sections of the document itself in addition to its preliminaries. The relevant international standard (ISO 5963:1985E), *Methods for Examining Documents, Determining their Subjects, and Selecting Indexing Terms*, recommends that important parts of the text need to be considered carefully, and particular attention should be paid to the following:

- the title
- the abstract, if provided
- the list of contents
- the introduction, the opening phrases of chapters and paragraphs, and the conclusion
- illustrations, diagrams, tables and their captions
- words or groups of words which are underlined or printed in an unusual typeface.

SUMMARY

The focus of this chapter has been the formatting and structuring of information through documents. We have given an overview of organizing and retrieving information, focusing first on the database and then on the document itself. We have considered some of the problems concerning documents: problems of definition and relationship, and of text analysis; and we concluded with an examination of document markup – instructions facilitating the storage and reuse of electronic documents – and metadata for facilitating access to documents.

REFERENCES AND FURTHER READING

Buckland, M. K. (1997) What is a 'document'? *Journal of the American Society for Information Science,* **48** (9), 804–9.

Burke, M. A. (1999) *Organization of Multimedia Resources: Principles and Practice of Information Retrieval.* Aldershot: Gower.

Dale, P. (ed.) (1997) *Guide to Libraries and Information Sources in Medicine and Health Care,* 2nd edn. London: British Library, Science Reference and Information Services. The Dublin Core Metadata Element Set Home Page <http://www.oclc.org:5046/research/dublin—core/>.

Ford, N. (1991) *Expert Systems and Artificial Intelligence.* London: Library Association.

Foskett, A. C. (1982) *Subject Approach to Information,* 4th edn. London: Bingley.

Heery, R. (1996) Review of metadata formats. *Program,* **30** (4), October, 345–53; (also at <http://www.ukoln.ac.uk/metadata/review>).

International Organization for Standardization (1985) *Documentation – Methods for Examining Documents, Determining their Subjects and Selecting Indexing Terms.* ISO 5963:1985. Geneva: ISO.

International Organization for Standardization (1986) *Information Processing – Text and Office Systems – Standardized Generalized Markup Language (SGML).* ISO 8879:1986. Geneva: ISO.

Kunze, J. *Guide to Creating Dublin Core Descriptive Metadata* <http://purl.oclc.org/metadata/dublin_core/guide.>.

Meadow, C. T. (1996) *Text Information Retrieval Systems.* San Diego: Academic Press, (especially chapters 1–3).

Mostafa, J. (1994) Digital image representation and access. *Annual Review of Information Science and Technology,* **29,** 91–135.

Rasmussen, E. M. (1997) Indexing images. *Annual Review of Information Science and Technology,* **32,** 169–96.

Schamber, L. (1996) What is a document? Rethinking the concept in uneasy times. *Journal of the American Society for Information Science,* **47** (9), September, 669–71.

Tillett, B. B. (1991) A taxonomy of bibliographic relationships. *Library Resources and Technical Services,* **35** (2), 150–58.

Vellucci, S. L. (1997) Options for organizing electronic resources: the coexistence of metadata. *Bulletin of the American Society for Information Science,* **24** (1) October–November, 14–17.

Vellucci, S. L. (1998) Bibliographic relationships. In J. Weihs, (ed.), *The Principles and Future of AACR: Proceedings of the International Conference on the Principles and Future Development of AACR, Toronto, Ontario, Canada, October 23–25, 1997.* Ottawa: Canadian Library Association, 105–47.

Vickery, B. C. (1997) Knowledge discovery from databases: an introductory review. *Journal of Documentation,* **53** (2), 107–22.

Weibel, S. (1997) The Dublin Core: a simple content description model for electronic resources. *Bulletin of the American Society*, **24** (1), October–November, 9–11.

Weihs, J. (ed.) (1998) *The Principles and Future of AACR: Proceedings of the International Conference on the Principles and Future Development of AACR2, Toronto, Ontario, Canada, October 23–25, 1997*. Ottawa: Canadian Library Association. For later developments, see the Joint Steering Committee's Web site: <http://www.nlc-bnc.ca/jsc/index.htm>.

Part II
Records

3   Describing documents

INTRODUCTION

This chapter looks at document representations and document surrogates: records that identify and characterize, and often serve as keys for retrieving the actual documents. You will learn the principles and problems of document representations and surrogates, including:

- the construction and use of citations
- the purposes of abstracts and related kinds of document summary
- record formats in abstracting and indexing services
- the nature of bibliographic records – that is, records primarily of books, but including other media
- how to prepare a bibliographic description according to Anglo-American Cataloguing Rules (AACR)
- the principles and structure of the Machine-Readable Cataloguing (MARC) bibliographic record format and of the Common Communications Format (CCF).

This chapter is concerned with document *representation*, not with document *access*, which is dealt with in Chapters 4 to 9. Metadata is also a form of document representation, but one which is invariably associated with the document itself, and for that reason it was described in Chapter 2.

CHARACTERISTICS AND PROBLEMS OF DOCUMENT REPRESENTATION

In many information retrieval situations, we are unable to work with documents themselves, but have to rely on representations, or document 'surrogates'. It is only in recent years that it has become technically and economically possible to directly retrieve documents. Previously, we constructed indexes consisting of brief records of documents, and retrieved those surrogates in advance of retrieving the actual documents. Library catalogues, citations, abstracts and bibliographies are typical examples. Hypertext links, classmarks, keywords and abstracts are other forms of surrogate, but are usually embedded in larger records. Identification keys – ISBNs, International Standard Serial Numbers (ISSNs) and URLs – are another type of document surrogate. All these document surrogates represent individual documents in an information retrieval system.

Document representation has a long and complex history, with many distinct strands, including:

1. *Cataloguing*: the compilation of lists of books in a collection. In its most basic form, this was an inventory for administrative purposes. It also became a finding list, to enable users to find items in the collection.
2. *Bibliography, historical and descriptive*. Historical bibliography is a tool of literary research, by which individual copies of books (particularly hand-printed books) are meticulously described, in order to establish the best text of an author. With descriptive (or systematic) bibliography the emphasis is not on the individual copy but on the definitive listing of works having some defining characteristic, often author, place of printing or subject.
3. *Citation*: the practice in research and scholarship of writers to list the works they have cited, thereby acknowledging the work of their predecessors.
4. *Indexing and abstracting services*, which are used to identify the documents – often journal articles – that are required to meet a specific subject request.
5. *Records management systems*, which are the responsibility of records managers and archivists to maintain an orderly collection of the records of an organization, in print or electronic format.
6. *Metadata*: data added to a networked electronic resource as a mechanism to enable it to be adequately described and located.

Some common and persistent characteristics and problems of document representation are:

1. *Defining the document*, as was discussed in Chapter 2.
2. *Identification*: any representation of a document or resource must be able to identify it uniquely.
3. *Granularity*, or breadth of bibliographic unit. At what level should a document be described and indexed? Should, for example, individual contributions to a journal be indexed separately? Similar questions arise in respect of (for example) papers in a set of conference proceedings; two or more musical works on one CD; a school resource kit containing pupils'

workbooks, wall charts, a teacher's book, etc.; or pages other than the home page of a Web site. Some considerations influencing the granularity of description include:

a) Is the more detailed description available within the document? For example, many books have contents pages and back-of-book indexes, or large Web sites may have an internal search engine.

b) Are there external sources that perform the same task? Most libraries for example do not record journal articles or contributions to published conference proceedings in their catalogues, as there are specialist indexing and abstracting services that perform this function.

c) Will the use justify the extra cost? Sometimes detailed description for rapid retrieval is vital, as with a television news service's film archive, or a fire service's database of information on hazardous materials. In other cases it may be cheaper to carry out time-consuming sequential searching for seldom required items, e.g. in archives of local history materials.

d) Will the extra detail merely lead to added complexity and near duplication? – as with some Web search engines when they record numerous hits, mostly to different parts of the same site.

4. *Selection*. The description must always uniquely identify the document it represents. Many representations go further, by indicating related documents, or by including information which characterizes the document. An important function of document representation is to act as a selection filter, enabling users to decide whether or not they wish to obtain the actual document.

5. *Search keys*. Document representations for manually searched databases need search keys: headings under which they are filed for manual searching. In the case of networked resources, 'semantic interoperability' requires such devices as metadata and the Z39.50 search and retrieve protocol.

6. *Location and accessibility*. A document representation loses much of its purpose if users are not given enough information to enable them to locate the document itself. In the case of books and journals, bibliographic control is well enough established for the conventional publication details to suffice for this purpose. In the case of non-print materials:

a) Bibliographic control is often less well organized than with printed materials

b) The extent of the item may not be immediately obvious in the way that it can be judged by counting or estimating the number of pages in a book or journal article

c) In many cases the material can only be used via some mechanical, optical or electronic device.

Networked resources may have specific hardware (e.g. free disc space) and/or software requirements (e.g. Adobe Acrobat). Locations may well be remote, unlike library catalogues, which typically list only locations within the institution. A networked resource may be available to all, or access may be restricted, e.g. to members of an organization or on payment of a fee.

RECORDS

The representation of an item comprises a record. A record contains the information relating to and describing one document. Other similar documents will also be represented by records. A database is a collection of similar records. Records are composed of a number of fields. The types of fields used, their length and the number of fields in a record must be chosen in accordance with a specific application.

There are two types of field: fixed length and variable length. A *fixed-length field* is one that contains the same number of characters in each record. Since field lengths are predictable, it is not necessary to signal to the computer where each field begins and ends. Fixed-length fields are economical to store and records using fixed-length fields are quick and easy to code. However, fixed-length fields may not adequately accommodate variable-length data. Fixed-length fields are ideal for codes, such as ISBNs, reader codes, product codes, bank account numbers, dates, and language codes where the length of the information will be the same in each record. With variable-length data variable-length fields are necessary. A *variable-length field* will consist of different lengths in different records. Here, the computer cannot recognize when one field ends and another starts, so it becomes necessary to flag the beginning and end of fields. In addition objects, such as pictures and video clips, may be stored as separate files linked to records that contain primarily fixed or variable length fields. Within fields, individual data elements or units of information may be designated as *subfields*. Subfields need to be flagged so that they can be identified. The discussion of the MARC record format, in the section on pages 85–9, has examples of the two types of field and subfields.

CITATIONS

We start with citations, as these have an honourable and familiar place in the academic world: the mechanism by which scholars acknowledge the work of their predecessors, and students ward off accusations of plagiarism in essays. Citations are a relatively uncomplicated form of document representation and one that every student, irrespective of discipline, is required to create. This section discusses the format of citations, and when to make them.

Citations form the basis for structuring the records used in indexing and abstracting services. The purpose and making of abstracts are described in the following section, and the records used in indexing and abstracting services are described in 'Bibliographic record formats' later in this chapter. *Citation indexes*, a method of retrieval based on the lists of references at the end of scholarly papers, are discussed in Chapter 2.

There are a number of published standards for ensuring uniformity, notably British Standards 5605:1990 *Recommendations for Citing and Referencing Published Material* and 1629:1989 *Recommendations for References to Published Material*; the *Chicago Manual of Style*; and K. L. Turabian's *A Manual for Writers of Term Papers, Theses and Dissertations*. In spite of the existence of standards, publishers of primary journals continue to maintain a wide range of house styles for citations and bibliographies.

For each reference it is essential to record sufficient information to identify precisely the source cited. There are a number of published standards for ensuring this, but there is at present no standard for citations to electronic documents, though one is in preparation. Two separate methods of referencing documents are permitted: the *Harvard* (name and date) system, and the

With this system, authors' names and dates of publication are given in parentheses within the running text or at the end of block quotations. They are keyed to a list of works cited, arranged alphabetically by author, and placed at the end of the text. Cited publications are referred to in the text by giving the author's surname and the year of publication:

In a recent study Schamber (1996) argued that . . .

In a recent study (Schamber 1996) it was argued that . . .

In their first work, Westlake and Clarke (1987) . . .

The more recent study by Farmer et al. (1998) . . . (For more than two authors)

To acknowledge direct quotations or to refer to individual pages of a particular book or article the page number(s) are given after the date, separated from it by a comma, and within the parentheses:

(Eason 1988, p.49)

The list of references is a single alphabetical list, at the end of the text. Date of publication appears immediately after the author's name:

Colley, A.M. and Beech, J.R., eds. (1989) *Acquisition and performance of cognitive skills.* Chichester: Wiley.

Cathro, W. (1997) Metadata: an overview. http://www.nla.gov.au/nla/staffpaper/cathro3.html

Ericsson, K.A. and Oliver, W.L. (1989). A methodology for assessing the detailed structure of memory skills. In: Colley, A.M. and Beech, J.R., eds. (1989), pp. 46–58

Rowley, J. (1988) *Abstracting and indexing.* 2nd ed. London: Bingley.

Rowley, J. (1998) *The electronic library.* London: Library Association.

Schamber, L. (1996) What is a document? rethinking the concept in uneasy times. *Journal of the American Society for information Science,* **47**(9), pp. 669–71.

Figure 3.1   Citation: The Harvard (name and date) system

With this system, cited publications are numbered in the order in which they are first referred to in the text. They are identified by a number given in square brackets (round brackets and superscript numerals are also found):

In a recent study, Schamber [5] argued that . . .

As Carson [7, p. 46] has argued . . .

A number of studies [2,3,4] have demonstrated . . .

Entries are listed in numerical order in the list of references to match the sequence of references cited in the text. Sources not specifically referred to in the text must be given in a separate list of sources or bibliography.

1. Cathro, W. (1997) Metadata: an overview. 1997. http://www.nla.gov.au/nla/staffpaper/cathro3.html
2. Colley, A.M. and Beech, J.R. Acquiring and performing cognitive skills. *In:* Colley A.M. and Beech, J.R., eds. *Acquisition and performance of cognitive skills.* Chichester: Wiley, 1989, pp. 1–10
3. Schamber, L. What is a document? rethinking the concept in uneasy times. *Journal of the American Society for Information Science*, **47**(9), 1996, pp. 669–71
4. Colley, A.M. and Beech, J.R. (ref. 2, p. 3)
5. Rowley, J. *Abstracting and indexing.* 2nd ed. London: Bingley, 1988
6. Ericsson, K.A. and Oliver, W.L. A methodology for assessing the detailed structure of memory skills. *In:* Colley and Beech (ref. 2), pp. 46–58
7. Rowley, J. *The electronic library.* London: Library Association, 1998

Figure 3.2 Citation: The Numeric (Vancouver) system

Numeric (Vancouver) system (Figures 3.1 and 3.2). The Harvard system is generally easier to apply, and is used in the majority of scholarly journals in the natural and social sciences. The Numeric system is more likely to be found in the arts and humanities.

COMPILING CITATION LISTS

Obtain data for citations from the following sources, in order of preference: (1) the title page, or a substitute (cover, caption, masthead, etc.); (2) any other source which is part of the item; (3) any other source which accompanies the item and was issued by the publisher (e.g. a container, a printed insert).

The citation elements are:

1. Primary responsibility (author, editor, etc.).
2. Year (the position of this element varies according to the display style chosen. This is the position if using the *Harvard* style).
3. Title.
4. Type of medium (if needed).
5. Publication details: place, publisher.
6. Year (the position of this element varies according to the display style chosen. This is the position if using the *Numeric* style.).
7. Series – normally only needed for reports, or where there might be confusion

between the title proper and the series title (as with some kinds of audio and visual material).

8. Numeration within the item (if the item is in more than one part, or if part of an item is cited).

9. Location of item (if unique, rare or otherwise difficult to locate).

NON-BOOK MATERIALS

Non-book materials, including computer software that can be handled like any other library material, e.g. CD-ROMs. The information given for printed media will need to be supplemented by as many of the following as are appropriate:

- the *medium* (e.g. filmstrip, video, compact disc (CD), CD-ROM)
- *how accessed*. With audio and visual materials, this information need in many cases only be given if a non-standard system is required (e.g. for Betamax videos)
- *duration* of films, videos, etc., if easily established
- frequency of *update* (e.g. for CD-ROM databases)
- Most materials that comprise a single intellectual unit can be treated broadly as books. Citations for databases in CD-ROM formats are based on citations of whole serials.

ELECTRONIC DOCUMENTS

Electronic documents, including electronic monographs, databases and computer programs, electronic serials, electronic bulletin boards, Web documents, and e-mail. As they exist only in electronic format, it is vital to show how the item can be accessed. In the case of Internet resources, the 'generic' location description is the URL. References are cited in the text in the usual way. If using the *Harvard* style, the list of references then follows the general form:

Author (year, date). Title (version) [medium]. Location. Place of publication: Publisher.

- *(Year, Date)*. Adding *Date* (month, day, even time of day) to the scheme overcomes the problem of transient or dynamically updated sources.
- *Version* is the online equivalent of *edition*. The *Date* may be optional if a particular version number is identified.
- *[Medium]* will be given as [Online] in the case of sources referenced over a telecommunications link. For non-networked formats use [CD-ROM], [Laserdisc], [Videodisc], [Disc], etc., as appropriate.

- *Page numbers* are not usually a feature of electronic documents, as page layout is dependent on the viewing method.
- *Location* refers to the URL in the case of Internet resources; otherwise a generic online location. ISO 690-2 (ISO, 1999) recommends the style: Available from *source*: *<location>*, e.g. Available from World Wide Web: <http://www.nlc-bnc.ca/iso/tc46sc9/standard/690-2e.htm>.
- On the Internet, anyone can be a publisher, and *Publisher* may be omitted where the author has self-published. However, electronic publishing online is becoming an industry in itself, and the position of publisher in the scheme needs to be retained.

CITATION PRACTICES

The following rules of thumb are offered as a general guide to good citation practice for students:

- Always acknowledge your sources.
- Keep a record of the bibliographical details of those sources as you consult them.
- If you have a significant number of sources, maintain a card or simple electronic listing of the sources you have used.
- Record all bibliographical details as indicated in this book.
- Be particularly attentive in recording details of electronic sources such as home pages – these can be surprisingly difficult to locate on subsequent occasions without the URL.
- Arrange your bibliography in alphabetical order by the author's surname or family name, irrespective of the form of document.
- Any items you have read, but not cited, may optionally be added under a heading such as 'Other sources'.

Many universities and departments have their own guidelines. Follow any local guidelines that may be issued.

PERSONAL BIBLIOGRAPHIC FILE MANAGEMENT SOFTWARE

A number of bibliographic file management programs are available for managing personal file collections such as those developed by researchers and other authors. Examples include Biblio-Link, End-Note Plus, File Maker Pro, Papyrus, Pro-Cite and Reference Manager. These packages are not primarily intended for information professionals, so it is important that they should be easy to use. Other desirable features include: predefined fields, the ability to import citations from external sources, so that online search results can be downloaded directly into the correct fields; adding extra fields for personal use, such as keywords and annotations; field or term search capability; detecting duplicates; editing globally; and predefined output formats for generating bibliographies in a variety of journal formats.

Notice that, while 'bibliographic' is properly confined to databases containing surrogate records of books, the word is also used more loosely in relation to surrogate records of all kinds of print materials and their databases.

ABSTRACTS

Abstracts are used by both readers of the primary literature and by users of secondary services. Within the primary literature, an abstract normally appears at the front of the item, usually immediately preceding the text. In this way, readers are able

> to identify the basic content of a document quickly and accurately, to determine its relevance to their interests, and thus to decide whether they need to read the document in its entirety. If the document is of fringe interest, reading the abstract may make it unnecessary to read the whole document.
>
> (ISO 214: 1976E)

Abstracts are recommended to accompany journal articles; also any other material in journals that has a substantial technical or scholarly content (e.g. discussions and reviews). It is normal for the writers of journal articles and similar primary material to include an abstract when submitting material for publication. Abstracts should also accompany reports (whether published or unpublished) and theses, monographs and conference proceedings (including chapter abstracts if each chapter covers different topics), and patents applications and specifications.

The other major use of abstracts is in secondary services (e.g. abstracting journals and their associated online and CD-ROM bibliographical databases). These services often use the original (author's) abstracts – either as they stand, or amended. Where these are lacking or considered unsuitable, an abstract has to be written from scratch, adding to the cost and often reducing the currency of the service.

There are many types of abstract (see Figure 3.3), according to the requirements of particular applications, as influenced by the language, length and readership of the document; the intended audience of the abstract; and the resources of the abstracting agency. For texts describing experimental work and documents devoted to a single theme, an *informative* abstract is recommended. This type of abstract presents as much as possible of the quantitative and/or

Below are four different types of abstracts relating to the same document: Rowley, J.E. Guidelines on the evaluation and selection of library software packages. A*slib proceedings*, **42** (9), September 1990, pp. 225–35.

Informative abstract
The evaluation and selection of a library software package (whether it be for library housekeeping, text retrieval or the selection of some other database) should be approached as a project. Strategies for the selection and evaluation of software packages can be based on systems analysis and design methodologies. Stages in the project should include: definition of objectives, evaluation of options, definition, selection and design, implementation, and evaluation and maintenance. The features to seek in text retrieval systems can be grouped into data entry, indexing, interactive information retrieval, output, current awareness, security, contract and other general issues. A checklist for library management systems also needs to encompass security, contract and similar general issues, but in addition needs to specify the features of the acquisitions, cataloguing and circulation control modules. Recent developments in database structures, retrieval facilities, the screen interface and integration with other systems must be noted.

Indicative abstract
The evaluation and selection of a library software package (whether it be for library housekeeping, text retrieval or the selection of some other database) should be approached as a project. Strategies for the selection and evaluation of software packages are considered. The following stages in the project are reviewed: definition of objectives, evaluation of options, definition, selection and design, implementation, and evaluation and maintenance. Some checklists of features to seek in text retrieval and library management systems are included. These are discussed in the context of new developments in software.

Extract
This article proposes a strategy for the selection and evaluation of library software packages. Two checklists review the key features of text retrieval software and library management systems.

Short abstract
Strategies for the selection and evaluation of software packages are outlined. Two checklists summarize the features to seek in text retrieval and library management software.

Figure 3.3   Examples of different types of abstract

qualitative information contained in the document. This includes in particular a note of the results and conclusions of any experimental work. Such an abstract can be a substitute for the full document when only a superficial knowledge is required. Informative abstracts can extend to 500 words or more, though 100–250 words is the norm.

An *indicative* abstract is usually much shorter: merely an indication of the type of document, the principal subjects covered, and the way the facts are treated. This type of abstract is often applied to opinion papers and papers generally which do not report research, or where the text is discursive or lengthy, such as broad overviews, review papers and entire monographs. A *short abstract* comprises only one or two sentences supplementing the title, and may be valuable in current awareness services where speed is essential.

In an *indicative-informative* abstract the primary elements of the document are written in an informative way, while the less significant aspects have indicative statements only.

A *slanted* abstract is one which concentrates on those topics within a document that are of interest to the abstracting service's user community. A development of this is the *critical* abstract: one that evaluates the abstracted item. Both types are expensive to produce, as the abstractor requires detailed knowledge of the subject and the user community as well as abstracting skills; so they are uncommon, and very seldom found in published abstracting services.

The location of abstracts is:

- in a *journal*: on the first page, between the title and author information and the text
- in a *report*: on the title page if possible; otherwise on a right-hand page preceding the table of contents
- in a *book* or *thesis*: on the right-hand page following the title page
- in a *secondary source*: immediately following the bibliographic citation for the original document.

The skills needed in an abstractor are essentially:

- a good standard of literacy, particularly the ability to write clearly and concisely
- detailed knowledge of the subject field of the material being abstracted
- an awareness of the patterns of text structures in the materials being abstracted
- an awareness of the kinds of people who will be using the abstracts, and of the environment of information access generally
- an ability to work methodically and accurately.

The tendency is for as much use as possible to be made of author-abstractors. Secondary abstractors often have formal qualifications in both information science and the subject field in which they are working. The larger abstracting services employ full-time abstractors, but many abstractors combine these tasks with other information-related duties – particularly information officers in industry and commerce, producing in-house information bulletins.

WRITING INFORMATIVE ABSTRACTS

- Most documents describing experimental work conform to the sequence *Purpose – Methodology – Results – Conclusions*. Readers in many disciplines are accustomed to this pattern.
- Begin the abstract with a topic sentence that is a central statement of the

document's major theme, unless this is already well stated in the document's title or can be derived from the remainder of the abstract.

- Give only a brief statement of methodology, unless a technique is new. Results and conclusions however should be clearly presented.
- If the findings are too numerous for all to be included, give the most important. Any findings or information incidental to the main purpose of the document but of value outside its main subject area may be included, so long as their relative importance is not exaggerated.
- Abstracts must be self-contained and retain the basic information and tone of the document. They must be clear and concise, and must not include information or claims not contained in the document itself.
- Unless the abstract is a long one, write it as a single paragraph. Write in complete sentences, and use transitional words and phrases for coherence.
- Use verbs in the active voice and third person whenever possible. Use significant words from the text. Avoid unfamiliar terms, acronyms, abbreviations or symbols, or define them the first time they occur.
- Include short tables, equations, structural formulas and diagrams only when necessary for brevity and clarity and when no acceptable alternative exists.

OTHER KINDS OF DOCUMENT SUMMARIES

An *annotation* usually appears as a note after the bibliographic citation of a document. It is a brief comment or explanation about a document or its contents, or even a very brief description.

An *extract* comprises one or more portions of a document selected to represent the whole – often a sentence or two indicating the results, conclusions or recommendations of a study. They are usually shorter than an abstract, and require less effort to produce.

A *summary* is a brief restatement of a document's salient findings and conclusions. It occurs within a document, usually at the end, less frequently at the beginning. Summaries are most often found in reports, where they are mainly intended for busy people who do not have time to do more than skim through the full text; and increasingly in the chapters of textbooks as an aid to orientation.

Other forms of text reduction, such as reviews, synopses, abridgements, digests, précis and paraphrases, have applications that are outside the scope of the present work.

RECORD FORMATS IN ABSTRACTING AND INDEXING SERVICES

For the large public databases, there has been little pressure to accept a standard format, and each database producer has in general chosen a record format to suit the particular database. The nearest applicable standard is the *UNISIST Reference Manual* (UNESCO, 1986). Even one database may emerge in different record formats according to the online search service on which it is mounted. Individual decisions are made concerning the fields to be included and the subject indexing made available. Yet another variable factor is the presence of full-text, and more recently multimedia, databases which demand a somewhat different record format from bibliographic records if the information is to be appropriately displayed.

Some examples of record formats in online search services are given in Figures 3.4 and 3.5.

BIBLIOGRAPHIC RECORD FORMATS

All records in one file have a standard format. In order to facilitate exchange of records between different computer systems, there have been attempts to develop some standard record formats. Such formats were seen to be particularly beneficial in cataloguing applications, where a standard format, which also

```
DIALOG(R)File 1:ERIC
(c) format only 1999 The Dialog Corporation. All rts. reserv.

EJ557261 IR536335
Automatic Text Structuring and Categorization As a First Step in Summarizing Legal Cases.
Moens, Marie-Francine; Uyttendaele, Caroline
Information Processing & Management; v33 n6 pp.727–37 Nov 1997
ISSN: 0306-4573
Language: English
Document Type: JOURNAL ARTICLE (080); PROJECT DESCRIPTION (141)
Journal Announcement: CIJJUN98
Describes SALOMON (Summary and Analysis of Legal texts for Managing Online Needs), a system
which automatically summarizes Belgian criminal cases to improve access to court decisions. Highlights
include a text grammar represented as a semantic network; automatic abstracting; knowledge acquisition
and representation; parsing; evaluation, including recall and precision; and future work. (Author/LRW)
Descriptors: Abstracting; Access to Information; *Automation; Computer System Design; *Court Liti-
gation; *Criminal Law; Evaluation Methods; Foreign Countries; Futures (of Society); *Information
Retrieval; Relevance (Information Retrieval); *Text Structure
Identifiers: Belgium; Knowledge Acquisition; Parsing; Semantic Networks
```

Figure 3.4 Citation with abstract

1/9/8
DIALOG(R)File 47:Magazine Database(TM)
(c) 1999 Information Access Co. All rts. reserv.

05302304 SUPPLIER NUMBER: 53621480 (THIS IS THE FULL TEXT)
Jackpot. (the economic aspects of the gambling industry) (Brief Article)
Stone, Peter H.
Mother Jones, 23, 6, 67(1) Nov, 1998
DOCUMENT TYPE: Brief Article ISSN: 0362-8841 LANGUAGE: English
RECORD TYPE: Fulltext
WORD COUNT: 560 LINE COUNT: 00047

TEXT:
Casino mogul Steve Wynn is behind millions in donations, but manages to stay off of the Mother Jones 400 One morning last November, a small jet owned by casino mogul Steve Wynn lifted off from Washington, D.C., bound for Las Vegas and carrying a trio of Senate GOP leaders: Majority Leader Trent Lott (R-Miss.), Mitch McConnell (R-Ky.), and Bill Frist (R-Tenn.). That evening they gathered for cocktails at Wynn's Shadow Creek Country Club, listening to him brag about all the jobs being created by the gambling industry.

But Wynn, who runs Mirage Resorts, did much more than just talk at the gathering: He had brought together a group of about three dozen gambling executives whose companies gave $100,000 to the GOP over the weekend. And, in the months that followed, the gaming industry poured $1.2 million into GOP coffers. Wynn headed the pack with a well-timed $250,000 contribution from Mirage in March: It arrived just days after the introduction of a measure that would have ended tax deductions for gambling losses. Leaving nothing to chance, the industry lobbied Lott and McConnell, who pressed the bill's sponsor, Sen. Dan Coats (R-Ind.), to pull the measure.

Tight relationships with prominent Senate leaders have made Wynn the gambling industry's most powerful political player. And Mirage has certainly led the charge, donating nearly $1 million since 1991, including contributions from Wynn, company executives, their spouses, and the company's PAC, according to the Center for Responsive Politics. He often gives through Mirage, and so he stays off lists such as the Mother Jones 400. (Others, such as Sheldon Adelson (No. 74), Stanley Fulton (No. 108), and Arthur M. Goldberg (No. 168) aren't as wise.)

Well known for his flashy style, perennial tan, and sleek coiffure, the 56-year-old Wynn demonstrates his political shrewdness by covering his bets with Democrats, too. In June, Mirage dropped a $200,000 check in the mail to the Democratic Party – just days after Sen. Robert Torricelli (D-N.J.), a longtime industry ally and an acquaintance of Wynn's, was quoted in the National Journal questioning why so much money was going to the GOP, given growing criticism of gambling from prominent conservative Republicans such as Gary Bauer and presidential candidate Sen. John Aschroft (see 'Reagan Redux,' page 27).

Such care and feeding of political leaders has paid off well: In 1996, when Congress and the Clinton administration created a National Gambling Impact Study Commission to probe the social and economic effects of gambling, Congress granted the commission only limited subpoena powers, and placed a number of strong industry allies on it. Still, the commission's final report is due next June, and casino interests are nervous about how critical it will be and whether it will lead to calls for federal regulation.

That sets the stakes high for the gambling industry – and, in particular, Wynn. Anyone wondering why Wynn would want friends covering his bets need only read about his latest and greatest venture: the $1.6 billion Bellagio, a lavish Las Vegas casino that houses an art collection worth a reported $300 million, with paintings by Gauguin, Van Gogh, and Monet, some of which he reportedly hopes to sell for a tidy profit.
COPYRIGHT 1998 Foundation for National Progress

DESCRIPTORS: United States. Congress. Senate—Political activity; Gambling industry—Economic aspects; United States—Politics and government
NAMED PERSONS: Wynn, Stephen A.—Practice
FILE SEGMENT: MI File 47

Figure 3.5 Full-text record

embodies an agreement on the elements of a bibliographic record, has been particularly attractive in allowing the exchange of cataloguing records. This exchange has minimized the need for local cataloguing, as libraries can make use of records that others have created. Accordingly, one of the fields in which a standard record format is best established is in the creation of cataloguing records.

The exchange of machine-readable records has necessitated the standardization of bibliographic record formats. There is an International Standard Bibliographic Description (ISBD) for most categories of material. These include ISBD(M) monographs, ISBD(S) serials, ISBD(PM) printed music, ISBD(CM) cartographic materials, and ISBD(CF) computer files – this is not by any means a complete list. All follow the general framework of ISBD(G), which recommends:

- what information should be given in the description, including the extent of detail required
- in what order the information should be given and, preferably,
- the punctuation needed to divide and distinguish between the elements of the description.

The programme of ISBDs has also brought about the reconciliation of two earlier sets of standards for bibliographical description: AACR, originally published in 1967 and extensively revised in 1978 (AACR2), and MARC, first implemented in 1968. Machine-Readable Cataloguing has proliferated into a range of formats. The UKMARC format is standard in Britain, but is being reconciled with the US format USMARC, which is now recognized as the standard format for the English-speaking world.

AACR2 is organized into two parts, the one entitled 'Description' and the other 'Headings, uniform titles and references'. These indicate AACR2's two distinct functions of document representation and document access. According to the plan of the present book, only the first of these is under detailed consideration in the present chapter. The MARC format however also incorporates AACR2's mechanisms for document access (which are discussed in Chapter 10). To further complicate matters, AACR2 excludes subject access whereas the MARC format makes provision for it. Three subject access systems are included in the USMARC record format: the Dewey Decimal Classification (DDC), the Library of Congress Classification (LCC), and Library of Congress Subject Headings (LCSH). These are described in Chapters 7 and 8.

BIBLIOGRAPHIC DESCRIPTION

The description of a document as part of a catalogue entry acts as a document surrogate. The word 'bibliographic' denotes the large degree of overlap between catalogues and bibliographies. The catalogues of major national libraries are often effectively major bibliographies in their own right, and the libraries themselves may be national agencies for preparing catalogue copy for distribution to subscribers.

The traditional functions of description are to:

- describe each document as a document – that is, to identify it
- distinguish it from other items
- show relationships with other items.

Again, notice that considerations of document access are excluded. In preparing the description of a document it is necessary to make certain preliminary decisions if different cataloguers are to produce identical records from the same document. These considerations include:

1. *The source of the information for the description.* A 'chief source of information' is designated, to ensure consistency among different cataloguers (for example, in the treatment of books whose title-page title differs from that found on the cover or spine). In order of preference, information is taken from: the item itself; its container; other accompanying material; other external sources. According to the material, a source of information may be unitary (a title page) or collective (the sequence of credits on a film or video). Specific sources of information are prescribed for different parts (areas) of the description. So for books, the prescribed source of information for the title and statement of responsibility is the title page, but for the physical description the whole publication is examined.

2. *Organization of the description.* The description is organized into eight *areas*, based on the layout of a catalogue entry as it has evolved over a century and a half. The areas are:
   a) Title and statement of responsibility
   b) Edition
   c) Material (or type of publication) specific details
   d) Physical description
   e) Series
   f) Note
   g) Standard number and terms of availability.
   The sequence of the areas is as shown. If an area is not applicable to an item, it is simply omitted. The areas are described in detail below. The organization of the MARC record format follows this sequence.

3. *Punctuation.* Consistent punctuation aids the recognition and rapid scanning of the various areas of the description in manually searched indexes, and is particularly important for the international exchange of records. In MARC

records, the prescribed punctuation for each area of the description is built into the subfield structure.

4. *Levels of detail in the description.* Different applications may demand different degrees of detail in the description. AACR2 identifies three levels of detail (see Figures 3.6 and 3.7). In a small general library simple records may be adequate, whereas a large research collection may require rather more detail. National bibliographic agencies may apply different levels of description to different categories of material, with, for example, fiction and books for children being catalogued at the simplest level.

Castles and palaces map of the British Isles. – Edinburgh: Bartholomew, [198-]. – 1 wall chart: col.; 101 x 75 cm (fold to 26 x 16 cm)

English madrigals/The King's Singers. – [London]: HMV Classics, c1995. – 1 sound disc (73 min.): digital, stereo; 4¾ in. + 1 leaflet (6 p.: col. ill.; 13 cm.). – (HMV Classics; 145). – Compact disc. – 'The principal composers in this collection are Thomas Morley and Thomas Weelkes' – accompanying notes. – HMV 5 69009 2

Frink: a portrait/Edward Lucie-Smith and Elisabeth Frink. – London: Bloomsbury, 1994. – 138p, [16]p of plates: ill (some col.).ports; 22 x 23cm. – Ill. on lining papers. – ISBN 0-7475-1572-7

Geoff Hamiltons [sic] 3D garden designer. – Computer program. – St Ives, Cambs: GSP, c1998. – 1 computer optical disc; 4¾ in. – System requirements: Windows 95 or higher. – Summary: Plant encyclopedia and graphic editor producing plans for gardens and parks. – GSPCD125

Mystic Meg's lucky numbers: for life, love and the lottery/illustrations by Caroline Smith. – London: Warner, 1996. – 289p : ill ; 18 cm. – ISBN 0-7515-1875-1

Rainfall in Birmingham, 1940–1979: a statistical analysis by weeks / J.Kings and B.D. Giles. – 2nd ed. – [Birmingham]: Department of Geography, University of Birmingham, 1982. – 87p: ill; 30cm. – (Occasional publication; no.14). – ISBN 0-7044-0575-X

Salmond and Heuston on the law of torts. – 20th ed. / by R.F.V. Heuston and R.A. Buckley. – London: Sweet & Maxwell, 1992. – 604p; 24cm. – ISBN 0-421-45980-8

Site layout planning for daylight and sunlight: a guide to good practice/P.J. Littlefair. – Watford: Building Research Establishment, 1991. – 85p: ill; 30cm. – (Building Research Establishment report; 209). – ISBN 0-85125-506-X

Soba: archaeological research at a medieval capital on the Blue Nile / by D.A. Welsby and C.M. Daniels; with a preface by Sir Lawrence Kirwan; and cont[r]ibutions by L. Allison-Jones . . . [et al.]. – London: British Institute in Eastern Africa, 1991. – 363p: ill, maps; 31 cm. – (Memoirs of the British Institute in Eastern Africa; no.12). – 2 maps on folded leaves in pocket. – Bibliography: pp. 356–60

Total eclipse / produced by Jean-Pierre Ramsey Levi. – London: Video Collection International, 1998. – 1 videocartridge (108 min.). – Cast: Leonardo DiCaprio (Arthur Rimbaud); David Thewlis (Paul Verlaine). – Credits: script: Agniezka Holland; music: Jan J.P. Kaczmarec; editor: Isbel Lorente. – Made in 1995. – VHS. – Summary: Chronicles the volatile relationship between the 19th century French poets Verlaine and Rimbaud. – VC3636

Figure 3.6 Descriptive cataloguing examples: Level 2

Castles and palaces map of the British Isles. – Bartholomew, [198-]. – 1 wall chart.

English madrigals/The King's Singers. – HMV Classics, c1995. – 1 sound disc. + 1 leaflet. – Compact disc. – HMV 5 69009 2

Frink/Edward Lucie-Smith and Elisabeth Frink. – Bloomsbury, 1994. – 138p. – ISBN 0-7475-1572-7

Geoff Hamiltons [sic] 3D garden designer. – Computer program. – GSP, c1998. – 1 computer optical disc; 4¼ in. – System requirements: Windows 95 or higher. – GSPCD125

Mystic Meg's lucky numbers. – Warner, 1996. – 289 p. – ISBN 0-7515-1875-1

Rainfall in Birmingham, 1940-1979 / J.Kings and B.D. Giles. – 2nd ed. – Department of Geography, University of Birmingham, 1982. – 87p. – ISBN 0-7044-0575-X

Salmond and Heuston on the law of torts. – 20th ed. – Sweet & Maxwell, 1992. – 604p. – ISBN 0-421-45980-8

Site layout planning for daylight and sunlight. – Building Research Establishment, 1991. – 85p. – ISBN 0-85125-506-X

Soba/by D.A. Welsby and C.M. Daniels. – British Institute in Eastern Africa, 1991. – 363p. – 2 maps on folded leaves in pocket. – Bibliography: pp. 356–60

Total eclipse/produced by Jean-Pierre Ramsey Levi. – Video Collection International, 1998. – 1 video-cartridge. – VHS. – VC3636

Figure 3.7 Descriptive cataloguing examples: Level 1

COMPONENTS OF THE DESCRIPTION

A bibliographic description compiled in accordance with ISBD and AACR2 is divided into a number of areas. The MARC bibliographic record format has corresponding groups of fields. These areas are discussed below.

Title and statement of responsibility

These form one area instead of two because one or the other may be lacking (as with anonymous works, or a book of reproductions of art works which has only the artist's name on the title page), or the two may be grammatically inseparable (e.g. *Poems of William Wordsworth*). In many cases, Author + Title proper + Date adequately identify an item, fulfilling the first purpose of description. Early cataloguers, who had to physically type or write each catalogue card, soon realized that time and card space could be saved by omitting the author's name from the description where it was recognizably the same as the author heading appearing immediately above the description (that is, in the great majority of cases), and this interdependence of description and heading has been built into the MARC record format.

The following elements are distinguished:

- title proper; this is transcribed exactly as found
- optionally, a general material designation: a word or short phrase from a prescribed list, indicating the type of material (e.g. [text], [music])
- parallel title: where the title appears in more than one language
- other title information: usually a subtitle
- statements of responsibility.

Optionally, a *uniform title* – a cataloguer's filing title, preceding the title proper – may be assigned in cases where different editions of the same work may appear under different titles (see Chapter 10).

The statement of responsibility is given as found within the chief source of information. Its purpose is to describe; it is not intended to serve as an access point. Access points use headings derived from the statement of responsibility according to a complex set of rules. These are described in Chapter 10. A heading is often permanently associated with a description, and in such cases Level 1 description permits the omission of the statement of responsibility when it is recognizably the same as the main entry heading.

The principles of description were laid down before online access became an everyday reality. Title keywords are now a significant access mechanism in OPACs and other computerized search systems. Subtitles are not required in a Level 1 description, but in view of their usefulness in keyword access it would be sensible to include them even in the most abbreviated formats.

Edition

The principal elements are:

- the edition statement as found in the document, except that abbreviations (e.g. Rev. ed.) may be used, and a statement of first edition is by convention omitted
- statements of responsibility relating to the edition.

The concept of the edition derives from the printed book in the days when type was set by hand. A new edition implied a resetting of the type, which usually implied some revision of the content. A valid distinction could thus be made between an edition and a *reprint*, a new printing from a photographic or mechanical copy of the text, with no change in the content. Today, many kinds of documents are produced from a machine-held file that can be updated instantly. For books, the idea of the edition still has some validity but, in general, edition statements are becoming more difficult to apply.

Material (or type of publication) specific area

This is used only to record:

- the scale and projection of maps and atlases
- optionally, the type of presentation of a piece of music, e.g. Miniature score
- computer file characteristics (e.g. number of records)
- the volume and part numbers and dates of issue of a serial.

Publication, distribution etc., area

The principal elements are:

- place of publication
- name of publisher, distributor etc.
- year of publication.

If the description is to be used for current bibliography – that is, as a selection tool – this area should give enough information to identify and locate the source from which the item may be obtained. For books, the publisher and distributor are usually one and the same, and directories of publishers are readily available, making it unnecessary to give more than the publisher's name for trade publishers. In other cases the full postal address may be required. Year of publication refers to the edition, and so if an item was published in 1894 and a library's copy is of a reprint dated 1912, AACR2 still regards its date as being 1894 – a view to which an antiquarian bookseller might not subscribe.

Physical description area

For books at any rate this is an uncomfortable area, in that the detail prescribed is more than is required for the general library purpose of conveying some idea of the extent of an item, but insufficient for the requirements of descriptive bibliography. For audio-visual and electronic materials on the other hand, this is a very important area, as these materials cannot be browsed like a book, so it is important to indicate accurately not only the extent of the item, but also what kind of equipment may be needed to use it. The principal elements are:

- extent of item, e.g. number of volumes or items in the bibliographic unit, pagination
- other physical details, e.g. illustrations
- dimensions.

Series area

The principal elements are:

- title proper of series; in many cases this is all that is required
- statement of responsibility only if necessary to identify the series
- numbering within the series.

The series statement helps to identify an item and to characterise it by giving some idea of its status and subject. Series can be problematical, in that it is not always easy to distinguish title proper from series title when both appear on the chief source of information. So one work might be catalogued as The Buildings of England: Suffolk, and another as Essex. – . . . (The Buildings of England). On many search systems a title or title keyword search will also retrieve series titles.

Notes area

Notes contain information considered necessary to fulfil the purposes of description but which cannot conveniently be given in one of the earlier, more formal, areas of the description. Notes may be taken from any available source: for all previous areas any information not derived directly from the item's prescribed chief source of information must be enclosed within square brackets. These are some of the commoner categories of notes:

- notes citing other editions and works
- notes describing the nature, scope, or artistic form of the work; or a list or summary of its contents
- notes expanding on the information given in the formal description
- notes on the particular copy being described, or on a library's holdings, or restrictions in its use.

Standard number and terms of availability area

In practical terms this means ISBN for books and ISSN for serials, as there are at present no standard numbering systems for other types of material. Terms of availability is an optional addition, serving the needs of current national bibliography rather than of library catalogues. Normally the price is shown. A standard number provides a check on an item's identity, provided one bears in mind some of the limitations of ISBNs in that different editions of a work will normally carry the same ISBN or, conversely, the same work may bear two or more ISBNs if it comes in hardback and paperback formats or is published jointly by two or more publishers.

DESCRIPTIVE CATALOGUING CHECKLIST

The full AACR2 provides for three levels of description; the Concise AACR2 approximates to Level 2 description. In the full AACR2, chapter 1 gives rules for describing materials generally, and these are expanded in chapters 2–12 for specific types of material, with the rules numbered in parallel with chapter 1.

UKMARC records currently use either Level 2 or Level 1 descriptions. Only the more common patterns are shown here: this checklist does not attempt to cover every eventuality. Level 3 description is identical to Level 2 for the majority of items. Only rarely will items be found where Level 3 prescribes more detail. Examples include second and subsequent place of publication and/or publisher, and parallel series title and/or other series title information.

Sources of information for the various areas (fields) of a description are rigidly prescribed. Any information that is taken from outside a prescribed source is enclosed within square brackets. The sources given below apply to books: consult AACR2 for other materials.

The areas (fields) follow an invariable sequence, as do the subfields within them. Fields or subfields not needed to describe a given item are simply omitted. Punctuation conforms to a rigid pattern (and, in UKMARC records, is generated by the system); for the most part it introduces the information that follows:

- *Overall layout* (1.0D; Concise 1C, 1D)
  Title and statement of responsibility. – Edition. – Material (etc.) specific details. – Publication etc. – Physical description. – Series. – Note. – Standard number
- *Title and statement of responsibility area* (1.1; Concise 2)
  Source: Title page.
  Level 2: Title proper: other title information / first statement of responsibility; each subsequent statement of responsibility.
  Level 1: Title proper / first statement of responsibility only if different from main entry heading.
- *Edition area* (1.2; Concise 3)
  Source: Title page, or a formal statement made by the publisher elsewhere in the item.
  Level 1: . – Edition
  Level 2: . – Edition / statement of responsibility for the edition
- *Material (or type of publication) specific area*. (1.3; Concise 4)
  Used as described above. Consult AACR2 for full instructions.
- *Publication, distribution etc area* (1.4; Concise 5)
  Source: Title page, or a formal statement made by the publisher elsewhere in the item.

Level 1:   . – First named publisher, year of edition

Level 2:   . – City of publication: first named publisher, year of edition

- **Physical description area** (1.5; Concise 6)

  Source: Anywhere in the item.

  Level 1:   . – Extent of item

  Level 2:   . – Extent of item: other physical details; dimensions. For books this mostly means:

  > . – Last numbered page: illustrations; height in cm.

- **Series area** (1.6; Concise 7)

  Source: Anywhere in the item.

  Level 1:   Not required at Level 1.

  Level 2:   . – (Title proper of series / statement of responsibility only if necessary to identify the series; numbering within the series).

- **Notes area** (1.7; Concise 8)

  Source: Any available source.

  Level 1/2:   . – Note. – Note (Repeat as needed)

- **Standard number** (1.8; Concise 9)

  Source: Any suitable source.

  Level 1/2:   . – ISBN 0-123-45678-9

SPECIAL PROBLEMS WITH NON-BOOK MEDIA

It was common in the past for libraries to maintain two catalogues, one for books and one for non-book media, or even separate sequences for each type of media. Practice today has moved towards integration, which AACR2 is designed to facilitate. Non-book media still present their own special problems, however. Problems of description or representation are on the whole are more acute than problems of access. The following list identifies a number of recurring problems, which vary from material to material.

- Many media cannot be browsed like a book. Equipment may be needed to view or play the item, which can be slow and calls for special expertise in the media and its equipment. The description may need to include a summary of the contents.

- Granularity can be difficult to establish, and a fine judgement is needed in deciding on the level at which to describe a composite item. Typical examples include a school teaching pack containing a range of separate items including audio-visual and printed, or a music CD with works by different composers or players on different tracks. Another aspect of this problem is that some materials are distributed in a complex pattern of series and subseries.

- Responsibility for the creation, production and distribution of non-book media can be complex and diffuse.
- There is far less standardization of presentation than with monographic materials. Titles may be difficult to establish, and other necessary information, for example date, may be difficult or impossible to establish. External sources of information – for example bibliographies and distributors' lists – may have to be consulted.
- There is no standard numbering system, and consequently less likelihood of finding a centrally produced record. Local indexing or abstracting is more likely to be required.
- Descriptions can be complex, with much necessary information that may not fit easily into the formal areas of description. Extensive notes are therefore often needed.

The following notes briefly characterize some of the problems specific to categories of media. The categories are those used by AACR2.

Cartographic materials

This category includes any representation of the whole or part of the earth or any celestial body, and extends to aerial photographs and three-dimensional maps and plans. These have a Mathematical data area, corresponding to the Material (or type of publication) specific area, to record scale and projection. Some examples are:

- Scale 1:50,000.
- Scale 1:23,000,000; Azimuthal equal-area proj.
- Not drawn to scale.

The physical description merits special attention. This will include: the number of physical units of an item, e.g. 1 map on 4 sheets; other physical details, to include: the number of maps in an atlas, the use of colour, the material from which it is made, if significant, and any mounting: e.g. 1 globe : col., wood, on brass stand. Finally, the dimensions of maps often mean height × width, e.g . 1 map: col., 35 × 50 cm.

Manuscripts

AACR2 gives a chapter to these, but as a manuscript is by definition unique and often of incalculable value, handling them demands specialist training, which places them outside the scope of the present work.

Music

This covers published music only; books about music and musicians are treated like any other book. Sound recordings are treated separately, but share some of the problems of music scores. Problems are more of access than of representation, for two reasons: (1) music publishing is highly international, and the music cataloguer is likely to be handling a disproportionate number of foreign language documents; and (2) classical music in particular may require a uniform title – see Chapter 10 for a brief description of these.

Sound recordings

Sound recordings share with printed music many problems of description and access. Physical description is a particular problem, because of the wide and changing range of formats. AACR2 has detailed instructions on such matters as: playing time; type of recording (analogue, digital, optical, magnetic etc.); the playing speed of discs and film; whether mono, stereo, or quad; and so on.

Motion pictures and video recordings

These even more than sound recordings are subject to rapid technological change. The physical description is along the same lines as sound recordings.

Graphic materials

AACR2 defines 20 types of graphic materials, from activity cards to wall charts, and taking in such categories as art reproductions, filmstrips, radiographs, and slides. Sources of information may be incomplete, and even titles may need to be supplied from external sources, or made up by the cataloguer. As always, the rules for physical description should be studied carefully; many of them are highly medium-specific.

Computer files

The AACR2 has incorporated recent extensions to these rules. The rules cover data and program files. They do not cover programs residing in the permanent memory of a computer, or firmware, or electronic devices such as calculators and little furry animals that die noisily if not looked after. (These are three-dimensional artefacts.) The chief source of information is the title screen, which means that the file has to be run in order to be catalogued. The edition statement is likely to use such words as *version* or *release*. Computer files require a Material (or type of publication) specific area, here called the File characteristics area. It indicates whether the file is a data or a program file, together with some indication of its extent. The Notes area provides for information on (among other things) the intended audience, and the need to provide a summary of the purpose and content of the item, together with a contents list and the nature and scope of the file. Other notes cover the system requirements; and the mode of access for files held remotely. This last implies the Internet, as some libraries are now incorporating selected Internet resources into their catalogues.

Three-dimensional artefacts and realia

Nine types are listed generically in the physical description area (art original, art reproduction, Braille cassette, diorama, exhibit, game, microscope slide, mock-up, model); otherwise the cataloguer has to state the specific name of the item. To this is added information on the extent of the item, its material, colour, dimensions and any accompanying material. The items are tangible enough, but chief sources of information may be lacking.

Microforms

Microforms are often reissues of ordinary full-sized materials. This gives two possibilities: to catalogue them as material in their own right (AACR2's implied preference), or to prepare a description based on the original, with a note indicating a microform reproduction, as is the Library of Congress's practice in USMARC records.

Serials

Serials differ from other forms of publication in that publication is intended to be continued indefinitely. If the title proper of a serial changes, a new description is made using the new title. Statements of responsibility tend to involve corporate bodies rather than personal authors, and exclude editors of serials. Serials have a Material (or type of publication) specific area, to record the chronological or numeric designation of the first issue. Here, as in the date and the 'extent of item' part of the physical description, an 'open' entry is normally made. A note records the frequency. The following example shows the general pattern:

> Jewellery international. – Oct./Nov. 1991– . – London:
> Jewellery Research and Publishing, 1991– . – v.: ill. –
> Six issues yearly. – ISSN 0961–4559

The bibliographic recording of serials is the responsibility of agencies reporting to the International Serials Data System (ISDS) in Paris. The British ISDS centre is the British Library's National Serials Data Centre (NSDC); the American centre is known as CONSER, having developed out of a Conversion of Serials project begun in 1973. Among their bibliographic control functions, centres assign ISSNs.

THE MARC RECORD FORMAT

The MARC record format was designed in the late 1960s as a standard format for representing bibliographic information, so that libraries could store, communicate and reformat bibliographic information in machine-readable form. It was first implemented in the USA by the Library of Congress in 1968 and in Great Britain by the British National Bibliography in 1971. The format was to be hospitable to all kinds of library materials, and is flexible enough to be used in a variety of applications not only in libraries and bibliographic agencies, but within the book industry and the information community at large. As more countries exploited MARC, variations in practices spawned deviations from the original format. The UNIMARC format was developed for international exchange of MARC records. National organizations creating MARC records have used national standards within the country and reformatted records to UNIMARC for international exchange. A generic MARC record conversion program called USEMARCON has been developed to assist this. Recently, however, a number of major suppliers of MARC records have agreed to use the USMARC format.

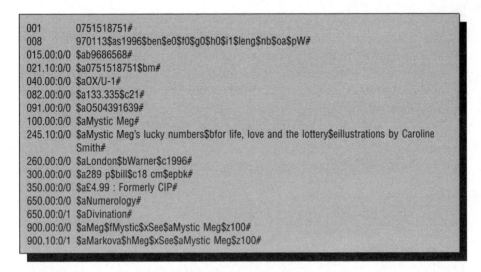

```
001        0751518751#
008        970113$as1996$ben$e0$f0$g0$h0$i1$leng$nb$oa$pW#
015.00:0/0 $ab9686568#
021.10:0/0 $a0751518751$bm#
040.00:0/0 $aOX/U-1#
082.00:0/0 $a133.335$c21#
091.00:0/0 $aO504391639#
100.00:0/0 $aMystic Meg#
245.10:0/0 $aMystic Meg's lucky numbers$bfor life, love and the lottery$eillustrations by Caroline
           Smith#
260.00:0/0 $aLondon$bWarner$c1996#
300.00:0/0 $a289 p$bill$c18 cm$epbk#
350.00:0/0 $a£4.99 : Formerly CIP#
650.00:0/0 $aNumerology#
650.00:0/1 $aDivination#
900.00:0/0 $aMeg$fMystic$xSee$aMystic Meg$z100#
900.10:0/1 $aMarkova$hMeg$xSee$aMystic Meg$z100#
```

Figure 3.8 Record in UKMARC format

The Canadian national format has already been fully harmonized, but more work remains to be done to harmonize the UKMARC (see Figure 3.8) and USMARC formats.

As well as the format for Bibliographic Data, there are USMARC formats for Community Information, Holdings Data, Classification Data and Authority Data. UKMARC also has a name authorities format. A joint authority file, the Anglo-American Authority File (AAAF), has been established.

The MARC record format complies with ISO 2709:1996 *Information and Documentation: Format for Information Exchange* (ISO, 1996), and with ISO 1001:1986 *Information Processing: File Structure and Labelling of Magnetic Tapes for Information Interchange* (ISO, 1986). The components of the format are:

- *Record label*: supplied by the program and placed at the beginning of the record. The label contains information about the record, such as, for example, its length and status (new, changed, etc.), type and class.
- *Directory*: a plan that lists, for every field, the tag, the number of characters in the field, and the starting character position within the record. Directories are also supplied by the program, and are not required to be input by the cataloguer.
- *Control field*: holds data for controlling the record. For books this is normally an ISBN.
- *Variable data fields*: these may be coded data fields or bibliographic data fields. Coded data is general data which is not unique to an item.

The following elements, called *field enumerators*, define the data content of each field:

1. *Tag*: a three-digit number within the range 000–945. The tags have a mnemonic structure in that they follow the order of a catalogue record, and the tags for added entries mirror those for main entry headings. The variable fields are grouped in blocks according to the first character of the tag:
   1xx Main entries
   2xx Titles and title paragraph (title, edition, imprint)
   3xx Physical description, etc.
   4xx Series statement
   5xx Notes
   6xx Subject access fields
   7xx Added entries other than subject or series
   8xx Series added entries
   9xx Local data.

Tags for specific fields are created by entering digits in the final two places, for example:

100	Personal author main entry heading
110	Corporate name main entry heading
240	Uniform title
245	Title and statement of responsibility
250	Edition and statement of edition author, editor, etc.
260	Imprint

A personal author's name generally has '00' in the second and third positions, so that:

100 is used for a main entry personal author heading

600 is used for a personal author subject heading

700 is used for a personal author added entry heading.

2. *Indicators*: two characters (normally digits) which follow the tag, and introduce the variable length fields that contain bibliographic data. Indicators are unique to the field to which they are assigned, and are used for such purposes as: to distinguish between different types of information entered in the same field; to provide for title-added entries; and to indicate the number of characters to be dropped in filing titles. For instance, in the field for main entry personal author heading, the following indicators are used in conjunction with the 100 tag, for the name of a person entered under:

100.00	A given name
100.10	A surname or single title of nobility
100.20	A compound surname or title, or one with a separate prefix, or an element of the name other than the first or last.

3. *Level*: a single digit introduced by a colon, indicating whether a separate entry has been made for a work contained in another publication (for example, individual plays in a collection).

4. *Repeat*: introduced by a slash, differentiating between two fields with the same tag, for example, if a work belongs to more than one series.

5. *Subfields*: indicating smaller distinct units within a field, which may require separate manipulation. Typical subfields in the imprint area are place of publication, publisher and date of publication. Subfields are preceded by a subfield code, which consists of a single non-alphanumeric symbol (e.g. '£') and a single letter. The imprint might be coded as: 260.00 £aLondon £bPitman £c1996. Subfield codes control such factors as appearance and (in UKMARC but not in USMARC records) punctuation. So, for example, the subfield coding just shown for the 260 field would generate the statement London: Pitman, 1996 in a Level 2 or Level 3 description, or Pitman, 1996 for a Level 1 description. Subfield codes are defined in the context of the field in which they are used, but similar codes are used in parallel situations. For example, the subfield codes for a person's name are constant, regardless of whether the name is main, or additional, author, or subject entry heading.

6. *Field mark*: a hash (#) representing the end of a field. This is necessary when variable length fields are used.

MARC records can be used in the following kinds of application:

1. *Information retrieval.* Most of the fields and subfields can be searched on, and together provide an exceptionally wide range of access points. In practice, different applications make their own selection of search keys from those available.
2. *Displaying citations.* Records are rarely displayed in their 'raw' MARC format, except for cataloguers. For most applications, the tags are either suppressed or replaced with appropriate verbal descriptions (for example, *Imprint:* in place of 260), and unnecessary fields and subfields suppressed. Many applications allow the data to be displayed or printed in more than one format.
3. *Cataloguing.* Cataloguers can call up MARC records using control numbers, or by the search keys available for information retrieval, or by acronym searches. Records may be selected online from a central database or from a CD-ROM, or by offline selection. Here, the user creates a request file of control numbers, which can be input by file transfer, or by e-mail, or sent on disc or tape to a processing agency. The Internet file transfer protocol (FTP) is increasingly being used to distribute the British Library's weekly BNBMARC file.
4. *Identifying new publications.* The major national bibliographic agencies operate Cataloguing-in-Publication (CIP) programmes. Arrangements are made with individual publishers to supply advance copies so that a skeleton MARC record can be made available in advance of publication. A full MARC record is made after publication and legal deposit, replacing the CIP record.
5. *Resource sharing.* The MARC format was designed from the start to facilitate the exchange of bibliographic data. Many library cooperatives have a central database in MARC format to which members can contribute records, and from which they copy records for local use. The Library of Congress is developing the MARC DTD project which aims to create standard SGML DTDs to support the two-way conversion of cataloguing data between the MARC data structure and SGML without loss of data. The MARC data structure is an international standard (ISO 2709), but is dauntingly specialized. SGML is widely used in publishing, and the project hopes to make MARC more attractive for use in less specialized environments.

How far will MARC DTD go towards providing a user-friendly MARC format? Like anything else, MARC is a product of its age, and its age was the 1960s – the age of the catalogue card. MARC's designers took a structuralist approach to bibliographic record format design: to try to think of every possible functionality that could ever be required of a catalogue card and devise a separate mechanism for each. It is instructive to compare the complexity of the MARC format with the minimalist approach of the Dublin Core, and to reflect that much of the input into the design philosophy of the Dublin Core was made by cataloguers.

Nevertheless, to the cataloguer, MARC's problems are not so much its complexity as its straitjacketing effect. Some problems are problems of detail – for example, Festschriften can be specified in the 008 field, but not large print books. Or there is the problem of redundancy, where identical or similar data can appear in different parts of the record. A perennial problem (which we discuss in Chapter 9) is that the format ties everybody to the main entry concept, which many would like to see buried. Others criticize its paucity of links with other records; or the difficulty of adapting it to a multi-tiered record structure – the list is endless. On the other hand, database vendors and others with large MARC databases to manage blanch at the thought of the slightest change to the format. By dint of everyday familiarity, cataloguers live with MARC's obsolete and inefficient features, just as we all live with similar features in QWERTY keyboards and English spelling.

THE COMMON COMMUNICATIONS FORMAT

There are many formats for bibliographic records. Rarely are two national formats sufficiently similar that they can be handled by the same computer programs. The bibliographic descriptions carried by these formats differ widely depending on their source. Abstracting and indexing services use different rules of bibliographic description to those followed in library cataloguing. The MARC format, which is used as an exchange format by major libraries, assumes the ISBD to be the standard. On the other hand, abstracting and indexing services may (but do not all) acknowledge the *UNISIST Reference Manual*, which prescribes its own content designators for the bibliographic descriptions of various types of materials. These two major formats define, organize and identify data elements in different ways and rely upon different sets of codes. Thus, it has been difficult or virtually impossible to mix in a single file bibliographic records from different sources. The CCF was thus designed with the aim of facilitating the communication of bibliographic data among the sectors of the information community.

In common with MARC, the CCF constitutes a specific implementation of ISO 2709. The CCF, then,

- specifies a small number of mandatory data elements that are recognized to be essential in order to identify an item
- provides mandatory elements that are sufficiently flexible to accommodate varying descriptive practices
- provides a number of optional elements
- permits the originating agency to include non-standard elements which are considered useful within its system
- provides a mechanism for linking records and segments of records without imposing on the originating agency any uniform practice regarding the treatment of related groups of records or data elements.

This last provision shows one difference with MARC. The CCF has been designed from the outset to link records at different bibliographic levels (e.g. Series – Monograph – Analytic), as this has always been an important feature of indexing services. Another difference is CCF's simplicity and permissiveness: rather than users adapt to the format, the format was designed to be adaptable to a range of practices.

RECORD FORMATS IN LOCAL SYSTEMS

Most of the centralized and shared cataloguing projects take account of and probably use the MARC record format. This degree of standardization is not the pattern outside this specific area of application. Essentially, there are two different categories of systems that may be encountered: publicly available databases, and local systems supported by software packages.

For the large public databases, there has been little pressure to accept a standard format, and each database producer has in general chosen a record format to suit the particular database. Even one database may emerge in different record formats according to the host on which it is mounted. Individual decisions are made concerning the fields to be included and the indexing to be made available. Yet another variable factor is the presence of full-text and, more recently, multimedia databases, which demand a somewhat different record format from bibliographical records if the information is to be appropriately displayed.

The record formats to be encountered in local systems that are supported by software packages are many and various. Most of these software packages offer cataloguing systems which will work in a MARC record format, or which produce records which are compatible with the MARC record format. Others do not offer such an option. Virtually all software packages offer the purchaser the opportunity to evolve a record format that suits a specific application. Thus, in local systems there may well be great variability in record format, as designs are implemented within the parameters set by the various software packages.

SUMMARY

This chapter has ranged widely across the formats for document representation. While representation and access are distinct topics, it must be remembered that the concept of access is built into most formats. Citations have an explicit filing element. More generally, most kinds of document representation can be entered into a retrieval system in such a way that the words they contain can be used as search keys in mechanized retrieval systems. Also, the record formats used in abstracting and indexing services (including MARC) are structured around access keys: titles, authors, classification codes and the rest.

This chapter has also considered records individually, whereas records are usually stored in databases along with other records of the same general type. We go on in Chapter 4 to look at databases, after which access in all its ramifications will be discussed.

REFERENCES AND FURTHER READING

ABSTRACTS AND ABSTRACTING

Cremmins, E. T. (1982) *The Art of Abstracting*. Philadelphia: ISI Press.
International Standards Organization (ISO) (1976) *Documentation: Abstracts for Publication and Documentation*. ISO 214:1976E. Geneva: ISO.
Jizba, L. (1997) Reflections on summarizing and abstracting: implications for Internet Web documents, and standardized library databases. *Journal of Internet Cataloging*, **1** (2), 15–39.
Lancaster, F. W. (1998) *Indexing and Abstracting in Theory and Practice*, 2nd edn. London: Library Association.
Rowley, J. E. (1988) *Indexing and Abstracting*, 2nd ed. London: Library Association.
Wheatley, A. and Armstrong, C. J. (1997) Metadata, recall, and abstracts: can abstracts ever be reliable indicators of document value? *Aslib Proceedings*, **49** (8), September, 206–13.

BIBLIOGRAPHIC RECORDS. MARC

Anglo-American Cataloguing Rules (AARC2) (1998) 2nd edn, revd. London: Library Association.
Attig, J. C. (1983) The concept of a MARC format. *Information Technology and Llibrarie*, 2, 7–17.
Avram, H. D. (1975) *MARC, its History and Implications*. Washington, DC: Library of Congress.
Burke, M. A. (1999) *Organization of Multimedia Resources: Principles and Practice of Information Retrieval*. Aldershot: Gower.
Byrne, D. J. (1988) *MARC Manual: Understanding and Using MARC Records*, 2nd edn. Englewood, CO, Libraries Unlimited.
Crawford, W. (1989) *MARC for Library Use*. Boston, MA: G. K. Hall.

Fecko, M. B. (1993) *Cataloging Nonbook Resources: A How-To-Do-It Manual for Librarians*. New York: Neal-Schuman.

Fritz, D. A. (1998) *Cataloging with AACR2R and USMARC: For Books, Computer Files, Serials, Sound Recordings, Video Recordings*. Chicago: American Library Association (ALA).

Furrie, B. (1998) *Understanding MARC: Machine Readable Cataloging*, 5th edn. Washington, DC: Library of Congress, Cataloging Distribution Service.

Gorman, M. (1989) Yesterday's heresy – today's orthodoxy: an essay on the changing role of descriptive cataloging. *College and Research Libraries*, **50** (6), 626–34.

Gredley, E. and Hopkinson, A. (1990) *Exchanging Bibliographic Data: MARC and Other International Formats*. London: Library Association.

Hagler, R. (1997) *The Bibliographic Record and Information Technology*, 3rd edn. Chicago: American Library Association.

Hill, J. S. (1996) The elephant in the catalog: cataloging animals you can't see or touch. *Cataloging and Classification Quarterly*, **23** (1), 5–25.

International Standards Organization (1986) *Information Processing – File Structure and Labelling of Magnetic Tapes for Information Exchange*. ISO 1001:1986. Geneva: ISO.

International Standards Organization (1996) *Information and Documentation – Format for Information Exchange*. ISO 2709:1996. Geneva: ISO.

ISBD(G) (1977): *General International Standard Bibliographic Description: Annotated Text*. London: IFLA.

ISBD(M) (1987): *International Standard Bibliographic Description For Monographic Publications*. Rev. edn. London: IFLA.

Lipow, A. G. (1991) Teach online catalog users the MARC format? Are you kidding? *Journal of Academic Librarianship*, **17** (2), 80–85.

McRae, L. and White, L. S. (eds) (1998) *ArtMARC Sourcebook: Cataloging Art, Architecture, and their Visual Images*. Chicago: American Library Association.

Spicher, K. M. (1986) The development of the MARC format. *Cataloging and Classification Quarterly*, **21** (3/4), 75–80.

UNESCO (1986) *UNISIST Reference Manual for Machine-readable Bibliographic Descriptions*, 3rd edn, compiled and edited by H. Dierickx and A. Hopkinson. Paris: UNESCO.

CITATION PRACTICES

British Standard 5605:1990 (1990) *Recommendations for Citing and Referencing Published Material*. London: British Standards Institution.

British Standard 1629:1989 (1989) *Recommendations for References to Published Material*. London: British Standards Institution.

Chicago manual (1993) *The Chicago Manual of Style: For Authors, Editors and Copywriters*, 14th edn. Chicago: University of Chicago Press.

International Standards Organization (ISO) (1999) *Information and Documentation – Bibliographic References – Part 2: Electronic Documents or Parts Thereof*. ISO 690–2. Geneva: ISO. Selections available from World Wide Web: <http://www.nlc-bnc.ca/iso/tc46sc9/standard/690-2e.htm>.

Turabian, K. L. (1996) *A Manual for Writers Term Papers, Theses and Dissertations*, 6th edn. Chicago: University of Chicago Press.

Part III
Access

4 Users and interfaces

INTRODUCTION

This chapter focuses on users and the user interface with knowledge-based systems. Since systems are designed to facilitate user access to information or knowledge, an important preliminary to systems design and creation is an understanding of the different kinds of users and the way in which users may wish to search or identify information. The chapter also explores some of the approaches to systems design. At the end of this chapter you will:

- understand ways of categorizing users
- appreciate the value of user models and cognitive modelling
- appreciate that indexing and searching processing are complementary
- be aware that users have different types of search patterns
- be aware of the different types of dialogue styles through which search strategies may be executed.

The earlier chapters in this book have focused on the information or knowledge that is to be organized, identifying some of its inherent structure and exploring the nature and context of the organization of knowledge. The next few chapters explore the range of approaches and devices that have been developed to assist users in exploring knowledge and meeting their requirements for knowledge or information. Understanding the user perspective has been a long-standing principle underlying the design of such systems. It is therefore appropriate that this chapter should consider the different categories of users, some of the purposes for which they might wish to organize knowledge or access information and their search processes. Search processes in electronic information systems are constrained by dialogue styles; accordingly, the chapter concludes with examples of the different dialogue styles in information retrieval systems.

As identified in the Introduction to this book, in systems, such as the Internet, in which the knowledge itself is weakly structured, the searcher encounters a messy information environment, in which it is necessary for them both to identify the range of sources that are appropriate, and to locate individual nuggets of information within those sources. In such a context, the organization of knowledge is increasingly user led. As users collect information, they create a model of the organization of information which it is necessary for them to refine over time, in other words, they learn, and that learning process is an important aspect of their ability to change and survive in an information society. Hence, the importance of the concept of experience in the categorization of users, and the recognition that previous experience influences user success in retrieving information, and in interacting with electronic information through specific dialogue styles.

USERS

The objective of any information retrieval system is that is should be used by the group of people for whom it has been designed. The field of human computer interaction has yielded the concept of usability in order to reflect this concern with users: 'The usability of a product is the degree to which specific users can achieve specific goals within a particular environment, effectively, efficiently and comfortably, and in an acceptable manner' (Booth, 1989, p. 110).

More specifically, the components of usability which were identified by Bennett (1984) and later operationalized by Shackel (1990) so that they could be tested, can be expressed in terms of:

- learnability, or ease of learning – the time and effort required to reach a specified level of use performance
- throughput or ease of use – the tasks accomplished by experienced users, the speed of task execution and the errors made
- flexibility – the extent to which the system can accommodate changes to the tasks and environments beyond those first specified
- attitude – the positive attitude engendered in users by the system.

Designers have also recognized that there are a number of different categories of users. Typical categories are: novice, expert, occasional, frequent, child, older adult, and user with special needs. Many users may fall into more than one of these categories, and none of the categories is mutually exclusive. The categories are used as stereotypes for ranges of experience with public access systems. More specifically:

- *Novice users* are users who have never used a specific system before. They need to learn how to perform information retrieval tasks quickly and easily.

Simple and intuitive interfaces are preferable. It is important to remember that whenever a system is changed all users become relative novices, although they may bring a conceptual framework based on their knowledge of other systems to the new system. Similarly, novice users of a particular system, who have used other similar systems will bring an underlying conceptual framework to their learning.

- *Expert users* use the system on a regular basis, and therefore are familiar with most functions and can negotiate any problems that might arise with the system. The expert user can complete the task quickly, but may be frustrated by wizards and menus and other features that slow down interaction with the system.

Many systems have more than one interaction mode to cater for these different categories of users. For example a number of OPACs and CD-ROM systems allow expert users to use short-cut keys rather than menus, and also offer 'expert user modes' so that individuals can execute complex search tasks.

Occasional users can often be viewed as near novice users in that, since they use the system infrequently on each occasion that do they use the system, they need to learn how to use the system again. Frequent users, on the other hand, are generally assumed to be expert users, although some frequent users will continue to limit the range of functions that they use, and thus never truly become expert users.

Another important category of user is users with special needs. Such users may be vision or hearing impaired, may have specific physical needs or learning disabilities. The system must be capable of supporting the user's special need. So, for example, for the user who is hearing impaired the interface must give clear visual cues.

Information managers and intermediaries who search systems on behalf of other users, can generally be expected to be expert users, but they may also require additional functionality so that it is easy to reformat and communicate information to the ultimate end-user.

COGNITIVE MODELLING

For users to make effective use of an information system, they must have a cognitive framework, or mental model upon which to hang their understanding. This mental model is a simplified mental 'picture' of what the system does, which assists the user through their interaction with aspects of the system. System designers also need to define these mental models. System design needs to recognize that there may be four models of an information systems:

- the user's mental representation of the system – the *mental model*

- the designer's conceptual framework for the description of the system – the *user model*
- the image the system presents to its users – the *system model*
- the psychologist's conceptual model of the user's mental model – the *conceptual model*.

The general aim is to produce a coincidence of these four models. Mental models are important in that they are owned by individual users. Every user develops a mental model of the system they use to build surrogates or metaphors that help them to understand complex concepts. Users of electronic information sources may find that their mental model, which has possibly been derived from a print equivalent, may or may not be relevant in the electronic environment. For example, users of library catalogues have found that OPACs differ considerably from the mental models which they may bring for card or microfiche catalogues (Slack, 1991). Problems may arise from the user's incomplete mental model of the catalogue database and the way in which the OPAC both holds the data and searches for the terms required.

Perceptual models of users describe the way in which users receive, perceive and process information. Users receive information from external sources, interpret the information based on previous experiences, identify a response to the received information and respond according to their decision. This basic 'human information processing model' has a number of key features that need to be considered in the design of public access database systems. These include:

- *perception*, which is concerned with the way in which the user interprets images or other stimuli
- *attention*, in which a user filters incoming stimuli to focus on what is perceived to be the most important information.
- *information processing*, or the stages and the task in the use of an information system
- *memory*, including both the short-term memory and long-term memory
- *learning strategies*, which will be employed by the user to enhance their use of the system. These may include learning through doing, active thinking, setting goals and creating plans, analogy, and learning from errors.

In summary, the cognitive frameworks which users bring to interaction with information systems, the use of mental models and the users' perceptual models are important aspects for the learning and recall of system functions.

THE PROCESSES OF SEARCHING AND INDEXING

Both indexing and searching, as performed by people, rather than machines, involve the same three stages:

Familiarization → Analysis → Translation

In systems where computer-based indexing is used, indexing is automatic in accordance with an algorithm, and these three stages are only relevant to the searching process. The user may, however, be called upon to exercise more skill in the design of a search strategy, in order to cater for some of the variability that arises in natural language indexing. We return to this issue in Chapter 5, and elsewhere, when we consider the differences between natural and controlled indexing languages. First we consider the nature of the processes of indexing and searching in a little more detail.

INDEXING

Indexing is the process whereby structure can be added to knowledge, in order to support more effective and more efficient retrieval.

The only totally adequate indication of the content of the document is the document in its entirety. Any other indications of document content, such as classification notation or alphabetical subject terms, are partial representations of content; they are surrogates for the document itself.

The objective of the three stages of indexing is to construct a *document profile* that reflects the document, usually with a focus on the subject of the document. Most documents have many characteristics that might be identified by a searcher as the criterion by which the document would be selected as relevant. Any set of search keys for a document can be described as a document profile. Different types of indexes and different user groups may require different sets of search keys (or different document profiles) to be developed in respect of any given document. The stages in framing a document profile are:

Step 1: Familiarization This first step involves the indexer in becoming conversant with the subject content of the document to be indexed. Documents are composed of words, and searchers and indexers use words to represent or convey concepts; at this stage, however, it is important for the indexer to attempt to identify the concepts that are represented by the words. In order to achieve good consistent indexing, the indexer must have a thorough appreciation of the structure of the subject and the nature of the contribution that the document is making to the advancement of knowledge. From time to time the indexer may need to consult external reference sources in order to achieve a sufficient understanding of the document for effective indexing. Certainly it will always be necessary to examine the document content, concentrating particularly on the clues offered by the title, the contents page, chapter and section headings and any abstracts, introduction, prefaces or other preliminary matter.

Step 2: Analysis The second step towards constructing an index involves the identification of the concepts within a document which are worthy of indexing. Any one document covers a numbers of different topics. Take, for example, a book entitled 'Wills and Probate'. This book contains sections on making a will, executors, administration of an estate, pension, tax, house ownership, grants and intestacy, to name but a few. Usually it is possible to identify a central theme in a document and to produce a summary of document content based upon this central theme. Frequently, but not always, this same process will have been attempted by the author when inventing the title, which explains why a title is often useful in indexing. Clearly, indexing must permit access to a document by its central theme, but to what extent should access be provided to secondary or subsidiary topics? This question can usually only be satisfactorily answered with reference to specific user groups and environments.

It is helpful to have such guidelines concerning the types, range and number of concepts to be indexed, but in many circumstances these choices may be at the discretion of the indexer. Many traditional indexing approaches have sought to find a label or indexing term which is co-extensive with the content of the document being indexed; that is, the scope of the indexing term and the document are similar. For example, for the book 'Wills and Probate', it would not be sufficient to index this book under the term 'Wills' alone, since this heading would not reveal the section of the book on 'Probate'.

Note: the term 'analysis' has been used here in its restrictive meaning. Some authors use 'analysis' to apply to all processes associated with the construction of a document profile of any kind. In this definition 'analysis' subsumes all of the processes associated with indexing, cataloguing, classification and abstracting.

Step 3: Translation Having identified the central theme of a document, this theme must be described in terms which are present in the controlled indexing language. This will involve describing concepts in terms of the classification scheme, thesauri or list of subject headings. For example, a free interpretation of the subject of a document might be: 'Social conflict and educational change in England and France between 1789 and 1848'. The concepts represented in this summary might be translated into an alphabetical description of the form: 'Education – History – England – Social Conflict – France', or into a classification notation such as, 942.073. To take another example: 'Radioactivity in the surface and coastal waters of the British Isles' might be converted to an alphabetical description such as, Water pollutants – Radioactive Materials – Great Britain, or into a classification notation such as, 628.16850941.

This translation involves not only labelling the subject, but possibly also indicating related subjects, as discussed in Chapter 5. The guiding principle in translating concepts into the indexing language of any given system must be that the terms selected and the relationships indicated are consistent with the 'normal' user's perspective on the subject. This coincidence between indexing and user approach is known as user warrant. In other words, the indexing system must be tailored to the needs of users. Given that different users may have different perspectives on the same subject, it is clear that different approaches to indexing and structuring knowledge will be applicable in different environments. To illustrate this point, consider, for example, medicine. The approach suitable in specialized structuring tools for medical research will need to be very specific in order to differentiate between closely related subjects. On the other hand, a collection of general medical books in a public library may deal with the same range of topics as the research databases, but the structuring will probably rely on broader categories, and the terms used for the same ailment may be different. What a doctor might refer to as 'rubella', will probably be called 'German measles' by the mother of the child with the complaint.

In general, it is important to recognize that there is a great variety of different approaches to indexing, and that this is inevitable, not only for reasons of history and indexer/organizational preference, but also because different situations require different approaches.

SEARCHING

Indexing and searching are complementary. The searcher uses the document profile created by the indexer as a basis for searching, but the searcher does not come to the search process with any knowledge of the specific document profiles of the documents that they might deem useful or relevant. There is great similarity between indexing and searching, and each involves the same three stages:

Step 1: Familiarization A searcher must be adequately familiar with what he or she wishes to retrieve. Although this may seem an obvious statement, there are many instances when the searcher is not fully aware of what can or might be retrieved. Two common circumstances may arise:
  a) The searcher is an information intermediary seeking to identify information or documents on behalf of someone else. Here familiarization can be partially achieved by conducting a reference interview with the end-user. The reference interview should ascertain both a clear subject profile

and also other characteristics of the required documents or information, such as any constraints on date, language, source or level. The intermediary also needs to be conversant with the sources to be searched.

b) The searcher may be the end-user, possibly approaching the search in some ignorance of their real requirements or the literature that might be available to meet those requirements. Some degree of ignorance of this kind is not unusual since the usual objective in consulting an information source is to become better informed. If the search is to be successful, the user will learn about the subject and its literature during the searching process. (Of course, an even more unfortunate situation is where the end-user, poorly informed about the information or documents required, briefs an intermediary, who is then in the position of conducting a search on the basis of incomplete or inaccurate information).

Step 2: Analysis When the objective is clear, the next step is to analyse the concepts present in a search. Sometimes, particularly for a straightforward search in a printed index, it will be sufficient to establish these concepts in the searcher's mind. On other occasions, where the search must be specified with a number of interacting concepts and other parameters, it will be necessary to write the concepts down. For example, if information is required on 'primary education' and this is a search term in a database, then the search profile merely involves the term primary education. If, however, the searcher seeks information on 'Recovering hydrogen from coal tar in a continuous electrofluid reactor' and is interested only in reports, books, or periodical articles that provide a review of the subject since 1990, then the search profile will be much more complex. Building a search profile has much in common with building a document profile during indexing. The search profile will comprise a series of search keys representing subjects and other characteristics of the search requirements that together indicate the scope and nature of the search.

Step 3: Translation Translation of the concepts in a search profile will involve reference to a thesaurus, classification scheme (or its index) or list of subject headings that has been used in constructing the index to be searched. Many computer-based systems make this process virtually automatic, and terms can, for instance, be selected from online thesauri. If such tools are not available, consultation of the inverted file that has been constructed for the indexing process may be useful, or reference to other sources of subject terminology, such as thesauri and dictionaries may be of assistance. The quality of translation depends considerably on the support that is available in the system being searched. In a printed index, guidance on indexing practices is useful. In computer-based systems, there will be a range of facilities which support searching on different parts of the record, including, often assigned subject terms, abstracts and the natural language of the text of the document. The development of a search profile is often an evolutionary process, and some approaches to this process are described in the next section.

Finally, it is essential not to forget that successful information retrieval does not only depend upon the effectiveness of indexing and searching in a single source. Most searchers need to use multiple information sources and knowledge structures to locate information and documents. This means that even if individual sources have been carefully indexed, through the use of controlled indexing languages, a user searching several sources, each of which has been indexed using a different controlled language, still has to negotiate a complex maze of different subject terms and subject relationships. Selection of the appropriate sources is key; no amount of searching a source that does not provide access to the information or documents that are being sought will produce a positive outcome!

SEARCH STRATEGIES

OBJECTIVES

The set of decisions and actions taken during a search is known as a search strategy. Some searchers are more methodical in the construction of search strategies than others, but every searcher aims to:

● retrieve sufficient relevant records

and avoid:

● retrieving irrelevant records
● retrieving too many records
● retrieving too few records.

DIRECTED SEARCHING VERSUS BROWSING

There is a spectrum of searches from the search for a specific document or item of information, (sometimes called known-item searching), through to the almost aimless or general browsing, over the Internet, or in a public library, for 'something interesting'. Many searches can be placed at some point in the middle of this spectrum; often the user is refining not only the search strategy, but also their information requirements as the search proceeds, so that, a search that may start with browsing may eventually have a very focused intended outcome. Alternatively, the visit to a library or the Internet search that starts with a very targeted objective, may open up other experiences and access to other sources, and suggest other lines of investigation or action that had not occurred to the user at the start of the search. Arguably one of the most important features of the Internet, as opposed to earlier avenues of access to electronic information sources, is the opportunity to browse. Directed searching and browsing can be differentiated thus:

- *Directed searching* is performed by users when they know what they are looking for, and usually possess some characteristic of the information or document (such as its author or a set of subject terms) which they can use as the basis of a specific search.
- *Browsing* is performed when the user has a less precise view of the information or documents that might be available and is not sure whether his or her requirements can be met or how they might be met. Browsing can be general or purposive. Purposive browsing occurs when the user has fairly specific requirements, whereas general browsing may be used as an opportunity to refine the user's perceptions of their requirements.

Knowledge structuring often needs to be able to cater for both directed searching and browsing.

In summary, it is important to recognize that the user's experience of the search for information, especially when it embraces a range of different sources, some of which are in print and others in electronic format, is essentially messy. It is likely that useless or irrelevant documents or information will be identified and discarded at various stages in any search experience, and considerations of recall and precision as explored in Chapter 13 are relevant in the individual search experience.

MORE ON BROWSING

Browsing is generally preferred to directed searching in situations in which:

- the search objective can not be clearly defined, usually because the searcher lacks sufficient information to be able to define it precisely
- the cognitive burden, including what the user needs to know about how to search, and how to search a specific system, is less than it might be for directed searching
- the system interface encourages browsing through the types of search facilities that it offers.

Browsing involves skimming information and making choices; it is extremely dependent on human perceptual abilities, as applied in the recognition of things of potential interest and the making of choices based upon that recognition.

104

Online search services that used command-based interfaces, and were used primarily by intermediaries, did not support browsing. However, as the range of systems interfaces has grown, many of these interfaces support scanning, and thereby offer the option to browse. Browsing is best performed in environments in which like things have been grouped together. The traditional context for browsing is books arranged on shelves in accordance with a classification scheme, in libraries. Onscreen browsing is facilitated by:

- highlighting, so that the user can identify salient words and objects
- scrolling, so that the user can scroll through information quickly
- menus of commands and lists of titles which summarize information.

Hyperlinks, as discussed further in Chapter 11, underlie the structuring of the Web. Browsing through networks of hyperlinks between documents allows users to navigate through cyberspace, in a non-sequential manner. Search histories can be useful in orientating the user; it is often possible to backtrack through a search to an earlier screen. Nevertheless, browsing can be time-consuming with large data sets, and it is easy for disorientation to result.

MORE ON DIRECTED SEARCHING

A common process is the broadening or narrowing of a search strategy on the basis of the outcome from the first search statement. This can be achieved by using any of the retrieval facilities reviewed below or by introducing different search terms. The effective development of a search strategy requires knowledge of the subject, databases and literature being searched.

Different search strategies might be appropriate for different kinds of searches. Five types of search strategies have been proposed:

1. *Briefsearch* – a 'quick and dirty' search – is a single search formulation, normally a Boolean combination of terms, to retrieve a few relevant items (see Figure 4.1). It is the fastest, simplest and least expensive approach to searching. Use this strategy:
   a) to retrieve a particular document known to be relevant to the problem
   b) to get a rough idea of what a database contains
   c) to retrieve a few records to examine the index terms which may later be formulated into a search expression for a more detailed search.
2. *Building blocks* is the most commonly used approach to online searching (see Figure 4.2). Terms used to represent a facet may be synonyms, near synonyms, narrower terms in a hierarchy or in some way related. These are grouped using OR to create a larger set. The facets representing the main concepts of the search are combined using AND (and on rare occasions OR

and NOT). Records should be examined for relevancy and the formulation can be modified in various ways using search heuristics aimed at increasing recall or precision, as necessary.

3. *Successive facets strategy* constructs each facet one at a time, successively and as needed (see Figure 4.3). At each step each new facet is intersected with the previous result. Consider using this approach:

    a) if you suspect that ANDing all facets will retrieve few (or no) records due to overspecification

    b) if you suspect that one facet is ambiguous in meaning.

4. *Pairwise facets*: the facets are ANDed a pair at a time, rather than all together (see Figure 4.4). Consider this strategy:

    a) if it is thought that all facets are well defined, each with sizeable literature, roughly equivalent in relevancy and specificity of definition of the search problem

    b) if it is considered that the intersection of all the facets at once will result in zero postings.

5. *Citation pearl growing* moves from high precision towards increasing the recall of the search (see Figure 4.5). A known highly pertinent document is used to select search terms to be formulated into a search expression. (Briefsearch can often be used to find a small number of relevant documents.) The resulting set can be examined and further search terms added to each facet, a process which can be cycled as many times as necessary. This is a fairly complex process. Consider this approach:

    a) if the terminology of the search problem is not well known

    b) if thesauri and word lists are not available.

CURRENT AWARENESS AND RETROSPECTIVE SEARCHES

Another important division is between searches for information to update a user's knowledge on a subject, and searches to find all of the information to date on a subject.

```
Search topic: Chinese blue and white porcelain

  ss chinese and blue and white and porcelain
1   2763 chinese
2   6539 blue
3   9734 white
4   538 porcelain
5   2 chinese and blue and white and porcelain
```

Figure 4.1   Briefsearch

Search topic: Redundant churches in East Anglia

```
   ss redundant or disused
1  22  redundant
2  35  disused
3  43  redundant or disused

   ss church? or chapel?
4  165  church?
5  54  chapel?
6  187  church? or chapel?

   ss east(w)anglia or norfolk or suffolk or cambrid? or essex
7  5634  east
8  15  anglia
9  18  east(w)anglia
10  68  norfolk
11  57  suffolk
12  155  cambrid?
13  96  essex
14  284  east(w)anglia or norfolk or suffolk or cambrid? or essex

   3 and 6 and 14
15  3 and 6 and 14
```

Notice particularly the third block, a topic (East Anglia) and its constituent counties. Listing them all in a search is laborious, and often overlooked by inexperienced searchers. (The truncation of Cambridgeshire cuts down both the drudgery and the chance of error. 'East' could probably have been omitted without ill-effect, as Anglia is not often used except in this combination.)

Figure 4.2 Building blocks strategy

Search topic: Sheltered housing for old people

```
   ss sheltered(w)housing
1  44  sheltered
2  3166  housing
3  34  sheltered and housing

   ss old or elderly
4  5054  old
5  654  elderly
6  5233  old or elderly

   3 and 6
7  22  3 and 6
```

However, it is only the old and the disabled, and predominantly the former, who need sheltered housing. Examination of the results of set 3 (i.e. omitting old and elderly from the search) should reveal that most of the titles will be potentially relevant to some extent. The second facet would therefore be better omitted from the search specification.

Figure 4.3 Successive facets strategy

107

Search topic: Satellites in weather forecasting

  ss satellite? and weather
1 264 satellite?
2 756 weather
3 16 satellite? and weather

  forecasting
4 538 forecasting

  1 and 4
5 11 1 and 4

  3 and 4
6 113 and 4

The first pair of facets (satellite? and weather) gives slightly higher recall than the second pair (satellite? and forecasting).

Figure 4.4 Pairwise facets strategy

A Briefsearch has retrieved from ERIC the following item, which is known to be relevant:

EJ521883 PS524404
The Role of Emotion in Children's Understanding and Emotional Reactions to Marital Conflict.
Crockenberg, Susan; Forgays, Deborah Kirby
Merrill-Palmer Quarterly; v42 n1 pp. 22–47 Jan 1996
Theme issue topic: 'Conflicts in Families and Between Children: Advances in Theory and Research.'
ISSN: 0272-930X
Available from: UMI
Language: English
Document Type: RESEARCH REPORT (143); JOURNAL ARTICLE (080)
Journal Announcement: CIJAUG96
Abstract: Tested a process model for the impact of children's exposure to marital conflict on their behavior adjustment with a sample of 28 couples and their 6-year-old children. Found that maternal conflict behavior and children's negative emotional reactions to fathers independently predicted children's behavioral adjustment. (MDM)
Descriptors: *Adjustment (to Environment); *Child Behavior; Conflict Resolution; *Emotional Response; *Family Problems; *Models; Predictor Variables; Sex Differences; *Young Children
Identifiers: *Marital Discord

Selected major (starred) descriptors can be used as the basis for further searches. By checking them against the ERIC Thesaurus, additional semantically related terms will be suggested for building blocks.

Figure 4.5 Citation pearl growing

Current awareness searches are performed when a well-informed user is concerned to locate the latest information on their topic of interest. For example, a doctor may be interested in the results of the latest research on the most effective treatments for cancer. A marketing manager may be interested in the market shares of the various competitor companies in the industry in which they are operating. Some of this information may be formally flagged as new information in newspapers, new issues of journals and newsletters. Current awareness services or alerting services are designed to make it easier for a user to keep abreast of new information in a range of different sources. Many users need to keep abreast of developments in a number of different areas.

Retrospective searches are undertaken when a user wishes to become informed of knowledge on a specific topic. Students may perform such a search when they need to prepare an essay or undertake a literature review for a research project. They may not be interested in locating all the information on a topic, but will be concerned to get a general picture of developments and of the concepts and ideas in the literature in their field of interest. Professionals, such as scientists, might perform a retrospective search when they commence a new project, and want to be sure that their work will not duplicate work that has already been performed elsewhere, and that thereby they will add to knowledge. The output from a retrospective search will include current information, but is likely to extent back over a longer period of time than the output from a current awareness search

INTERFACE DESIGN

Search processes in electronic information systems are constrained by interface design. The search interface is the context in which information searching and seeking is conducted. Interfaces must:

- be easy and quick to learn
- allow users to issue instructions quickly, and respond quickly to that instruction
- minimize errors
- be easy to remember
- make it easy for the user to perform the tasks that they wish to perform.

Interface design has come a long way since the early command-based interfaces. There is an extended range of input devices, including mouse and touch screen, higher resolution monitors, faster processors and more sophisticated software environments. There are a number of different interface styles, but most knowledge-based systems now operate with a graphical user interface (GUI) or Web-based interface. A GUI embraces:

- direct manipulation
- windows
- dialog boxes

- form filling
- question and answer
- menus
- buttons and checkboxes
- icons
- command languages.

We explore these components below, and Figure 4.6 illustrates the development of a search strategy in a GUI.

There are still a few applications that use one or more of these dialogue styles in non-GUIs or Web-based interfaces. In early systems the emphasis was on command-based interfaces and menu-based interfaces. Until a few years ago all information retrieval systems were command based. These systems were regarded as impenetrable for the inexperienced user. The need to learn the command language was aggravated by the fact that nearly every software package used a different command language. Menu-based interfaces were introduced as a means of making systems more accessible to the new and occasional user. They first emerged in CD-ROM, OPAC and some specialist online applications, and later were adopted by online search services as interfaces for their services that are marketed directly to end-users. The first menu-based systems were very simple full-screen menus, but most systems now have full GUI-based interfaces. Menu-based systems often embed the use of commands in a menu-based environment, by offering the searcher a list of commands from which the appropriate commands can be selected. This still requires the searcher to have some appreciation of the effect that the application of a specific command may have, but eliminates the requirement for the searcher to remember the exact form of a command for a given information retrieval system. In information retrieval applications, features of GUI which facilitate the search process include:

- the ability to move more easily between applications, so, for example, through the one interface, the user might perform a search on an external databases, download some information, and enter a word-processing package to reformat that data, and then, finally, communicate the reformatted data to a colleague through an e-mail system
- the use of windows, so that a user can build a search strategy in one window, while consulting a thesaurus or a help system in another window. Once the search has been completed, the search strategy window can remain on display, while the records are displayed
- the use of direct manipulation and the ability to click on hypertext links in a document
- much more visually appealing and easy to understand interfaces

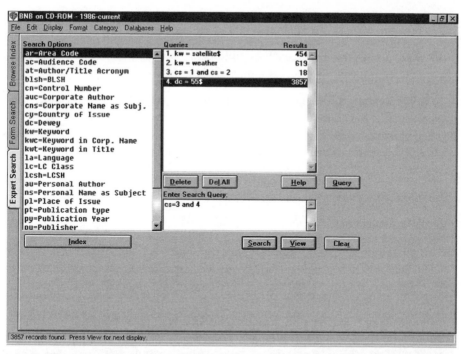

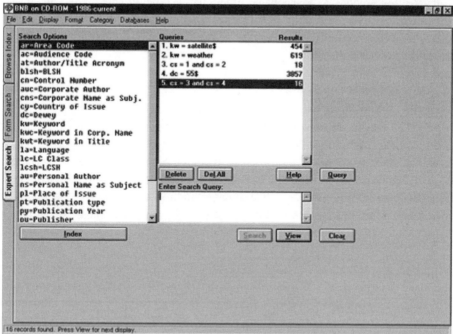

Figure 4.6 Development of a search strategy in a GUI

111

- ease of navigation through different menus and actions available within the system
- opportunities for the display of multimedia documents with, for example, an onscreen display of photographs and video.

In general, then, GUIs have made information retrieval systems much more user-friendly, but there are some public access environments, particularly those where a kiosk is used for public access, where the use of the full functionality of a GUI would be seen as confusing by a significant proportion of the users.

COMPONENTS IN GUIs

Direct manipulation

The idea of direct manipulation is that the user's actions should directly affect what happens on the screen, in the sense that there is a feeling of physically manipulating objects on the screen. Typically, direct manipulation systems have icons representing objects that can be moved around the screen and manipulated by controlling a cursor with a mouse, for example, in moving a file by clicking on an icon representing the file and dragging it to a new location. This makes it easy for novices to learn basic functionality quickly, and experienced users can work extremely rapidly to carry out a wide range of tasks

Windows

A window is a rectangular area on the screen in which an application or document can be viewed. Most windows can be opened, closed, moved and sized. Several windows can be opened simultaneously and most windows can be reduced to an icon, or enlarged to fill the entire desktop. Sometimes windows are displayed within other windows. There are two types of windows: tiled and overlapping. Tiled windows are where the screen is divided up in a regular manner into subscreens with no overlap. Overlapping windows can be nested on top of one another. Windows have a number of uses. Screen areas can be separated for error messages, control menus, working area and help.

Dialog boxes

A dialog box is a special window that appears temporarily to request information. Many dialog boxes contain options that you select to tell the software to execute a command. A dialog box requests information from the user. For example, the user may need to select certain options, type some text or specify settings.

Dialog boxes can form the basis of a question and answer or a form-filling dialogue.

The user of a *question and answer* dialogue is guided through his interaction by questions or prompts on the screen. The user responds to these by entering data through the keyboard. Often questions may require only a simple 'yes' or 'no' response, but on other occasions the user may be required to supply some data, such as a code, a password, their name or other textual data. Usually, however, one-word responses are expected. On receiving the user's response, the computer will evaluate it and act accordingly. This may involve the display of data, additional questions or the execution of a task such as saving a file. The prompt information can easily be tailored to the requirements of the user, and this dialogue style may therefore suit novice and casual users. The main drawback of this dialogue mode is that since an input data item must be validated at each step before continuing with the dialogue, the interaction can be slow. Question and answer dialogue is widely used in a simple form in GUIs where a question might be posed in a dialog box and the user is expected to respond by clicking the Yes or No button.

In a *form filling* dialogue the user works with a screen-based image of a form. The screen form will have labels, and space into which data are to be entered. It should be possible to move a cursor to any appropriate position on the form for the entering of data. Labels will normally be protected from amendment or overwriting and some users may be able to amend only certain fields, so that others are protected. Form filling is a useful dialogue for inputting records and blocks of data. In searching it is used in Query by Example interfaces. All data input should be validated and errors reported to the user. Form filling, because it may involve large amounts of data entry, can take a lot of user's time and can be a source of frustration and errors. In form filling dialogues the user has little control over the dialogue, but the approach has the advantage that the user rarely needs to remember commands or their syntax. Form filling can be speeded up by the use of a drop down box from which an option can be selected for entry into the form.

Menus

Menus present a number of alternatives, or a menu on the screen, and ask the user to select one option in order to proceed. The menu options are usually displayed as commands, or as short explanatory pieces of text. Pictures or icons may also be used to represent the menu options. The appropriate option is selected by keying in a code (often a number or letter) for that option, or by pointing to the required option with a mouse or other pointing device. Menus are generally recognized to be a sound approach for the occasional or novice

113

user. Additional help is rarely necessary and little data entry is required of the user. The system designer has restricted the total set of options, and thus the novice user has less potential for mistakes. Menu-based interfaces must be closely defined with the user in mind. This involves careful consideration of menu structure, key presses required and menu bypass techniques. For example, expert users should have the option of accessing a specific screen or making a selection without necessarily passing through all previous menu selections.

Where there are many possible commands and displaying them all might be difficult, menus are sometimes organized hierarchically in tree-like structures. In other words, a menu might not only contain commands, but also routes to other menus. For example a Format command in a word-processing package, when selected from a menu, might display a further menu which listed the options of items for formatting, such as characters or paragraphs.

Today's interfaces use a number of different types of menus, often in combination. Commonly encountered menu types include:

- *Single option menus*, often used to request a confirmation of a response offered by a user.
- *Pop-up menus* pop up or appear, often in the centre of the screen, and request a response or a selection.
- *Pull-down menus* are often attached to a main menu across the top of the screen. When a user clicks on a menu option on the main menu bar, a further menu appears showing a number of options.
- *Step-down menus* are a series of menus. So, for example, a user may click on an option on the main menu bar at the top of a screen to display a pull-down menu. Options on this menu that will lead to the display of further menus may be indicated, for example, with three dots e.g. Field. . . . Clicking on these options leads to a further menu. This is known as a step-down menu. These menus can be particularly helpful when there is a series of actions to perform, since they can remind the user of the sequence in which these actions must be completed.
- *Main menu bars* appear at the top or bottom of the screen and remain on the screen while the user performs other functions and displays other menus. They may have pull-down menus attached as indicated above or may simply display some common menu options such as Help, Save, and Exit.
- *Full screen menus on the Web* Some Web search environments use menus that occupy windows that cover much of the screen. Users need to proceed through these menus through a hierarchy, in a similar way to the way in which they might have interacted with full screen menus.

In most of the above uses of menus, the user is free to choose the order in which they issue commands. This requires that the user recognizes the order in which commands need to be executed and appreciates the effect of issuing a command.

Buttons and check boxes

Buttons and check boxes are similar in that you click on them to select an option or to choose a command.

There are two types of buttons, command buttons and option buttons. Command buttons allow you to choose a command, such as Save or Help. Command buttons appear as images of keys. Command buttons displayed with . . ., such as Set-up, will display a further dialog box when clicked. Option buttons are usually shown as small circles. When clicked and selected the circle is filled with a smaller filled-in circle.

Check boxes are shown as small boxes. When selected the box is filled with an X and clicking on the box turns the option on or off. Often a series of check boxes may be shown in a dialog box to allow the user to set a number of options or settings.

Icons

Icons are graphical representations of various elements in Windows, such as disc drives, applications, embedded and linked objects and documents. An icon can be chosen by double-clicking on it. For example, the Main window in Windows shows the main applications that are included in Windows, such as File Manager, Control Panel, Print Manager, Clipboard Viewer, MS-DOS Prompt, Windows Set-up, PIF Editor, and Read Me. Group icons represent other groups of icons. Icons often cover a subset of the commands available through menus, and are a faster route to the issuing of instructions than menus.

Command languages

Command languages are one of the oldest and most widely used dialogue styles. In dialogues based on commands the user enters instructions in the form of commands. The computer recognizes these commands and takes appropriate action. For example, if the user types in PRINT 1-2, the computer responds with a prompt to indicate that the command has been carried out or a message stating why the command cannot be executed.

The command language must include commands for all of the functions that the user might choose to perform and, therefore, since different systems perform different functions, it is inevitable that command languages will differ between systems. Some attempts have been made to adopt standard command languages for systems that perform similar functions, and one result of this is the Common Command Language used by some of the online search services. However, standardization is difficult and an inherent feature of command-based dialogues is the need for users to become familiar with the command language used. An intermediate option that is widely used in GUIs, and is suitable for users with some familiarity with the system, is the use of commands in menus, so that the menus prompt users in their use of commands. This is not, however, effective for new users because they cannot be expected to know what the commands displayed on the menus mean. Commands are useful because they offer direct addressing of objects and functions by name, and the flexibility of system function which a combination of commands can provide. Command languages are preferred by many experienced searchers of online search services. In addition, Web search engines use a range of symbols, for example, to truncate search terms, and to specify adjacency searching (see Figure 11.6).

VOICE-BASED DIALOGUES

All of the dialogue styles considered so far are concerned with screen-based communication, with the aid of keyboards, mice, touch screens and similar devices. There are many circumstances in which a voice-based dialogue would be most convenient for the user, and this is another option for knowledge-based systems. Such dialogues would be attractive to the occasional user inputting only 'yes' and 'no' and other one-word answers, and also to the user inputting large quantities of textual data. Voice-based dialogues might be voice to voice (i.e. computer and person talk to each other), screen to voice (i.e. person talks, computer shows responses on screen), or voice to keyboard (i.e. computer talks, person operates keyboard).

With voice-to-voice dialogues communication may be remote from a workstation, through a telephone receiver and telecommunications link. All of these modes may have their applications, and the dialogue modes outlined above (e.g. menu, command, form filling) might be employed in a voice-based dialogue. Although there are some applications of such systems, they are limited and further development is to be expected.

MULTIMEDIA INTERFACES

Multimedia interfaces present interesting challenges to the interface designer with regards to how best to incorporate sound, video, still graphics, text, numbers and animation. Multimedia interfaces can be viewed as having two components:

- the navigational interface, which exhibits many of the characteristics of a GUI, such as buttons and windows.
- the graphics elements that contribute to the appearance of the application, including backgrounds, textures, colours, the way that the type is displayed on the screen and how the stills, graphics and videos are displayed.

These components need to be integrated so that, for example, the complementary colours of the design may be used to match a still graphic, or the lighting of a sequence of video may be designed to match the look and feel of the rest of the presentation.

There are a number of unanswered questions concerning how people use multimedia interfaces. This may depend on the nature of the application for which the multimedia is being used; application areas embrace entertainment, marketing, information provision and education.

WEB INTERFACES

Figure 4.7 compares the Web-based interface and the GUI for access to a specific search service. This illustrates that most of the features that are available in Windows-based GUIs are also available in Web interfaces. Such interfaces, for example, feature form filling, check boxes, menu bars and icons. In addition, they feature hyperlinks, often displayed in a different colour (e.g. red in otherwise black text), which when clicked on allow the user to 'link' to other documents. Web screens look a little different from Windows GUI screens, since they are written in HTML. One feature that they do not have is direct manipulation, with associated features such as drag and drop.

COLOUR IN INTERFACE DESIGN

Colour is widely used in today's systems. Colour can be an effective mechanism for communicating alerts, drawing attention and defining relationships. In a number of database systems, colour is used to draw attention to specific parts of records. In general, colour can be used to:

- draw attention to warnings
- improve legibility and reduce eyestrain
- highlight different parts of the screen display, such as status bars and menus
- group elements in menus or status bars together so that, for instance, an instruction is associated with the number of its function key.

Nevertheless, colour must be used with care and with an understanding of how

117

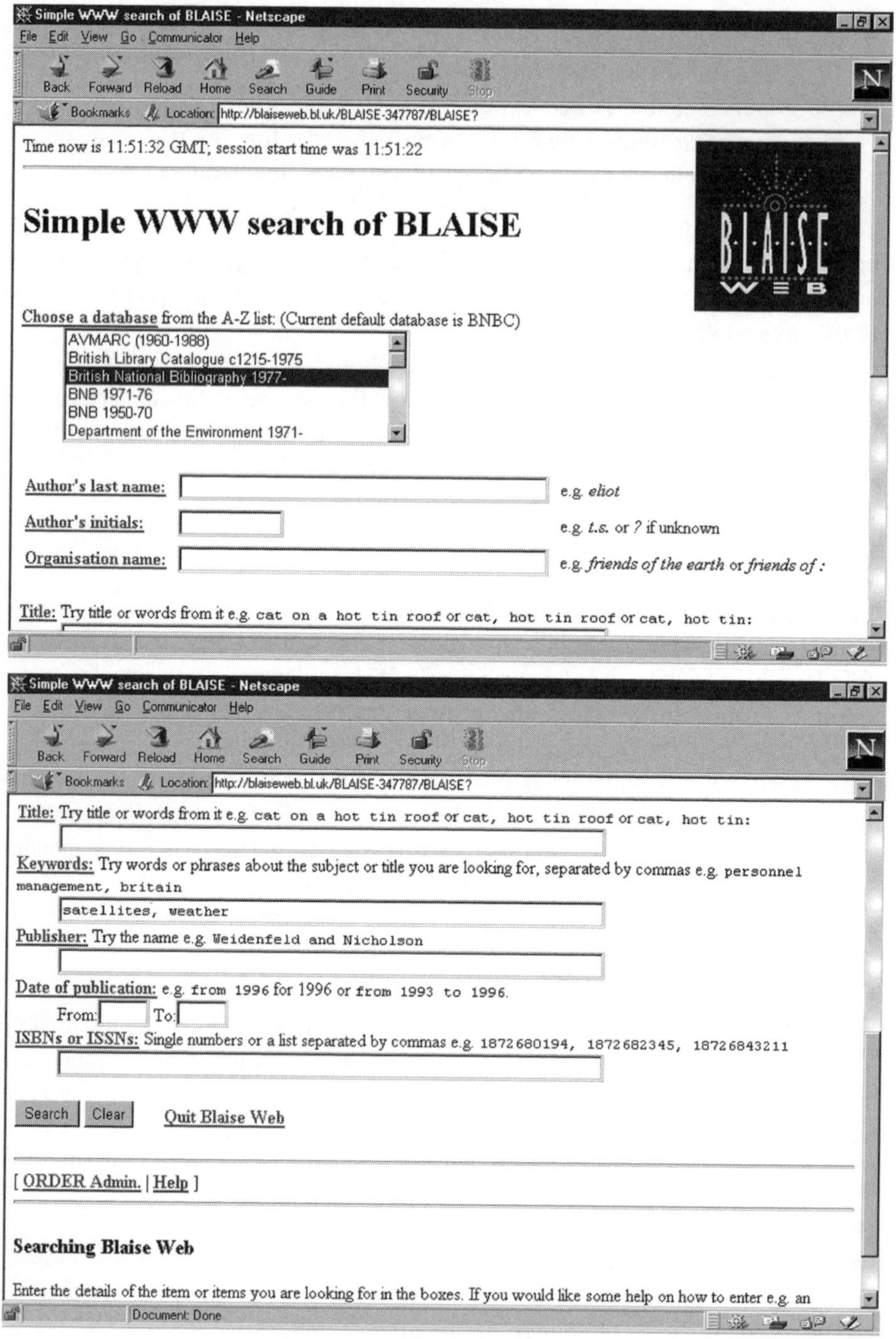

Figure 4.7 Web-based interface
Compare this with Figure 4.6

Continued

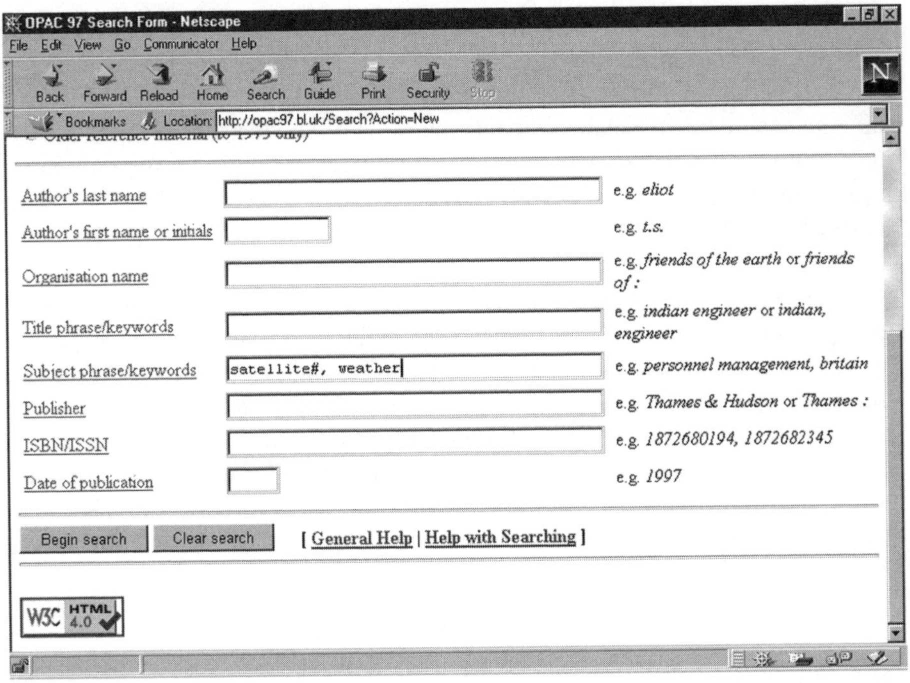

Figure 4.7 *Concluded*

potential users see colour differences and obtain information from colours. Colour used inappropriately can be distracting, confusing or objectionable.

Z39.50 AND SR

Z39.50 and SR are standards for information retrieval. Z39.50 is a national US protocol developed by the American National Standards Institute (ANSI), whilst SR or ISO 10162/3 Search and Retrieve is the international standard emanating from the International Standards Organisation. Z39.50 and SR are compatible, but Z39.50 is more frequently used because it has greater functionality.

Z39.50 is an application layer protocol which supports the construction of distributed information retrieval applications (the protocol which relates to data processing). The implementation of the Z39.50 standard allows users of different software products to communicate with each other and to exchange data. Most significantly, the local familiar interface can be made available for searching other remote databases. This means that, for instance, a user can search a remote OPAC mounted under a different library management system, through the interface available in their local library.

Z39.50 functions in a client-server environment. In this context the client is

119

known as the origin and the server as the target. At the client end, a request from the user application is translated into Z39.50 by the origin and sent to the target. At the server end, the target translates the request into a form understandable by the database application, which processes the request, locates the required information and returns it to the target which, in turn, passes it back to the origin. The reciprocal translation process accommodates returning information.

Many, but not all systems suppliers offer Z39.50 clients and/or servers. Z39.50 is used in a number of library management systems, OCLC's FirstSearch service, for document delivery and interlibrary loan, in the online search services offered by Mead Data Central, and Dialog, and SilverPlatter have embedded it in their Electronic Reference Library. Also, while Z39.50 allows the use of a local search interface, this does not mean that all search facilities normally offered by that interface are available. Since the remote database application performs the search, the user is restricted to the facilities of that system. There are also some restrictions imposed by the protocol itself. For example, the protocol does not cover relevance ranking.

SUMMARY

Since systems are designed to facilitate user access to information or knowledge, an important preliminary to systems design and creation is an understanding of the different kinds of users and the way in which users may wish to search or identify information. Users are often categorized on the basis of their level of experience with a given system; more experienced users generally need less support and more powerful applications than novice users. Cognitive models are also important in an appreciation of the way in which users understand and learn to use information systems. Indexing and searching are complementary processes. There are a number of different types of search strategies that may be adopted by different users. Search processes are also constrained by interface design. Most systems have GUIs and/or Web-based interfaces. GUIs use a combination of direct manipulation, windows, dialog boxes, menus, buttons and check boxes, icons, form filling, question and answer and command languages. Voice-based dialogues and multimedia interfaces are also important in some applications. Z39.50 and SR are important standards for information retrieval, which support the construction of distributed applications. Z39-50 allows the use of a local search interface when searching a remote database.

REFERENCES AND FURTHER READING

Allen, B. (1991) Cognitive research in information science: implications for design. In M. E. Williams (ed.), *Annual Review of Information Science and Technology*, **26**, pp. 3–37. Medford, NJ: Learned Information.

Armstrong, C. J. and Large, J. A. (1999) *Manual of Online Search Strategies*, 3rd edn. Aldershot: Gower.

Barker, A. L. (1997) DataStar Web: living up to the hype? An evaluation of the interface and search system. In *Online Information97: Proceedings of the 21st International Online Information Meeting, London, 9–11 December 1997*, pp. 213–22. Oxford: Learned Information.

Bastien, J. M. C. and Scapin, D. L. (1995) Evaluating a user interface with ergonomic criteria. *International Journal of Human Computer Interaction*, **7** (2), 105–21.

Bennett, J. L. (1984) Managing to meet usability requirements. In J. L. Bennett, D. Case, J. Sandelin and M. Smith (eds), *Visual Display Terminal: Usability Issues and Health Concerns*. Englewood Cliffs, NJ: Prentice Hall.

Beaulieu, M. (1997) Experiments on interfaces to support query expansion. *Journal of Documentation*, **53** (1), 8–19.

Berkman, R. I. (1994) *Find it Online*. New York: Wondcrest/McGraw-Hill.

Booth, P. (1989) An introduction to human–computer interaction. Hove: Lawrence Erlbaum.

Borgman, C.L. (1996) Why are online catalogs still hard to use? *Journal of the American Society for Information Science*, **47** (7), 493–503.

Borgman, C. L., Hirsh, S. G., Walter, V. A. and Gallagher, A. L. (1995) Children's searching behaviour on browsing and keyword online catalogs: the Science Library catalog projects. *Journal of the American Society for Information Science*, **46** (9), 663–84.

Bosch, V. M. and Hancock-Beaulieu, M. (1995) CDROM user interface evaluation: the appropriateness of GUI's. *Online and CD-ROM review*, **19** (5), 255–70.

Butcher, D. R. and Rowley, J. E. (1989) The Searcher/Information Interface Project 2: manual and on-line searching-pilot study. *Journal of Information Science*, **15**, 109–14.

Dempsey, L. (1994) Distributed library and information systems: the significance of Z39,50. *Managing Information*, **1** (6), 41–2.

Dempsey, L., Russell, R. and Kirriemuir, J. (1996) Towards distributed library systems: Z39.50 in a European context. *Program*, **30** (1), 1–22.

Galitz, W. O. (1997) *Essential Guide to User Interface Design: An Introduction to GUI Design: Principles and Techniques*. New York: Wiley.

Head, A. J. (1997) A question of interface design: how do online service GUI's measure up? *Online*, **21** (3), 20–29.

Hewitt, S. (1997) The future for mediated online search services in an academic institutions: a case study. *Online and CD-ROM Review*, **21** (5), 281–4.

Hsieh-Yee, I. (1993) Effects of search experience and subject knowledge on the search tactics of novice and experienced searchers. *Journal of the American Society for Information Science*, **44** (3), 161–74.

Jasco, P. (1995) WinSPIRS : Windows software for SilverPlatter CD-ROMs. *Online*, **19** (1), 74–81.

Kearsley, G. and Heller, R. S. (1995) Multimedia in public access settings: evaluation issues. *Journal of Educational Multimedia and Hypermedia*, **4** (1), 3–24.

Large, A. (1981) The user interface to CD-ROM databases. *Journal of Librarianship and Information Science*, **23** (4), 203–17.

Mandel, T. (1997) *The Elements of User Interface Design*. New York: Wiley.

Marchionini, G., Dwiggins, S., Katz, A. and Lin, X. (1993) Information seeking in full text end-user oriented search systems: the roles of domain and search expertise. *Library and Information Science Research*, **15** (1), 35–69.

McGraw, C. L. (1992) *Designing and Evaluating User Interfaces for Knowledge Based Systems*. New York and London: Ellis Horwood.

Mohan, L. and Bryne, J. (1995) Designing intuitive icons and toolbars. *UNIX Review*, 49–54.

Preece, J. (1994) *Human–Computer Interaction*, Woking.

Puttapithakporn, S. D. (1990) Interface design and user problems and errors: a case study of novice searchers. *RQ, 30* (2), 195–204.

Quint, B. (1991) Inside a searcher's mind: the seven stages of an online search – Part 1 *Online, 15* (3), 13–18.

Rowley, J. E. (1995) Human–computer interface and design in Windows based CD-ROMs: an early review. *Journal of Library and Information Science, 27* (2), 77–88.

Rowley, J. E. and Butcher, D. R. (1988) The Searcher Information Interface Project – final report. *Journal of Information Science, 14*, 355–63.

Rowley, J. E. and Slack, F. (1997) The evaluation of interface design on CD-ROMs. *Online and CD-ROM Review, 21* (1), 3–14.

Rowley, J. E. and Slack, F. S. (1998) *Public Access Interface Design*. Aldershot: Gower.

Russell, R. (ed.) (1996) *Z39.50 and SR*. LITC Report No 7. London: LITC.

Saracevic, T., Kantor, P., Chamis, A. Y. and Trivison, D. (1988) A study of information seeking and retrieving. *Journal of the American Society for Information Science, 39* (3) 161–96.

Shackel, B. (1990) Human computer interaction: whence and whither? *Journal of the American Society for Information Science, 48* (11), 970–86.

Shaw, D. (1991) The human–computer interface for information retrieval. *Annual Review of Information Science and Technology, 26*, 155–95.

Shneiderman, B. (1992) *Designing the User Interface: Strategies for Effective Human–Computer Interaction*, 2nd edn. Reading: Addison-Wesley.

Shuman, B. A. (1993) *Cases in Online Search Strategy*. Englewood, CO: Libraries Unlimited.

Slack, F. E. (1991) OPACs: Using enhanced transaction logs to achieve more effective online help for subject searching. PhD thesis. Manchester Polytechnic (unpublished).

Stuart, R. (1996) *The Design of Virtual Environments*. New York: McGraw Hill.

Vaughan, T. (1994) *Multi-Media; Making it Work*, 2nd edn. Berkeley, CA and London: Osborne McGraw Hill.

Vickery, B. and Vickery, A. (1993) Online search interface design. *Journal of Documentation, 49* (2), 103–87.

Wade, A. (1996) Training the end-user. Case study 1: Academic libraries. In R. Biddiscombe (ed.), *The End-User Revolution: CD-ROM, Internet and The Changing Role of the Information Professional*, pp. 96–109. London: Library Association.

Yee, M. M. (1991) System design and cataloguing meet the user: user interfaces to online public access catalogs. *Journal of the American Society for Information Science, 42* (2), 78–98.

Yuan, W. (1997) End-user searching behaviour in information retrieval: a longitudinal study. *Journal of the American Society for Information Science, 48* (3), 218–34.

5 Indexing and searching languages

INTRODUCTION

This chapter introduces a range of principles associated with the concept and use of indexing and searching languages. The primary focus of this chapter is on indexing languages that are used to represent subjects. Accordingly the chapter starts by exploring the concept of a subject. Next the types of indexing languages are introduced and, finally, a range of principles that apply to the application and use of indexing languages. At the end of this chapter you will:

- recognize the complexities associated with naming subjects and the need to identify relationships between subjects
- be familiar with different approaches to indexing and with associated concepts such as specificity and exhausitivity
- understand the difference between natural and controlled languages
- be aware of the principles of vocabulary control
- understand the principles of thesaurus construction
- be familiar with the search facilities that are available to support post-coordinate searching.

APPROACHES TO SUBJECT RETRIEVAL

Users often approach information sources not with names in mind, but with a question that requires an answer or a topic for study. Users seek documents or information concerned with a particular subject. This is a common approach to information sources and, in order to provide for it, the document or document representation must include enough data to ensure that items on specific subjects are retrieved.

What is a specific subject? A rabbit is a rabbit; but is it? Europeans will have in mind the European rabbit, Americans the cottontail; they belong to different genera. A rabbit is a concrete entity – that is, we can see it and pick it up (preferably not by its ears) and define it by its physical characteristics (long ears, furry, weighs around a kilogram) and behaviour (hopping movement, digs burrows, breeds freely). Abstract concepts can be more difficult to pin down. Some are fairly straightforward, like Music (encyclopaedia definition: 'the organized movement of sounds through a continuum of time'); some, like Geography ('the science that deals with the distribution and arrangement of all the elements of the earth's surface') look straightforward until we think of the vast scope of the subject; while Games defies definition – the philosopher Wittgenstein concluded after a long study that the subject could only be defined through its examples. Not only may subjects be in themselves difficult to define, we must remember that they do not exist in isolation in the way that named entities do. If we are looking for information on William Shakespeare, Mount Everest or Microsoft, we can be sure when we have found it that we have come to the right place as these are all 'classes of one'. Common subjects, on the other hand, form networks of conceptual relationships with other subjects. If we are trying to identify a rabbit, we may not be entirely sure that what we saw was not a hare; the reader in a library looking for the geography books is likely to be directed to at least three widely separated sets of shelves; and library readers everywhere are notorious for asking for the games section when what they are looking for is information on chess. Any system of subject retrieval must then have a mechanism for directing users to other, closely related, subjects.

WHY INDEX?

Now that cheap online storage and retrieval of full text are commonplace, the value of indexing has been questioned. If the individual words in a text are immediately accessible in any combination, why go to the trouble of constructing indexes at all? Why not simply search for combinations of words from the text? The assumption behind this attitude is that a text is 'about' what it mentions. Fairthorne put his finger on the weakness of this assumption:

> *Moby Dick* is about a whale, *Othello* is about a handkerchief, and about other things. The difficulties are to identify which of the things mentioned refer to relevant topics, and how to deal with topics of the document that are not mentioned explicitly ... Parts of the document are not always what the entire document is about, nor is a document usually about the sum of the things it mentions.
>
> (Fairthorne, 1969, p. 79)

In other words, this paragraph has just mentioned a whale and a handkerchief, but nobody would suggest that it is *about* those things. It is the indexer's job to ensure that a document's overall topic and, perhaps, its major constituent themes are adequately represented.

WHAT IS A DOCUMENT ABOUT?

Information retrieval is in general concerned with what a text is *about* rather than what it *means*. What is meaning? One point of view holds that that meaning is inferential: a scientific paper may be *about* a statistical correlation between tobacco smoking and lung cancer; what it *means* is that the one may cause the other. Another argument states that indexers should adopt a neutral position and not attempt to impose upon the reader their views on what a document means. There is also the point of view – grounded in literary theory – that meaning is interactive (and to that extent subjective), the result of the interaction between the text and the individual reader. Perhaps the most powerful argument against indexers attempting to represent the meaning of documents is economic: it would simply take too long to do. A trained indexer can grasp what a document is about by scanning it rapidly. To attempt to extract its meaning would involve a far closer study, as well as requiring expert subject knowledge.

APPROACHES TO INDEXING

An indexing language can be defined as the terms or codes that might be used as access points in an index. A searching language can be defined as the terms that are used by a searcher when specifying a search requirement. If the terms or codes are assigned by an indexer when a database is created, then the indexing language is used in indexing. The same terms or codes may also be used as access points to records during searching. While the indexing language may be distinct from the searching language, clearly, if retrieval is to be successful, the two must be closely related. Indexing languages may be of two different types: controlled-indexing languages or assigned-term systems, and natural-indexing languages or derived-term systems. Each of these is briefly discussed below.

Controlled-indexing languages (assigned-term systems)

With these languages a person controls the terms that are used as index terms. Controlled-indexing languages may be used for names and other labels but much emphasis is placed upon languages with terms that describe subjects. Normally an authority list identifies the terms that may be assigned. Indexing involves a person assigning terms from this list to specific documents on the basis of subjective interpretations of the concepts in the document; in this process the indexer exercises some intellectual discrimination in choosing appropriate terms.

There are two types of subject-based controlled-indexing languages: alphabetical-indexing languages and classification schemes. In alphabetical-indexing languages, such as are recorded in thesauri and subject headings lists, subject terms are the alphabetical names of subjects. Control is exercised over which terms are used, and relationships between terms are indicated, but the terms themselves are ordinary words. In classification schemes each subject is represented by a code or notation. Classification schemes are particularly concerned to place subjects in a framework that crystallizes their relationships one to another. More generally though, classification is implicit in all indexing. A document in which content is wholly or partially specified in the index term RABBITS is thereby classed with other documents to which the same specification has been applied. Controlled-indexing languages take the process of classification one stage further, by displaying semantic links, between rabbits and hares for example. Formal bibliographic classification schemes, such as the DDC and LCC classifications, display these relationships in a systematic manner. They are able, in addition, through their notation to exclude particular connotations of meaning: thus DDC's 599.322 denotes rabbits as zoological entities, but not as pets (which would be 636.9322).

Thesauri have always been a feature of the document management systems that have been designed to manage larger collections. They are increasingly featuring in OPACs and other information retrieval environments, and their applicability for Internet applications is of interest. Thesauri typically show the controlled indexing term, with related, narrower and broader terms, as shown in Figure 5.6. They may be displayed in a window during search strategy formulation, to aid a user in the selection of terms. Often terms can be selected from the thesaurus listing simply by clicking on them. Hypertext links in thesauri listings can be used to move between different occurrences of the same term in the list. Another application of thesauri is as a basis for automatic indexing. All terms in the documents that appear in the thesaurus will generate an entry in the inverted index. Related applications of thesauri are in the creation of semantic nets and semantic knowledge bases.

Natural-indexing languages (uncontrolled or derived-term systems)

These languages are not really a distinct or stable language in their own right, but rather are the 'natural' or ordinary language of the document being indexed. Strictly, natural language systems are only one type of derived-term system. A derived-term system is one where all descriptors are taken from the document being indexed. Thus, author indexes, title indexes and citation indexes, as well as natural language subject indexes, are derived-term systems. Any terms that appear in the document may be candidates for index terms. Emphasis has traditionally been on the terms in titles and abstracts, but increasingly the full text of the document is used as the basis for indexing. Natural language indexing using the full text of the document may be very detailed, and in some systems some mechanism for deciding which terms are the most important in the indexing of a given document may be appropriate. Such mechanisms are often based upon statistical analysis of the relative frequency of occurrence terms. Natural language indexing can be executed by a human indexer, or automatically by the computer. The computer might index every term in the document, apart from a limited stop-list of very common terms, or may only index those terms that have been listed in a computer-held thesaurus.

Natural language indexing and controlled language indexing are used extensively in many information retrieval applications. Both are used in retrieval on CD-ROM, via the online search services, in document management systems and in online public access catalogues. Controlled-indexing languages are claimed to be more consistent and therefore more efficient and straightforward for the searcher, but research has failed to prove this convincingly. The dilemma facing systems designers is that to offer anything other than natural language indexing in the context of the huge databanks available through the Internet would be prohibitively expensive. On the other hand, controlled language indexing is seen as valuable in a supportive environment for inexperienced users because they do not need to navigate all the variations inherent in natural language. Significant effort is being directed towards the development of system interfaces that manage this variability, either implicitly or explicitly, on behalf of the user. Many databases include terms from controlled indexing languages (often including both alphabetical indexing languages and classification schemes) and also support searching on the text of the record, thus covering all options.

FEATURES OF RETRIEVAL SYSTEMS

EXHAUSTIVITY AND CONTENT SPECIFICATION

It was suggested above that indexes attempt to specify content by means of single words or phrases. Clearly, the *whole* of the subject content cannot be specified by anything less than the complete text (and may well require more, in the way of footnotes and other glosses, as with the heavily annotated editions of classic writers). Indexing has to try to sum up the salient points, while ignoring the non-essentials. This can be done at a number of levels, which, even

Advantages of Uncontrolled Indexing Languages
- Low input cost
- Full database contents searchable
- No human indexing errors
- No delay in incorporating new terms
- High specificity gives precision. Excels in retrieving individual terms – names of persons, organizations, etc.
- Exhaustivity gives potential for high recall. Does not apply to title-only databases

Disadvantages of Uncontrolled Indexing Languages
- Greater burden on searcher, particularly with terms that have many synonyms and several species
- Information implicitly but not overtly included in text may be missed
- Absence of specific to generic linkage
- Vocabulary of discipline must be known
- Syntax problems. Danger of false drops through incorrect term association
- Exhaustivity may lead to loss of precision.

Advantages of Controlled Vocabulary Indexing Languages
- Eases searching through:
  - control of synonyms and near synonyms
  - qualification of homographs
  - provision of scope notes
  - display of broader, narrower and related terms
  - expresses concepts elusive in free text.
- Overcomes syntax problems with compound terms and other devices
- Normally avoids precision loss through over-exhaustivity
- Maps areas of knowledge

Disadvantages of Controlled Vocabulary Indexing Languages
- High input cost
- Possible inadequacies of coverage
- Human error in interpretation and application of index terms can occur
- Possible out-of-date vocabulary
- Difficulty of systematically incorporating all relevant relationships between terms
- Lack of specificity
- Lack of exhaustivity
- The searcher needs to become acquainted with the language

Figure 5.1 Comparing uncontrolled and controlled indexing languages

though they are presented here as distinct strata, form a continuum. *Exhaustivity* of indexing is the name given to the depth of indexing which it is the policy of a given indexing system to employ. Exhaustivity is therefore a management decision. The level of exhaustivity at which a system operates can either be built into the system (for example, by restricting the number of fields available for index terms), or it can be controlled operationally, by giving instructions to indexers.

Summarization refers to the process of conveying the overall subject content of a document in a single word or a short phrase or structured heading: for example, RABBITS, or BREEDS OF RABBITS – BREEDS. Indexing at the level of summarization is commonly applied to graphic material – photographs and the like – which convey information perceptually; and also – particularly – to books, which normally have their own detailed indexing systems in the form of back-of-book indexes and contents lists. Library catalogues and published bibliographies are nearly always indexes at the level of summarization. So, too, are some published indexes to periodical literature: for example, *British Humanities Index* and the range of indexes – *Humanities Index, Education Index,* etc. – published by the H. W. Wilson Company.

A second level of exhaustivity is found in many databases that are indexes to collections or to periodical literature, and select the most significant subjects in the text – often around six to twelve controlled descriptors. In addition, the words in the title and abstract are available for searching. Contents lists operate at this level.

Even more exhaustive are back-of-book type indexes: indexes to individual documents, which should list every subject discussed in the text (Figure 5.2). The ultimate level of exhaustivity is provided by the text itself. In full-text retrieval systems any word or phrase is potentially available for searching. (Most systems have a *stop-list* of very common words that have not been indexed and cannot therefore be retrieved.) At this point we have a concordance rather than an index.

Figure 5.3 gives examples of indexing the same journal article at different levels of exhaustivity.

Compare the Abstract, Descriptors, and Identifiers in each. (NB: ERIC and PsycInfo define 'Identifiers' differently.) ERIC's abstract has 44 words; PsycInfo's has 96. For Descriptors and Identifiers the word counts are 20 and 46.

Specificity

Specificity is an aspect of controlled language systems. It refers to the vocabulary of the system, and denotes the extent to which we are able to specify subject content when indexing. Dewey Decimal Classification, for example, specifies rabbits as domestic animals at class 636.9322. This class is, however, unable to specify individual breeds of rabbit: there are no subclasses for lop-eared or Angora rabbits or any other breed. Neither can this class distinguish between rabbits kept as pets and rabbits grown for meat or for their fur. A specialist manual on keeping pet Angora rabbits has to be classed with all other works on rabbits as domestic animals. This clearly makes searching less precise, as the searcher has to sift through a number of marginally relevant items all classed

1. Summarization

Subject heading: Indexing (*supplied by the Library of Congress*)

Title: Indexing books

Series title: Chicago guides to writing, editing and publishing

2. Most significant subjects

Chapter headings:
1. Introduction to book indexing
2. The author and the index
3. Getting started
4. Structure of entries
5. Arrangement of entries
6. Special concerns in indexing
7. Names, names, names
8. Format and layout of the index
9. Editing the index
10. Tools for indexing

3. Detailed subject specification

Index (*part*):

Abbreviations
  alphabetizing, 130
  of company names, 177, 180–81
  cross-references to and from, 102, 128–29
  double-posting, 130
  explaining, 12, 70
  spelling out, 128-29
  for states in U.S., 175–76
access points
  converting subentries to main headings, 219
  main heading as primary, 77, 217
  multiple, with double posting, 75, 76, 221
accuracy of entries, assessing, 230
acronyms
  alphabetizing, 130

4. The full text

Text: Alphabetizing of Abbreviations and Acronyms

Abbreviations and acronyms should be alphabetized in the same way as the other entries in the index, whether letter-by-letter or word-by-word. They are not usually alphabetized as if they were spelled out. An exception that many publishers allow is that the abbreviation U.S. may be alphabetized as though spelled out. This allows a term like *U.S. Bureau of Reclamation* to interfile with other entries such as *United States Coast Guard*.

Figure 5.2 Levels of exhaustivity within a single work
Source: Mulvaney, 1994.

Example from ERIC and PsycInfo, showing how one research paper has been indexed and abstracted by the two services.

ERIC:
EJ521883 PS524404

The Role of Emotion in Children's Understanding and Emotional Reactions to Marital Conflict.
Crockenberg, Susan; Forgays, Deborah Kirby
Merrill-Palmer Quarterly; v42 n1 pp. 22–47 Jan 1996
Theme issue topic: 'Conflicts in Families and Between Children: Advances in Theory and Research.'
ISSN: 0272-930X
Available from: UMI
Language: English
Document Type: RESEARCH REPORT (143); JOURNAL ARTICLE (080)
Journal Announcement: CIJAUG96
Abstract: Tested a process model for the impact of children's exposure to marital conflict on their behavior adjustment with a sample of 28 couples and their 6-year-old children. Found that maternal conflict behavior and children's negative emotional reactions to fathers independently predicted children's behavioral adjustment. (MDM)
Descriptors: *Adjustment (to Environment); *Child Behavior; Conflict Resolution; *Emotional Response; *Family Problems; *Models; Predictor Variables; Sex Differences; *Young Children
Identifiers: *Marital Discord

PsycInfo:
01416789 1996-01718-002

The role of emotion in children's understanding and emotional reactions to marital conflict.
Author: Crockenberg, Susan; Forgays, Deborah Kirby
Author Affiliation: U Vermont, Dept of Psychology, Burlington, VT, USA
Journal: Merrill-Palmer Quarterly , Vol 42(1) , 22–47 , Jan , 1996
Special Issue: Special Issue: Conflicts in families and between children: Advances in theory and research.
ISSN: 0272-930X
Document Type: Journal Article; Empirical Study
Special Features: References
Record Type: Abstract
Language: English
Population Group: Human; Male; Female **Age Group:** 100 (Childhood (birth–12 yrs)); 180 (School Age (6–12 yrs)); 300 (Adulthood (18 yrs & older)) **Population Location:** USA
Abstract: (Presents a process model that identifies children's processing of marital conflict as an essential mediator between the conflict and behavioral maladjustment. 28 mothers (aged 27–42 yrs) and fathers (aged 21–44 yrs) assessed their 6-yr-old child's adjustment with the Child Behavior Checklist and questionnaires. Children viewed videotapes of their parents working toward conflict resolution. Children's perceptions indicate ability to distinguish behavior of fathers from mothers during marital conflict. Children report negative emotional reactions to mothers when fathers exhibit negative behavior. Maternal conflict behavior and children's negative emotional reactions to fathers independently predict children's behavioral adjustment. ((c) 1997 APA PsycINFO, all rights reserved)
Descriptors: *Child Attitudes; *Emotional Responses; *Marital Conflict; *Human Sex Differences; *Parents ; Adjustment; Childhood; Psychosocial Development; School Age Children; Adulthood
Identifiers: perceptions of & emotional reactions to mother's vs father's behavior during marital conflict, behavioral adjustment, male vs female 6 yr olds & their 21–44 yr old parents
Subject Codes & Headings: 2820 (Cognitive & Perceptual Development)
Release Date: 19970101

Figure 5.3 Indexing at different levels of exhaustivity

at the same place. Specificity thus improves the precision of a search: that is, its ability to sift out unwanted material.

Special systems (i.e. systems confined to one subject area or other field) often use differential levels of specificity. Topics that are central to the subject field are indexed at a higher level of specificity than peripheral subjects. For example, if Domestic Animals is a system's principal subject field, it would be quite likely to make specific provision for the various breeds of rabbit. If the subject field is something remote, however, there might be no specific provision even for rabbits: we might have to include them under a more general term, like Pets.

Specificity and exhaustivity are related to the extent that in practice greater exhaustivity needs to be matched by greater specificity in the indexing terms. Most book indexes, for example, are both specific and exhaustive. The combination of specificity and exhaustivity is often referred to as *depth of indexing*.

Complex topics

A final set of definitions concerns the way complex topics are handled. A document may not be simply about rabbits or apples or chess; it may very well deal with some more precise aspect, like breeds of rabbits, or the effect of pre-storage heat treatment on the shelf life of apples. The traditional method of dealing with complex topics has been to encapsulate as much of the topic as possible into a single heading, RABBITS – BREEDS for example, or APPLES – SHELF LIFE – *EFFECT OF* – HEAT TREATMENT. Indexes of this kind are known as *pre-coordinate* indexes, because the topics that comprise a heading are strung together or coordinated by the indexer in advance of any searches that may be carried out on any of the topics represented within the heading. These indexes require elaborate rules for the consistent construction of headings, and will be considered in Chapter 6. Because of this lack of flexibility many systems employ a quite different method of handling complex topics. Here the subject of a document is represented by a number of one-concept terms – these are the descriptors in Figure 5.3 – and the searcher is able to combine as many or as few of them as are required, using Boolean logic: for example, CHILD ATTITUDES AND MARITAL CONFLICT. Systems employing this method of indexing and searching are known as *post-coordinate* systems. The earliest of these systems were card-based, using specialized stationery and other equipment, but nearly all systems in use today are computerized.

User-friendliness

In 1960 Calvin Mooers expounded his famous law:

An information system will tend not to be used whenever it is more painful and troublesome for a customer to have information than for him not to have it.

The corollary of this is that the use of information systems and services will be increased if steps are taken to improve their user-friendliness. Some of the factors influencing user-friendliness are:

- *Accessibility*: the service should be physically accessible to users.
- *Ease of use*: the service should be within the intellectual capabilities of its users. While great strides have been made in improving user interfaces (see Chapter 4), there is always a trade-off between ease of use and system capabilities. The more powerful the functionality of a system, the more complex the instructions and protocols for using it, and its proneness to error on the part of the user.
- *System error*: as opposed to user error. This includes system malfunctions, and output errors caused by inadequacies in the system, as with some automatic indexing and retrieval systems.
- *Form of output*: output may be in the form of actual documents, or document surrogates; if the latter, output may or may not be downloadable. The least convenient output is non-downloadable document surrogates, for example, with manually searched catalogues.
- *Delay*: whether in accessing the service, or in obtaining the search results.

SEARCH FACILITIES IN POST-COORDINATE SEARCHING

SEARCH LOGIC

Search logic is the means of specifying combinations of terms that must be matched for successful retrieval. Boolean search logic is employed in searching most systems. It may be used to link terms from either controlled- or natural-indexing languages, or both. The logic is used to link the terms that describe the concepts present in the statement of the search. As many as 20 to 30 or more search terms may be linked together by search logic in order to frame the search statement. Search logic permits the inclusion in the search statement of all synonyms and related terms, and also specifies acceptable and unacceptable search-term combinations. Search strategies often need to be more complex with natural language terms, in order to accommodate all the potential spelling variations and near-synonyms. In an online search the search statements are evolved one at a time, and feedback is available at each stage. The searcher specifies a search statement and the computer responds with the number of relevant records. With this type of search facility, the search strategy can be refined to yield a satisfactory output.

The Boolean logic operators are AND, OR and NOT.

AND reduces the number of items retrieved:

CHILDREN AND PARENTS retrieves items in which *both* terms occur.

OR increases the number of items retrieved:

CHILDREN OR PARENTS retrieves items in which *either* term occurs.

NOT subtracts the second term from the first.

CHILDREN NOT PARENTS retrieves items in which *only the first term* occurs.

The operators are subject to some variation. A few systems use AND NOT or ANDNOT. Also, operators may often be abbreviated, so that on Dialog * can be used to represent AND and + for OR.

It is common to use more than one operator in a search statement, as in for instance: CHILDREN AND PARENTS AND CONFLICT OR DISCORD. Once more than one operator has been introduced, the priority of execution needs to be considered. In the example above it is necessary to specify whether the search should be conducted as (CHILDREN AND PARENTS AND CONFLICT) OR DISCORD or as CHILDREN AND PARENTS AND (CONFLICT ORDISCORD). This latter is the expected order of execution, and must be specified by the use of parentheses.

The use of parentheses in formulating a search statement is often known as *nesting*. Each software package (or search service) has its own priority rules (for example, AND may always be processed before OR), and successful searching depends on heeding these rules, and making appropriate use of parentheses. Nesting forces priority, and offers a clear specification from the searcher's perspective.

RELEVANCE (CONFIDENCE) RANKING AND BEST MATCH SEARCH LOGIC

A weakness of Boolean searching is that it returns straight hit or miss responses, and items that partially fulfil the search specifications are excluded. For example, a search on CHILDREN AND PARENTS AND (CONFLICT OR DISCORD) would not return items containing the terms PARENTS AND CONFLICT but not CHILDREN. Many search systems now relevance rank results, listing items matching *any* of the search terms, with the best matches first. This can be done in a variety of ways, e.g.:

CHILDREN AND PARENTS AND CONFLICT
CHILDREN AND PARENTS AND DISCORD
CHILDREN AND CONFLICT
CHILDREN AND DISCORD

PARENTS AND CONFLICT
PARENTS AND DISCORD
CHILDREN AND PARENTS
CHILDREN
PARENTS
CONFLICT
DISCORD

A variation common in Web search engines is to use *implicit OR*, then relevance rank the results so that AND combinations are ranked before OR combinations, and adjacency before either. (This is one reason for the huge search sets generated by many simple Web searches.) The user could for example simply enter CHILDREN PARENTS CONFLICT DISCORD.

In most search statements it is possible to designate certain concepts as being more significant than their neighbours. In its role in formulating search profiles, weighted-term logic may be introduced either as a search logic in its own right, or as a means of reducing or ranking (relevancy ranking) the search output from a search whose basic logic is Boolean.

In an application where weighted-term logic is the primary search logic, each search term in a search profile is allocated a weight. These weights can be allocated by the searcher, but more commonly are allocated automatically. Automatic allocation of weights is usually based on the inverse frequency algorithm which weights terms in accordance with the inverse frequency of their occurrence in the database. Thus common words are not seen to be particularly valuable in uniquely identifying documents. A further refinement considers both the frequency and the positioning of the terms – i.e., words in important positions (titles, headers, early in the document) are given a higher ranking than words appearing elsewhere. If the weights are assigned by the searcher, they are associated with a relevance rating on a document which is found containing that term as a search term. Search profiles combine terms and their weights in a simple sum, and items rated as suitable for retrieval must have weights that exceed a specified threshold weight. A simple Selective Dissemination of Information (SDI) type profile showing the use of weighted-term logic is shown below:

Search description: The use of radioactive isotopes in measuring the productivity of soil.

A simple search profile (which does not explore all possible synonyms) might be:

8 Soil	4 Plants
7 Radioisotopes	3 Food

7 Isotopes	2 Environment
6 Radioactive	2 Agriculture
5 Radiation	1 Productivity
5 Agricultural chemistry	1 Water

A threshold weight appropriate to the specificity of the searcher's enquiry must be established. For instance, a threshold weight of 12 would retrieve documents with the following combinations of terms assigned, and these documents or records would be regarded as relevant:

Soil and Plants
Soil and Radioisotopes
Soil and Agricultural chemistry
Radioisotopes and Agricultural chemistry
Soil and Food and Agriculture

Documents with the following terms assigned would be rejected on the grounds that their combined weights from each of the terms identified in the records did not exceed the pre-selected threshold:

Productivity and Water
Food and Soil
Radioactive and Agriculture

Alternatively no threshold weight may be used, and then users will simply be presented with records in ranked order, and can make their own choice as to how far down the list they choose to scan.

Weighted-term search logic may also be used to supplement Boolean logic. Here weighted-term logic is a means of limiting or ranking the output from a search that has been conducted with the use of a search profile that was framed in terms of Boolean logic operators. In the search, and prior to display or printing, references or records are ranked according to the weighting that they achieve, and records with sufficiently high rankings will be deemed most relevant, and be selected for display or printing. In this application, relevancy ranking is most often achieved through an analysis of the number of occurrences of search terms or hits in the document.

The inverted indexes that need to be created to support Boolean searching, and relevance ranking, respectively, are different. An inverted index may be stored in the form of a large matrix, with each row corresponding to an individual term, and each column to an individual record. A Boolean search simply requires that each of these cells in the matrix have a value of 1 or 0. A mechanism that uses some type of term-weighting scheme will require the cell of the matrix to have a value n, where n is the result of a more complicated function of a number of variables. These values may be calculated on the basis of term occurrences. Each record may be considered as a vector or sequence of values.

SEARCH FACILITIES

Standard retrieval facilities are available in most information retrieval applications. These facilities have been developed to cater for a text-based environment, where the user does not know what documents are available and/ or does not know the terms by which records can be retrieved. In other database applications, where records can be retrieved through pre-assigned codes, many of the facilities listed below are not necessary. These facilities cater for the uncertainty in document-based systems, such as those of the external online search services, document management systems, CD-ROM applications and online public access catalogues. In command-based systems these faciltities are accessed through the use of an appropriate command; in GUIs the options are likely to be embedded in pull-down menus, or buttons and check boxes on dialog boxes.

Set-up facilities

These facilities set up the environment in which the search will proceed and are therefore environment-dependent. Help and news are common, as well as connection facilities sometimes in the form of logon and logoff facilities. Web-based interfaces often also offer access to information about the search service, its databases and customer service arrangements. The selection of database is usually a further preliminary.

Selecting search terms

Identification of search terms can be assisted by the display of search-term or index listings. The display may show index or search terms and, sometimes, their number of postings.

Entering search terms

Once a search term has been selected it must be entered. This may merely involve clicking on the term in a search-term listing, typing the term in, or using the term as a component in a more complex search statement entering the term itself, or a specific command might need to be issued. The system responds by creating a set of records indexed by that term and display the search term and the number of records in the set.

Combining search terms

Search terms may be combined into search statements with the aid of a search logic as discussed previously in this chapter. Boolean search logic or relevance ranking is common.

Entering phrases

Many search engines and OPACs allow the user to enter a search phrase, such as PURCHASING BOOKS ON THE INTERNET. As discussed above the system will often treat this as an implicit OR search, although some search engines may process phrases as if each of the terms were linked together with AND. Thus the above phrase would be searched as: PURCHASING AND BOOKS AND INTERNET.

Specifying sections of documents or fields in records to be searched

The ability to search for the occurrence of terms in a specific section of a document or in specific fields in a record facilitates more precise searching. For example, through the specification of whether a search might be conducted on a subject field or author field it may be possible to differentiate between documents on an a person (say SHAKESPEARE) as subject and as author. In order to be able to specify appropriate field labels, it is necessary to know the fields in a given database and which fields are indexed for successful field-based searching. Often it may be possible to search on a combination of fields or sections.

Truncation and search-term strings

Truncation supports searching on word stems. By using the truncation character at either end of a word, the system can be instructed to search for a string of characters, regardless of whether that string is a complete word. For example, if the user asks for a search on COUNTR* this would retrieve records including words such as Country, Countries, Countryside and Countrywide. The use of truncation eliminates the need to specify each word variant, and thus simplifies search strategies. This is particularly useful in natural language information retrieval systems where word variations are uncontrolled.

The most basic truncation is right-hand truncation where characters to the right of the character string are ignored. Left-hand truncation can be useful in circumstances where a variety of prefixes might occur. This is particularly useful in searching chemical databases. For example, *CHLORIDE might retrieve records of 'chloride' with various prefixes. Truncation, or masking as it is called in this context, is sometimes also available in the middle of words. Here truncation can be useful to cater for alternative spellings. So, for example, NA*IONAL will search for records with National and Nacional.

In order to control the array of word variants that might be retrieved as the result of a truncation, in some systems it is possible to specify the number of characters that are to appear after the truncated string. For example, EMPLOY??? might select terms with a maximum of three additional characters.

Proximity, adjacency and context searching

Often a subject is best described by a phrase of two, three or more words. Subjects such as Information Retrieval and Competitive Advantage need two words to describe them. It is useful if a search can be performed for such phrases. One obvious option is to search for the two words ANDed together, for example, INFORMATION AND RETRIEVAL. This should retrieve records containing the phrase but will also retrieve other records where these two words appear, but where they do not appear next to each other. This method, then, only allows crude phrase searching.

Another option is to store such terms as phrases, possibly by inserting hyphens to mark phrases. Then, for example, INFORMATION-RETRIEVAL would be stored as one term in the inverted file. This method is satisfactory but is primarily applicable to controlled indexing; phrases must be marked at input, and searchers must enter the term in exactly the form in which it was originally entered.

A more flexible option is the use of proximity operators. There are various different kinds of proximity operators. These can require that:

- two words appear next to each other; for example 'INFORMATION RETRIEVAL', INFORMATION ADJ RETRIEVAL, INFORMATION (N) RETRIEVAL, depending on the search system
- two words appear within the same field, sentence or paragraph. The first of these is available on most search systems, and is obligatory on some
- two words be within a specified distance of one another, with the maximum number of words to come between the two words indicated by the user; e.g. Dialog has INFORMATION (W.3) RETRIEVAL
- two words be within a specified distance of one another, with the maximum number of words to come between the two words set by the system. The operator NEAR is found on many Web search engines.

Range searching and limiting

Range searching is particularly useful when selecting records on the basis of numeric or data fields. They might, for instance, be used to select records according to a price field or publication data field. Fairly common range operators are:

EQ	equal to	LT	less than
NE	not equal to	NL	not less than
GT	greater than	W	within the limits
NG	not greater than	OL	outside the limits.

Although range searching is not appropriate in these contexts, examination of the contents of specific field may allow searches to be limited by document type, language or source.

Displaying search or results sets

Shows the user how many documents, search terms and references were found, and thereby indicates whether it might be appropriate to further refine the search.

Displaying records

Once a successful search has been performed, it is necessary to display the records. OPACs first display one-line records and then allow the user to display the full record. Online search services offer a variety of commands for displaying records on the screen, offline printing and downloading. Default formats are the norm, but user-defined formats are becoming more common. These allow users to specify the range of fields to be displayed in the records, and other features of the display. In addition to specifying the record format, users need to be able to specify which records are to be displayed. OPACs tend to let users select records and display them one at a time. CD-ROM and online search services have commands or options that allow the set of records for display to be indicated.

Storing search sets

Many retrieval systems store sets of search specifications by assigning them a running number. The sets can then be reused within the same search session. This permits the user to construct the search in stages, combining search sets by number:

Set 1:   CONFLICT
Set 2:   DISCORD
Set 3:   1 OR 2
Set 4:   CHILDREN
Set 5:   PARENTS
Set 6:   4 AND 5
Set 7:   3 AND 6

This may look long-winded, but it reduces typographical errors and gives the searcher the opportunity to reuse any of the terms in different combinations in order to refine the search. A search statement in the form CHILDREN AND PARENTS AND (CONFLICT OR DISCORD) will generate only one search set, and the terms cannot be reused in other combinations.

With systems that do not store search sets, a search has to be entered as a single statement, and once the user moves on to the next search the old search is lost. There may be a facility for refining a search (by performing a search on the set of search results instead of on the whole database), or for storing searches for reuse.

Search management

Search management includes opportunities to review the search strategy that has been adopted and, permanently or temporarily, to save a search profile for subsequent use. Search profiles may be saved temporarily of permanently. Temporary saves are useful for searches where a searcher might wish to reflect on a search, or otherwise come back and complete the search at a later point in time. Permanent saving of the search profile is usually associated with current awareness of selective dissemination of information. The search profile will be run on behalf of the user at regular intervals in order to identify new material, and this will be sent to the user as current awareness notifications. Intelligent agents and other push technologies that refine profiles over a period of time are a recent innovation in this area.

Advanced display options

Records in full-text databases are long, and a full record usually occupies several screens. In such circumstances, special display facilities can support browsing through relevant portions of the text. The ability to stop as soon as the screen is full is useful, as are facilities for moving backwards and forwards through the document. If the text is divided into numbered paragraphs, it is possible to select paragraphs for display. Another approach is to use a KWIC facility, which shows relevant index terms with bits of adjacent text in small windows. Another option that might prove useful is the ability to sort a set of records into order before displaying. Numeric or financial data may be best displayed in reverse or descending order. Some financial databases offer statistical presentation and analysis.

Multi-file searching

Where, as with the online search services, there are a number of databases that might generate relevant records in response to one search, multi-file search facilities are beneficial. The most user-friendly multi-file search option is when other databases can be searched without reformulating the strategy. This requires the system to make the appropriate adjustments in search terms and fields to be searched. The most refined multi-file searching then goes on to produce an integrated set of records drawn from several databases, and with duplicate records eliminated. Many online search services have a database of databases, such as Dialog's Dialindex (File 411). Available databases are grouped by subject. The searcher specifies a subject group to be searched and enters a search specification. The system returns the number of hits for each database.

Displaying the thesaurus

Where a controlled-indexing language has been used to provide index terms, a thesaurus will often be available in both printed and online formats. This thesaurus displays the controlled vocabulary used and relationships between terms, and is therefore a useful tool in narrowing or broadening searches. It is useful if the thesaurus can be displayed in a window to assist users as they attempt to develop a search strategy. Free-language thesauri that show relationships between terms may be available on some systems, but these take considerable effort to set up. GUIs offer fascinating opportunities for the display of graphical thesauri, showing multiple tree structures and explode options.

Hypermedia

Many systems, including the WWW, offer hypermedia searching. True hypertext searching relies upon an indexer establishing conceptual links between documents. Creators of Web pages often do this when they indicate which terms are to be used as links to other pages. However, in a large database this is very labour-intensive. An alternative is to rely upon the content, including the text and other objects in the record and use the occurrence of objects or terms as the basis for hypermedia links. Thus if the same term or object appears in two records or documents, the user may move from one record to another by, say, clicking on the term or object and without explicitly returning to the index.

PRINCIPLES OF LANGUAGE CONTROL

At its simplest, a controlled language is a list (known as a *thesaurus*) of permitted terms and terms which are semantically related. All controlled languages have an alphabetical display sequence. There may also be a *systematic* (classified) sequence, either as the principal display or as an adjunct to the alphabetical display.

The vocabulary of a controlled language comprises the available terms used for indexing. Such terms describe the content of a document, and so are called *descriptors*. These may be words, or they may be coded into the notation of a classification schedule, where the notation translates the concepts behind the words. In either case, any relationships between the terms are fixed and permanent.

How does vocabulary control work in practice? Consider the term *wagon*. The word has a plural, *wagons*, as well as an alternative spelling, *waggon(s)*, so we must opt for one or other spelling, and have some means of alerting those who use other forms of the word. A wagon is a wheeled vehicle for transporting freight; but it can denote a range of specific vehicles, according to whether the transport is by rail or by road and, if the latter, whether it has an engine or is drawn by a horse or tractor. So for indexing purposes we may well wish to limit our definition to just one of these. If road vehicles, they are often known by their manufacturer's name and perhaps the name of the model. Finally, there are other words or phrases whose meaning is synonymous or nearly so (*cart, truck, lorry*), or which belong to the same category but have a wider or narrower meaning (*road vehicle, pick-up truck*), or which, while not strictly belonging to the same category, are an essential part of the definition of a wagon (*freight, goods*). With this in mind, let us look at the formal rules of vocabulary control. The basic source is the International and (identical) British Standard Guide to *Establishment and Development of Monolingual Thesauri* (ISO 2788:1986, BS 5723:1987 – ISO, 1986).

METHODS OF VOCABULARY CONTROL

The methods of vocabulary control are:

- The form of a term (e.g. its grammatical form and spelling) is controlled.

- A choice is made between two or more synonyms or near synonyms to express the same concept.
- A decision is made on whether to admit proper names.
- A term may be deliberately restricted in meaning to the most effective meaning for the purposes of the thesaurus.

A thesaurus uses a range of symbols to indicate semantic relations. The commonest list is:

SN	Scope Note
USE	Use [another term in preference to this one]
UF	Used For
BT	Broader Term
NT	Narrower Term
RT	Related Term

CONSTRUCTION OF DESCRIPTORS

Terms used in indexing (descriptors) conform to one of the following types:

- Concrete entities:
  things and their physical parts: *Reptiles, Feet, Microforms, Tropical regions*
  materials: *Solvents, Leather, Iron.*
- Abstract entities:
  actions or events: *Frost, Walking, Sleep*
  abstract entities and properties: *Hardness, News, Feminism, Poverty*
  disciplines or sciences: *Archaeology, Physics*
  units of measurement: *Kilometres.*

If a candidate term does not conform to one of these types, it should not be used as it stands. In many cases, a term can be made to conform by being modified in accordance for controlling word forms. These rules are:

- Avoid **verbs**: use *Cookery, Opposition* not *Cook, Oppose*
- Do not use attributes (**adjectives** or **adverbs**) on their own, but only to help define an entity: *Yellow fever, Fast food*; but not *Yellow* or *Fast* on their own. Very occasionally an attribute may be found on its own as a descriptor, if a noun is implied, e.g. *Baroque [style].*
- Avoid adjectives or adverbs of **degree**, unless they have a technical meaning: *Small firms, Very high frequency.*
- Use **nouns** and **noun phrases**, including adjectival and prepositional phrases as appropriate: *Women workers, Prisoners of war.*
- Use the **plural** number for 'count' nouns (how many?): *Buildings, Paintings*;

also for substances or materials treated as a class with more than one member: *Plastics, Poisons*

- Use **singular** for non-count nouns (how much?): *Snow, Painting* (notice that it is possible to use both singular and plural if their meanings are distinct), *Physics* (which is not a plural!); also for parts of the body which occur singly: *Mouth, Respiratory system,* but *Lips, Lungs*

- Use the most widely accepted **spelling**: *Romania,* not *Roumania.* However, 'widely accepted' begs the question: by whom? Some readers will already have noticed the British (rather than American) English spellings of *Archaeology* and *Kilometres* above.

- Use **slang** or **jargon** only if well established and there is no acceptable alternative: *Hippies* have been with us for long enough to become established (except that they now seem to be transforming themselves into New Age travellers), but the *Yuppies* of the 1980s fell victim to economic depression. The application of this rule requires a fine judgement. The English language is full of neologisms, which journalists are quick to seize on. Indexers however are a cautious breed, loath to admit a new word that may drop out of fashion after a year or two. *Art index* did not accept *Art nouveau* as a heading until the 1950s, and the Library of Congress indexed computers as *Electronic calculating machines* until 1973. These are extreme cases, but serve to illustrate the fact that controlled vocabularies are poor at keeping up with changes in terminology.

- Use **abbreviations** and **acronyms** only if they are unambiguous and in common use within the subject field. Words like *Radar* have ceased to be regarded as acronyms, and it saves space and time to list bodies such as *UNICEF* as acronyms; but *WHO* or *BP* can only lead to ambiguity and misunderstanding. Again, there are grey areas: *CD-ROMs? URLs?*

- Differentiate **homographs** by a qualifier within parentheses: *Cranes (lifting equipment); Cranes (birds).* Homographs have the same spelling but different meanings. In a specialist thesaurus only one meaning might apply, and will be clear from the context.

- Use a **scope note (SN)** to exclude possible alternative meanings; or where the meaning is not immediately apparent; or to instruct indexers how a term is to be used. Scope notes in subject headings lists often start with a stock phrase, such as 'Here are entered . . .', as in this example from LCSH:

Conditionality (International relations)

Here are entered works on the requirement that nations meet certain conditions, such as restructuring their economies or respecting human rights, to be eligible to receive foreign aid or loans, or to have normal relations with other nations.

Classification schedules may use SN or some other formula. This example shows some of the kinds of instructional note that may appear after a DDC heading:

Grammar
Descriptive study of morphology and syntax
Including case, categorial, generative, relational grammar
Class here grammatical relations; parts of speech; comprehensive works on phonology and morphology, on phonology and syntax, or on all three
Class derivational etymology in 412

- Do not **invert** phrases: *Storage batteries* not *Batteries, storage*. (This particular example also carries the risk of ambiguity.)

The inversion rule is quite explicit. Compound terms, that is, multi-word concepts, have for many years been the bugbear of controlled language systems. The problem is whether to invert phrases and, if so, to what extent. In manually searched indexes, inversion brings a useful collocation, as the eye can run down a list from (say) *Dogs* to *Dogs, gun, Dogs, sporting* or *Dogs, working*. The problem is that this construction could be extended to *Dogs, hot*, which would benefit nobody. Inverted headings are inherently unpredictable, and a distraction to searching. Today's rules of thesaurus construction presuppose machine-searched indexes, which with keyword access are indifferent to word order and are not intended for sequential searching.

Compound terms then should not be inverted. Other restrictions also apply, notably that they are to be avoided altogether if a noun phrase can be factorized down:

Garage doors	use instead	*Garages* AND *Doors*
Coal mining	use instead	*Coal* AND *Mining*
Animal behaviour	use instead	*Animals* AND *Behaviour*

Factorizing is used when each separate word retains its original meaning. Factorizing should not be used for terms where the original meaning has been lost (*Deck chairs*), where a different type of entity is denoted (*Silk flowers*), where one term is used metaphorically (*Elbow joints*) or where one or both terms are semantically empty on their own (*Family problems*). Where compound topics like *Coal mining* are admitted, they are in effect pre-coordinated terms, and are described as having a *high pre-coordination level*. Normal principles of thesaurus construction require compounds to be reduced to their constituent elements (e.g. *Coal mining* is retrieved by a Boolean search on COAL AND MINING). Occasionally a single descriptor may pre-coordinate two or more concepts, as with *Life satisfaction* (a search on LIFE AND SATISFACTION would be likely to generate all manner of false coordinations); or *Student evaluation of teacher performance* (to make it clear who is evaluating whom). *Child behaviour* is another instance. It could be factorized into CHILDREN AND BEHAVIOUR without loss of meaning; but the phrase is one that is widely used and understood, so that the convenience and precision of having a ready-made phrase could be considered to outweigh the disadvantage of making the vocabulary larger than is strictly necessary.

SEMANTIC RELATIONSHIPS

Next, semantic relationships must be considered. Semantic relationships between terms are, as their name implies, built into the meanings of the terms. They are permanent, in that they do not change according to whatever document is being indexed or searched. Semantic relationships are stable, i.e., they remain constant within an indexing language and do not change to accommodate the indexing requirements of particular documents. In theory, they ought to be transferable between indexing languages, but in practice other considerations (e.g. disciplinary bias and the degree of specificity required) often militate against this. The rules govern the relationships in meaning between pairs of words (for example *Seas/Oceans, Legs/Knees, Food/Diet*) – or more precisely how the meaning of the second word relates to the first. There are three basic types of relationship: Equivalence, Hierarchical, and Associative.

Equivalence relationships

Equivalence relationships are relationships where two or more terms are regarded as having the same meaning. One is the preferred term (descriptor); all others are non-preferred terms (non-descriptors). Non-preferred terms are indicated in a thesaurus by the instruction:

Non-preferred term USE *Preferred term*
Asses USE Donkeys

Under the preferred term is placed the reciprocal of this instruction:

Preferred term
　UF *Non-preferred term*
Donkeys
　UF Asses

which serves as a check for both indexers and searchers. Older subject headings lists replace USE and UF with **see** and **x**, i.e.:

Asses **see** Donkeys   Donkeys **x** Asses

The first of these is displayed both in the subject headings list and in indexes based on it. The reciprocal **x** serves only as an aid to the indexer, and appears in the subject headings list only, and not in the index.

The following subcategories of equivalence relationship have been distinguished:

1. *Variant spellings, word forms, abbreviations, etc.* These exemplify the rules for word form control shown above.

   Rumania USE Romania   Romania UF Roumania
   ROM USE Read Only Memory   Read Only Memory UF ROM
   Mouse USE Mice   Mice UF Mouse

   Singulars and plurals are distinguished if the plural is irregular and would file a considerable distance away from the singular.

   Selling USE Sale   Sale UF Selling
   Sea food USE Seafood   Seafood UF Sea food

   because of the filing implications. Filing sequences are often 'word by word' as opposed to 'letter by letter'

   Coal mining USE Coal AND Mining
   This is an example of 'semantic factoring'.

2. *Synonyms.* Synonyms are rarely if ever completely interchangeable. In these examples, the co-reference is exact, but they differ in their usage.

   Asses USE Donkeys   Donkeys UF Asses
   Noble gases USE Inert gases   Inert gases UF Noble gases
   Wireless USE Radio   Radio UF Wireles
   Elevators USE Lifts   Lifts UF Elevators
   German measles USE Rubella   Rubella UF German measles
   Tax planning USE Tax avoidance   Tax avoidance UF Tax planning

3. *Quasi-synonyms.* These are terms whose meanings are different but overlap in ordinary usage, but are treated as synonymous for indexing purposes.

   Deceleration USE Acceleration   Acceleration UF Deceleration
   Softness USE Hardness   Hardness UF Softness

   The above two examples are antonyms: they represent different viewpoints of the same property continuum. The following two examples might or might not be regarded as equivalent, depending on subject field:

Fostering USE Adoption   Adoption UF Fostering
Barley USE Cereals   Cereals UF Barley

These would only be regarded as synonymous if they were on the fringe of the subject field of the thesaurus, where the generic level is set rather higher than for central themes. A thesaurus on social welfare would almost certainly have *Fostering RT Adoption* (an associative relationship), and one on agriculture would have *Barley BT Cereals* (a hierarchical relationship). This last is an example of 'upward posting': treating a narrower term as if it were equivalent to, rather than a species of, its broader term.

In a classification schedule synonyms are often shown in parentheses, e.g. DDC's 796.334 Soccer (Association football). Quasi-synonyms may be shown by an inclusion note, e.g. 796.33 Inflated ball driven by foot. Example: pushball – where Pushball is not given a specific place in the classification. (Note in passing that in classifications like DDC that are primarily designed for shelf arrangement, headings like 'Inflated ball driven by foot' are not intended as a verbal approach: their purpose is to define precisely and unambiguously the scope of a class together with any subclasses it may have.)

Hierarchical relationships

Here both terms are permitted terms (descriptors) and are linked in a broader-to-narrower hierarchy. This use of 'hierarchy' and 'hierarchical' is precise and technical, and is not to be confused with common, looser usages that denote any kind of descending sequence. Indexers are able to select the most specific term available to index concepts within the document. Searchers can extend a search by transferring from a first access term to a broader (more general) or narrower (more specific) term. Hierarchical relationships are indicated by BT (broader term) and NT (narrower term), e.g.

Sparrows BT Birds   Birds NT Sparrows

There are three subcategories of hierarchical relationship:

1. *Generic* relationships are easiest to spot: they can be verified by the rule-of thumb: *some* As are B; *all* Bs are A:

Protest NT Rebellion   Rebellion BT Protest
Reptiles NT Snakes   Snakes BT Reptiles

But not:

Pets NT Budgerigars

149

Why does this not qualify? Because not all budgerigars are pets. Most hierarchies are unique (a snake is a reptile and not any other kind of living creature), but the next example is a *polyhierarchy* (as is the Brain example below).

Rocks NT Coal	Coal BT Rocks
Fossil fuels NT Coal	Coal BT Fossil fuels

2. *Partitive*, or whole–part relationship. This applies only if the part is unique to the whole:

Science NT Chemistry	Chemistry BT Science
Head NT Brain	Brain BT Head
Central nervous system NT Brain	Brain BT Central nervous system
Canada NT Ontario	Ontario BT Canada

But not:

Buildings NT Doors

A door is a necessary part of any building, but cars, railway carriages etc. also have doors.

3. *Instance* (class-of-one). Proper names may be acceptable or not, according to policy. (Sometimes they are regarded as *identifiers* rather than descriptors, and as such excluded from the thesaurus.)

Mountain regions NT Alps   Alps BT Mountain regions

Hierarchical relations *modulate*, i.e. they move a step at a time through their hierarchy, e.g.:

Science NT Chemistry	Organic chemistry BT Chemistry
Chemistry NT Organic chemistry	Chemistry BT Science

and not, e.g., Science NT Organic chemistry. If an intermediate step is omitted, there is a very real likelihood that a search will skip over potentially useful material.

Older subject headings lists use **see also** and its reciprocal **xx**, e.g.:

Science **see also** Chemistry
Chemistry **xx** Science

The first of these would appear both in the subject headings list and in indexes based on them. The reciprocal **xx** serves only as an aid to the indexer, and appears in the subject headings list only and not in the index. By convention, indexes display **see also** references only in a downwards (generic-to-specific) direction. Users of these indexes are presumed to be aware that (e.g.) Chemistry is part of Science. **See also** does not distinguish hierarchical and associative relationships (see below).

In a classification schedule indentation is used to indicate hierarchical relationships, often with different typefaces. There *may* be a corresponding lengthening of the notation for more specific terms; but many bibliographic classification schemes either do this inconsistently (e.g. DDC) or do not set out to do it at all, as with the LCC and Bliss Bibliographic Classification (BC; 2nd edition, BC2).

Associative relationship

This relationship is not easy to categorize. The International Standard offers two useful clues:

> One of the terms should be strongly implied, according to the frames of reference shared by the users of an index, whenever the other is employed as an indexing term ... It will frequently be found that one of the terms is a necessary component in any explanation or definition of the other.
>
> (ISO, 1986, p. 17)

As with hierarchical relationships, both terms are descriptors. *RT* (related term) is the thesaural symbol, and its reciprocal is the same. The following are typical:

Buildings RT Doors   Doors RT Buildings

This is the more usual kind of partitive relationship, where the part is not unique to the whole, and is therefore regarded as an associative relationship rather than as hierarchical.

Entomology RT Insects   Insects RT Entomology
Illumination RT Lamps   Lamps RT Illumination
Programming RT Software   Software RT Programming
Harvesting RT Crops   Crops RT Harvesting
Poisons RT Toxicity   Toxicity RT Poisons
Insects RT Insecticides   Insecticides RT Insects
France RT French   French RT France

Adjectives are not normally permitted as descriptors. Here, 'French' can be used as a noun, to denote the people of France; or as the first word of a phrase, e.g. French music.

Silk flowers RT Flowers   Flowers RT Silk flowers

A silk flower is not a flower!

151

Handicapped children RT Schools for handicapped children

Nested phrases of this kind do not require a reciprocal RT. (Notice in passing that the phrase would now be considered socially unacceptable. A more acceptable phrase today would be: Schools for children with special needs.)

Subject headings lists have in the past used **See also** and **xx**. These are the same symbols as are used to denote hierarchical relations, and are used in the same way. It is not uncommon for associative **see also** references to appear in one direction only.

Classification schedules are by their nature set out hierarchically. There may occasionally be found references to associated topics in other parts of the schedule, e.g. in DDC:

790 Recreational & performing arts
Class the sociology of recreation in 306.48

There is often a temptation to enter RTs as BT/NT (broader term/narrower term). In some cases it is very difficult to determine whether a relationship should be entered as BT/NT or RT/RT. A rule of thumb is to check whether both terms belong to the same basic type (abstract or concrete entities). If they do not, the relationship cannot be hierarchical, and must be associative (if it is to be admitted at all): e.g., Entomology is a discipline or science (an abstract entity), and cannot therefore belong to the same hierarchy as Insects (which are concrete entities).

Another temptation is to make RTs indiscriminately. The principle of RTs is that there must be an immediate and necessary relationship between the two terms. If the relationship is not direct or not necessary, then the terms either should not be related at all, or at best should be linked indirectly, through a third term. Consider the following:

Authors
    RT   Books
     *   Publications
            Textbooks

Books and Textbooks are hierarchical to Publications. It would be enough therefore to make the one reference

Authors RT Publications

and let users find their own way if they wish to pursue the references through Publications NT Books and Books NT Textbooks. It is also tempting to link topics that are only indirectly connected, e.g., by sharing a common BT. So there is little point in links such as Mice RT Hamsters, simply because they share the common BT Rodents. Subject headings lists have in the past been guilty of some highly tendentious **see also**s, such as Journalism **see also** Libel and slander, with its implication that journalists go around libelling people for a living; or Psychical research **see also** Personality disorders, suggesting that only those with personality disorders engage in psychical research.

FACET ANALYSIS

The simplest way to present a thesaurus is to arrange all the descriptors with their relationships into a single alphabetical sequence. Many thesauri are of this kind. However, much of the effectiveness of a thesaurus is lost if this alphabetical display is not backed up by means of some kind of systematic display. Because alphabetical order scatters subjects indiscriminately, it is not possible to obtain an overview of the way the subject matter of the thesaurus is structured. The most widely used technique for creating systematic displays is *facet analysis*.

Facet analysis involves:

1. A set of terms representing simple concepts: that is, the descriptors created by applying the rules of thesaurus construction.
2. The grouping of the terms into a number of mutually exclusive categories, called *facets*, using just one characteristic of division at a time.
3. Organizing the facets into a limited number of *fundamental categories*. These are generalized categories which can be adapted to any subject field, and define the role of a term within the overall scheme of the thesaurus. Some examples of fundamental categories are given in Figure 5.4.

    In a working thesaurus these categories will inevitably be heavily adapted to the subject-matter in hand. The *Art and Architecture Thesaurus* for example calls Concrete entities its Objects facet, and Time, its Styles and Periods facet. The *Multilingual Egyptological Thesaurus* has an even more specialized list of facets: Acquisition; Present Location; Category; Provenance; Dating; Material; Technique; State of Preservation; Description; Language; Writing; Category of Text; Text Content; Divine Names; Royal Names.
4. In many cases, a *notation* will be required to fix the filing value of each term in a systematic sequence.

> **Entities**
> Abstract: *Archaeology, Kilometres, News*
> Concrete:
>   Naturally occurring: *Titanium*
>   Living: *Birds*
>   Man-made: *Paintings*
>   Complex: *Buildings*
> Properties (Attributes): *Speed, Elasticity*
> Materials, Constituents: *Adhesives*
> Parts: *Limbs, Doors*
>
> **Actions**
> Processes (internal, intransitive): *Glaciation*
> Operations (external, transitive): *Marketing, Cookery*
>
> **Place** (location, environment): *London*
>
> **Time**: *Nineteenth century, Summer*

Figure 5.4 *Examples of fundamental categories*

DISPLAYING THE THESAURUS

The principal symbols denoting functions and relations have been described in 'Principles of language control' above. To recap, they are:

- SN: Scope note, defining or restricting the meaning of a word within the indexing language
- USE: The term preceding this symbol is a non-preferred term. The preferred term follows this symbol.
- UF: The reciprocal of USE. The term that follows this symbol is a non-preferred term.
- BT: The term that follows is a broader term: another preferred term, but having a more general meaning.
- NT: The term that follows is a narrower term: another preferred term, but having a more specific meaning.
- RT: The term that follows is a related term: another preferred term, having a meaning that is associated with the term preceding the symbol, but not one of the types described above.

By convention, the symbols are listed after each term in the above order. The International Standard permits other symbols in addition to BT/NT if finer distinctions are considered necessary for denoting hierarchical relations:

- TT: the term that follows is the top term in the hierarchy to which the term preceding this symbol belongs.
- BTG: broader term (generic)
- NTG: narrower term (generic)
- BTP: broader term (partitive)
- NTP: narrower term (partitive). See 'Principles of language control' above for explanations of generic and partitive.

It also mentions the possibility of completely language-free symbols, e.g. < for BT and > for NT, but these refinements and alternatives are little used. (The *INSPEC Thesaurus* uses TT, and the British Standards Institution *Root Thesaurus* uses < etc.) Individual thesauri may use symbols other than these, either instead of the recommended symbols (e.g. the *American Psychological Association Thesaurus* abbreviates to U, B, N and R) or to denote something else, for example a classification code, or the date a term was introduced.

Figure 5.5 shows a typical thesaurus record (from ERIC).

ALPHABETICAL DISPLAY

Because alphabetical order is self-evident, every thesaurus has an alphabetical display of terms and their relations. Usually this is the principal display. Not infrequently it is the only display. Often, though, the alphabetical display is supplemented by other displays.

ROTATED DISPLAY

Where phrases comprise a high proportion of preferred terms, a second alphabetical display may be found, usually a machine-generated rotated display of terms, to ensure access to embedded words in phrases. This form of display (see Figure 5.6) is confined to printed thesauri, as keyword access is normally available in machine-held thesauri.

SYSTEMATIC DISPLAY

Alphabetical subject order is unfortunately quite arbitrary: 'catalogue' is followed in one encyclopaedia by Catalonia, Catalpa (a tree), and Catalysis. To counteract this, by bringing related topics together, various forms of systematic display are frequently found. They may or may not involve facet analysis. Representative examples include:

- *Subject group displays* (see Figure 5.7). These are looser associations than

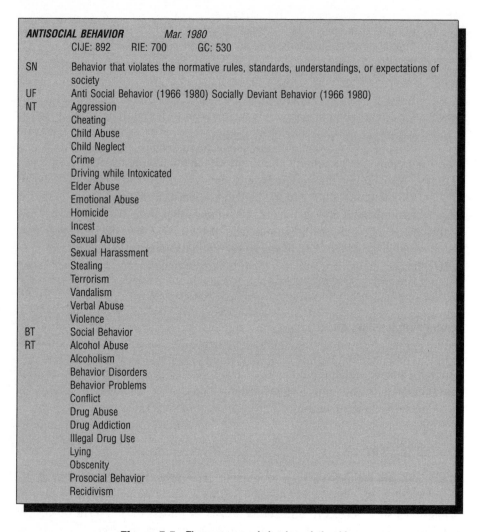

ANTISOCIAL BEHAVIOR   *Mar. 1980*
CIJE: 892   RIE: 700   GC: 530

SN   Behavior that violates the normative rules, standards, understandings, or expectations of
      society
UF   Anti Social Behavior (1966 1980) Socially Deviant Behavior (1966 1980)
NT   Aggression
      Cheating
      Child Abuse
      Child Neglect
      Crime
      Driving while Intoxicated
      Elder Abuse
      Emotional Abuse
      Homicide
      Incest
      Sexual Abuse
      Sexual Harassment
      Stealing
      Terrorism
      Vandalism
      Verbal Abuse
      Violence
BT   Social Behavior
RT   Alcohol Abuse
      Alcoholism
      Behavior Disorders
      Behavior Problems
      Conflict
      Drug Abuse
      Drug Addiction
      Illegal Drug Use
      Lying
      Obscenity
      Prosocial Behavior
      Recidivism

Figure 5.5   Thesaurus record showing relationships

hierarchical term displays, and for that reason are more common in the social sciences. *ERIC*'s Group display is a typical example.

- *Hierarchical term displays* (see Figure 5.8). These may start at the top term of a hierarchy (hence the use of TT in the alphabetical display), successive narrower terms being shown by indentation. Medical Subject Headings (MeSH) has 'tree structures': hierarchical displays with notations, so that the alphabetical display shows only the notational codes for the tree structures, and the user has to consult the tree structures to expand a search. (Most search systems for Medline have an EXPLODE command which ORs

ANTI SEGREGATION PROGRAMS (1967 1980) Use
RACIAL INTEGRATION
ANTI SEMITISM

ANTI SOCIAL BEHAVIOR (1966 1980) Use ANTISOCIAL
BEHAVIOR

ANTISOCIAL BEHAVIOR

ANTITHESIS

ANXIETY

COMPUTER ANXIETY

MATHEMATICS ANXIETY

SEPARATION ANXIETY

TEST ANXIETY

Figure 5.6 Thesaurus display: rotated display

ANTISOCIAL BEHAVIOR

. . .
CHEATING
CHILD ABUSE
CHILD NEGLECT
COMMUNITY PROBLEMS
CONFLICT
CRIME
CRIMINALS
DELINQUENCY
DELINQUENCY CAUSES
DISCIPLINE PROBLEMS
DRIVING WHILE INTOXICATED
DRUG ABUSE
DRUG ADDICTION
ELDER ABUSE
EMOTIONAL ABUSE
FAMILY PROBLEMS
. . .

Figure 5.7 Thesaurus display: subject group display

NTs automatically to the search specification.) A few thesauri include a complete hierarchical display under each descriptor in the alphabetical sequence. The *Thesaurus of Scientific, Technical and Engineering Terms* is of this type. The *ERIC Thesaurus* has a two-way hierarchical display in a separate sequence.

- *Systematic display* (see Figure 5.9). The hierarchical term display described

157

```
: : BEHAVIOR
: SOCIAL BEHAVIOR
ANTISOCIAL BEHAVIOR

  .  AGGRESSION
  .  CHEATING
  .  CHILD ABUSE
  .  CHILD NEGLECT
  .  CRIME
  .  DELINQUENCY
  .  INTERNATIONAL CRIMES
  .  DRIVING WHILE INTOXICATED
  .  ELDER ABUSE
  .  EMOTIONAL ABUSE
  .  HOMICIDE
  .  INCEST

  .  SEXUAL ABUSE

  .  RAPE
  .  SEXUAL HARASSMENT
  .  STEALING
  .  PLAGIARISM
  .  TERRORISM
  .  VANDALISM
  .  SCHOOL VANDALISM
  .  VERBAL ABUSE
  .  VIOLENCE
  .  FAMILY VIOLENCE
```

Figure 5.8 Thesaurus display: hierarchical term display

above supplements the main alphabetical display of the thesaurus. It is, however, sometimes desirable to reverse the roles of these two displays, so that the hierarchical display becomes the principal display and the alphabetical display functions as an index to it. Categories of terms, which share properties in common but may not necessarily belong to the same hierarchy, are placed in as close juxtaposition as the limitations of linear sequencing will allow. The sequence of this systematic display, while helpful to indexer and searcher alike, is however not self-evident. In order to fix the sequence and link it to the alphabetical index, an address code using alphanumeric symbols must be attached to each descriptor.

There are a number of advantages to a systematic display. While it cannot juxtapose every semantic relation, complete hierarchies are displayed and many other related terms are to be found in the vicinity. It is economical of space, in that there is no repetition of hierarchical information. Finally, the

PSYCHOLOGY	11

SN – Used here to encompass psychological and/or physiological processes

- **behaviour** — 11-A
  RT personality traits 11-ND
  RT behavioural disorders 12 -KE

- - **biological behavioural influences** — 11-AA

- - - **innate behaviour** — 11-AAA

- - - **heredity** — 11-AAB

- - **environmental behavioural influences** — 11-An

- - - **home environment** — 11-ABA

- - - **stress** — 11-ABB

- - - **early experience** — 11-ABC

- - **social behaviour** — 11-AC

- - - **aggressive behaviour** — 11-ACA

- - - **anti-social behaviour** — 11-ACB
      RT behavioural disorders 12-KE

- - - - **disruptive behaviour** — 11-ACB-O

- - **play behaviour** — 11-AD
    BT play 00

- - **range behaviour** — 11-AE
    SN – used to refer to children's ranges from home

- - **behavioural disorders** — 11-AF
    BT psychological disorders 12-K
    RI anti-social behaviour 11-ACBLS

- **communication** — 11-C
  RT communication disorders 12 -KD

Figure 5.9 Thesaurus display: systematic display (Thesaurus of play terms)

arrangement of the principal sequence is by address codes and not by language. This independence of language makes systematic arrangement ideally suited to a multilingual thesaurus.

With systematic display there are many loose ends to watch. The arrangement can only take care of one hierarchy at a time, so polyhierarchical terms must have their additional broader terms specially written in. The symbol BT(A) is sometimes used to denote an additional broader term. Scope notes, non-preferred terms, and associative relations must all be written in – usually into the systematic display, but some thesaurus compilers prefer to write these into the alphabetical display, to give both displays a more equal signifi-

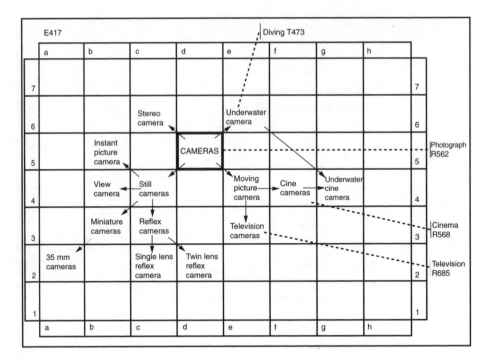

Figure 5.10 Thesaurus display: graphic display

cance. Finally, unless the systematic sequence is very basic it will need guidance in the form of 'node labels'.

- *Graphic display* (see Figure 5.10) of semantic relations are of two basic kinds: tree structures and arrowgraphs. With both, hierarchical relations are displayed in a two-dimensional format. The example is of the sample arrowgraph in BS 5723:1987.

THESAURUS USE

A thesaurus may be used in the indexing and/or searching of databases in three possible ways:

- *In indexing but not in searching*: this is the 'indexing thesaurus', where the database is mostly used for simple searching, often by less expert searchers. Retrieval is helped if a wide range of terms is used to index each record. Some electronic systems will automatically map a user from the 'unpreferred' to the preferred term.
- *In searching but not in indexing*: this is the 'searching thesaurus'. The

160

thesaurus assists the searching of a free-text database by suggesting additional search terms. This can be done automatically ('query expansion') if the thesaurus is available online. A searching thesaurus tends to provide a wider set of terms as entry vocabulary than a traditional thesaurus, and make greater use of automatic construction techniques. Many experienced searchers use a thesaurus when carrying out natural language searches, especially on full-text files. The thesaurus is used, not as a source of indexing terms, but as a reminder of semantically related terms to be added to a building block for searching.

- *In both indexing and in searching*: this is the traditional way in which a thesaurus is used. The same thesaurus is used for indexing (by the database compilers) and for searching (by users who know how to use a thesaurus and have one available). This kind of use presumes expert searchers. In indexing or in searching, terms may be added to the descriptor list or to the search statement without the explicit knowledge of the indexer or searcher.

SUMMARY

This chapter has explored issues associated with subject retrieval, and specifically introduced indexing and searching languages. The two main kinds of indexing languages are controlled and natural language. Systems designers need to decide when to use each of these. Other features of retrieval systems are exhausitivity and content specification, specificity, and the way in which complex topics are represented. Search facilities in post-coordinate searching are important in supporting users in their searching of controlled and natural language. Boolean search logic is widely used, but relevance ranking and best match search logic are becoming more significant. Other search facilities include: truncation, proximity searching, range searching and search sets. Thesauri are one way of recording controlled languages. They establish the terms that are to be used as descriptors for subjects, and relationships between subjects. Relationships are of three types: equivalence, hierarchical and associative. Facet analysis is useful in offering a perspective on the structure of relationships between subjects. The main means for displaying thesauri is the alphabetic display, but there are also a variety of approaches to systematic display that are useful in displaying relationships.

REFERENCES AND FURTHER READING

Basch, R. (1989) The seven deadly sins of full text searching. *Database*, **12** (4), August, 15–23.

Basch, R. (1991) My most difficult search. *Database*, **14** (3), June, 65–7.

Bates, M. J. (1977) Factors affecting subject catalog search success. *Journal of the American Society for Information Science*, **28** (3), 161–9.

Bates, M. J. (1989) Re-thinking subject cataloguing in the online environment. *Library Resources and Technical Services*, **33** (4), October, 400–412.

Brenner, E. H. (1996) *Beyond Booleans: New Approaches to Information Retrieval*. Philadelphia, PA: National Federation of Abstracting and Indexing Services.

British Standards Institution (1985) *BSI Root Thesaurus*, 2nd edn. Milton Keynes: British Standards Institution.

Chang, S. J. and Rice, R. E. (1993) Browsing: a multi-dimensional framework. *Annual Review of Information Science and Technology*, **28**, 231–76.

Clausen, H. (1997) Online, CD-ROM and the Web: is it the same difference. *Aslib Proceedings*, **49** (7), 177–83.

Cleverdon, C. W. (1967) The Cranfield tests on index language devices. *Aslib Proceedings*, **19**, 173–94.

Cousins, S. A. (1992) Enhancing subject access to OPAC's: controlled vocabulary versus natural language. *Journal of Documentation*, **48** (3), 291–309.

Creth, S. D. (1995) A changing profession: central roles for the academic librarian. *Advances in Librarianship*, **19**, 85–98.

Ellis, D. (1991) Hypertext: origins and use. *International Journal of Information Management*, **11** (1), 5–13.

Ellis, D. (1992) The physical and cognitive paradigms in information retrieval research. *Journal of Documentation*, **48** (1), 45–64.

Ellis, D. (1996) *Progress and Problems in Information Retrieval*. London: Library Association Publishing.

Ellis, D, Furner-Hines, J. and Willett, P. (1994) On the creation of hypertext links in full text documents: measurements of inter-linker consistency. *Journal of Documentation*, **50** (2), 67–98.

Enser, P. G. B. (1993) Query analysis in a visual information retrieval context. *Journal of Document and Text Management*, **1** (1), 28–52.

Fairthorne, R. A. (1969) Content analysis, specification and control. *Annual Review of Information Science and Technology*, 4: 71–109.

Fidel, R. (1991) Searchers' selection of search keys: II Controlled vocabulary or free-text searching. *Journal of the American Society for Information Science*, **42** (7), 501–14.

Fidel, R. (1992) Who needs controlled vocabulary? *Special Libraries*, **83** (1), 1–9.

Ingwersen, P. (1992) *Information Retrieval Interaction*. London: Taylor Graham.

INSPEC Thesaurus. (Annual.) London: INSPEC.

International Standards Organization (1986) *Documentation – Guidelines for the Establishment and Development of Monolingual Thesauri*. ISO 2788:1986. Geneva: ISO.

Khan, K. and Locatis, C (1998) Searching through cyberspace: the effects of link display and link density on information retrieval from hypertext on the World Wide Web. *Journal of the American Society for Information Science*, **49** (2), 176–82.

Lancaster, F. W. (1977) Vocabulary control in information retrieval systems. *Advances in Librarianship*, **7**, 1–40.

Lancaster, F. W. (1986) *Vocabulary Control for Information Retrieval*, 2nd edn. Arlington, VA: Information Resources Press.

Lancaster, F. W. and Sandore, B. (1997) *Technology and Management in Library and Information Services*. London: Library Association Publishing.

Lancaster, F. W. and Warner, A. J. (1993) *Information Retrieval Today*. Arlington, VA: Information Resources Press.

Large, J. A., Beheshti, J., Breuleux, A. and Renaud, A. (1994) A comparison of information retrieval from print and CD-ROM versions of an encyclopaedia by elementary school students. *Information Processing and Management*, **30** (4), 499–513.

Marchionini, G. (1995) *Information Seeking in Electronic Environments*. Cambridge: Cambridge University Press.

Markey, K., Atherton, P. and Newton, C. (1980) An analysis of controlled vocabulary and free text search statements in online searches. *Online Review*, **4** (3), 225–36.

Milstead, J. L. (1995) Invisible thesauri: the year 2000. *Online and CD-ROM Review*, 19 (2), 93–4.

Milstead, J. C. (1993) Thesaurus management software. *Encyclopedia of Library and Information Science*, **51**, 389–407.

Mulvany, N. C. (1994) *Indexing Books*. Chicago: University of Chicago Press.

Nicholson, S. (1997) Indexing and abstracting on the World Wide Web: an examination of six Web databases. *Information Technology and Libraries*, **16** (2), 73–81.

Rowley, J. E. (1990) A comparison between free language and controlled language indexing and searching. *Information Services and Use*, **10** (3), 147–55.

Rowley, J. (1994) The controlled versus natural indexing languages debate revisited: a perspective on information retrieval practice and research. *Journal of Information Science*, **20** (2), 108–19.

Thesaurus of Psychological Index Terms. Arlington, VA: American Psychological Association.

Webber, S., Baile, C., Cameron, A. and Eaton, J. (1994) *UKOLUG Quick Guide to Online Commands*, 4th edn. London: UKOLUG.

Weinberg, B. H. (1995a) Library classification and information retrieval thesauri: comparison and contrast. *Cataloging and Classification Quarterly*, **19** (3/4), 23–44.

Weinberg, B. H. (1995b) Why postcoordination fails the searcher. *Indexer*, **19** (3), April, 155–9.

Welsh, T., Murphy, K., Duffy, T. and Goorum, D. (1993) Accessing elaborations on core information in a hypermedia environment. *Educational Technology Research and Development*, **41** (2), 19–34.

Willpower Information. *Comparison of Thesaurus Management Software for PCs*. Available from World Wide Web: <http://www.willpower.demon.co.uk/thestable.htm>.

6 Pre-coordination and subject headings

INTRODUCTION

Chapter 5 considered the principles of language control and the construction and use of thesauri. Here we are still concerned with language control. This chapter develops the idea of pre-coordination and its application in subject headings, where the approach is predominantly verbal. At the end of this chapter you will:

- understand syntax in indexing languages
- know the uses and limitations of post-coordination and pre-coordination
- understand the importance of significance order and citation order in pre-coordinate systems
- be aware of the development of subject heading theory and practice
- understand the main features of the Library of Congress Subject Headings
- know some of the principal considerations in formulating subject headings.

In the previous chapter we suggested that a person's natural inclination is to describe subjects in documents by means of title-like phrases: Laboratory techniques in organic chemistry, Skin diseases in dogs, and the like. These examples, and many others, are of compound concepts: in the language of information retrieval, they are pre-coordinated. However, thesauri as described in Chapter 5 deal in simple concepts only – laboratory techniques; organic chemistry; skin; diseases; dogs – and are designed for use with post-coordinate indexing and searching methods.

Verbal subject headings apply the principles of the thesaurus – controlled terms together with the semantic relations between them – to both simple and compound concepts. So verbal subject headings are pre-coordinate. Subject headings lists are lists of index terms, normally arranged in alphabetical order, which have been given authority for use in an index, catalogue or database for retrieving records by their subject content. In manually searched indexes, the subject headings are used to file the records in alphabetical order. When these are interfiled with entries representing titles and authors in a library, the result is known as a *dictionary catalogue*.

Subject headings lists also make recommendations about the use of references for the display of semantic relationships, in order to (a) guide the cataloguer or indexer to the most suitable subject heading, and (b) guide users between connected or related terms.

Some writers on information access contrast thesauri with subject headings lists, others are more concerned with pointing out the similarities. The terminology is not chiselled in stone, however, and a number of thesauri have been designed for either post-coordinate or pre-coordinate use.

SYNTAX AND PRE-COORDINATION

Pre-coordination is the combination of index terms at the *indexing* stage. The indexer constructs a heading containing as many terms as are required to summarize as much of the subject content of the document as the indexing system permits, and the searcher has to accept this heading in its entirety. This reflects and systematizes our natural tendency to think of subjects as phrases, like 'Drug abuse treatment in Britain'. The LCSH for this topic is: Drug abuse – Treatment – Great Britain.

A pre-coordinate indexing system is one which, like LCSH, sets out to create *compound* headings – i.e., headings which may contain two or more elements or facets. Traditionally, two forms of manually searched index have used pre-coordination: *dictionary* and *classified* indexes. Also, library classification schemes are pre-coordinate systems. Older library classification schemes used pre-coordination intuitively, as does LCSH. All these are controlled language systems. Natural-language pre-coordinate systems are also found, mainly keyword in context (KWIC) indexes. (All these are described in Chapter 12.)

Pre-coordinate indexes are essentially for manual searching. By the time machine searching became the norm, and post-coordinate searching became the more usual way of accessing databases, pre-coordinate indexing systems were deeply and permanently embedded into many of our largest and most highly institutionalised bibliographic databases. Machine-searchable indexes (with a few exceptions) use inverted files to decompose subject headings, titles, etc. into their constituent keyword elements. These can then be searched individually, using the standard techniques of post-coordinate searching. For example, a record carrying the subject heading Drug abuse – Treatment – Great

Britain would be retrieved by a search on any Boolean combination of individual words: ABUSE AND BRITAIN, and so on.

After specificity, pre-coordination is the most powerful device for improving the precision of a search – far more precise than the crude AND of Boolean searching. A few systems (MeSH, Compendex) permit limited pre-coordination in a Boolean search. The method typically consists of applying a subheading to the descriptor for a system or organ (e.g., KIDNEYS – LESIONS). In natural language searching, phrase searching and the use of adjacency and proximity operators are forms of pre-coordination.

Pre-coordination is an aspect of the wider field of *syntax*: the study of the way we put words together to make sentences. Formally, syntax comprises the rules defining valid constructions in a language. These include rules for such elements as word order and punctuation, neglect of either of which reduces intelligibility. In the English language, a great deal of syntax is about word order: alter the order of 'Dog bites man' and you either reverse its meaning or create something unintelligible. Similarly with an indexing language. Here are two typical subject headings:

History – Teaching
Teaching – History

Anyone familiar with the English language coming across either would intuitively understand its meaning: the teaching of history, and the history of teaching. The syntax of indexing languages normally tries to eliminate prepositions and other link words (because they make for untidy filing). A few indexing languages include such link words systematically; their indexes are known as *articulated indexes*. They are described in 'Facet analysis and subject headings' in this chapter.

SIGNIFICANCE ORDER

We all have well-organized minds, and tend naturally to think of the most significant elements of a subject first, and to establish a pecking order from the most important to the least important. This principle is fundamental to the way we structure knowledge in any medium, and can be seen, for example, in many onscreen menu trees. In most pre-coordinate systems, significance order is the basis on which index terms are combined, and is particularly important where:

- a pre-coordinate system is in use *and*
- La manual system of searching is in use *and*
- items (citations or actual documents) are located in *one place* only.

These conditions are mainly to be found in:

167

- library classification, where open access encourages users to browse the shelves
- traditional printed and card catalogues, whether in dictionary or classified formats
- the hard-copy versions of many bibliographies, indexes, and abstracts.

Significance order determines filing order. If a document was given the subject heading SOCCER – CUP COMPETITIONS, it would generally be far more useful if it could be sought in a filing sequence which included:

SOCCER – CUP COMPETITIONS

SOCCER – FRIENDLY MATCHES

SOCCER – LEAGUES

etc., than in a filing sequence which looked like this:

CUP COMPETITIONS – GOLF

CUP COMPETITIONS – NETBALL

CUP COMPETITIONS – RUGBY LEAGUE FOOTBALL

CUP COMPETITIONS – SOCCER

CUP COMPETITIONS – TENNIS

etc. – a person is more likely to be interested in Soccer in all its aspects than in cup competitions across a range of sports. Also, anyone searching library shelves or 'one place' indexes, having noted the sequence SOCCER – CUP COMPETITIONS would reasonably expect the same pattern to be observed for items on cup competitions in other sports.

Significance order cannot be left entirely to intuition. The intuitions of two cataloguers in the Library of Congress, presumably working separately and at different times, gave the world not only the heading Drug abuse – Treatment – Great Britain, but also Drug abuse – Great Britain – Prevention. A more systematic set of syntactic rules is needed if this kind of inconsistency is to be avoided. These rules are known as *Citation order.*

Citation order is the order in which the facets of a compound subject are set down (i.e., cited) in a pre-coordinate system. The elements may combine to make up a verbal subject heading or a classification notation. Traditionally, citation order has always been based on significance order. In making up a subject heading, as many of the facets are used as are required, or as the system permits (if the system in use does not permit facets to be combined freely), e.g.:

SOCCER – REFEREEING

SOCCER – CUP COMPETITIONS

SOCCER – CUP COMPETITIONS – REFEREEING

```
[Discipline – in bibliographic classification only]
– Key system (things acted on, objectives, end products
  – Kinds [in verbal systems, often forms a phrase with Key system]
    – Parts (of key system)
      – Materials  (recursion is possible from here on)
        – Properties (of key system)
          – Processes (from within key system)
            – Operations (from outside)
              – Agents
                – Common facets: subject
                                 place
                                 time
                                 form
```

Figure 6.1 Standard citation order

The principles of citation order were largely evolved in the 1960s, and are based on the fundamental categories of facet analysis described in Chapter 5. Citation order also underpins the construction and use of library classification schemes, which will be described in the next chapter. The present section thus forms a bridge between Chapters 5 and 7.

The intention of 'standard' citation order was to form a set of readily understood and generalizable principles for determining facet sequence across all subjects. The elements of citation order are shown in Figure 6.1.

The following notes and comments are to be read in conjunction with Figure 6.1.

- *Discipline.* General classification schemes all use *discipline* as their primary facet: e.g. in DDC the topic HORSES is expressed as Zoological sciences – horses (599.725), Animal husbandry – horses (636.1), etc. The descriptor in a verbal system (e.g. LCSH) would be, simply, HORSES.
- *Key system.* A question-begging term for 'whatever seems most significant'. Often it conveys the idea of *purpose, end product* etc. Key systems are always passive, and represent what is being influenced or acted upon. Examples: Testing the hardness of *metals*; Software packages for *machine knitting*; Group theory in *physics*; *Road* construction in developing countries; The conquest of *California* by the USA. A key system in one context may not be so in another: e.g. MAPS is the key system of the topic The cataloguing of *maps*; but if the topic had been The cataloguing of maps in *university libraries*, then the key system would be UNIVERSITY LIBRARIES, and MAPS would be Materials.
- *Kinds.* Whatever differentiates a term (focus), e.g. PORTABLE PRINTERS where PORTABLE differentiates such printers from other printers. Most alphabetical

169

systems now treat these semantically, i.e. they would use the single heading PORTABLE PRINTERS. (Technically, PRINTERS is known as the *focus* and PORTABLE the *difference*.) A classification system on the other hand would differentiate printers by establishing subfacets:

Printers

(by portability)	*(by method of operation)*	*(by colour)*
fixed	ink-jet	monochrome
portable	laser (etc.)	colour

- *Parts.* These are often treated semantically (i.e. using BT and NT). Here we are concerned with those instances where the part is not unique to the whole, and so has to be entered syntactically in pre-coordinate systems, e.g. GARAGES – DOORS. As well as physical parts, this category includes constituent parts, e.g. Recruitment of *personnel* to the Civil Service.
- *Materials.* These are fairly self-explanatory, e.g. *Glass* for windows; though in practice this category is often subsumed under Kinds or Parts, and in verbal systems is often treated as a phrase (STEEL DOORS). (*Recursion* is the programmer's term for a procedure which calls itself, as in the tale of the fairy who grants you two wishes. Your first wish is to be granted two wishes . . . The point here is that it is possible to have *kinds* of materials (GALVANIZED STEEL DOORS), parts of materials, etc.; and the same applies to the facets which follow: e.g. an agent can have kinds, parts, etc.)
- *Properties.* Whatever qualities a key system possesses, e.g. Testing the *hardness* of metals; The development of *reading skills* in children.
- *Processes.* These occur *within* the key system, and do not require any external agency: e.g., *Diseases* of mice, *Development* of reading skills in children.
- *Operations.* These imply an agent (which need not always be named), e.g., *Coaching* children in reading, The *conquest* of California by the USA, Road *construction* in developing countries.
- *Agents.* The agent or instrument which carries out an operation, e.g. *Roundworms* as vectors of virus diseases in potatoes; The marketing of prepackaged consumer goods by *multinational companies*; The conquest of California by the *USA*.
- *Common facets* are concepts that are applicable to a wide range of topics. Most pre-coordinate indexing systems have lists of such concepts, so they can be tacked on to the end of a heading. They may be:
  - *subjects* like Research or Psychology, which exist as disciplines in their own right, but are also applicable to any subject.
  - *places*, where they limit the context of a topic (e.g., Road construction in *developing countries*)
  - *time*, often a more restricted view of the common subject History (e.g.,

The conquest of California by the USA, *1846–1850*), but sometimes including other temporal concepts (e.g., *weekly*).

– *form*, a catch-all which includes physical form (e.g. *videos*), literary form (e.g. *poetry*), and form of presentation (e.g. *manuals*) or arrangement (e.g. *dictionaries, tables, programmed texts*). They are most closely associated with headings for use in library catalogues and bibliographies of books.

As with fundamental categories, citation order often has to be adapted to the subject in hand, particularly within the humanities and social sciences. For example, in Education it is generally agreed that the key system is the Educand: the person being taught. However, in the literature of education it is not always easy to distinguish the Educand from the schools and colleges where education takes place. Some systems regard them as one; others distinguish them. The next most important facet concerns what is taught, i.e., Curriculum subjects, which correspond nearly enough to the generalized Materials facet. Under Processes we can subsume Student learning, but Teaching implies an Agent (the Teacher), so it is more properly an Operation; but teaching and learning are not always distinguishable in the literature.

LIMITATIONS OF PRE-COORDINATION

There are six possible ways to arrange a subject string containing three elements ($3 \times 2 \times 1$); a five-element string can be arranged in 125 different ways. Therefore, in pre-coordinate systems, strings become exponentially more difficult to handle as the number of elements in them increases. More generally, they require more intellectual effort at the input stage, and are therefore costly to produce. They make too for bulky indexes, as they create cumbersome networks of references; and unless the index is 'articulated' (i.e. includes linking words such as 'for', 'in', 'of' etc. to clarify relationships), a long subject string can be difficult to interpret. Thus the exhaustivity possible with pre-coordinate systems is low, and they can only operate at the level of summarization.

In practice, many systems limit the amount of pre-coordination they permit. The following degrees of pre-coordination can be found:

- Heading + single subheading, e.g. FOOTBALL – INJURIES . Examples: *Index medicus (MeSH); Engineering index (Compendex)*. Here, pre-coordination is essentially a means for improving precision in post-coordinate searches.
- Heading + a variable number of subheadings, but rarely exceeding three facets in all. Examples: any catalogue or index based on the LCSH or the DDC. Also most H. W. Wilson indexes, e.g., *Cumulative Book Index, Library Literature*.
- Fully faceted systems, allowing complete flexibility to express complex sub-

jects. Examples: the PRECIS system, used to index the *British National Biography* (*BNB*) between 1971 and 1990; the revised BC2; *Abstracts in New Technology and Engineering* (*Applied Social Sciences Index and Abstracts – ASSIA –* uses the same system).

WHO NEEDS PRE-COORDINATION?

Citation order is important in that it determines the degree of collocation and scattering in one-place pre-coordinate systems. In particular, it is (after Discipline) the second most important factor affecting the physical ordering of items on library shelves. As machine searching of indexes has become the norm, the importance of citation order in indexes has diminished. Pre-coordination is important only in the printed versions of indexes; and most indexing and abstracting services now regard their hard-copy formats as incidental by-products of the machine-held database. Their indexing systems are often designed primarily for online searching, and users of the printed versions are left to manage as best they can with indexes that are relatively unsophisticated.

Another inherent problem with pre-coordination is that the searcher has to make do with the sequence of topics imposed by the system's citation order. To some extent, multiple entry indexing systems can alleviate this problem. These, however, are inherently bulky, and unsuited to all situations – in particular they cannot be applied to shelf classification. A classification scheme that is sensitive to its users can provide alternative citation orders to serve the needs of different users. For example, DDC permits law books to be arranged by jurisdiction within broad topic headings (i.e. Broad topic – Jurisdiction – Problem), rather than by the preferred citation order, which is Broad topic – Problem – Jurisdiction. Another measure is the differential facet: part of a subject being treated differently from the rest. Thus in DDC curriculum subjects are distributed around the classification, using standard subdivision – 071, giving (e.g.) Mathematics teaching 510.71. This reflects the fact that in secondary education and above, subjects are taught by specialist teachers. This does not hold in elementary (primary) schools, however, where class teachers are normally responsible for all subjects. DDC recognizes this by classing elementary education in specific subjects within elementary education (372), at 372.3–372.8, e.g., Mathematics at 372.7.

A summary of the relative merits of pre-coordinate and post-coordinate techniques is given in Figure 6. 2.

Pre-coordination:

- improves the precision of searching
- makes for indexes that are familiar to users, in that they present a more-or-less complete statement of the subject
- is traditionally used for user-conducted searches in manual systems
- is available in well-tried, 'standard' systems (particularly LCC, DDC and LCSH in MARC records)
- in A–Z order make one-stage 'dictionary' indexes, which can be used with little or no training
- as classification systems is the only practical way to arrange the stock of open-access libraries.

BUT:

- a fixed citation order leads to complications in collocation and searching
- pre-coordinate indexes are only effective at summarization level, because large numbers of terms in a string become very difficult to handle
- indexing in controlled language systems is slow and costly. (This is not the case with title-derived KWIC and KWOC indexes).

Post-coordination:

- permits indexing to any level of exhaustivity
- accommodates different kinds of searching pattern
- makes it easy to add or discard terms when searching
- is syntax-free (i.e., has no citation order), and so indexing is faster and therefore cheaper
- is the normal method of machine searching.

BUT:

- it cannot be used for shelf arrangement
- a limited range of syntactic relationships is shown, and false coordinations are difficult to avoid when searching
- the searcher has to input terms individually, and does not see a full statement of the subject
- indexing to higher levels of exhaustivity can lead to an excess of recall, with large numbers of marginally relevant items being retrieved
- formulating Boolean searches, and the protocols of machine searching, can be complicated, even in menu-driven systems
- command-driven online systems are user-unfriendly, and may require an intermediary.

Figure 6.2 Summary of pre-coordination and post-coordination

TRADITIONAL CUTTER-BASED SUBJECT HEADINGS LISTS

Verbal subject headings began to be systematized well over a century ago, in 1876, when Charles Ammi Cutter published his *Rules for a Dictionary Catalog* (Cutter, 1904). Cutter's system was as much of an advance on preceding systems as was Melvil Dewey's *Decimal Classification* (which also dates from 1876; see Chapter 8 for a full discussion and listing of editions etc.). Around the turn of the century, the Library of Congress thoroughly reorganized its cataloguing procedures, adopting and developing Cutter's *Rules*, and inaugurated its printed card distribution service. Its dictionary catalogue, based on Cutter's principles, was quite simply the best available at the time. Library of Congress Subject

173

Headings has continued with only evolutionary alterations (most of them since 1975) until the present day.

Cutter's *Rules* thus still retains its relevance (as well as its readability). Cutter lists among the objectives of a catalogue:

1. To enable a person to find a book of which the subject is known; and
2. To show what the library has on a given subject and in a given kind of literature.

The techniques used to achieve these ends are:

- Subject entry under the most specific word or phrase expressing the subject. In Cutter's words: 'Put Lady Cust's book on "The cat" under CAT, not under ZOÖLOGY or MAMMALS, or DOMESTIC ANIMALS.' This establishes the principle of alphabetico-direct as opposed to alphabetico-classed entry. Many catalogues and indexes of the time used the method known as alphabetico-classing, where subject entries display two or more hierarchical levels, a broad topical heading with a specific subheading, like DOMESTIC ANIMALS – CATS.
- A work may have two or more subject entries if the subject cannot be fully specified in one. Composite subjects were less prevalent in Cutter's day. Cutter did not recognize subheadings: a work on social conditions in rural England might have entries under SOCIAL CONDITIONS, RURAL CONDITIONS and ENGLAND. This principle is still to be found in LCSH: while subheadings are permitted there, such a work would now have the headings ENGLAND – RURAL CONDITIONS and ENGLAND – SOCIAL CONDITIONS.
- The wording of subject headings must reflect usage. Cutter selected headings on the basis that they should be terms in general usage and accepted by educated people. In addition to problems with new subjects that lacked accepted or established names, this guiding principle engendered inconsistency in the form of headings. Equally, Cutter's devotion to natural language posed problems with multi-word terms. Direct order was preferred, but inverted phrases were acceptable when it could be established that the second term was definitely more significant, leaving it to the individual to judge when to apply this. The well-intentioned vagueness of these rules has been inherited by LCSH.
- A uniform heading for each subject, with references from synonymous terms. This technique states for once and for all the guiding principle of vocabulary control and, together with specific entry, is Cutter's most lasting contribution to indexing theory and practice.
- *See also* references linking related subjects. While Cutter's system of references has been refined, the main features of semantic relations are clearly laid down.

174

LIBRARY OF CONGRESS SUBJECT HEADINGS

Library of Congress Subject Headings is the pre-eminent authority list for subject headings. First published in 1909, it is used not only by the Library of Congress but widely throughout the English-speaking world. The headings form the verbal subject approach in USMARC records and also in UKMARC records since 1997 (and sporadically before then), as well as in centrally produced records from Canada, Australia and some other countries.

STRUCTURE AND APPLICATION

Library of Congress Subject Headings is firmly based on Cutter's *Rules for a Dictionary Catalog*. The most important developments of Cutter to have been introduced by LCSH are subdivided headings and the use since 1988 of the thesaurus conventions BT, NT etc. to express semantic relationships in place of Cutter's *see*, *x*, *see also* and *xx*.

Library of Congress Subject Headings was developed well before modern ideas about thesaurus construction were developed. It has been tidied up considerably since the mid-1980s in the light of modern theory, but is still full of inconsistencies. Like DDC, it is so well entrenched in library practice that it is unlikely to be replaced for many years. Paradoxically, online searching and OPAC have made LCSH more effective, as keyword access has ironed out many of its inconsistencies.

It is well to remember that LCSH is the head of a large family of subject heading systems derived from Cutter and sharing the same principles. Other examples include *Sears List of Subject Headings* – virtually an abridgement of LCSH – and the subject headings used in the various indexes published by the H. W. Wilson Company.

TYPES OF HEADING

Most headings are mapped to their equivalent LCC class numbers. The simplest form of heading is a single noun, e.g. Advertising; Heart; Railroads; Success.

A heading may be followed by a *parenthetical qualifier*, usually to distinguish homographs e.g. Cold (Disease) or explain terms not widely known, e.g. Dodoth (African tribe). Some qualifiers simply limit or qualify their heading by discipline, e.g. Divorce (Canon law); Bread (in religion, folk-lore, etc.) – the precise form of the qualifier can vary. A few, like Cookery (Chicken), are idiosyncratic forms of pre-coordination.

Phrase headings will usually be in direct order, often Adjective + Noun, e.g.

Nuclear physics; American drama; Mining machinery. Other examples are: Children's art; Chevrolet automobile (LCSH does not always follow thesaural recommendations as to singular and plural); and the notorious One-leg resting position (used once only, for a 28-page pamphlet published in 1942). Occasionally, following Cutter's (1904, p. 69) instruction that phrases may be inverted 'where the second term seems decidedly more significant' we find such headings as: Education, secondary and Functions, Abelian – unfortunately the headings Adult education and Bessel functions also occur. Editorial policy is to reduce the number of inverted headings, and many have been eliminated: e.g. Gas, Natural has become Natural gas.

Conjunctive phrase headings link overlapping topics by means of 'and' or 'etc.', e.g.: Literary forgeries and mystifications; Mines and mineral resources; Law reports, digests, etc. As well as being used for the conjunction of A and B, this type of heading can also be used to express a relationship between A and B, e.g.: Good and evil; Television and children; Literature and society. Because of their inherent looseness, this type of heading has now been discontinued and some headings simplified, e.g.: Cities and towns, Ruined, extinct, etc. is now simply: Extinct cities.

A final form of heading is the *prepositional phrase heading*, e.g.: Fertilization of plants; Radar in speed limit enforcement; Automobile driving on mountain roads; Cooperative marketing of farm produce; Mites as carriers of disease; Bread in literature.

Headings for *named entities* – persons, families, places, corporate bodies – are established where possible in accordance with AACR2, and can usually be checked in the Name Authority File, as LCSH lists them only sporadically. To this extent, LCSH is an open system, allowing individual users to create headings for named entities.

Many headings have *scope notes*. These usually start with the formula 'Here are entered works . . .', and go on to define or explain the heading, indicate its application, and often to indicate the line of demarcation with related headings.

A heading may be a *topical heading* (what the work is about) or a *form heading* (indicating the work's physical form or its form of presentation and arrangement). A heading such as Short stories might apply to a collection or to a work of criticism. In some but not all cases a subdivision may clarify which is which.

SUBDIVISIONS

The subdivision of headings is LCSH's principal advance on Cutter, and the pre-coordination they provide greatly increases the precision of headings. Subdivisions are introduced by a hyphen. A large number of subdivisions are enumerated under their headings, but many more are designated *free-floating*. These are commonly used subdivisions which can be added to headings as required, and do not appearing specifically after their headings in LCSH. They can be of general or restricted application. There are around 40 different categories of these latter. They are controlled by *pattern headings* (i.e. representative headings for personal names, other proper names, various ethnic and national topics, and certain everyday objects, and serving as a pattern for all entries of the same type). Subdivisions are of four types: topical, form, geographic, and period.

Topical (i.e. subject) *subdivision*, often follows standard citation order, e.g.: Heart – Diseases; Herbicides – Research – Technique; Shakespeare, William, 1564–1616 – Characters – Children. There are (as always) anomalies: Automobiles – Motors – Carburetors (Thing – Part – Part) looks suspiciously like alphabetico-classing. (English readers should note both the terminology and the spelling. UKMARC records take LCSH as it comes, with no concessions to British English.)

Form subdivisions are the everyday common facets denoting common subject or form, e.g.: Engineering – Dictionaries; Mathematics – Study and teaching; France – History – Revolution, 1789–99 – Fiction; Suffolk – Description and travel – Guidebooks.

Geographic subdivisions are the common facets of place, e.g.: Probation – Northern Ireland; Music – England – Manchester; Geology – England – Peak District; Churches – England – Suffolk – Guidebooks. 'Indirect' subdivision (the name of the place is preceded by the name of the country in which it is situated) is often used for places smaller than a country to improve collocation.

Period subdivisions are the common facet of time. Mostly however they are not free-floating but are tailored to their topic (DDC often behaves in much the same way), e.g.: Great Britain – History – to 1485; Great Britain – History – Victoria, 1837–1901; France – Politics and government, 1589–1610; English fiction – nineteenth century; English drama – Restoration, 1660–1700; English language – Dictionaries – Early works to 1700. Occasionally, period is expressed in ways other than by a subdivision, e.g.: Art, Renaissance.

It will be seen from the above examples that more than one subdivision may be applied. There are usually specific instructions for particular combinations, to maintain control over the use of subdivisions. Recent policy has been to replace subdivisions with a phrase heading if possible, e.g., Railroads – Stations has become Railroad stations. In the application of subdivisions the following should be noted:

Order of heading and subdivision. Most headings conform to standard citation order (Entity – Action or process), e.g.: Kidneys – Diseases; but with occasional exceptions, e.g. Advertising – Cigarettes, which places the process before the product, presumably on the grounds that advertising is advertising whatever the product.

Topic versus Place. Usually topic comes first; but there are many occasions, particularly in the social sciences, where place takes precedence. To confuse matters further, cities are treated differently from regions, e.g. Nottingham (Notts) – Hospitals; but Hospitals – Nottinghamshire.

Geographic names may serve as headings, as part of a heading, as a subdivision, or as a qualifier, e.g.: Manning Provincial Park, BC; Jamaica – description and travel; Paris in literature; Building permits – Belgium; Japanese in San Francisco.

The filing sequence of headings and subheadings in card indexes and printed lists can be complex. An example appears in Figure 12.2.

REVISION OF HEADINGS

A new edition of the printed *LCSH* appears annually, and now extends to five volumes. It is available in other formats, notably as part of the *Cataloger's Desktop* CD-ROM. There is a weekly computer tape distribution service of new and changed headings, a cumulated file of which is accessible on the Library of Congress's (LC's) Web site. There are also various printed and fiche lists. *CDMARC Subjects* is a quarterly CD-ROM update of the complete subject authority file. The *L.C. Cataloging Service Bulletin* gives information on selected new and cancelled headings.

Editorial policy has always been to create new headings as needed. Because of varying editorial policies stretching back for nearly a century, there are many inconsistencies in the formulation of headings. Where there has been a change of policy, normal practice was to leave existing headings alone, and apply the new policy only to headings established after the change of policy, with retrospective revision undertaken only when the pressure to change became intolerable, as when Negroes was changed to Blacks, or Electronic calculating machines to Computers. This conservatism was understandable and indeed necessary with card catalogues. Now that increasingly software is able to accommodate global changes to the catalogue database, current practice is to replace headings systematically.

REFERENCES IN LCSH

The former reference symbols *See, x, sa* and *xx* have since 1988 been replaced with:

USE
UF   Used for
BT   Broader topic
NT   Narrower topic
RT   Related topic

Library of Congress Subject Headings's references (see Figure 6.3) have been tidied up considerably in recent years. The symbols follow thesaural practice, and denote Equivalence, Hierarchical and Associative relationships. Note however the subtle use of *topic* (acknowledging that some headings are pre-coordinate) instead of *term* (which in a thesaurus normally indicates a simple concept).

SA (*see also*) is still used, but is limited to general references. The following general reference appears under the heading Bibliography:

> SA names of literatures, e.g. American literature; and subdivision Bibliography under names of persons, places and subjects; also subdivision Bibliography – Methodology under specific subjects, e.g. Medicine – Bibliography – Methodology; and subdivision Imprints under names of countries, states, cities, etc.

References are used in two ways. The *cataloguer* uses the references in the List to help locate the correct heading. References to headings in a catalogue or bibliography are interfiled with the headings. The *catalogue user* uses the refer-

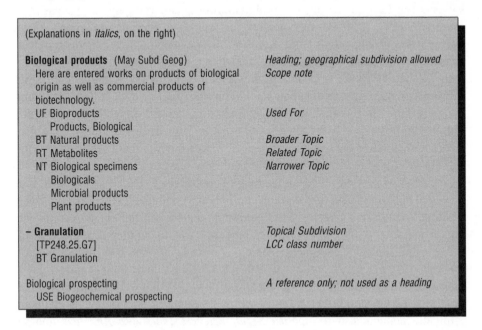

Figure 6.3 LCSH heading with its references

ences to help locate the correct heading for a topic; also as a means of moving between related topics. This use of references is becoming obsolete. It was normal usage with card and printed catalogues and bibliographies; but it is very unusual to include references in computerized catalogues and bibliographies (whatever their format)

FACET ANALYSIS AND SUBJECT HEADINGS

Library of Congress Subject Headings and other subject headings lists are known as *enumerative* systems. They are thus named because many headings – Fertilization of plants, and Radar in speed limit enforcement are two examples among many – list, or enumerate, compound topics in an *ad hoc* way, without system. So, for example, Fertilization of plants is not matched by any corresponding heading for (say) the fertilization of roses; and there are no corresponding headings for the use of cameras or police helicopters to discourage motorists from exceeding speed limits.

Developments since Cutter in the theory and practice of subject headings have largely taken place outside the USA, where the authority and wide availability of Library of Congress printed cards discouraged experimentation. In England, J. Kaiser's *Systematic Indexing*, published in 1911, suggested that many composite subjects can be analysed into a combination of a 'concrete' and a 'process'; for example, SHIPS – SERVICING to represent the topic 'The servicing of ships'. While Kaiser made an important contribution to the development of citation order in subject headings, his work had little influence for nearly half a century.

In the late 1950s E. J. Coates took Kaiser's work as his starting point, and combined it with the contribution to classification theory of S. R. Ranganathan. Ranganathan was the first to fully articulate the analytico-synthetic principle. This is the process of facet analysis (described later in this chapter) by which a summarization of the subject content of a document is analysed into its constituent facets, which are then synthesized into a subject heading according to the rules of whichever indexing language is being used. He also developed the theory of fundamental categories and citation order with his PMEST (Personality – Matter – Energy – Space – Time) formula, and devised chain procedure for organizing subject indexes to files of citations. Coates further developed facet analysis and applied it to subject headings. For over 30 years from 1963 Coates's theories on the construction of subject headings and their references – expounded in his book *Subject Catalogues* (Coates, 1960) – were put into practice in *British Technology Index* (*BTI*), of which Coates was editor. They were subsequently applied also to *Applied Social Sciences Index and Abstracts* and to *BTI*'s successor *Current Technology Index,* now *Abstracts in New Technology and*

Engineering (ANTE). Unlike Cutter and *LCSH*, Coates held that headings should be coextensive with a summarization of the subject. Multiple subject headings were, and are, forbidden. As the system is used to index technical subjects, some headings assume a daunting complexity. One knack is to read them backwards, inserting prepositions as required. The following are examples of subject headings as structured by Coates and his successors:

Steel, Low alloy: Welding, Electron beam
Piles; Concrete, Bored: Testing: Ultrasonics
Motor cars – Bodies – Paint – Spraying – Robots
Compact video discs – Image compression – Decoding – Multimedia micro-computers – Window systems – Replay systems – Expansion cards

The system has historical importance as the first large-scale working example of the use of computers to manipulate subject strings. It had some interesting subtleties – notice the use of punctuation as role indicators in the first two examples: commas introduce *kinds*, and semicolons *materials*. (The third and fourth examples show current practice, which is not to use differential punctuation.)

ARTICULATED SUBJECT INDEXES

Articulated subject indexes have had some popularity as a less formal and intimidating technique than Coates for computer-generated subject indexes. Articulation means the insertion of link words into subject headings in order to bring them closer to natural language. Articulation is a purely syntactic device. It is for individual users to decide whether or not to employ a controlled vocabulary.

In an articulated subject index, the entry consists of a subject heading and a modifying phrase; these can be combined to form a title-like phrase. Modifying phrases are arranged alphabetically under a subject heading. The words or strings of words may be machine selected or drawn manually from a controlled vocabulary. The structure of the phrases is analysed, and various connectives and prepositions cause the generation of different arrays of entries. Note that prepositions are retained in the index. Figure 6.4 gives an example of string manipulation to form a set of articulated subject index entries.

PRECIS

Coates's *BTI* helped pave the way towards a new system of subject indexing that was to serve UKMARC records well for twenty years from 1971. The development of MARC in the late 1960s forced the *British National Bibliography* to rethink its indexing policies. Hitherto it had based its indexing on a locally

181

Topic: Testing of bored concrete piles by ultrasonics

The indexer inserts manipulation codes into this string, i.e.:
  <Testing> of <Bored <Concrete <Piles>>> by <Ultrasonics>
which the computer turns into a set of index entries:

  Testing of Bored Concrete Piles by Ultrasonics
  Bored Concrete Piles. Testing by Ultrasonics
  Concrete Piles. Bored. Testing by Ultrasonics
  Piles. Bored. Concrete. Testing by Ultrasonics
  Ultrasonics. Testing of Bored Concrete Piles

This example is based on Craven's NEPHIS (NEsted PHrase Indexing System).

Figure 6.4 Articulated subject index

expanded version of DDC. However, irregularities in the structure of DDC made it unsuitable for the machine generation of subject index entries, and the lack of specificity of a classification whose primary purpose was (and is) shelf arrangement was held to be inimical to good indexing practice. Additionally, good indexing practice was felt to require a more friendly and explicit procedure than chain indexing.

A completely new indexing system was therefore commissioned. The criteria laid down were that the system was to be based on a single coherent logic. The indexer was to produce, by intellectual effort, an input string of terms and role operators. The generation of index entries from this string, and any other subsequent operations, were to be computerized. Each entry under every significant word in the string was to provide a full subject statement – unlike LCSH, and unlike Coates's system also, where only one entry was coextensive with the subject, access from other terms being by references. Entries were to be as close as possible to natural language. Finally, the new system was to make a firm distinction between semantic and syntactic relations (chain procedure linked to a classification schedule is unable to distinguish them), and was to have a machine-held thesaurus that would automatically produce *see* and *see also* references to the terms in each string. Effectively, what was to be devised was an articulated subject indexing system having a controlled vocabulary.

The result was called Preserved Context Index System (PRECIS). Its syntax is based on a system of over 30 role operators and other manipulation codes. These have three functions. They indicate the role of each term within the subject statement or string. They determine the citation order. Finally, they pass instructions to the computer for the precise pattern of rotation of the index entries under each lead term, as well as their typography, punctuation and capitalization.

Title: Education and the Third Age in the South-West

Subject in natural language: Education of the elderly in Devon to 1990.

PRECIS concept string: (0) Devon √
                                (1) old persons √
                                (2) educationv $d to 1980 √

where (0), (1) and (2) are role operators denoting Environment, Key system, and Action / Event respectively, and $d is a manipulation code introducing date. ☐ against a term indicates that a lead (entry) is required under that term. The indexer rewrites these instructions as a machine-readable *manipulation string*:

$z01030$dDevon$z11030$aold persons$z21030$aeducation$dto 1990

Index entries are generated from these coded instructions:

Devon.
    Old persons. Education, *to 1990*

Old persons. Devon
    Education, *to 1990*

Education. Old persons. Devon
    to 1990

References are recalled automatically from a machine-held thesaurus:

Aged persons *see* **Old persons**

Elderly persons *see* **Old persons**

England
    see also Names of individual counties

Great Britain
    see also Names of individual countries, regions and districts

Figure 6.5 PRECIS worked example

Figure 6.5 shows a fairly simple subject string; the system is capable of far greater complexity. While indexes produced by PRECIS are models of clarity and precision, the system was essentially designed for printed output and manual searching. With the move to machine searching, it became difficult to justify the costly complexity of formulating input strings, and UKMARC records now use LCSH as their only means of controlled language subject access.

PRECIS is an example of an *open* indexing system. Many indexing systems are *closed*: that is, individual users have no autonomy to add new headings as required, but have to wait until the next official amendment list from the system's compilers or other responsible authority. Any system with a classified display is likely to be closed, as new headings have to be inserted into their correct classified position. PRECIS as a purely alphabetical system simply sets out the rules for the construction of headings and references, and allows users to construct and maintain their own authority files.

ACCESS FROM SUBORDINATE TERMS IN SUBJECT HEADINGS

Many subject headings consist of a single concept only, but many more contain two or more concepts, or facets. In machine-searched systems any facet is equally retrievable, but manually searched indexes need to provide some mechanism for gaining access from terms that are not in the lead (filing) position. Most indexes employ some form of *rotation*: a subject heading consisting of the facets ABCD, and filed at A, can also be retrieved by means of references or additional citations at B, C and D.

There are a number of different ways of rotating subject headings. All of the following are commonly found in indexes:

- *Cycling*: Successive index entries move the final term across to the lead position:

  Football. Clubs. Management. Scotland.   [*citation or address*]
  Management. Scotland. Football. Clubs.   [*citation or address*]
  Clubs. Management. Scotland. Football.   [*citation or address*]
  Scotland. Football. Clubs. Management.   [*citation or address*]

- *Keyword out of Context (KWOC)*. With this technique (which has many variations) the lead term is followed by either the whole of the string, or (as in the example) the remainder of the string:

  Football. Clubs. Management. Scotland.   [*address*]
  Clubs. Football. Management. Scotland.   [*address*]
  Management. Football. Clubs. Scotland.   [*address*]
  Scotland. Football. Clubs. Management.   [*address*]

- *Rotation, or Keyword in Context (KWIC)*. The whole string is slid forward in successive index entries, so that each term in turn appears in the lead position:

  Football. Clubs. Management. Scotland.
  [*address*]
  Football. **Clubs.** Management. Scotland.   [*address*]
  Football. Clubs. **Management.** Scotland.   [*address*]
  Football. Clubs. Management. **Scotland.**   [*address*]

- *Shunting*. This method is used by PRECIS, and has a two-line format:

Scotland.
    Football. Clubs. Management.   *[citation or address]*
Football. Scotland.
    Clubs. Management.   *[citation or address]*
Clubs. Football. Scotland.
    Management.   *[citation or address]*
Management. Clubs. Football. Scotland.   *[citation or address]*

(PRECIS determines citation order by context dependency; hence the different ordering of the string.) KWIC and Shunting preserve the citation order of the original string; other methods based on rotation distort the citation order. This can occasionally cause relevant entries to be overlooked when conducting a manual search. To counteract this, some have suggested *permutation*: creating references under all possible combinations of the facets. This however is prohibitively bulky: a four-facet string would generate 24 references (4! factorial 4, i.e. $4 \times 3 \times 2 \times 1$). There is a modified form of permutation called Selective Listing in Combination (SLIC), which bears a similar relationship to permutation as chain procedure (see below) does to rotation. Even this generates an unacceptably large number of references.

CHAIN PROCEDURE

Rotated indexes are usually generated by computer program. Chain procedure was originally devised by Ranganathan as an economical method for the manual production of subject indexes, but it is equally amenable to computer-generated indexes. It became popular in Britain in the 1960s as an economical method of organizing the subject indexes to classified library catalogues, and so was often adapted for use with DDC. The essentials of this will be described below. However, chain procedure in its original and purest form uses verbal headings alone. We will use the same subject heading as in the previous examples:

    Football. Clubs. Management. Scotland.

This heading would be followed by a citation. Every other approach is a reference:

    Scotland. Management. Clubs. Football. *see* Football. Clubs. Management. Scotland.

Notice that the reference *reverses* the order of the original string. Then, each successive reference truncates the string by removing its last facet (the first facet of the back to front string):

Management. Clubs. Football. *see* Football. Clubs. Management.
Clubs. Football. *see* Football. Clubs.

The reference under Management has dropped Scotland, so that the reference can be used as it stands for items on the management of football clubs in England, Milan, or wherever, as well as for the management of football clubs generally. In the same way, the reference

Clubs. Football. *see* Football. Clubs.

will serve for items on all aspects of football clubs, and not just their management.

This describes the original system of references. As it was rather bulky, it has subsequently been simplified (Figure 6.6).

Again, observe in the above example that (a) the references *reverse* the citation order of the heading, and (b) each successive reference drops a facet, so that only the first reference is specific to the subject. Note that until the reference is followed up, the searcher does not know exactly how detailed the subject is;

Example from *ANTE*. Abstracts are arranged under specific subject headings under broad subject groups. The abstract at the following heading comes within Group 16: Transport, mechanical handling and packaging.

1224   Motor cars – Bodies – Paint – Spraying – Robots

where 1224 is the abstract number. There is a separate index, with entries at:

Robots
Spraying – Paint – Bodies – Motor cars: 1224

Spraying
Paint – Bodies – Motor cars: 1224–1225

Paint
Bodies – Motor cars: 1224–1227

Bodies
Motor cars: 1222–1230

Notice that only the index entry under Robots is specific. Each of the others drops a facet in succession. As the index entries become more general in scope, they refer to more abstracts.

The index entries are interfiled with other index entries and with references:

Automobiles *see* Motor cars
Cars *see* Motor cars
Motor vehicles *narrower term* Motor cars
Vehicles *narrower term* Motor vehicles
Transport *see also* Vehicles

Coatings *narrower term* paint

Figure 6.6   Subject index by chain procedure

and what looks like a reference to a general topic may lead only to an item on one small aspect of it. This situation happens all the time with post-coordinate searches, where searchers are aware that they are working with keywords, and the actual searching is done by computer. Searchers are therefore less likely to mind if their search yields a highish proportion of dross along with the nuggets. Greater precision is usually expected with manual searching, however, as it is far more laborious; and pre-coordinate headings look as if they ought to mean what they say, so that searchers are rightly disappointed if they find that they do not. This is a typical instance of greater recall in a search leading to loss of precision.

Chain procedure and the classified catalogue

The adaptation of chain procedure to the classified catalogue relies on classifications like DDC having a notation that is largely hierarchical. The technique was widespread from the 1960s on in Britain, where the great majority of libraries of all kinds had classified catalogues; and there are still many library catalogues, including OPACs, whose subject indexes are based on (or at least pay lip-service to) chain indexing. The technique is described in Figure 6.7.

A big limitation of this method when applied to DDC is that the classification is often too inflexible to express all facets of a subject. The nearest that DDC

Example 1: for items classed at 821:

Step 1: Deconstruct the notation into its constituent elements:

    800   literature
    820   English
    821   poetry.

Step 2: Reverse the citation order: Poetry – English – Literature.

Step 3: Reference this to its notation: Poetry – English – Literature *see* 821

Step 4: Make any necessary adjustments to the wording, punctuation, etc. As these are obviously references, it is usual to omit *see*:

       Poetry: English Literature **821**

Step 5: Work down the chain, making sure that each truncation of the index entry is matched by a shortening of the notation:

       English literature   820
       Literature   **800**

The index entries have to be imagined as being sorted into alphabetical order and interfiled with other entries.

Figure 6.7 Chain indexing applied to a DDC classified catalogue

can get to the Football example is 796.3340681 (Soccer – Management). As the other elements (Clubs, Scotland) are absent from the notation, it becomes very difficult to express them in the indexing. Thus, anyone using a library catalogue that purports to be based on chain procedure should not expect too much from it. Library subject indexes of this kind provide a rough and ready guide to the whereabouts of the various topics; for serious searching they are a starting point and nothing more.

ASSIGNING SUBJECT HEADINGS

As subject headings are pre-coordinated, and can often be used as they stand, it is easy to think that assigning them is simply a matter of picking from a list. In reality there are a number of issues to be considered. These include:

1. Policy issues:
    a) Are subject headings to be assigned:
        i) only to complete works?
        ii) to partial contents, where a substantial part of a work deals with a distinct topic?
        iii) to individual chapters, articles, etc.?
        iv) to parts of a work, as analytical entries, where a work consists of a small number of discrete items?
    b) What is the maximum number of subject headings that can be assigned to a work?
    c) Are there any categories of work to which no subject headings are to be assigned? (Possible examples include fiction and general periodicals.)
    d) If a specific heading is not available, is there a mechanism for creating a new heading?
    e) If keyword access is available on the OPAC, do the subject headings complement the keywords available elsewhere in the record, or are they searchable independently of them?
2. In working situations, headings and their references are recorded in a Subject Authority File (see Chapter 14).
3. Specific entry: use the most specific heading that will accommodate the subject content of the work. If there is no specific heading, and a new heading cannot be created, use the nearest broader heading.
4. Multiple headings: consider whether more than one subject heading is needed to cover the major aspects of the subject content. Occasionally, depending on policy, additional subject headings may be assigned to express subordinate themes within the work.

5. Multi-topical works: if a work deals separately with two or three distinct topics, assign separate subject headings to each topic, provided that the topics do not together constitute a more general topic (e.g., a work dealing with inorganic and organic chemistry is assigned the single heading Chemistry).
6. Follow any *scope notes* governing correct usage.
7. Apply subdivisions judiciously, paying attention to LCSH's often subtle rules governing their application and sequencing (where more than one subdivision applies). Again, check any scope notes, as distinctions between subdivisions (e.g., between Social conditions and Social life and customs) can be fine.

SUMMARY

Subject headings have had a topsy-turvy history. Library of Congress Subject Headings in particular was for many years a target for abuse (and indeed offered some very easy targets). Ultimately it was saved by a combination of factors: the sheer weight of the resources behind it; apprehensions about the intellectual effort required to apply its strongest contender PRECIS; some much needed updating; and above all the change to OPACs with their keyword facility. In recent years the use of subject headings has been extended: both territorially (through the UKMARC record format) and in the range of documents indexed, as works of the imagination are now given subject headings, and new systems of headings have been developed for fiction.

Library of Congress Subject Headings and other subject heading systems are limited by the inability of pre-coordinated systems to express anything more than a broad summarization. While they are unlikely to offer more than a general indication of subject, their sturdiness and familiarity will ensure their survival even in an age of machine searching.

REFERENCES AND FURTHER READING

Bates, M. J. (1989) Rethinking subject cataloging in the online environment. *Library Resources and Technical Services*, **33** (4), October, 400–412.

Calderon, F. (1990) Library of Congress Subject Headings: vested interest versus the real needs of the information society. *Cataloging and Classification Quarterly*, **11** (2), 85–94.

Chan, L. M. (1990) Subject analysis tools online: the challenge ahead. *Information Technology and Libraries*, **9** (3), September, 258–62.

Chan, L. M. (1995) *Library of Congress Subject Headings: Principles and Practice*, 3rd edn. Englewood, CO: Libraries Unlimited.

Chan, L. M., Richmond, P. A. and Svenonius, E. (eds). (1985) *Theory of Subject Analysis: A Sourcebook.* Littleton, CO: Libraries Unlimited.

Coates, E. J. (1960) *Subject Catalogues: Headings and Structure.* London: Library Association.

Cutter, C. A. (1904) *Rules for a Dictionary Catalog,* 4th edn. Washington, DC: Government Printing Office (and later reprints).

Drabenstott, K. M. and Vizine-Goetz, D. (1994) *Using Subject Headings for Online Retrieval: Theory, Practice, and Potential.* San Diego, CA: Academic Press.

Dykstra, M. (1987) *PRECIS: A Primer.* London: Scarecrow.

Franz, L. (1994) End-user understanding of subdivided subject headings. *Library Resources and Technical Services,* **38** (3), 213–26.

Kaiser, J. (1911) *Systematic Indexing.* London: Pitman.

Langridge, D. W. (1989) *Subject Analysis: Principles and Procedures.* London: Bowker-Saur.

Library of Congress. Cataloging Policy and Support Office. (1966–) *Subject Cataloging Manual: Subject Headings.* Washington, DC: Cataloging Distribution Service, Library of Congress.

Miksa, F. (1983) *The Subject in the Dictionary Catalog from Cutter to the Present.* Chicago: American Library Association.

Rolland-Thomas, P. (1993) Thesaural codes: an appraisal of their use in the Library of Congress Subject Headings. *Cataloging and Classification Quarterly,* **16** (2), 71–91.

Sear's list of Subject Headings (1997) 16th edn. New York: H. W. Wilson.

Shubert, S. B. (1992) Critical views of LCSH – ten years later: a bibliographic essay. *Cataloging and Classification Quarterly,* **15** (2), 37–91.

Studwell, W. E. (1991) Of eggs and baskets: getting more access out of LC subject headings in an online environment. *Cataloging and Classification Quarterly,* **13** (3/4), 91–6.

7 Classification and systematic order

INTRODUCTION

This chapter brings together, and builds on, strands from the preceding two chapters. In it you will learn:

- the place of classification in the scheme of controlled languages
- the differences between natural and bibliographic classifications
- the functions of bibliographic classification
- the component parts of a bibliographic classification scheme: schedules, notation, index
- the differences between the enumerative and faceted approaches to bibliographic classification
- some practical guidelines for classifying documents.

CATEGORIES, HIERARCHIES AND SYSTEMATIC ARRANGEMENT

The formation of categories is one of the most fundamental of human learning activities. Many of us have observed small children in their attempts to categorize the everyday world, and can supply instances – a typical one being the two-year-old who classified birds as pigeons if they were flying and ducks if they were walking or swimming.

In Chapter 6 we learnt how to categorize pairs of terms in three basic ways: where term A is considered equivalent to term B; where A and B are in an hierarchical relationship; and where there is such a close association between A and B that the one forms part of the definition of the other. The skills we acquire in recognizing these relationships are essentially classificatory skills.

We use these skills, often unconsciously, in a number of ways when accessing information. Some examples are:

- Many menu-based user interfaces are hierarchically organized. We start with a broad area, and narrow it down in hierarchical steps to find the required information.
- In traditional alphabetical indexes, if we wish to expand a search to a term that is hierarchically broader, the reference structure usually gives no help: we have to think of the broader term ourselves.
- Conversely, in machine searching, if we wish to search on terms that are hierarchically narrower, we *may* be able to make use of an EXPLODE function, but more usually have to enter the narrower terms individually and OR them together.

SYSTEMATIC ARRANGEMENT

Humankind's attempts to classify the world are as old as knowledge itself – the biblical story of the Creation is an exercise in classification. Much of the human learning process is through classification – Bernard Palmer once gave a series of lectures on classification and published them (they are still worth reading) under the title *Itself an Education*. It is by classifying the objects and activities of the everyday world that children develop their world-knowledge, and this process is constantly being added to and fine-tuned throughout the life cycle. Most of us have seen the attempts of very young children to categorize the world. The 18-month-old who looked at the television screen showing King Kong tearing down skyscrapers and said 'Doggy' was merely trying to fit the unknown into his personal classification schema. The two-year-old who categorized all birds as pigeons if they were flying and ducks if they were walking or swimming had a slightly more sophisticated schema. As we learn, we extend and refine our personal classifications of the world around us.

Classifications of the objects of the everyday world are often known as taxonomies. Their archetype is Linnaeus' systematic ordering of the world of botany. Such classifications work by grouping things together on the basis of their similarities and dissimilarities. Thus onions, leeks, shallots, chives and garlic are grouped together under the family name of Alliaceae.

The systematic arrangement of knowledge, or of the documents in a collection or index, has two important functions:

- It gives us an overview of the subject field covered.
- It makes it possible for information on a subject to be retrieved without having to search the whole file.

Most contents pages of books are effectively classifications of their contents. *Encylopaedia Britannica* has a classification of the whole of knowledge to introduce readers to its scope and organization. Other classifications are not hard to find. Governments maintain official classifications of occupations and industries; educationalists have classifications of schools and of exceptional children; supermarkets group their wares on their shelves, and so on.

Information professionals use classified order in many ways. One common use is to arrange current bibliographies. Users who are interested in keeping up to date on developments in a particular subject field can turn straight to it, either by turning the pages of a printed bibliography or by keying in its class code in a machine-retrieval system. Another use is in designing the knowledge bases for expert systems. Yet another is to give structure to data archives and knowledge repositories held by business and other organizations, so packages of relevant knowledge can be directed to users. An application that is increasingly important today is the design of menus for interactive searching. However, the longest established use of classified order is for the arrangement of the stock of libraries. A number of classification schemes have been devised for this purpose. Chief among them are the DDC, its offshoot the Universal Decimal Classification (UDC) and the LCC.

Library classifications have much in common with the taxonomic groupings of the everyday world, but there are important differences:

- Taxonomic groupings of the everyday world are limited to generic relationships. Documents, as we have seen in Chapter 3, deal with combinations of topics, e.g. a *report* on the *prevention* of *diseases* in *onions*.
- The classification of documents is governed by *literary warrant*: the actual or probable existence of documents that are about the topic for which a class has been defined. This principle has not always been recognized: DDC used many years ago to provide a specific class for library hat-stands (under the broader class Public conveniences), ignoring the extreme improbability of there ever being a literature on that topic.
- Documents can only be arranged in a one-dimensional, linear order. This makes it possible for shelf arrangement to show only one kind of relationship at a time. Catalogues and indexes are necessary to supplement shelf order.

'Library' classification is to some extent a misnomer, as the same schemes are often used to arrange bibliographies (*British National Bibliography, American Book Publishing Record* among others are arranged by DDC) and latterly for the grouping of electronic files also: an example is the Web directory BUBL (*Bulletin Board for Libraries*), which also uses DDC. The term *bibliographic classification* is more accurate.

BIBLIOGRAPHIC CLASSIFICATION

FUNCTIONS OF CLASSIFICATION

Traditionally, bibliographic classification has two functions:

1. Linking an item on the shelves with its catalogue entry. An item's classmark forms part of its shelf mark (also known as call number and book number), which enables items located within a library catalogue to be retrieved from the shelves.
2. Direct retrieval by browsing. If we know where a subject is classed, we can locate it without having to search the whole collection; and can moreover expect to find related subjects nearby. However, because of the limitations of linear order, not all like subjects can be collocated. It is the function of a classification to group together the topics that the users of the collection are most likely to want grouped together (library shelves and, increasingly, virtual collections also).

These two functions taken together are sometimes referred to as marking and parking. The qualities that a bibliographic classification requires in order to achieve these ends are a helpful collocation and sequence, and a brief and memorable notation. Detail is not in itself a requirement, so long as there is enough of it to spare users from having to scan long sequences of items carrying the same classmark. The detailed retrieval of items through the catalogue is achieved through a verbal indexing language. Classification and subject cataloguing are thus seen as distinct and separate.

Some would give classification a third function. Many librarians of special collections have developed detailed, specialized classifications – detailed enough for the topics in the classification, translated back into words, to be used as the basis for compiling the subject catalogue. Traditional enumerative classifications were by and large incapable of supporting this function; but UDC, supplemented by Ranganathan's development of faceted classification in the 1930s, greatly extended the ability of classification to support pre-coordination, to the extent that it became possible for even highly specialized research libraries to base subject indexes on the classification.

The techniques used to construct faceted classifications and their accompanying subject indexes were essentially the techniques of thesaurus construction with systematic order and pre-coordination thrown in. By this argument, thesauri, subject headings and classifications are all manifestations of the same 'deep' index language structure (which, broadly, is the position taken by this book). These new theories and practices were seized on with eagerness, mainly by the British library community, to the extent that classification was held to be the key to all information retrieval; and a lot of energy was expended in the pursuit of the will-o'-the-wisp of a truly universal classification scheme that could be drawn on for use in any kind of information retrieval situation. In recent years there has been some reconciliation of these opposing perspectives on classification and information retrieval generally.

GENERAL AND SPECIAL CLASSIFICATION SCHEMES

A classification may be *general* or *special*. A general classification covers all subjects. A special classification concentrates on a narrower range of topics, typically the goods manufactured or services provided by the organization for which it has been developed. Some general classifications, notably UDC and BC2, have been developed in sufficient depth to enable them to be adapted to special collections.

COMPONENT PARTS OF A CLASSIFICATION SCHEME

Why classification *scheme*? A classification is simply a systematically arranged list. To be of practical bibliographic use a classification needs additional features, and these are what make it into a scheme. A classification scheme has three components:

- the *schedules*, in which subjects are listed systematically showing their relationships. This grouping is not self-evident, and therefore it requires:
- a *notation*, a code using numbers and/or letters, that have a readily understood order which signals the arrangement of the schedules, and
- an *alphabetical index* to locate the terms within the classification.

It is often stated that a classification requires a fourth component: an *organization* to develop it and maintain its currency. This is true, but such a mechanism is not unique to classification, but is a feature of all controlled language systems.

SCHEDULES

Classification schedules comprise the following elements:

- the division of classes by a single characteristic at a time
- main classes
- facets, generated by facet analysis (as described in Chapter 6)

195

- subfacets (arrays), formed by the subdivision of the facets by a single characteristic at a time
- notation, a numeric, alphabetical or alphanumeric code to fix the position of each topic within the the the schedules
- alphabetical index, for accessing the schedules.

These will now be described in turn.

DIVISION OF CLASSES

Division of classes must be by one principle (characteristic) of division at a time. That is, all the subclasses have the same attribute. For example, garments can first be divided according to function (e.g., overcoats, dresses, underwear), and then within these functional groups, or classes, there will be further principles of division, such as size or material.

Failure to observe this principle (see Figure 7.1) reduces the predictability of the system and can lead to cross-classification, which could be problematic if you know of a tame stray dog or an embalmed sucking pig. More plausibly perhaps, DDC's Architecture class (720) has subdivisions 722–724 for schools and styles, and 725–728 for types of structure. Ancient Egyptian architecture is at 722.2, and Temples and shrines at 726.1. Where to class a book on ancient Egyptian temples? The schedules have a clear instruction to use the latter number, and provide we know that types of structure take precedence over schools and styles, all is well.

There are two approaches to the division of classes: *enumerative*, and *analytico-synthetic* or *faceted*. Historically, bibliographic classifications have followed Linnaean principles. Linnaeus divided the plant kingdom into Orders: flowering and non-flowering plants; and then proceeded by successive subdivision to enumerate the various genera and species of plants in their classes and subclasses. Such a

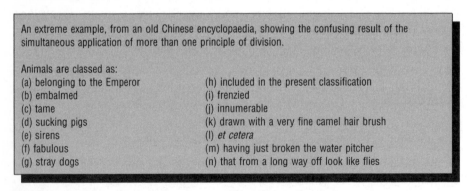

An extreme example, from an old Chinese encyclopaedia, showing the confusing result of the simultaneous application of more than one principle of division.

Animals are classed as:
(a) belonging to the Emperor
(b) embalmed
(c) tame
(d) sucking pigs
(e) sirens
(f) fabulous
(g) stray dogs
(h) included in the present classification
(i) frenzied
(j) innumerable
(k) drawn with a very fine camel hair brush
(l) *et cetera*
(m) having just broken the water pitcher
(n) that from a long way off look like flies

Figure 7.1 Principles of division

Example from DDC showing enumeration of different types of relationship.

628.16833 Protection of the water supply from pollution by oil spills

600 Technology (Applied sciences) [*Discipline facet*]
620 Engineering and allied operations [*NT*]
628 Sanitary and municipal engineering. Environmental protection engineering [*NT*]
　.1　Water supply [*RT of Sanitary engineering. Key system facet*]
　.16　Testing, analysis, treatment, pollution countermeasures [*Operations facet*]
　.168　Pollution countermeasures [*NT*]
　.1683　Countermeasures for industrial wastes [*Agents acet*]
　.16833　Oil spills [*NT*]

This is a typical DDC *chain*, comprising four facets, and with the classmark including both semantic and syntactic relations in a single seamless whole. The same classmark could be represented thus, with hierarchical (semantic) relationships represented vertically, and syntactic relationships horizontally:

Discipline	Key system	Operation	Agent
Technology			
Engineering		Testing . . .	Countermeasures for industrial wastes
Sanitary engineering	Water supply	Pollution countermeasures	Oil spills
628	.1	68	33

Figure 7.2 Enumerative classification 1

top-down, deductive procedure applied to documents results in an *enumerative* classification. Both LCC and DDC are essentially enumerative classifications. This method of compiling a classification brings with it a number of problems:

1. Successive subdivision of classes can only properly cover one kind of relationship – the hierarchical. Other semantic relationships, and all syntactic relationships, have to be assimilated as best they can. This in practice means that relationships of different types are listed in the schedules in a way that makes them look hierarchical when they are not. Figure 7. 2 shows how a single DDC class can include associative as well as hierarchical relationships, together with a range of syntactic relationships.

2. Successive subdivision of classes carries the temptation to continue subdividing for the sake of it, ignoring literary warrant, as with the library hat-stands.

3. Another problem with enumerative classification is that of repetition. Subordinate topics have to be enumerated every time, which bulks out the schedules (Figure 7.3).

> Example from DDC showing (a) enumeration of complex topics, and (b) repetition of data.
>
> 379   Public policy issues in education
>   .1   Specific elements
>   .11   Support of public education
>   .112   Support of public elementary education
>   .113   Support of public secondary education
>   .114   Public support of adult education
>   .118   Support of public higher education
>   .119   Public support of special education
>   .12   Support by specific level of government
>   .121   Support by national governments
>   .1212 National support of elementary education
>   .1213 National support of secondary education
>   .1214 National support of higher education
>   .1215 National support of adult education
>   .1216 National support of special education. . . .
>   .3   Public policy issues in private education
>   .32   Public support of private education
>   .322   Public support of private elementary education
>   .323   Public support of private secondary education
>   .324   Public support of private higher education
>   .326   Public support of private adult education
>   .328   Public support of private special education
>
> Notice in passing the little variations of order in array (adult-higher and higher-adult) and notation (2-3-4-8-9; 2-3-4-5-6; 2-3-4-6-8). These are characteristic of an enumerative classification which has developed piecemeal over many years. It would clearly be more flexible and more economical of space to list the array elementary – secondary – adult – higher – special once only, and to provide instructions for synthesizing it with other topics as required.

Figure 7.3   Enumerative classification 2

4.   Enumerative classifications behave in a very similar way to enumerative subject headings lists, in that they may permit only a limited amount of pre-coordination. Just as a work on the architecture of wooden church buildings would carry the LCSH headings *Church architecture* and *Wooden buildings,* so the best that an enumerative classification like DDC can offer is 721.0448 Architectural structure – Specific materials – Wood, and 726.5 Buildings associated with Christianity (class here church buildings), with no provision for combining the two. However, whereas an item can carry more than one subject heading, we are forced to make a choice between two non-specific classmarks. There is a very real danger of cross-classification, the classing of works on the same subject at two different places. (DDC is good at anticipating this kind of problem: at 721 there is an instruction to 'class architectural structure of specific types of structures in 725–728'.)

198

The topic: *Stability and power structure in small groups* can be analysed into three facets: 1) Small groups [*Key system*]; 2) Power structure [*Property*]; Stability [*Property*].

The topic in DDC (an enumerative classification)
300   Social sciences
301   Sociology and anthropology
302–307   Specific topics in sociology and anthropology
302   Social interaction
   .3   Social interaction within groups
   .34   Social interaction in primary groups.

This shows the principal features of an enumerative classification:

(1) Compound topics are enumerated in the schedules.
(2) Only those compounds that are enumerated can be classed specifically. The concept Power structure has to be subsumed under the more general Social interaction. The third facet – Stability – cannot be expressed at all.

The topic in BC2 (a faceted classification). BC2 analyses the topic into three facets, shown here with their hierarchies and notations:

1.   Social units – Individuals in society – Collectivities – Groups – Primary groups – Small groups: KMD
2.   Social processes – Social action – (Special forms of behaviour) – Social interaction and social relationships – Social relationships – Power and influence – Power structure: KGM R
3.   Social processes – (Types of processes) – (Change and equilibrium) – Equilibrium, social equilibrium, stability: KCS

These three notations are combined according to the rules of the scheme (see Figure 7.8) to give: KMD GMR CS.

Figure 7.4   Enumerative and faceted classifications compared

Faceted classifications are constructed in an inductive, bottom-up manner, as was described in Chapter 6.

Figure 7.4 shows the principal features of a faceted classification:

- Compound topics are formed by synthesis.
- The classification is infinitely hospitable to new compounds. All facets can be expressed. Suppose, for example, someone made a study of resistance to change in the power structure of small groups. No problem: simply alter the final facet to KCT X Resistance to change, giving KMD GMR CTX.

SUMMARY OF ENUMERATIVE AND FACETED CLASSIFICATION

Enumerative classification

- There is a temptation to dismiss enumerative classification as antiquated and inflexible. While there is some truth in this, it need not be dismissed out of hand. Dewey Decimal Classification and LCC go back a long way and have solid institutional support, and the story of DDC in particular over the past generation has been one of careful and sympathetic improvement, and the piecemeal incorporation of faceted features. These vary in extent: 780 Music is fully faceted, but 150 Psychology has very few such features.

- Dewey Decimal Classification and LCC are sophisticated, well developed and widely used schemes.
- Perhaps the strongest inherent advantage of enumerative classification is that it is constructed and displayed in a way that can be intuitively understood. If we take a topic like 'Stability and power structure in small groups' we think of it like that: as a phrase, not as three facets to be stuck together. And if we cannot find the precise topic, we look for the nearest match, in the spirit of compromise that is part and parcel of everyday life. In spite of its many faceted features, and sometimes labyrinthine instructions, DDC can be picked up and understood in its main features with little preliminary training, and LCC is even more thoroughly enumerative than DDC.
- Enumerative classification is incapable of the depth of pre-coordination (hospitality in chain) of faceted classification. This is not often a problem provided a generally helpful sequence of topics is maintained, and the system is not used in the compilation of verbal subject indexes.
- It is true that it is unsystematic in application. Synthesis is unevenly developed, and methods vary from class to class.
- Enumerative schemes are more difficult to revise, because enumerated compounds have to be relocated.
- Schedules tend to be bulky, because the enumeration of compound topics leads to much repetition of data. This, however, is becoming less of a practical (i.e., weight!) problem now that electronic access to schedules is available.

Faceted classification

- Faceted classification has largely been developed since the 1950s.
- Schemes can be daunting at first appearance, as the construction of compound subjects requires both knowledge of the methods of synthesis used and looking up two or more places in the schedules.
- It offers hospitality in chain to any degree, subject only to the overall limitations of pre-coordination.
- Schedules are compact, as only simple topics are listed, with little repetition of data.
- Application is systematic and predictable. With familiarity, the classifier can work with speed and confidence.
- Schemes can be more easily kept up to date.

- Faceted classification has had an incalculable influence on the development of controlled languages over the past half century, but the schemes themselves are largely confined to a few specialist applications. DDC and LCC have an iron grip on general libraries, and BC2 has been developed too late and with insufficient resources to make a significant impact. The rapid growth of mechanized post-coordinate retrieval methods has meant that classification can get by without the level of detail that is required to support a subject index.

MAIN CLASSES

General classifications, whether enumerative or faceted, must have an initial system of broad classes, called the *main classes* or *primary facet*. All current classifications base their main classes on *disciplines*. Disciplines are ways of looking at the world. The narrowest definition of disciplines postulates a small number – perhaps six or seven – of fundamental disciplines, and contrasts them with *phenomena*, the objects of the world, any of which can be studied from more than one disciplinary viewpoint. Many of the traditional disciplines of professional and academic life are, according to this perspective, subdisciplines: a fundamental discipline applied to a particular group of phenomena. So biology is science applied to living organisms, social science is science applied to human groups, and so on. Bliss Bibliographic Classification, second edition, is constructed in this way (see Figure 7.5).

The use of disciplines raises a number of questions and problems:

- There is a large body of literature, often but by no means exclusively written for children, the focus of which is a phenomenon treated from a range of

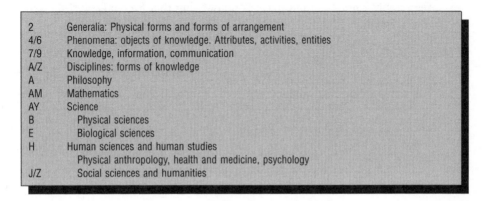

2	Generalia: Physical forms and forms of arrangement
4/6	Phenomena: objects of knowledge. Attributes, activities, entities
7/9	Knowledge, information, communication
A/Z	Disciplines: forms of knowledge
A	Philosophy
AM	Mathematics
AY	Science
B	Physical sciences
E	Biological sciences
H	Human sciences and human studies
	Physical anthropology, health and medicine, psychology
J/Z	Social sciences and humanities

Figure 7.5 Order of main classes in BC2

disciplinary viewpoints: Water, Colour, Life underground, and so on. (BC2 reserves class 3 for such topics.)

- There needs to be provision for topics that are too general in scope to fall within the disciplinary structure. Traditionally, such topics have been placed in a main class labelled Generalia. These may include:
  - the vehicles for communicating information: books, journals and so on
  - documents with no subject limitation, which may be classed by their format or arrangement: encyclopaedias, general newspapers, and the like
  - the tools of knowledge: systems, computers
  - the disciplines associated with any of these: publishing, information science, librarianship, bibliography.
- Not all disciplines are clear-cut. Geography for example is a loose aggregate of topics.
- Disciplines are by no means static, but are constantly evolving and being added to, often by the fusion of distinct fields of study, as with biochemistry or psycholinguistics – there was a book published some years ago with the title *Biological and Social Factors in Psycholinguistics*. Where such topics have to be accommodated within an existing disciplinary framework, anomalies and second thoughts can result, as with DDC's recent relocation of the sociology of education from 370.19 (within Education) to 306.43 (aspects of the sociology of culture).
- The number and order of main classes are determined by:
  - philosophical and scientific considerations. Bliss studied for 40 years to find a 'scientific and educational consensus' on which to base his classification. Francis Bacon and Hegel are both said to have influenced Dewey in his choice of main classes.
  - the practicalities of the notation. In theory, anyone constructing a classification should determine the number and order of the classes first, and then apply a notation; but there is no denying that Melvil Dewey thought of the notation first and adapted the schedules to it.
  - other considerations, from the pragmatic to the ideological. For example, the Library of Congress's primary function is to serve Congress, and a basic function of government is national defence. The LCC accordingly has a main class for military science. Or take Colon Classification (CC): to its deviser Ranganathan, mysticism was the pinnacle of human experience, so he created a main class for it, gave it a suitable notational symbol – the Greek letter delta (Δ) – and located it at the very centre of his classification.

FACETS

A vocabulary of terms organized into *broad facets* is the defining structural feature of a faceted classification. The terms are derived from the literature, using the technique of facet analysis outlined in Chapter 5. An important difference between the terms of a classification schedule and a verbal system is that the terms of a classification represent the *concepts* defining each class, whereas the terms in a verbal system are *labels* for retrieval. In many cases these are identical. Where they are not so, classes can be defined by means of headings such as Secondary forms of energy, Persons by miscellaneous social characteristics, or Postage stamps commemorating persons and events, which would be unacceptable (except as node labels) in a verbal system. As they are collected, many of the terms will tend to organize themselves into groups. These are the broad facets of the classification. A facet is the total subset of classes produced when a class is subdivided by a single broad principle or characteristic.

SUBFACETS OR ARRAYS

Once the broad facets have been determined, each must be examined to see if it can be further subdivided by a more specific principle into *subfacets*, or *arrays*. The order of classes within an array can often be determined intuitively, the guiding principles being that (a) any hierarchies must be indicated, and (b) alphabetical order is used only as a last resort. More specifically, the following arrangements have been found useful:

- chronological, e.g. for history and literature; also for operations carried out sequentially, e.g., the sequence of agricultural operations from ploughing to harvesting
- evolutionary, e.g., the stages in the life cycle
- increasing size or complexity, e.g., for musical ensembles
- spatial, with the proviso that classification is one-dimensional, making it impossible to maintain full geographic contiguity. Thus, in DDC's Table 2 (Geographic areas), the first area enumerated under -4 Europe is -41 British Isles, from where the table crosses the North Sea to Germany and tours the central European states as far as Hungary (-439); after which it skips to France (-44), Italy (-45), Spain and Portugal (46); then an even greater leap to Russia and Scandinavia. (It is perhaps comforting to find that 611 Human anatomy is better ordered.)

Enumerative systems such as DDC also recognize subfacets. For example, 011 Bibliographies has these divisions:

.1   Universal bibliographies

.2   General bibliographies of works published in specific languages
.3   General bibliographies of works published in specific forms
.4   General bibliographies of works exhibiting specific bibliographic characteristics other than form [eg rare books, reprints]
.5   General bibliographies of works issued by specific kinds of publishers
.6   General bibliographies of works for specific kinds of users and libraries
.7   General bibliographies of works having specific kinds of content

However, whereas a faceted classification would be able to express as many of these characteristics as required (e.g., serial publications from underground presses, or rare books in microform), with DDC it is only possible to express one characteristic.

Unless a classification is intended for in-house use only, it is helpful to allow alternative locations where user feedback suggests that other collocations might be preferred. For example, in DDC much the greatest part of class 200 is given to the Christian religion. No fewer than five different options are offered to users who wish to give preferred treatment to a specific religion.

CITATION ORDER

The principles are precisely the same as for pre-coordinate systems generally (see Chapter 6) except that in general classifications discipline forms the primary facet.

Alternative citation orders are sometimes offered. An example from DDC is subject bibliographies (016), where the preferred citation order is *Bibliographies – Subject*, as 016.61 for a bibliography of medicine. The alternative treatment scatters subject bibliographies by topic instead of keeping them all together, as 610.16.

FILING ORDER

Filing order is the actual sequence of books on shelves, citations in bibliographies, etc. There is an apparent paradox here. Schedules are arranged from general to specific, which means that the *least* significant facet is listed first and the most significant last. In other words, filing order is the *reverse* of the citation order. This is known as the *principle of inversion*, and maintains the principle of filing general topics before special in syntactic as well as in semantic relationships (Figure 7.6). In DDC the principle is seldom specifically acknowledged, but often followed in practice, in 'class elsewhere' and 'preference' instructions. For example, when classifying the book on ancient Egyptian temples referred to earlier, there is an instruction at 722–724 to 'class specific types of structures

Citation order:				
Literature by origin – Periods – Authors – Literary forms – Literary movements				
Schedule – *inverting* the citation order				
B Literary mov'ts B2 Naturalism B4 Romanticism	D Literary forms D2 Poetry D4 Drama D42 Comedy D44 Tragedy	F Authors *Arrange* *alphabetically* *within facets* *K and H*	H Periods H2 Classical H4 Modern H41 15th century H45 19th century	K Lit. by origin K2 English K4 French K6 Classical K61 Greek K62 Latin

Filing order, showing general-to-special order:

Romanticism in literature	B4
Poetry	D2
Romanticism in poetry	D2B4
Nineteenth-century literature	H45
Nineteenth-century poetry	H45D2
English literature	K2
Romanticism in English literature	K2B4
Romanticism in nineteenth-century English literature	K2H45B4
Romanticism in nineteenth-century English poetry	K2H45D2B4
The poetry of John Keats	K2H45FKeats
Romanticism in the poetry of John Keats	K2H45FKeatsB4

Figure 7.6 Citation order and filing order

regardless of school or style in 725–728' – that is, at the *later* class. For the bibliographies at 011, there is the preference instruction: 'class a subject with aspects in two or more subdivisions of 011.1–011.7 in the number coming last, e.g. Russian-language newspapers on microfilm 011.36 (not 011.29171 or 011.35)'.

OTHER COMPONENTS

NOTATION

Notation is a code applied to topics in order to fix their arrangement. Thus notation or code may be used in organizing books on shelves, files in a filing cabinet, entries in a catalogue or bibliography, or electronically held resources or their representations. The term 'notation' is generally used of document arrangement for shelf retrieval and for manually searched files. The more general term 'code' is used in machine retrieval.

Notation fixes a pre-existing arrangement: that is, it is applied to the schedules of a classification system *after* the subjects to be included, and their order, have been settled. It is necessary because systematic order is not self-evident.

205

After fixing the order of classes, the next important function of notation is hospitality: the ability to accommodate new subjects. For manual searching, a notation should be easy to use. Finally, there is the question of expressiveness: it is open for a notation to express the hierarchical structure of the classification, and also to express the facet structure of compound topics. These considerations will now be discussed in turn, together with a brief consideration of shelf notation.

Showing the order of classes

The purpose of notation is to give each class an address that fixes its order within the classification. The ordinal values of Arabic numbers and roman letters are widely understood and form the basis of all notations. Where more than one kind of symbol is used – a *mixed notation* – filing precedents may have to be set, and here the ASCII sequence of numbers – upper case – lower case is used. Where non-alphanumeric characters are used, they are assigned arbitrary ordinal values.

Hospitality

Notation must be hospitable to the insertion of new subjects. There are two methods by which this can be achieved:

1. Unassigned notation within an array. If the new topic is coordinate, all is well if a suitable gap has been provided. DDC20 classed Roller skating at 796.21, with 796.22 unused; DDC21 has appropriated 796.22 for Skateboarding.
2. Subdivision of the notation. If the notation is hierarchical and the new topic is by nature subordinate, it can be slotted in naturally. DDC20 used 004.67 for wide area networks (WANs), and DDC21 has inserted a class for the Internet at 004.678. However, if the array of subordinate topics has a larger number of classes than the notational base can accommodate, then the hierarchical nature of the notation is inevitably compromised. Greece recently set up 12 new regional government areas, for which provision has been made in DDC21's Table 2, where some of the regions have four digits and others five, as the notational base is too short to allow them all notations of the same length.

Any more extensive revision in an established scheme is likely to involve the reuse of existing numbers with new meanings. The recent revision of DDC's Life sciences class has tried to reduce the burden on individual libraries by leaving unassigned class 574, which was very heavily used in previous editions.

Ease of use

A notation should be easy for users to remember, copy, and shelve books by. To a large extent this is a function of *brevity*: the shorter the notation the easier it is to remember. Length of notation is determined by:

- The *notational base*. There are over twice as many letters as numbers, so a lettered notation will be shorter than one that uses numbers alone.
- The *allocation* of notation to the literature. This particularly affects established classification schemes, whose main classes may have been established for a century or more, and where the original allocation becomes less balanced with time and the emergence of new subdivisions. Growth subjects like electronic engineering tend to have long notations (621.38 in DDC), which gives all topics within that class even longer notations: 621.389332 is the number for Hi-fi systems. Conversely, some subjects have little or no growth. The classic instance is Logic (160 in DDC). It is a salutary exercise to go round any general library making a note of the length of shelving taken up by each main class.
- Provision for *synthesis*: the more facets, the longer the notation. In DDC this can lead to some very long notations, especially in classes such as 338 Production, where the synthesis of Topic + Industry + Place leads to prodigious notations: a history of the Merseyside ship repair industry is classed at 338.476238200288094275. Where synthesis is systematic, as in faceted classifications, the notation for a facet will be consistent. In BC2 for example 28 introduces Place, so that 28S will always denote Japan. In DDC synthesis is anything but systematic: Africa is often denoted by -096, but 344.096 denotes Laws relating to religion; a class mark ending in -03 often denotes a dictionary or encyclopaedia, but 697.03 denotes central heating.
- *Mnemonics*, where the same notational symbol is consistently used to denote the same topic, is properly an aspect of synthesis. Occasionally a classification having a lettered notation may be able to use *literal mnemonics* based on the initial letter of a subject. BC2 has AL Logic, AM Mathematics, C Chemistry, among others. There is however a temptation on the part of the designer of classifications to allow literal mnemonics to distort the order of the schedules; and they can raise false expectations among users – for example that B should denote Biology. (In BC2 B is Physics, and Biology is E.) At worst, it can lead to the use of alphabetical order as a lazy substitute for classification.
- *Chunking*: long notations are more memorable if broken up into shorter groups in the manner of telephone numbers. Many classifications (DDC, UDC, BC2) use groups of three symbols separated by spaces or points.

Expressiveness

The notation *may* express the hierarchy of classes, and if it is intended for machine manipulation, this is a requirement, as with the EXPLODE function with MeSH tree structures. With manual systems, anyone familiar with DDC tends to expect this: there is an intuitive satisfaction in observing that, say, 636 denotes animal husbandry, 636.1 horses, and 636.12 racehorses. However, maintaining hierarchical expressiveness has certain problems:

- It can lead to excessively long notations.
- It is impossible to maintain if the number of terms in an array exceeds the notational base (as with the regions of Greece mentioned above).
- Human perspectives on hierarchical structures can change over time. Relationships between subjects change as knowledge develops.

Figure 7.7 shows a notation that is deliberately non-hierarchical.

The notation *may* also express the facet structure of classes. In a faceted classification, there is often an expectation that this will be achieved. Even DDC makes some use of facet indicators, both generally throughout the scheme, for example where 09 often (but by no means invariably) introduces place or time,

---

This example uses the first facet (KMD) of the topic in Figure 7.4: Stability and power structure in small groups.

K	Society
K9Z	Social phenomena
KK	Social structure
KLI Y	Social units
KLJ	Individuals in society
KLK	Collectivities
KLM	Groups
KMC	Primary groups
KMD	Small groups

A mixed notation: numbers file before letters in BC2. 2–9 are used for the common facets; but some locations towards the end of the sequence are used for other topics, including Sociology at K9V and Social anthropology at K9W.

Notice how the notation shows the order of topics, but not the hierarchical structure. Indeed, KLI Y has a longer notation than KLJ (compare classes AY and B in Figure 7.5), reflecting the amount of literature on these topics.

Hierarchies in BC2 are notable in that they are rigorously defined and do not cut any corners in the way that older classifications often do. A fully hierarchical notation for Small groups would have at least nine digits.

Figure 7.7 Retroactive notation in BC2

BC2 observes the principle of inversion, so the facets are cited in the reverse order of their appearance in the schedules. The notation is synthesized retroactively in the same way.

Topic: Stability and power structure in small groups.
Chain: Small groups – Power structure – Stability
Notations: KMD   KGM R   KCS

In the subordinate facets, any initial letters which duplicate the initial letters of the preceding facet are dropped: KMD KGM R KCS
Completed notation: KMD GMR CS

Figure 7.8 Non-hierarchical notation in BC2

and in individual classes, notably 780 Music, where both 0 and 1 are used only as facet indicators. A few classifications, notably UDC and CC, use non-alphanumeric symbols to introduce particular facets. Universal Decimal Classification, for example, encloses places between parentheses and uses the colon to introduce a whole range of relationships. This complicates filing, as it is not self-evident whether, say, 63:31 Agricultural statistics will file before or after 63(31) Agriculture in ancient China. Another drawback is that facet indicators make the notation longer. A simple way to avoid both problems is to use a lettered notation, the initial letter of each class being in capitals and the rest in smalls, e.g. TjgLmEs for a (hypothetical) notation containing three facets. A variation of this technique is shown in Figure 7.8. Douglas Foskett (Foskett and Foskett, 1974) used a pronounceable notation in his London Education Classification, with some wickedly memorable features, e.g. the notation for Students was Sad, and for Sex education, Pil.

Shelf notation

The notation inscribed on the back of books may usefully be shorter than that used in catalogues and other indexes. Dewey Decimal Classification notation supplied by central bibliographic agencies is often segmented: that is, one or two points are shown at which the notation could be cut off. So the 21-digit class appearing above could be shortened to 338.4762382 or even 338.4 (the maximum allowed in the Abridged DDC).

The notation forms the basis of an item's *call number* or *shelfmark*, the actual symbol on the spine of the item which determines its place on the shelves and which the catalogue uses to locate it. This has three elements:

- a symbol denoting any special shelving sequence, e.g. oversize items (usually omitted for items within the main sequence)

- the classmark proper (full length or shortened)
- a device to denote the item's position within that class. This may be a Cutter number – a letter followed by one or more numbers as a coded representation of the author's name – or some other (usually simpler) device.

Cutter numbers are used by LC to arrange books alphabetically within a class number. They consist of the initial letter of the main entry heading followed by one or two numbers that represent the second or subsequent letter of the name. The precise distribution of the numbers depends on the initial letter. For most names beginning with a consonant the second letter:

a e i o r u y is represented by the number: 3 4 5 6 7 8 9

So the name Davidson might be represented by .D3, Deakin by .D4, and so on. The numbers may be expanded decimally, using the third letter of the name, so Dean might be .D42. Further expansion is applied as required. The system is collection-specific: two libraries applying Cutter numbers independently would be likely to assign different numbers to the same work. Hence the tendency to rely on numbers supplied by LC.

Cutter-Sanborn Author Tables are a modification, using three digits. For large collections, Cutter numbers provide a better collocation than systems based on the first three letters of the heading, or on the initial letter followed by a running accession number.

ALPHABETICAL INDEX

The index to the classification schedules has two purposes:

- to locate topics within the classification
- to bring together related aspects of a subject which appear in more than one place in the schedules. (Indexes to classification schemes are sometimes known as relative indexes.)

Faceted classifications need only index the simple concepts appearing in the schedules. Related aspects are uncommon, but do occur (essentially they reflect polyhierarchies): for example, the index to class K Society of BC2 gives two locations for Ethnomethodology. Enumerative classifications must show enumerated compound subjects: examples from DDC were given in Figures 7.2 and 7.3. Additionally, DDC's index also includes a selection of synthesized compounds: Pines, Elms and Eucalyptus for example have subheadings for Ornamental arboriculture, whereas Apples, Firs and Yews do not.

REVISION

Bibliographic classifications are inherently out of date. In part this is due to the tendency of all controlled language systems to lag behind the times. Additionally with classification:

1. Classifications are necessarily *closed* rather than open systems. The *ordering* of a new topic is not automatic, as it is with verbal systems: only a controlling organization can determine the correct placing of a new topic within the schedules.
2. Any revision of the order of topics involves the physical removal of books from shelves, the altering of their shelf numbers, and their replacement – a far more labour-intensive operation than the altering of surrogate records.

So classification schemes tend to be revised on the principle of doing only as much as the market will bear. The point is stressed here to explain how it is that, even though modern faceted principles have been shown to be far superior to traditional enumerative classifications, the great majority of libraries use enumerative classifications. The Library of Congress Classification is almost entirely enumerative. The Dewey Decimal Classification is largely enumerative but with variable proportions of faceted features. The Universal Decimal Classification is a faceted system grafted on to an enumerative base. The Bliss Bibliographic Classification, second edition, is thoroughly faceted, but is incomplete and little used. Colon Classification, the original faceted classification, has few users outside its home country.

THE CLASSIFICATION PROCESS

These guidelines are based on DDC, but can be adapted to apply to any classification.

ANALYSE THE SUBJECT

- Use *title* and *subtitle, contents list* and scan the *author's introduction* for any paragraph describing the purpose of the book. Treat *blurbs* with caution – their primary objective is to sell the book.
- In working situations you have *outside sources*: reviews, bibliographies (e.g., *BNB*, MARC records), subject experts, etc.
- Make a mental note of the word or phrase which most precisely describes the subject: e.g. if it is on combine harvesters, note it as such, not as agricultural machinery.

211

NOW GO TO THE CLASSIFICATION SCHEDULES

- The most reliable way to classify is to start at the most appropriate discipline in the *summary tables* and work downwards through the schedules.

WHAT IS THE DISCIPLINE?

If the work appears to fall between two (or more) main classes, then:

- class at the discipline which receives the greater emphasis
- watch the schedules for instructions on classing interdisciplinary works
- check the DDC *index*. If the first index entry has a classmark on the same line (and not after an indented subheading), that is probably the place to classify a topic covering more than one discipline (but check the schedules).

WHICH ASPECT OF THE SUBJECT FIRST?

- Check the schedules carefully for any *table of precedence, class here* note, or *class elsewhere* note. If necessary, check the broader containing headings for your subject (e.g., for 305.4 check 305, 302–307, and 300 – this is why it is always best to work downwards from the main class whenever you can.)
- In any given subject, there is an expectation that the more important facets of a subject will be listed *after* the less important: e.g., class Norman castles at 728.81 castles rather than at 723.4 Norman architecture.
- Class at the *passive* system: i.e., at whatever is at the receiving end of any process or operation: e.g. a book on bovine medicine with cattle (636.2) rather than veterinary medicine (636.0896).
- Follow any *add* instructions (e.g., to give 636.20896), but *never* try to combine two numbers from the schedules if there is no specific instruction to do so.
- Anything normally falling within the scope of DDC's *standard subdivisions* is classed last: i.e.,
  - common subject aspects, e.g., historical aspects of X; also biography, management, philosophy, psychology, psychology, statistics, computer applications, etc.
  - the subject in relation to a particular *place*
  - the subject written for a class of users who would not normally be the target readership, e.g. Anatomy *for nurses*
  - the way the subject is arranged or presented, e.g. dictionary, humorous treatment.

MORE THAN ONE SUBJECT

(A + B, where A and B are independent themes treated together in a work).

- If one is clearly subordinate, ignore it (e.g. Chess and draughts).
- If two equal subjects, class at the earlier one, unless there are contrary instructions.
- If three or more within the same general subject field, class at the first more general class that will accommodate all of them.
- If necessary, apply a combination of these rules.

FINAL CHECK

- Always check a classmark upwards through every stage of its hierarchy. If doing so leads to a heading that is irrelevant or misleading, there is a strong possibility that you have selected an inappropriate number (another reason for starting with the main class and working downwards).

SUMMARY

This chapter has led us from a discussion of classification as a fundamental human activity to an introduction to the theoretical features of a bibliographic classification and some practical hints on how to apply a classification scheme. Our account is necessarily brief, and should be supplemented by at least a selection of the fuller studies listed below.

In studying a construct as complex, abstract and highly organized as bibliographic classification, it is all too easy to lose sight of the principles among the plethora of detail. Much of this chapter has elaborated principles introduced in Chapter 5. It may help to keep the following three principles from Chapter 5 firmly in mind:

1. Bibliographic classification is not something apart, but is in essence a means of organizing a controlled vocabulary. Turn back to the principles of language control section in Chapter 5, as a reminder of how the trio of basic semantic relationships – equivalence, hierarchical, associative – are displayed in classification schemes.
2. Facet analysis, introduced in Chapter 5, lies at the core of modern classification theory.
3. The systematic display that forms the most obvious feature of a bibliographic classification indicates its main purpose: to achieve the sequence of topics that is most helpful to the users of the system. The section 'Displaying the

thesaurus' in Chapter 5 took us in steps from a simple alphabetical display to systematic displays which are at the threshold of bibliographic classification.

The present chapter has been at pains to take most of its examples from published general classification schemes, especially DDC. Much of modern classification theory was conceived as an antidote to the traditional classification schemes, and there was a tendency to treat classification theory and DDC and its companions as totally separate entities: theory on the one hand which bore little relationship to practice, and practice on the other which was entirely devoid of theory. This is not a helpful attitude, and it is particularly unjust to DDC, which has striven over the past generation to adapt itself to modern ideas. It is now time to look at the individual schemes in more detail.

REFERENCES AND FURTHER READING

Beghtol, C. (1998) Knowledge domains: multidisciplinary and bibliographic classification systems. *Knowledge Organization*, **25** (1/2), 1–12.

Buchanan, B. (1979) *Theory of Library Classification*. London: Bingley.

Cochrane, P. A. (1995) New roles for classification in libraries and information networks. *Cataloging and Classification Quarterly*, **21** (2), 3–4.

Foskett, A. C. (1996) *The Subject Approach to Information*, 5th edn. London: Clive Bingley; Hamden, CT: Linnet Books.

Foskett, D. J. and Foskett, J. (1974) *The London Education Classification: A Thesaurus/Classification of British Educational Terms*, 2nd edn. London: University of London Institute of Education Library.

Hunter, E. (1988) *Classification Made Simple*. Aldershot: Gower.

Hurt, C. D. (1997) Classification and subject analysis: looking to the future at a distance. *Cataloging and Classification Quarterly*, **24** (12), 97–112.

Langridge, D. W. (1992) *Classification: Its Kinds, Systems, Elements and Applications*. London: Bowker-Saur.

McIlwaine, I. C. (1997) Classification schemes: consultation with users and cooperation between editors. *Cataloging and Classification Quarterly*, **24** (1–2), 81–95.

Marcella, R. and Newton, R. (1994) *A New Manual of Classification*. Aldershot: Gower.

Mills, J. (1969) Bibliographic classification. In *Encyclopedia of Library and Information Science*, vol. 2, pp. 368–80. New York: Dekker.

Mills, J. and Broughton, V. (1977) Organizing information and the role of bibliographic classification; and, The structure of a bibliographic classification. Both in *Bliss Bibliographic Classification*, 2nd edn. Vol. titled *Introduction and Auxiliary Schedules*, pp. 29–34, 35–48. London: Butterworths.

Palmer, B. (1971) *Itself an Education: Six Lectures on Classification*. London: Library Association.

8 Bibliographic classification schemes

INTRODUCTION

The three major general classification schemes are DDC, its offspring UDC, and LCC. These will be described in some detail in this section. Two other schemes: BC (and its successor BC2) and CC, will be discussed briefly because of their influence on current theory and practice. At the end of this chapter you will:

- understand the structure and principal features of the three major general classification schemes
- appreciate the salient contributions to classification theory and practice made by BC and CC
- be aware of the arguments for and against modifying published classification schemes
- understand the place of special classification schemes.

The three major schemes were all introduced before the ideas of facet analysis were developed. They are thus basically enumerative schemes, though all have some analytico-synthetic features. In the case of UDC these are very extensive, less so with DDC – though DDC has embraced the principles of facet analysis and is incorporating more synthetic features. With LCC they are a minor feature.

THE DEWEY DECIMAL CLASSIFICATION

In 1876 Melvil Dewey, a 25-year-old college librarian, published anonymously *A Classification and Subject Index for Cataloguing and Arranging the Books and Pamphlets of a Library*, with 12 pages of introduction, 12 pages of tables and 18 pages of index. It had three novel features:

- Books were to be shelved by relative instead of fixed location. With fixed location (which can still be seen in a few places), books were given a fixed place on a numbered shelf, and any new books on the subject represented by that shelf had to be filed at the end. When the shelf became full, a new sequence had to be started elsewhere. With relative location, the books are numbered in relation to each other and not to the shelves. The whole collection could grow as required, and a more detailed subject specification became possible – Dewey's 999 classes were a great advance on anything that had gone before.

- A simple decimal notation instead of the cumbersome notations (often involving roman numbers) previously used. Indeed, Dewey is said to have thought of the notation first. Certainly the notation was an important factor in the early and continued success of the scheme.

- A detailed subject index, made necessary by the detail of the classification.

The second edition of 1885 established three further principles:

- Decimal subdivision: the first edition used the decimal point only to introduce a book number. This greatly increased the ability of the scheme to support specific detail.

- Integrity of numbers: Dewey had made some quite sweeping relocations in the second edition, and to sugar the pill announced that future editions would expand but not relocate: a policy that was followed until 1951. This policy, however reassuring to users and potential users, inevitably meant that the structure of the scheme became more and more outmoded over time.

- Synthesis, in the shape of (a) a table of 'form divisions' representing some of the common facets, which could be appended to any number; and (b) 'divide like' instructions, the forerunner of the present 'add' instructions, where all or part of one number may be added to another in order to specify an extra facet.

By 1951 it was clear that the policy of integrity of numbers could not be maintained, but that each new edition would have to radically restructure one or more classes. Complete revision has to date been applied to: 546 and 547 Inorganic and Organic chemistry (sixteenth edition, 1958); 150 Psychology (seventeenth edition, 1965); 340 Law and 510 Mathematics (eighteenth edition, 1971); 301–307 Sociology and 324 Political process (nineteenth edition, 1979); 780 Music (twentieth edition, 1989); and 350–354 Public administration, 570 Biology, 583 Dicotyledons (twenty-first edition, 1996). These complete revisions were formerly known as phoenix schedules. Also, classes may be extensively revised, keeping the main outline but reworking subdivisions. 370 Education and all the rest of 570–590 Life sciences were thus revised in the twenty-first edition, and 001–006 Knowledge, systems and data processing in the twentieth; 004–006 has had to be further revised and expanded in the twenty-first edition.

SCHEDULES

Division of classes

With DDC the notation is everything. This may seem an odd way to start a discussion of the division of classes in DDC, but the evidence is that Dewey fitted his classification to the notation rather than the other way round. The magnificent simplicity of a pure numeric notation is achieved at the cost of the most tightly constricted notational base of any classification. Each stage in the subdivision of the universe of knowledge permits only nine divisions. A three-digit notation allows for only 999 classes, and Dewey used them all. As the universe is not organized on regular decimal lines, it is inevitable that each 1–9 subdivision will more often than not include topics from more than one facet or subfacet. With very few exceptions, classes are divided top-down on the enumerative principle. This again has resulted in many classes being divided according to more than one principle of division at a time. This is further discussed below.

Another way of saving notational space is the use of pseudo-hierarchies. One class is used as an umbrella heading for a miscellaneous collection of loosely associated topics. Some examples are:

380	Commerce, communications, transportation
387	Water, air, space transportation
646	Sewing, clothing, management of personal and family living
646.7	Management of personal and family living. Grooming
629.28	[Vehicle] tests, driving, maintenance and repair.

In a few places the original division of classes omitted steps in hierarchies and left no space in the notation for a necessary broader term to be added later. One instance is the sequence 385–388, which denoted rail, canal, sea and land transport without providing a place for transportation generally. For some years a niche was found at 380.5, which preserved the general-to-special order but introduced a yawning gap between transportation and its subdivisions. Recently however, transportation generally has been classed at 388, sacrificing general-to-special in order to keep the subject together. Prose literature is another instance where no provision was originally made: it is found in a number of places (808.888, 818.08 etc.) but always at the *end* of the sequence of prose forms (essays, letters etc.).

217

```
000  Generalities (88 pages)
100  Philosophy, paranormal phenomena, psychology (62 pages)
200  Religion (160 pages)
300  Social sciences (549 pages)
400  Linguistics (38 pages; 45 including Table 4, which is specific to this class)
500  Natural sciences and mathematics (302 pages)
600  Technology (Applied sciences) (508 pages)
700  The arts. Fine and decorative arts (226 pages)
800  Literature (Belles-lettres) and rhetoric (64 pages; 96 including Table 3, which is specific to this
     class)
900  Geography, history and auxiliary disciplines (204 pages)
```

Figure 8.1   DDC Main Classes

Main classes

Advances in knowledge over the past century and a quarter have made an unequal development of the main classes inevitable. Figure 8.1 names the classes and gives an idea of their relative sizes. The classes are based on disciplines, with occasional exceptions, notably 770 Photography that includes both technical and artistic aspects.

Facets

Dewey himself had only an inchoate awareness of facets. Consistency in facet structure tended to be subordinated to the notation. Sometimes the notation lent itself to a coherent facet structure, as in classes 400, 800 and 900. More often it did not, causing the facets to be jumbled together. In 370 Education we find:

- 371 Schools and their activities (itself a hotchpotch of assorted facets with Special education tagged on at the end)
- 372, 373, 374 Stages of education: elementary, secondary, adult – with Higher education separated from these at 378
- 375 Curricula
- 379 Public policy issues in education.

Where there is notation left at the end of an array, it may be used for another array with a different principle of division. 720 Architecture has already been mentioned: the arrays are:

- 721 Architectural structure
- 722–724 Architectural schools and styles
- 725–728 Specific types of structures

218

624.1 Structural engineering and underground construction
 .15 Foundation engineering and engineering geology [Key system]
 .151 Engineering geology [NT. Properties, processes, operations]
 .152–.158 Foundation engineering *[Centred heading]* [NT]
 .152 Excavation [Operations]
 .153 Foundation materials [Materials]
 .154–.158 Specific types of foundations *[Centred heading]* [Kinds]
 .16 Supporting structures other than foundations [Key system]
 .17 Structural analysis and design [Operations]
 .171 Structural analysis [Operations]
 .172–.176 Loads, stresses, strains *[Centred heading]* [Processes]
 .177 Structural design and specific structural elements
 .1771 Structural design [Operations]
 .1772–.1779 Specific structural elements [Parts]
 .18 Materials [in structural engineering][Key system, Materials]
 .19 Underground construction [Key system]

DDC here follows standard citation order quite closely – remember that in an inverted schedule you read the facets *upwards*.

Figure 8.2 Facet structure and centred headings in DDC class 624.1

- 729 Design and decoration of structures and accessories.

In many places some kind of order is imposed by the use of centred headings, which serve as facet indicators, showing where a facet occupies a spread of notation; 722–724 and 725–728 are examples. Figure 8.2 is a more thoroughgoing example, mapping the implied facet structure onto the schedule.

Since the eighteenth edition determined efforts have been made to regularize the facet structure. Some classes have been completely revised. Elsewhere, ambiguities in the facet structure are dealt with in one of the following ways:

1. 'Add' instructions, which always make clear the citation order. In DDC20 we found 370.11 Education for specific objectives, and 372 Elementary education, with no indication of where to class a work on elementary education for specific objectives. DDC21 has provided a new class 372.011, with an 'add' instruction to add to this number the subdivisions of 370.11. Thus, 370.115 denotes Education for social responsibility, and Elementary education for social responsibility will be classed at 372.0115.
2. Preference instructions, which indicate which facet is to be preferred and which is to be ignored. Class 155 is Differential and developmental psychology; 153.9 is Intelligence and aptitudes with the instruction: Class factors in differential and developmental psychology that affect intelligence and aptitudes in 155. In 624.1 (see Figure 8.2), 624.17723 is Beams and girders, and 624.1821 Iron and steel. There is an instruction at 624.182: Class specific

structural elements in metal in 624.1772–624.1779, so that Structural steel girders would be classed at 624.17723.

Subfacets or arrays

Arrays were given cavalier treatment by Dewey, and later attempts to tidy up the structure have been variably successful. The example in Figure 8.3 shows part of Sociology, which was completely revised in the eighteenth edition. 305 Social groups has 13 subfacets (Figure 8.3)

Most structural problems in DDC are hangovers from Dewey's original assignment of topics to classes. Some classes, notably 400 Language, are quite consistently constructed. The schedules that have been completely revised also have a far more regular structure, though the degree of synthesis varies greatly: 780 Music is almost fully faceted (to the extent that users are said to be put off by it); 340 Law and 350–354 Public administration allow a high degree of synthesis. 150 Psychology, 301–307 Sociology and 510 Mathematics on the other hand are thoroughly enumerative. Editors of DDC have to tread a very fine line between what revisions are theoretically desirable and what users are prepared to accept. 370 Education has been extensively revised in the twenty-first edition, but has retained many of its structural anomalies. While there is no shortage of models of good classification structure in education, to incorporate them would have forced users to make hard decisions on whether or not the extensive

.2	Age groups (2)
.3–.4	Groups by sex (3)
.5	Social classes (4)
.6	Religious groups (5)
.7	Language groups (7)
.8	Racial, ethnic, national groups (6)
.904	Persons by kinship (8)
.9063	Persons by cultural level (9)
.9065	Persons by marital status (10)
.9066	Persons by sexual orientation (11)
.9069	Persons by special social status (e.g. aliens, offenders) (12)
.908	Persons by physical and mental characteristics (1)
.909	Persons by occupation (13)

A preference table instructs the classifier which subfacet to choose. Numbers in parentheses indicate the preference order, e.g. black Roman Catholic middle-class male youths within 305.2 (specifically, 305.235), rather than in 305.3, .5, .6 or .8.

This being an enumerative classification, all the other subfacets are ignored. A faceted classification like BC2 is able to specify all subfacets: compare Figure 8.12.

Figure 8.3 Subfacets in DDC class 305 Social groups

reclassification involved is worth the candle. Better a half-hearted revision than one that nobody has the resources to adopt.

Citation order

Many of the vagaries of DDC's citation order have already been examined. However, to correct any impression that all is chaos, it must be stated that the schedules have about them a sturdy pragmatism reinforced by an awareness in recent editions of classification theory. Time and again it is possible to find synthesis and standard citation order. More and more use is being made of synthesis by means of 'add' instructions (see Figure 8.4), and in nearly every case

A specific instruction in the schedule reads: 'Add to base number XXX the numbers following YYY in ZZZ'

Example: Let's get publicity: public relations in voluntary organizations. Class: 659.288

659.2 Public relations
  .28 In specific kinds of organizations
      Add to base number 659.28 the numbers following 658.04 in 658.041–658.049, e.g. corporations 659.285
658.048 Non-profit organizations

Some people find it helpful to draw a vertical line after the base number. The added part is aligned beneath it, then pulled up to tack onto the end of the base, i.e.:

  659.28¦ → 659.28¦8 → **659.288**
  658.04¦8 → 658.04¦ ↑

A less common variant of the Add instruction is to add the whole of the second number to the first. This can **only** be done where the 'Add' instruction specifically allows this: anyone attempting to string together two DDC numbers where this is not specifically permitted will soon make nonsense of the classification.

Example: Public relations management in universities. Class: 659.29378

659.2 Public relations
  .29 In organizations producing specific kinds of products and services
      Add to base number 659.29 notation 001–999
  378 Higher education

Another variant is synthesis by 'add as instructed' footnotes. An asterisk or other mark in the schedules leads to a footnote saying 'Add as instructed under' followed by the place in the schedules (almost always an *earlier* place) where there will be found a table in small print beginning 'Add to notation for each term identified by * [or whatever] as follows':

Example: Marine reinsurance. Class: 368.220122

368.22 *Ocean marine insurance
        *Add as instructed under 368.1–368.8
  01 General principles
            Add to 01 the numbers following 368.01 in 368.011–368.019
  .012 Underwriting
    2 Reinsurance

Figure 8.4 Synthesis by means of 'add' instructions

the number to be added comes *earlier* in the schedules – a sure sign that, intuitively or consciously, schedule inversion is being applied.

'Add' instructions are applied *ad hoc* (though the principle involved in dropping initial digits is very close to BC2's). More systematic synthesis is provided through the auxiliary tables in Volume 1 of the schedules. These comprise:

- Table 1: Standard subdivisions, which can be applied to any number from the schedules. The oldest of the auxiliary tables, covering the common facets of form and subject. The sequence is chaotic, reflecting the practical difficulties of undertaking a thorough revision.
- Table 2: Geographical areas etc. The longest by far of the tables. Typically (but not invariably) applied after -09 from Table 1.
- Tables 3 and 4 are special auxiliary tables for use with class 800 Literature and 400 Languages respectively.
- Tables 5 (Racial, ethnic and national groups), 6 (Languages) and 7 (Groups of persons) can only be applied where instructed.

NOTATION

Dewey Decimal Clasification's notation is at once its greatest strength and its greatest weakness. The concept of numbers used decimally is simple and universally understood; but at the same time DDC's constricted base and lopsided allocation have led to many excessively long numbers. Another recurring result of the short base is the use of -9 as an overspill class for 'other' topics. This is very common indeed. Examples include:

290	Comparative religion and other religions
299	Other religions
629	Other branches of engineering
679	Other [manufacturing] products of specific materials
759.9	[Painting and paintings of] other geographic areas.

Even worse is DDC's practice of allowing the notation to dictate the order of subjects. Instances have already been given. In some places the notation even dictates the citation order. In particular, DDC's notation cannot satisfactorily accommodate an open-ended list of named persons, so individuals as subjects can only come at the very end of the citation order. In 800 Literature it is impossible to subdivide works by or about individual authors (other than by a local adaptation of the optional table for Shakespeare at 822.33). The revised 780 Music had as its main model Coates's (1960) *British Catalogue of Music Classification*. Here, composer was the primary facet for treatises on music; but 780 has been unable to follow this, except as an option at 789.

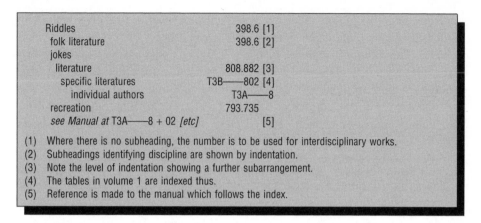

Riddles	398.6 [1]
folk literature	398.6 [2]
jokes	
literature	808.882 [3]
specific literatures	T3B——802 [4]
individual authors	T3A——8
recreation	793.735
see Manual at T3A——8 + 02 *[etc]*	[5]

(1) Where there is no subheading, the number is to be used for interdisciplinary works.
(2) Subheadings identifying discipline are shown by indentation.
(3) Note the level of indentation showing a further subarrangement.
(4) The tables in volume 1 are indexed thus.
(5) Reference is made to the manual which follows the index.

Figure 8.5 DDC Relative index

ALPHABETICAL INDEX

Dewey Decimal Classification's index is called a relative index: originally, it seems, because it indexed the new relative as opposed to fixed-place classes; but latterly because it relates subjects to disciplines. Figure 8.5 shows a sample index entry.

There are also see-also references to synonyms and broader terms, but only where three or more new numbers are to be found.

The CD-ROM version *Dewey for Windows* has a fuller index than the printed index. Nevertheless, the index does not – could not – claim to be exhaustive. Indeed, DDC's summary tables make it unnecessary to use the index except in the most intractable cases. There are three summary tables of the whole classification, showing the ten main classes, the hundred divisions, and the thousand sections. These appear at the beginning of Volume Two. They are supplemented by summaries at the beginning of each of the ten main classes and their divisions, and additionally as required – complex sections like 616 Diseases or 621 Applied physics may have up to six summary tables each. It is sound practice for classifiers to classify from the schedules as far as possible, using the excellent guiding and summary tables, and to keep the index as a last resort. Bibliographic databases in USMARC format, which have both DDC classmarks and LCSH headings, offer another approach, using LCSH as an entry vocabulary to DDC classmarks.

ORGANIZATION, REVISION AND USE

Control of the scheme was assigned by Dewey himself to the Lake Placid Club Educational Foundation, a not-for-profit body which he set up 'to restore to helth [sic]and educational efficiency teachers, librarians and other educators of moderate means, who have becum [sic] incapacitated by overwork' (*Dewey Decimal Classification*, 14th edn, p. 48). (Simplified spelling was one of Dewey's many interests.) The club owned Forest Press, DDC's publisher, which gave the scheme a sound financial footing. After some vicissitudes an editorial office was established within the Library of Congress, ensuring both literary warrant for the scheme and the inclusion of DDC class numbers in USMARC records. In 1988 the Forest Press was sold to OCLC, and editorial work is now done by the Library of Congress under contract with OCLC Forest Press. There is a broadly based Editorial Policy Committee, which includes members from Canada, Australia and the UK, and advises the editorial team. Other experts are also consulted as required. Dewey Decimal Classification's literary warrant has been improved through becoming part of OCLC, as OCLC's Online Union Catalog is now accessed electronically as part of the revision process. This, being based on a very wide range of working collections, gives a better idea of the range of titles that libraries actually acquire than could be obtained from a single legal deposit collection.

The schedules are published in four well-designed volumes. A Manual, containing detailed class-by-class advice for the classifier, information on major revisions, and explanation of classification policy and practice, is included in the fourth volume, following the index. New editions are published every seven years. One or two major divisions are recast completely, with piecemeal alterations elsewhere. The major revisions in the current (twenty-first, 1996) edition were described above. Advance notice of changes is published annually in *Decimal Classification Additions, Notes and Decisions*, abbreviated to *DC&*, which is distributed to subscribers. The DDC database does include additional information including a wider range of index entries. These appear in the CD-ROM version, *Dewey for Windows* – a fine tool for the practising classifier, but too complex for those learning the scheme.

A single-volume abridged edition is published alongside every full edition, currently the thirteenth Abridged. There is also a further abridgement: *Dewey Decimal Classification for School Libraries*. Translations into eight foreign languages are available (most recently Russian), and into at least 30 languages if translations no longer current are included. Although libraries may classify new stock by the latest edition of DDC, earlier editions remain important because many libraries are reluctant to reclassify, and thus leave stock classified by earlier editions long after they have been superseded.

The use of DDC in the *British National Bibliography* has been important in establishing DDC in British libraries. The *British National Bibliography* began publication in 1950, and from 1971 has been produced from the UKMARC database. Normal practice is to apply the latest edition of DDC from the January after its publication. There has also been some retrospective conversion of earlier records. There is now a USMARC format for classification data, which incorporates fuller information about DDC classmarks than was previously available. This includes:

- a history of changes between editions, making it easier for users to track relocations
- the components of synthesized numbers, making it possible to carry out machine searches on classes formed by 'add' notes. Thus in the examples in Figure 8.3 above, a search on 658.048 Non-profit organizations could be made to lead to 659.288, which is synthesized from 659.28 and the final digit of 658.048.
- a field for centred headings, making it possible to systematize the hierarchical broadening or narrowing of machine searches on DDC classmarks.

These developments are a practical result of the link-up between DDC, the Library of Congress and OCLC, and help to ensure the continued success of DDC. In other respects, editorial policy is concentrating on:

- user convenience: making the schedules easier to apply
- regularization: the gradual elimination of irregular developments of standard subdivisions which occur at a number of places throughout the schedules
- 'faceting': the increased use of notational synthesis
- ensuring that terminology is kept up to date, for example by replacing 'physically handicapped persons' with 'persons with physical disabilities'
- catering for international needs, e.g., by reducing the American and Christian bias in the classification, and by expanding the area tables and the historical and literary periods for a number of countries.

LIBRARY OF CONGRESS CLASSIFICATION

The detailed classification scheme of the Library of Congress was occasioned by the library's removal to new premises in 1897. The scheme consists of 21 main classes set out in over 50 volumes. Publication began in 1899 and was virtually complete by 1910 – apart from class K Law, publication of which did not commence until 1969 and was not completed until 1993. There are revised editions of most classes (Q Science is in its seventh edition). Recent editions are published in the USMARC format for classification data, and the full schedules together with LCSH are available as *Classification Plus* on CD-ROM.

The scheme's name describes it precisely: it is the classification of the Library of Congress. It exists to serve the needs of that body. It was developed, under the general editorial direction of the Librarian, Herbert Putnam, and his Chief Classifier, Charles Martel, on a class-by-class basis by the staff of the library's subject departments, who also implemented the classification. It was, and is, an in-house classification. However, as the classification of the world's largest library, its suitability to other large academic and research collections was soon recognized, and was greatly advanced by the library's decision in 1901 to make its printed catalogue cards available for sale to other libraries.

SCHEDULES

The scheme was based on the long defunct *Expansive classification* of Charles Ammi Cutter. Its main classes (Figure 8.6) are clearly tailored to the needs of the LC, as they were perceived a century ago. Like everything else about LCC, the order of the main classes is thoroughly pragmatic, avoiding the idiosyncrasies of DDC. Each class was compiled separately, and could be used independently. It follows that the classification is almost entirely enumerative, with much repetition of detail, making the schedules very bulky in hard copy.

Classes are divided in a broadly hierarchical manner; but as the scheme was compiled piecemeal at a time when classification theory barely existed, one must not expect the consistent application of either hierarchies or a facet structure, even within a single class. As the most enumerative of all the schemes, LCC can only be learnt by practice. It cannot be learnt by the application of

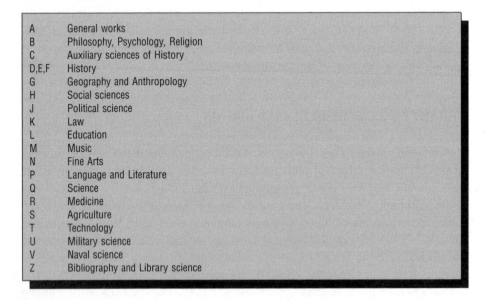

A	General works
B	Philosophy, Psychology, Religion
C	Auxiliary sciences of History
D,E,F	History
G	Geography and Anthropology
H	Social sciences
J	Political science
K	Law
L	Education
M	Music
N	Fine Arts
P	Language and Literature
Q	Science
R	Medicine
S	Agriculture
T	Technology
U	Military science
V	Naval science
Z	Bibliography and Library science

Figure 8.6 LCC main classes

principles, because there are none. Library of Congress Classification's great strength is that every class exists because subject specialists have perceived the need for it, and the order and detail of the classes have been developed, again by specialists, to meet the requirements of an exceptionally large working collection operating under exacting conditions. There are a number of recurring themes, including:

- A tendency to file common form and subject facets *before* general works on a topic. A common sequence (derived from guidelines laid down by Martel) is some kind of variant on:
  - Periodicals, Societies
  - Collections, Dictionaries
  - Theory, Philosophy, Congresses
  - History
  - General works
- Alphabetical subdivision – which purists would object is the negation of classification – is frequently used, the precise method being by Cutter numbers. These allow individual classifiers great flexibility, provided that sufficient authority control is exercised to avoid cross-classification. For example, class HJ4653 Income tax – United States – Special, A–Z has subdivisions that include .C3 Capital gains and .E75 Evasion. Which subdivision is to be used for evasion of capital gains? If a title is published on tax avoidance, how do we know not to create a new Cutter number for it under .A? In these respects, the success of LCC depends on its being based on a single authoritative institution that applies authority control on behalf of all other users.
- A variable amount of *ad hoc* synthesis, which never has any application outside its main class (so there is no one table for the common facets). Methods vary from elaborate tables – class P has a truly wondrous table of subdivisions under individual authors, separately notated according to the amount of notation allocated to an author – to brief one-line instructions to divide one spread of numbers in the same way as another.

NOTATION

The general pattern of LCC's notation can be observed in the examples above: one or two (very occasionally three) capital letters followed by up to four digits used numerically rather than decimally. Hospitality is achieved by leaving gaps in the notation. Where these have been filled, the notation is then expanded decimally. It is all very clear and workmanlike, like the numberplate of a car.

H	Social sciences
HM–HX	Sociology
HV	Social pathology. Social and public welfare. Criminology
HV 6001–9920	Criminology
HV 6254–6773	Special crimes
HV 6435–6492	Offenses against the public order
HV 6435–6453	Illegal organizations
HV 6441–6453	Outlaws. Brigands. Feuds

Vendettas are not specifically named, but their close relation Feuds is lumped together in a class containing both concrete and abstract topics, after the manner of LCSH's conjunctive phrase headings. Contrast LCC's hierarchy with BC2's (Figure 8.10), where Vendettas are correctly classed as a social phenomenon (not necessarily criminal) and minutely categorized by hierarchy. LCC will have none of this soft sociological nonsense: feuding's a crime, and that's the end of it!

(Some would see the heading and collocation at HV as more insidiously tendentious, with their implication that anyone receiving public welfare benefit is not far removed from being a criminal. These are characteristic instances of *critical classification*.)

Figure 8.7 LCC sample topic: Vendettas

The use of Cutter numbers adds to the complexity of the notation, however. There is also an official manual giving guidance on shelf-listing.

Classmarks assigned by the Library of Congress and appearing in USMARC records always include the full shelfmark, so that every LCC classmark ends with a Cutter number – or, in the many places where A–Z topical subdivision is prescribed, with two in succession. Many libraries perceive this as an advantage, as they can use Library of Congress shelfmarks as they stand, thus eliminating one stage of book preparation. Some American libraries have migrated from DDC to LCC because of this.

ALPHABETICAL INDEX

For many years there was no official comprehensive alphabetical index, but only the indexes to each volume. Library of Congress Subheading served as a rough and ready index, however, as many headings have relevant LCC classmarks. The CD-ROM has a comprehensive index.

ORGANIZATION AND REVISION

As the in-house classification of a huge legal deposit library, LCC assigns new classmarks as the need arises. A list is published weekly in the Library's *Information Bulletin,* and the CD-ROM is updated annually. Revision is thus continuous, unlike DDC's. Radical revision of individual classes is very much the exception. The following official manuals are published: *Subject Cataloging*

Manual: Classification; *Subject Cataloging Manual: Shelflisting*; *LC Cutter Table*. These are available electronically on the *Cataloger's Desktop* CD-ROM, along with other publications on cataloguing topics. The CD-ROM is designed to be used in conjunction with *Classification Plus*.

The scheme is primarily used by LC itself and by other extensive research collections such as large academic libraries, mainly North American but also in other English-speaking countries, including a significant minority of British university libraries. The resources behind the scheme, and the size of the collections that currently use LCC, are sufficient to ensure its stability throughout the foreseeable future. United Kingdom MARC records currently include LCC classmarks, though with some gaps in the case of retrospective UKMARC records. They do not however include shelfmarks (i.e. Cutter numbers) for individual items.

OTHER GENERAL CLASSIFICATIONS

UNIVERSAL DECIMAL CLASSIFICATION

Universal Decimal Classification emerged from an attempt in 1894 by two Belgians, Paul Otlet and Henri LaFontaine, to commence the compilation of a 'universal index to recorded knowledge'. A classified rather than an alphabetical approach was necessary in the index because of the many languages involved, and because an internationally acceptable notation was important. The Dewey Decimal Classification was already in its fifth edition, and Melvil Dewey's permission was obtained to extend the scheme. A conference in 1895 established the Institut International de la Bibliographie (IIB) to be responsible for the index. The first edition of UDC was published in French between 1904 and 1907.

The First World War and the unfavourable climate after it led to the demise of the index, but UDC continued with a second edition in French and a third in German. The IIB eventually became the Fédération International d'Information et de Documentation (FID). The British Standards Institution, the official English editorial body, published an abridged English edition in 1961. Publication of a full English edition had begun in 1943 but was not completed until 1980. Since 1992 all rights and responsibilities for UDC have been vested in the UDC Consortium, representing various international and national organizations. There now exists a machine-readable Master Reference File containing some 60 000 classes (compared with 220 000 classes in the full editions), from which the International Medium Edition, English Text, second edition was published in 1993. There are also editions in various combinations of Full, Medium and Abridged in around 20 other languages – French, German and English are

Topic	DDC	UDC
Psychology	150	159.9
Sociology	301–307	316
Commerce, communications, transport	380–388	Vacated. UDC classes Commerce at 339, Communications 338.47, Transport and postal services 656
Languages	400	Within class 8. Class 4 is vacant.
Literatures of individual languages	820–890	Does not use: classes are formed by synthesis within class 8.

Figure 8.8 Principal differences between DDC and UDC schedules

UDC's official languages. A revised edition of the official *Guide to the Use of UDC* was published in 1995.

Schedules

The overall outline of the schedules follows DDC, with the main differences shown in Figure 8.8.

It will be apparent from this that UDC's attitude towards disciplines is more relaxed than DDC's. The schedules and notation are largely hierarchical, though hierarchies are less clearly indicated than in DDC. There is no indentation. Bold type is used, but is applied mechanically to notations of six digits or fewer, the shorter the number the larger the typeface. In the Medium edition many classes have headings describing aggregates of topics, e.g., 675.25 Mechanically treated leathers. Including: Embossed leather. Buff. Perforated, punched leather. The Full edition provides subclasses for each of these. The schedules include some pre-coordinated classes, for example:

341.345	Internment of military personnel in neutral countries
551.588.5	Influence of ice on climate
664.71	Milling of wheat and rye
664.782	Processing of rice. Rice milling
664.784	Processing of maize. Maize milling (corn milling)
664.785	Processing of oats. Oat milling

While many enumerated compounds do occur, the principal means of pre-coordination is by synthesis. Within the schedules, 'special auxiliary subdivisions' are frequently to be found. These often indicate a Processes or Operations facet, and are introduced by .0 (less frequently by a hyphen or an apostrophe). They apply only to their class. For example, under 636 Animal husbandry, 636.082 is

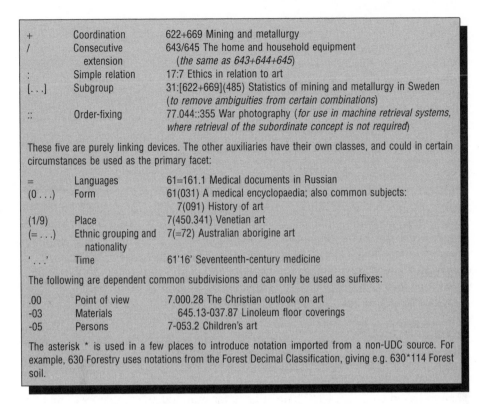

+	Coordination	622+669 Mining and metallurgy
/	Consecutive extension	643/645 The home and household equipment *(the same as 643+644+645)*
:	Simple relation	17:7 Ethics in relation to art
[...]	Subgroup	31:[622+669](485) Statistics of mining and metallurgy in Sweden *(to remove ambiguities from certain combinations)*
::	Order-fixing	77.044::355 War photography *(for use in machine retrieval systems, where retrieval of the subordinate concept is not required)*

These five are purely linking devices. The other auxiliaries have their own classes, and could in certain circumstances be used as the primary facet:

=	Languages	61=161.1 Medical documents in Russian
(0 ...)	Form	61(031) A medical encyclopaedia; also common subjects: 7(091) History of art
(1/9)	Place	7(450.341) Venetian art
(= ...)	Ethnic grouping and nationality	7(=72) Australian aborigine art
'...'	Time	61'16' Seventeenth-century medicine

The following are dependent common subdivisions and can only be used as suffixes:

.00	Point of view	7.000.28 The Christian outlook on art
-03	Materials	645.13-037.87 Linoleum floor coverings
-05	Persons	7-053.2 Children's art

The asterisk * is used in a few places to introduce notation imported from a non-UDC source. For example, 630 Forestry uses notations from the Forest Decimal Classification, giving e.g. 630*114 Forest soil.

Figure 8.9 UDC Common auxiliary tables

the special auxiliary for the breeding of animals. 636.1 denotes Horses, and 636.16 Ponies, which would give 636.1.082 and 636.16.082 for the breeding of horses and ponies respectively. In a few places an equivalent of DDC's 'Add' instructions is to be found, indicated by ≅, for example 378.18 Student life, customs etc ≅ 71.8 – classifiers have to work out for themselves which part of the number to bring across. There are also ten Common auxiliary tables (Figure 8.9).

Most of the auxiliaries can if required be repeated or combined with one another, so a high degree of synthesis is possible. The colon is the general purpose relational indicator: when UDC was used to compile subject indexes, before machine retrieval became the norm, it was common to find hugely lengthy notations containing four or more facets strung together with colons.

Uniquely among general classifications, UDC allows the individual user a large degree of autonomy in selecting the citation order. Standard citation order is officially recommended, however, and in many places it is built into the schedules through the special auxiliaries. There is an obvious need for the individual user to follow a consistent citation order, and the maintenance of an authority file is particularly important.

UDC contains a number of devices to enable a user to modify standard citation order. Notation may be reversed round the colon, e.g., 17:7 (Ethics of Art) may be expressed as 7:17 making Art rather than Ethics the primary facet. Any auxiliary that has both an opening and a closing notation can be moved to other positions, e.g., instead of 343(410.5) Criminal law – Scotland, a user may prefer 34(410.5)3 Law – Scotland – Criminal, to keep all Scottish law together.

UDC's filing order is complicated by the range of non-alphanumeric characters in the notation, and by the possibility of many auxiliaries being used independently, so that a class number could conceivably begin with a bracket, equals sign or double-quote. That aside, the coordination and extension symbols + and / widen the scope of a class, so they file *before* the simple class number. Thereafter, the filing order is (broadly): (colon), then = (equals), then (. . .) (bracketed auxiliaries), then '. . .' (double quotes). This is not an exhaustive listing: the *Guide* has a mind-boggling table with over 20 entries, including the sequence .00 -0 -1/-9 .0 which is equally incomprehensible to machine and human filing.

Notation

Though based on DDC, UDC's notation is far more complex, thanks to its non-alphanumeric auxiliaries. Thanks also to these, the finer aspects of showing the order of classes are not always apparent. There are other differences from DDC. Main classes and their divisions are not filled out with zeros to a three-digit minimum: Technology and Agriculture are 6 and 63 respectively. Where final zero is used, it is significant: 630 denotes Forestry; (41) is the auxiliary for the British Isles, (410) for Great Britain as a political entity. A point is inserted after every third digit of the notation, as 629.454.22 Railway sleeping cars.

The notation is completely hospitable through the use of decimal expansion. As UDC has been largely developed for use in scientific and technical contexts, the allocation of the notation is even more skewed than DDC's, and classes 5 and 6 comprise almost two thirds of the schedules. For more specific subjects the notation can be extremely long.

Alphabetical index

The single-volume Abridged and two-volume Medium editions have their own complete indexes. As with DDC, classifiers are recommended to work primarily from the schedules, and to use the index as a check on the validity of a selected number or the locations of related classes. In particular, many UDC numbers are obtained by synthesis, and the index does not show synthesized numbers.

Organization and revision

UDC's revision structure has in the past been notoriously slow. The setting up of the UDC Consortium, together with the machine-readable Master Reference File, can be seen as measures to streamline the revision process. Much work remains to be done in ironing out UDC's anomalies to make it entirely suitable for machine searching. There are currently some interesting projects for developing UDC for computer retrieval, and prospects for the successful rejuvenation of the scheme do appear brighter than in the fairly recent past.

Prior to the 1970s UDC was frequently to be found in large card indexes in special libraries and sometimes in abstracting and indexing tools. Computer-based indexing systems have largely rendered obsolete UDC's detailed indexing function (which essentially is why development is now concentrating on the Medium rather than the Full editions). UDC remains very popular for shelf classification, particularly in the libraries of continental Europe. It is also used to arrange various bibliographies and indexing services (for here the length of the notation is less of a problem than on the spines of books), including Walford's *Guide to Reference Material*, the *British National Film and Video Catalogue*, and the national bibliographies of over 20 countries. The omission of UDC class numbers from MARC records of North American and UK origin is a serious limitation.

BLISS BIBLIOGRAPHIC CLASSIFICATION

Henry Evelyn Bliss (1870–1955) made classification his life's study, and wrote two major theoretical works before his classification was published in stages between 1940 and 1953. Though published by the H. W. Wilson Company, his work had little impact in the USA, but had a small but enthusiastic following in Britain and elsewhere, particularly in the specialist fields of education, social welfare and health. A Bliss Classification Association was formed in Britain to sustain and develop the classification, and the decision was made to undertake a major revision on analytico-synthetic principles, using and developing the work of the Classification Research Group towards the elusive goal of a completely new general classification scheme. Bliss's original classification had many synthetic features, but was essentially enumerative in structure, and chiefly notable for the care taken over the order of classes. The revision (BC2) was to retain much of this macrostructure, but otherwise is effectively a new classification. It is this

```
K       Society
KC        Social processes
KCY         Social action
              (Types of action by consequences for society)
KIB           Divisive processes
KIC             Conflict
                  (Types of conflict)
                  (By instruments used)
KII X             Force
KIJ                 Violence
KIJ V                 Feuds and vendettas
KIJ X                   Vendettas
```

Figure 8.10 BC2's hierarchy for Vendettas

version that is discussed here. The schedules are being published class by class. Publication began in 1977, and is still not quite complete.

Schedules

As BC2 is entirely faceted, only simple concepts appear in the schedules. The schedules are rigorously hierarchical (Figure 8.10).

While the notation is not hierarchical, hierarchies are clearly indicated by indentation and by summaries at the head of every column. Subfacets are shown within parentheses.

BC2's basic citation order is Disciplines – Phenomena. Phenomena that are treated in a non-disciplinary manner are given a numbered notation, to make them file *before* the disciplines. The main classes are little changed from BC, and continue to embody Bliss's principles of following the 'educational and scientific consensus', placing general before special, 'gradation in speciality', and the collocation of related subjects. Figure 8.11 shows the main classes, with approximate DDC equivalents.

The schedules are relentlessly faceted, and all facets and subfacets are carefully indicated. The complexity of the facet structures of many classes can give the schedules a daunting appearance, and a clear head is needed when approaching them from cold. For example, the facet formula for class K Society is:

(1) Collectivities (KLK/KV)
(2) Parts and properties (KLK KW)
(3) Institutions (KK/KLC)
(4) Social processes (KC/KJ)
(5) Environmental bases (KA/KB)

234

(DDC equivalents are approximate.)	
2/3	Physical forms and forms of arrangement of documents (DDC 030, 050 etc)
4/6	Phenomena: objects of knowledge (no DDC equivalent)
7/9	Knowledge, information, communication (001)
A/Z	Disciplines: forms of knowledge
A	Philosophy (100)
AM	Mathematics (510)
AY	Science (500)
B	Physical sciences (530)
C	Chemistry (540)
D	Astronomy (520), Earth sciences (550–560)
E	Biological sciences (570–590)
H	Human sciences and human studies. Physical anthropology, health, medicine, psychology (599.9, 360, 610, 150)
J/Z	Social sciences and humanities
J	Education (370)
K	Social sciences (300, 390)
L/0	History (900)
P	Religion (200), the Occult (130), Morals and ethics (170)
Q	Social welfare (360)
R	Political science (320, 350)
S	Law (340)
T	Economics (330, 380)
U	Technology (600; also 355–359, 790)
V	Arts, fine arts (700)
W/Y	Philology: language and literature (400, 800)
Z	(Alternative to P)

Figure 8.11 Order of main classes in BC2

(6) Operations on phenomena (KA/KB)

(7) Common facets (K2/K9)

Even in a 'soft' science like sociology, many of the elements of standard citation order are discernible. As always, the order of the schedules is the *reverse* of the citation order.

Figure 8.12 below gives an example of BC2's subfacets. For an example of subfacets within a single classmark, see the breakdown of class KIX J Vendettas in Figure 8.10.

Notation

BC2's notation uses both numbers and letters (capitals only; BC used both capitals and smalls). As has been seen, numbers and letters are used together in the listing of main classes. Otherwise, numbers are used only as facet indicators for the common subdivisions:

Subgroups
  By time factors
  By space factors
  By number in group
  Reflecting particular social processes
  Territorial groups
  Stratification (class etc.) groups
  Age groups
  Sex-groups
  By personality attributes
  Advantaged / disadvantaged groups
  Occupational groups
  By political status
  Religious groups
  Linguistic groups
  Ethnic and racial groups

The above are given in *schedule* order (*least* important first). Unlike DDC's treatment of the same subject (see Figure 8.3), BC2 is able to combine subfacets. The following example uses the same topic (Black Roman Catholic middle-class male youths) as in Figure 8.3:

KNB	Middle classes
KNR	Youths
KNX	Males
KPB R	Catholics
KPF BF	Blacks (from Table 3A)

Class number synthesized retroactively, omitting notation that duplicates the previous subfacet:
KPF BF + KPB R + KNX + KNR + KNB.
This gives: KPF BF BR NX R B, expressed as KPF BFB RNX RB.

Figure 8.12 Principal subfacets for social groups (KLM-KV) in BC2

2   Physical form
3   Forms of presentation and arrangement
4/9   Common subject subdivisions

These are the only facet indicators; the standard method of building classmarks is by retroactive notation. The notation is remarkably brief, and can pack a goodly number of facets into a small compass. Brevity is assured by means of:

● a long notational base
● sensible allocation of notation to the classes (with the reservation that out of deference to BC too much space is allocated to History and not enough to Science and Technology)
● a non-hierarchical notation
● absence of facet indicators.

For easier use, the notation is split into groups of three characters. An (extreme) example of BC's synthesis in action is given in Figure 8.12.

For anyone used to DDC, BC2 has some oddly notated hierarchies. Being non-hierarchical, the notation is required only to show the order of topics. The length of the notation reflects the estimated literature on a topic, and not the degree of subordination. Thus, in the above examples, AY Science appears to be – but is clearly not – a subdivision of A Philosophy, and its first subdivision – B Physical sciences – has a shorter notation.

Alphabetical index

As with UDC, BC2's indexes show simple concepts only. Each volume of the schedules has its own index: there is no general index. It is thus up to the classifier to decide on an item's main class before it is possible to have recourse to the index. Every volume contains two outline schedules of the whole classification; the second outline has around 100 classes: much the same level of detail as in DDC's second outline.

Organization and revision

Both BC and BC2 have been dogged throughout their lives by a chronic lack of resources. BC2 was conceived at a time when there was an enthusiastic following, at least in Britain, for the idea of a highly specific general classification that would form the basis for all forms of information retrieval. A generation later the world has moved on, and BC2 is still only half-published. Its intrinsic qualities may make it the benchmark by which other classifications may be judged, but quality is not in itself enough to attract users and ensure its future. Besides being ill resourced, the physical production of many of the schedules is user-unfriendly, and considerable intellectual effort is required to become fluent in using the schedules. Most importantly today, BC2 classmarks do not appear on centrally produced MARC records.

Paradoxically for a classification calling itself Bibliographical, it may be that BC's future is to be used predominantly not as a library classification but as a quarry for others to mine. More than any other general classification, BC2 resembles the systematic display of a thesaurus. Its specificity is such that the great majority of its headings can be used as they stand as thesaurus descriptors, and reorganizing the semantic relationships for a thesaurus is largely a mechanical exercise (but by no means altogether so – see Figure 8.13).

As well as being a potent source for thesaurus compilers, BC2 with its immense detail and regular and explicit structure would lend itself to machine manipulation better than UDC, and there have been suggestions that the develop-

237

Class KIJ X Vendettas shows how easily BC2 adapts as a thesaurus, and also how some professional input is needed. Only the immediate hierarchy is shown here.

Classification
KIJ   Violence
                   * Application of injurious physical force
                   * For War, see Political science R
KIJ K   Intimidation [further classes follow]
KIJ V   Feuds & Vendettas
                   * Lasting mutual homicidal relationship between two groups
KIJ W   Feuds
                   * Socially regulated, terminable peacefully
KIJ X   Vendettas
                   * Not socially regulated

Thesaurus:
Feuds
   SN   Lasting mutual homicidal relationship between two groups, socially regulated,
                   terminable peacefully
   BT   Violence
   RT   Vendettas
Vendettas
   SN   Lasting mutual homicidal relationship between two groups, not socially regulated
   BT   Violence
   RT   Feuds
Violence
   SN   Application of injurious physical force
   BT   Conflict
   NT   Feuds
                Intimidation
                Vendettas
                [etc.]
   RT   War

Figure 8.13 Adapting BC2 as a thesaurus

ment of UDC could borrow some leaves from BC2's book. (There is already some collaboration with UDC.) More generally, the study of classification schedules is recognized to be an excellent starting-point for anyone who needs to learn how a subject is structured, and the detail and rigorous analysis of BC2's schedules make it especially useful in this respect.

COLON CLASSIFICATION

The CC devised by S. R. Ranganathan is little used outside the Indian subcontinent and in the Western world is chiefly of historical interest for its development of facet analysis. First published in 1933, subsequent editions have introduced quite drastic changes. The current edition is the seventh (1987, and still lacking an index).

CC's facet formula is simple, sturdy and hauntingly memorable: PMEST, i.e. Personality, Matter, Energy, Space and Time. Personality is (broadly) Key system; Matter is Materials; Energy is Processes and Operations; and Space and Time are two of the common facets. Mapping these onto standard citation order gives:

Key system	Personality
Kinds	
Parts	
Materials	Matter
Properties	
Processes	Energy
Operations	
Agents	
Common facets	Space
	Time

As this is clearly an incomplete formula, Ranganathan postulated two further devices. His fundamental categories can apply at different *Levels*. These are (again broadly) what we would call subfacets, but can be used to specify basic facets such as Kinds, Parts and Properties. The other device is *Rounds* where the PME formula can begin a second round at some subordinate position in the citation order – typically to introduce Agents. Every class has its own facet formula, based on PMEST with different Levels and Rounds as required. This is difficult enough, and is not made easier by Ranganathan's adherence to his *Law of Parsimony* – trained as a mathematician, he believed in giving information succinctly, to the point of desiccation. Neither is it made easier by CC's notation, which is of a desperate complexity. It uses a range of non-alphanumeric characters as facet indicators in a manner comparable to UDC. However, whereas UDC otherwise confines itself to numbers, CC also has upper and lower case letters, as well as using a few letters as honorary numbers to extend the notational base.

While Ranganathan is undoubtedly the father of modern classification theory, and one of the fathers of the theory of controlled languages generally, his CC has few users in Western contexts. However, PMEST remains a very worthwhile mnemonic in a range of professional applications.

MODIFYING PUBLISHED CLASSIFICATION SCHEMES

A published classification scheme is a complex package, and whatever scheme is in use for a particular application, there is a good chance that its managers will feel dissatisfied with some aspects, and contemplate modifying it. Reasons may include:

- Providing extra specificity for applying a general classification to a special collection.
- Giving a special collection a shorter base notation.
- Altering the citation order, to bring together distributed relatives (e.g. in DDC in an academic library, to bring together all aspects of Geography, or to arrange literary works by Language – Period – Author instead of DDC's preferred Language – Form – Period – Author).
- To simplify the classification.

Modifications are of two kinds:

- Making use of one or more of the scheme's own published alternatives. For example, DDC has an option that permits literary works to be classified at –8 under each language irrespective of literary form.
- Buying in or developing an unauthorized modification.

In either case, the implications must be carefully considered:

- Many libraries use centrally produced bibliographic records that include DDC and/or LCC class numbers. Resources must be allocated to identify records whose class numbers require modifying, as well as to apply the local modification.
- In the past, many modifications, certainly in British libraries, were made with the objective of providing extra detail to support subject indexing. This function is today done more effectively by other means.
- If there is pressure from users to modify parts of the scheme, for example the better to reflect patterns of academic study, can the objective be met by other means, for example by guiding or user education?
- Are the publishers of the scheme preparing an official revision? Local alterations to individual classes can be overtaken by a future edition of the classification.
- Have identical or similar problems been encountered elsewhere? If so, how have they been addressed?

Some of these implications are managerial, others technical. Modifications to classification schemes were more commonly undertaken a generation or more ago, when published schemes and central bibliographic agencies were both less well developed than today, and when classification (at least in Britain) was expected to do more than arrange books on shelves and was propagated in some quarters almost as a panacea. Today, managers should satisfy themselves that their problem is real, unique, and incapable of resolution by other means before tampering with published schemes.

SPECIAL CLASSIFICATION SCHEMES

The general classification schemes that have been considered so far attempt to encompass all of knowledge. Special classification schemes are to be found in the following environments:

- bibliographies, indexing and abstracting services and their associated databases: for example INSPEC, PsycInfo
- shelf arrangements of special collections. These may be business, industrial and research libraries, specialist government libraries, organizations within the voluntary sector, or special collections within general libraries, especially local studies collections in public libraries. Special classifications for these purposes were often devised with indexing as an additional objective
- shelf arrangement of a particular class within a general classification: for example, Elizabeth Moys's (1982) *Classification Scheme for Law Books*, originally to stand in for LCC's then unpublished class K Law
- thesaurofacets: a thesaurus having its systematic display developed with notation and rules for pre-coordination, enabling it to be used as a shelf classification as well as for post-coordinate retrieval. The eponymous original was the English Electric *Thesaurofacet* of 1969
- records management systems where files are stored in a topic-related order.

In general, schemes aim to cover just one subject area, or to meet the interests of one user group. More specifically, their types include:

- schemes restricted to a conventional subject area or discipline: for example, music, insurance, chemistry
- schemes devised for other associations of topics: for example, local collections, industrial libraries, archives
- schemes for a certain type of user: for example, children, general browsers
- schemes for documents in a particular physical form: for example, pictures, sound recordings; or restricted to a certain form of publication: for example, patents, trade catalogues
- schemes for classifying the subject content of works of the imagination: for

example, fiction, paintings. Conventional classification schemes classify these only by non-subject characteristics.

The rationale for applying a special classification scheme is essentially the same, writ large, as that for modifying a published classification, and the same caveats apply. The heyday of special classification schemes was in the 1960s and 1970s, when (as noted above) general classifications and central bibliographic agencies were relatively undeveloped, and classification was often expected to support an indexing function. Additionally, the great expansion of libraries at that time coincided with the flowering of post-war classification theory. For anyone setting up a special collection, a special classification tailored to its needs seemed the natural choice. Special classifications were made and published in great numbers, and their compilation by library school students was an exercise that was held to be both professionally relevant and academically rigorous, like learning Latin. Since the 1970s many such schemes have fallen by the wayside. Today library or database managers would be well advised to contemplate using an existing special classification only when satisfied that none of the major general classifications is viable, and to construct a special classification as an absolute last resort. The focus of activity has moved: in many cases it will be found that a thesaurus, locally maintained as an authority file, and perhaps based on a published thesaurus, will be all that is required for specific subject retrieval, and a published classification scheme will suffice for shelf arrangement.

SUMMARY

The three major general classification schemes have all been in existence for upwards of 90 years. All have enjoyed some measure of official backing by government agencies, and this is undoubtedly of prime importance to their continuing success. The move over the past generation towards centrally produced records with classmarks centrally applied has led to a lower emphasis today on modifying published schemes. This, together with the virtual demise of the indexing function of classification, has reduced the need for special classification schemes.

REFERENCES AND FURTHER READING

Forest Press publish a range of materials for DDC, including a Dewey Audiocassette, Poster, Bookmark, and Cartoon Booklet. 'Try the Dewey Rap, an 8½-minute audiocassette that uses the solid beat and easy to remember rhyme of rap music to teach the DDC system. Or choose the cartoon Dewey poster for children and its companion bookmark. Also available is "I've Got Your Number", a four-page comic-style Dewey booklet for grades K–5. All are teaching tools that are both educational and entertaining. Bookmarks available in English and Spanish.' For information on these and other products, see the Dewey Web site at <http://www.oclc.org/fp>.

Aitchison, J. (1986) A classification as a source for a thesaurus: the Bibliographic Classification of H. E. Bliss as a source of thesaurus terms and structure. *Journal of Documentation*, **42** (3), 160–81.

Batty, C. D. (1992) *An Introduction to the Twentieth Edition of the Dewey Decimal Classification*. London: Library Association.

Chan, L. M. (1990) The Library of Congress classification system in an online environment. *Cataloging and Classification Quarterly*, **11** (1), 7–25.

Chan, L. M. (1995) Classification, present and future. *Cataloging and Classification Quarterly*, **21** (2), 5–17.

Chan, L. M., Comaromi, J. P., Mitchell, J. S. and Satija, M. A. (1996) *Dewey Decimal Classification: A Practical Guide*, 2nd edn, revised for DDC21. Albany, NY: Forest Press.

Coates, E. J. (1960) *British Catalogue of Music Classification*. London: British National Bibliography.

Comaromi, J. P. (1990) Summation of classification as an enhancement of intellectual access to information in an online environment. *Cataloging and Classification Quarterly*, **11** (1), 99–102.

Dewey Decimal Classification and Relative Index (1996) 21st edition, 4 vols. Albany, NY: Forest Press. (The Introduction in Vol. 1 explains DDC's basic principles and structure; and the Manual in Vol. 4 offers detailed advice on practical problems of implementation.)

Drabenstott, K. M. (1983) Searching and browsing the Dewey Decimal Classification in an online catalog. *Cataloging and Classification Quarterly*, **7**, 37–68.

Foskett, A. C. (1996) *The Subject Approach to Information*, 5th edn. London: Library Association.

Marcella, R. and Newton, R. (1994) *A New Manual of Classification*. Aldershot: Gower.

Miksa, F. M. (1998) *The DDC, the Universe of Knowledge and the Post-Modern Library*. New York: Forest Press.

Mills, J. and Broughton, V. (1977) *Bliss Bibliographic Classification*, 2nd edn, vol. titled *Introduction and Auxiliary Schedules*. London: Butterworths.

Moys, E. (1982) *Moys Classification Scheme for Law Books*, 2nd edn. London: Butterworths.

Satija, M. P. (1990) A critical introduction to the 7th edition (1987) of the Colon Classification. *Cataloging and Classification Quarterly*, **12** (2), 125–38.

Sweeney, R. (1983) Historical studies in documentation: the development of the Dewey Decimal Classification. *Journal of Documentation*, **39** (3), 192–205.

Thomas, A. R. (ed.) (1995) *Classification: Options and Opportunities*. New York: Haworth. (Also published as *Cataloging and Classification Quarterly*, **19** (3/4)).

9 Access points in catalogues and bibliographies

INTRODUCTION

This chapter draws together strands from earlier chapters. Chapter 3 examined document *representation*, including record formats, bibliographic description and the structure of the MARC record. This chapter examines document *access* in the context of catalogues and bibliographies. Access points, called *headings*, in catalogues and bibliographies use a special kind of controlled language: one that is confined to proper names and is governed not by a thesaurus but by cataloguing rules. Cataloguing rules are quite different in structure and appearance from thesauri; and whereas there exists a large range of special purpose thesauri, in most of the world there is just one cataloguing code: the *Anglo-American Cataloguing Rules*, first published in 1967, extensively revised in 1978 (AACR2), and reissued with minor revisions in 1988 and 1998. As was explained in Chapter 3, Part 1 of AACR2 addresses document description. Part 2, entitled 'Headings, Uniform Titles, and References', addresses document access.

This chapter, then, aims to give you a critical awareness of cataloguing rules governing access points. You will learn:

- the functions of catalogues, and the conflict between the 'direct' or 'finding list' and 'collocative' or 'bibliographic' functions
- the structure of Anglo-American Cataloguing Rules
- the 'cases' and 'conditions' approaches to catalogue rule construction
- the principles of main and added entries
- how headings for persons, corporate bodies and uniform titles are structured
- how to make and use references in catalogues.

> **Mystic Meg**
> Mystic Meg's lucky numbers : for life, love and the lottery / illustrations by Caroline Smith. – London
> : Warner, 1996. – 289 p : ill ; 18 cm. – ISBN 0–7515–1875–1
>
> 133.335

Figure 9.1 Sample catalogue entry

WHAT IS A CATALOGUE?

A catalogue is a list of the documents in a library, with the entries representing the documents arranged for access in some systematic order. Catalogues, today, are often held as a computer database, usually called an OPAC. Otherwise, a catalogue may be held as a card catalogue, or on microform, or as a printed book.

A catalogue comprises a number of entries, each of which is an access point for a document. A document may have several entries, or just one.

The entry shown in Figure 9.1 has, like all catalogue entries, three sections:

- heading: this is the access point, the element under which the record is filed
- description, identifying and further characterizing the item
- shelfmark: a mark identifying the physical location of the item within the collection.

The presence or absence of a shelfmark is the most obvious distinguishing feature between a record in a catalogue and one in a bibliography. Bibliographies are not normally limited to items in one collection, and so the records in a bibliography do not carry shelfmarks.

The entry is derived from a MARC record: the same record that was used in Figure 3.8, and is displayed again in Figure 9.2.

In this MARC record, the access points are determined as follows:

100.00:0/0	the 100 field determines a personal author main entry heading.
245.10:0/0	1 in the first indicator position of a 245 (title) field indicates that an entry is required under the title.
900.00:0/0	This field shows that references are required. The first reference is from an inverted form of the author's name. The second is from her real name to her given name.

The MARC record also gives subject access points (field 650), which were described in Chapter 6.

In an author/title catalogue or bibliography, entries for persons, corporate bodies, and titles are filed alphabetically, together with references from unused

```
001   0751518751#
008   970113$as1996$ben$e0$f0$g0$h0$i1$leng$nb$oa$pW#
015.00:0/0  $ab9686568#
021.10:0/0  $a0751518751$bm#
040.00:0/0  $aOX/U-1#
082.00:0/0  $a133.335$c21#
091.00:0/0  $aO504391639#
100.00:0/0  $aMystic Meg#
245.10:0/0  $aMystic Meg's lucky numbers$bfor life, love and the lottery$eillustrations by Caroline
            Smith#
260.00:0/0  $aLondon$bWarner$c1996#
300.00:0/0  $a289 p$bill$c18 cm$epbk#
350.00:0/0  $a£4.99 : Formerly CIP#
650.00:0/0  $aNumerology#
650.00:0/1  $aDivination#
900.00:0/0  $aMeg$fMystic$xSee$aMystic Meg$z100#
900.10:0/1  $aMarkova$hMeg$xSee$aMystic Meg$z100
```

Figure 9.2 MARC record from which the catalogue entry in Figure 9.1 was derived

names or forms of a name. Figure 9.3 shows a mini-catalogue containing just five works, all taken from the example in Figure 3.6. (For simplicity, Level 1 descriptions have been used for the added entries):

FUNCTIONS OF CATALOGUES

As explained in Chapter 6, the functions of a catalogue were systematically defined over a century ago by Charles Ammi Cutter, whose *Rules for a Dictionary Catalogue* (fourth edition, 1904) is one of the seminal works of the information and library profession – and remains highly readable today. Cutter's is the classic analysis, and is still widely accepted, at least as the starting-point for a definition of the functions of a catalogue:

1. **To enable a person to find a book of which either**

    the author
    the title   } **is known**
    the subject

Cutter oversimplifies. No single one of these attributes (except sometimes the title) can be relied on to find a book. In practice two are needed: author + title, or author + subject, or title + subject. With the increased availability of keywords as identifying elements in online searches, it is no longer necessary to know the first word of an author, title or subject heading.

Otherwise, Cutter's basic definition of the catalogue as a finding list to the

247

Castles and palaces map of the British Isles. – Edinburgh: Bartholomew, [198-]. – 1 wall chart: col.;
101 × 75 cm (fold to 26 × 16 cm)   728.810941

English madrigals / The King's Singers. – HMV Classics, c1995. – 1 sound disc. + 1 leaflet. –
Compact disc. – HMV 5 69009 2   782.543

Frink / Edward Lucie-Smith and Elisabeth Frink. – Bloomsbury, 1994. – 138p. – ISBN 0–7475–1572–7.
                                                                                                                                            730.92

Geoff Hamiltons [sic] 3D garden designer. – Computer program. – St Ives, Cambs: GSP, c1998. – 1
computer optical disc; 4¼ in. – System requirements: Windows 95 or higher. – Summary: Plant
encyclopedia and graphic editor producing plans for gardens and parks. – GSPCD125   712.6

Hamilton, Geoff Geoff Hamiltons [sic] 3D garden designer. – Computer program. – GSP, c1998. – 1
computer optical disc; 4¼in. – System requirements: Windows 95 or higher. – GSPCD125   712.6

King's singers English madrigals / The King's Singers. – [London]: HMV Classics, c1995. – 1 sound
disc (73 min.) : digital, stereo.; 4¼in. + 1 leaflet (6 p.: col. ill.; 13 cm.). – (HMV Classics; 145) . –
Compact disc. – "The principal composers in this collection are Thomas Morley and Thomas Weelkes"
– accompanying notes. – HMV 5 69009 2   782.543

Lucie-Smith, Edward Frink : a portrait / Edward Lucie-Smith and Elisabeth Frink. – London:
Bloomsbury, 1994. – 138p, [16]p of plates : ill (some col.).ports ; 22 x 23cm. – Ill. on lining
papers. – ISBN 0–7475–1572–7.   730.92

Frink, Elisabeth Frink / Edward Lucie-Smith and Elisabeth Frink. – Bloomsbury, 1994. – 138p. –
ISBN 0–7475–1572–7.   730.92

Markova, Meg see Mystic Meg

Meg, *Mystic* see Mystic Meg

Morley, Thomas English madrigals / The King's Singers. – HMV Classics, c1995. – 1 sound disc. +
1 leaflet. – Compact disc. – HMV 5 69009 2   782.543

Mystic Meg Mystic Meg's lucky numbers : for life, love and the lottery / illustrations by Caroline
Smith. – London : Warner, 1996. – 289 p : ill ; 18 cm. – ISBN 0–7515–1875–1   133.335

Mystic Meg's lucky numbers. – Warner, 1996. – 289 p. – ISBN 0–7515–1875–1   133.335

Smith, Edward Lucie- see Lucie-Smith, Edward

Weelkes, Thomas English madrigals / The King's Singers. – HMV Classics, c1995. – 1 sound disc.
+ 1 leaflet. – Compact disc. – HMV 5 69009 2   782.543

Figure 9.3 Author/title catalogue

contents of a library or library system still holds good, but with the reservation
that in recent years attitudes to retrieval have become access based rather than
collection based, so that many catalogues range more widely than their own
collections. Also, most library catalogues now include not only books but other
materials as well, particularly audiovisual materials (films, videos, tapes, slides,
etc.); only occasionally are there separate catalogues for these. Catalogues did
not and do not normally list the contents of books or serials. For serials normally
only the title of the serial as a whole is catalogued, and other indexes identify
the individual articles.

The catalogue is primarily a finding list for known-item searches. It gives direct access to a specific document, details of which are known to the searcher, and in the past often constituted a library's administrative record of its stock. This type of catalogue has been variously labelled a *direct* catalogue, *finding-list* catalogue, or *inventory* catalogue. This group of functions is valid for both manual and machine-searchable catalogues. The latter usually offer extended facilities for known-item searches (e.g., author/title acronym; title keywords; control number).

Card catalogues in the UK traditionally only provided title access points for a small proportion of their stock. Many UK catalogues were described as name catalogues, containing entries under authors and under personal names as subjects.

A subject search is not usually a known-item search, unless the subject is the only retrievable fact known about a half-forgotten item ('. . . a slim green volume on fly-fishing, written by J. R. somebody-or-other . . .'). Since Cutter's day, subject and author approaches have come to be contrasted. In the one, the requester usually has a specific item in mind. In the other, there is only an information need, and no specific item or items can be identified until a selection of hopefully relevant items has been found. Catalogue codes after Cutter have excluded the subject approach.

2. To show what the library has: by a given author . . .

This has caused, and continues to cause, endless confusion in catalogues. Many authors use or are known by variants on their name (George Bernard Shaw; Bernard Shaw; G. B. Shaw; even G.B.S.) or even by two or more completely different names (Anthony Eden; Earl of Avon). Cutter implies that all the works of a given author must appear in a catalogue under a single unique and uniform heading.

A catalogue that sets out to fulfil these functions is called a *collocative* or *bibliographic* catalogue. This group of functions has long been recognized as being far subordinate to the *finding-list* function (Figure 9.4). Advances in bibliography over the past century have meant that there is now far less need for a catalogue to provide this kind of service than there was in Cutter's time. However, much networked catalogue copy is produced by national bibliographic agencies (e.g., the British Library), whose primary function is to produce a national bibliography which will correctly and uniquely ascribe each work to its author.

Current cataloguing rules (AACR2) try to reconcile this tension (see the discussion at the end of this chapter); but essentially the bibliographic tail continues to wag the finding-list dog in the majority of our catalogues.

Characteristics of a *direct* or *finding list* catalogue include:

- Authors' names in headings are as found in the item.
- Forenames may be shortened to initials.
- No more descriptive detail is required than is necessary for identification.

Characteristics of a *collocative* or *bibliographic* catalogue include:

- Authors are given a single uniform heading irrespective of the way in which their names appear in catalogued items.
- To avoid the possibility of one heading being used for more than one author, additional distinguishing features may be appended to headings most commonly, unused forenames and dates of birth and death.
- Uniform titles are used to bring together works where different editions, translations etc. have appeared under various titles.
- Descriptive detail may be expanded to include reference to related works.

Figure 9.4 Direct and collocative catalogues

. . . on a given subject . . .

Nearly all catalogues offer a subject approach. 'On a given subject' is a delightfully simple phrase, implying that the subject of a published item can be adequately summed up in a single word or short phrase. This might have sufficed a century ago, but it is ill equipped to express the complexities of current publishing and scholarship. However, such is the weight of tradition that it is largely through Cutter's influence that the subject approaches available in library catalogues today are simplistic, crude and superficial. (Notice, again, that AACR2 does not deal with the subject approach.)

. . . in a given kind of literature.

Catalogues are mostly well equipped to tell the user if a book is prose or poetry, or even (say) German poetry. In other respects (e.g., all books written in German; all humorous books; all biographies) catalogues today are less helpful. The MARC record format does however provide for these (and other) approaches.

3. To assist in the choice of a book:
   #### as to its edition . . .

It is basic to the function of a catalogue to be able to identify each item uniquely, and the need for catalogues to indicate the edition of a work is undisputed. Beyond this, full descriptive cataloguing (AACR2's Levels 2 and 3) provides for considerably more detail than is needed for identification. Such elements as subtitle, series title, physical description (pagination etc.) and (usually) notes serve to characterize rather than to identify, and some library catalogues exclude them as a matter of policy.

... as to its character (literary or topical)

Cutter had annotations in mind when he wrote this. A century ago, libraries kept their stock on closed access, and every item had to be individually requested. Under these conditions, suitably annotated catalogue entries were considered well worth while in giving readers some better idea of what they were requesting, and so saving the time and shoe-leather of library clerks scurrying to and fro in the stacks. Open access and plastic jackets have removed the need to annotate catalogue entries routinely. The practice survived sporadically into the 1960s, but is now confined to special subject lists in libraries, and to catalogue entries for videos, CD-ROMs and similar non-browsable materials.

Access to items of information by the names of the persons responsible for their intellectual content has a long and complex history. The need for a code of practice was powerfully established a century and a half ago by Antonio Panizzi, who as Keeper of Printed Books in the British Museum Library had to persuade the trustees of the need for the complex rules he was proposing to introduce. This he did by sending each of them off separately with copies of the same books, to catalogue them; and on their return he pointed out to them how each of them had done it quite differently.

The problems of personal names, as of corporate bodies, are, as Panizzi told his trustees, essentially two: agreeing on the name to be used, and establishing its entry element and other factors affecting its filing position in an alphabetical list. (In these respects the rules governing the author approach are the standard thesaural rules of vocabulary control extended to proper names.) These problems are as real today as they were in Panizzi's day, though societal and technological changes have emphasized different aspects of them. With personal names, the problems addressed by Panizzi and his successors as compilers of catalogue codes for a full century were predominantly historical: what name to use for a nobleman; how to enter classical writers; whether to use the vernacular or Latinized form of name of writers like Linnaeus, and so on. We today tend to be more occupied with the problems of reconciling all the varied traditions of contemporary personal names in the global society. In the case of factors affecting filing, technology has removed many of the old problems. With keyword access, the filing element of Muhammad Ali or Chiang Kai-shek is no longer an issue.

While the author approach is traditionally associated with library catalogues, listings other than author indexes or catalogues also involve the arranging of entries according to the names of persons or organizations. Telephone directories are an obvious example, and there are many trade directories and similar publications that are alphabetically arranged. Even in this era of machine searching, there is still a significant place for manually searched, alphabetically arranged databases.

ANGLO-AMERICAN CATALOGUING RULES

Two early sets of cataloguing rules have been mentioned so far: Panizzi's British Museum Rules of 1841, and Cutter's *Rules for a Dictionary Catalog*, first published in 1876. Other significant codes of rules have included the Anglo-American Code of 1908 (AA1908), and the American Library Association Code of 1949 (ALA1949).

These codes were all based on the 'cases' approach whereby specific procedures were ordained to deal with specific problems (see Figure 9.5), and cataloguers faced with a problem that was not specifically covered by a rule had to proceed as best they could by analogy – there were even published special interleaved editions of the rules for cataloguers to add their marginal glosses.

The futility of the 'cases' approach was exposed in detail in 1953 by Seymour Lubetzky. He proposed instead a simpler set of 'conditions' or principles to guide the cataloguer. These were debated in detail by an International Conference on Cataloguing Principles held in Paris in 1961 – a landmark in the history of

Early codes, such as AA1908 and ALA1949, provided rules on specific problems case by case, as the following extracts from ALA1949 show: 46. Married women. Enter a married woman under the latest name unless, as specified below, she has consistently written under another name . . .

A. When a woman uses her husband's forenames or initials in place of her own . . . enter under her own name . . .

B. Omit the name of an earlier husband in the heading unless it continues to appear in the form of name which the author customarily uses. (An exception to an exception!)

C. Enter a married woman who continues to write under her maiden name under the maiden name . . .

D. Enter a woman who remarries but continues to write under the name of a former husband . . .

E. When a divorced woman resumes her maiden name, enter under the maiden name . . .

F. Compound names consisting of a combination of the surnames of husband and wife are frequently found . . .

What was not appreciated was that all these specifics, and many others (rule 47 has two pages on Saints; followed by Popes, Patriarchs, Cardinals, Ecclesiastical princes, Bishops, and more besides) are simply instances of the condition of a name that has changed. The circumstances are irrelevant, and need not be listed. AACR2 recognizes the condition of having to choose among different names (rule 22.2), and despatches the problem in just ten lines.

Figure 9.5 The 'cases' approach to catalogue code compilation

universal bibliographic control. The code which eventually emerged – the Anglo-American Cataloguing Rules of 1967 (AACR1) – is based on the 'conditions' approach. The Anglo-American Cataloguing Rules received a thorough revision in 1978 (AACR2), and was reissued with minor revisions in 1988 (AACR2R) and 1998. This last is available in print (AACR2R2) and CD-ROM (AACR2e). A Concise AACR2 is also published. AACR2R2 incorporates a number of corrections and changes authorized by the Joint Steering Committee of AACR since the 1988 revision. (The acronym becomes more and more unwieldy with each successive issue. We shall refer simply to AACR2.)

STRUCTURE OF AACR2

Throughout this section, Concise AACR2 equivalent rules are given in italics. This section will be easier to understand if a copy of AACR2 is to hand.

The rules follow the sequence of cataloguers' operations, and proceed throughout from general to specific. The sequence is:

- *Description*: The first step is to create a description based on the chief source of information (e.g., title page) of the item being catalogued. The description will normally contain enough information to explain the access points (headings) under which it is filed.
- *Choice of access points* thus follows description. An access point may be a person, a corporate body, or a title. A work is likely to have more than one access point, typically two or three.
- *Headings*. The cataloguer may have to choose between different names, or variant forms of the same name, or between different entry (filing) elements for any of the chosen access points.
- *References*. Finally, references are needed for the guidance of catalogue users who approach the catalogue under a name or filing element other than the one that has been used.

CHOICE OF ACCESS POINTS

The concept of the access point belongs to manually searched indexes, and is arguably irrelevant to databases with search systems allowing keyword access. In manual indexes where every access point requires physical space, it is economically only possible to list a work in a limited number of places – very seldom more than five or six. The general principle is to provide access points under the significant persons and corporate bodies, and under titles, shown in the description.

One of these access points is traditionally designated the main entry, and all other approaches are by definition added entries. The original concept of main entry was partly administrative, partly intellectual. Administratively, the main entry in a card catalogue might carry 'tracings' – notes at the foot, or on the reverse, of the card, showing where the added entries were filed, so that the catalogue could be properly updated whenever a work was discarded or its catalogue entry amended. Intellectually, main entry was selected on the basis of the author 'chiefly responsible for the creation of the intellectual or artistic content of a work' (21.1A1). This principle is extended to works of corporate bodies. For the great majority of items, the main entry consists of a single personal author, which in a catalogue entry is followed immediately by the title – which follows our normal everyday practice of citing a work by its author and title.

The idea of main entry is thus a deep-rooted one, even though there is general acceptance that it has little relevance to modern cataloguing practice, and survives largely through being built into the structure of the MARC record. In most libraries, however, the main entry heading determines the shelving position of an item, as some kind of abbreviation (e.g., a Cutter number) forms part of the shelfmark.

Most of Chapter 21 (i.e., 21.1–21.28) (21–28) is concerned with establishing Main Entry and distinguishing it from Added Entries. Do not overlook sections 29 and 30 (29), which deal specifically with added entries, as the rules for main entry include instructions for added entries only where these are specifically covered by the rule.

GENERAL RULE: 21.1 (23)

Main entry under a personal author or corporate body has to be justified on criteria of responsibility for the existence of the work; otherwise main entry is under title.

WORKS OF SINGLE RESPONSIBILITY: 21.4 (19)

Single person   21.4A (24A)
Single corporate body   21.4B (24B)
Problems and special cases   21.4C–D

Personal authors are straightforward to define; corporate bodies ('no body to kick, no soul to be damned') are more elusive. AACR2 defines a corporate body as 'an organization or a group of persons that is identified by a particular name and that acts, or may act, as an entity'. The designation of corporate *author* is studiously avoided. Instead, works are described as 'emanating from' one or more corporate bodies – the desperate verb, with its connotations of spiritualism and drains, warns of the many hair-splitting and sometimes arbitrary distinctions that are inevitably associated with corporate bodies. The general intention of rule 21.1B (main entry under corporate body) is clear enough: works dealing with the policies, procedures, operations or resources of the body, or which record or report its collective thought or activity. The specific rules on the other hand are fraught with provisos and special cases, making their consistent application very difficult in practice.

Here, as throughout AACR2, the examples are essential reading. They show how the problem or condition set out in the rule is applied to individual cases.

WORKS OF UNKNOWN OR UNCERTAIN AUTHORSHIP, OR BY UNNAMED GROUPS: 21.5 (23C)

Main entry is under title. The second example under 21.5A (A Memorial to Congress against an increase of duties on importations/by citizens of Boston and vicinity) illustrates the definition of a corporate body: the group acted as an entity, but is not identified by a particular name. (Some earlier codes tried to invent a name: Boston. Citizens.)

WORKS OF SHARED RESPONSIBILITY: 21.6 (25)

Shared responsibility is where two or more persons (or occasionally corporate bodies) have performed the same kind of activity. In cases where principal responsibility is indicated (usually by layout or typography), main entry is straightforward. Otherwise, an arbitrary rule is applied: if there are two or three contributors, main entry is under the first named, with added entries for the second and/or third. If there are four or more authors, main entry is under title, with an added entry for the first named person or body only.

Citation practice is to name two authors, e.g., Aitchison, Jean and Gilchrist, Alan. Headings of this kind are not authorized by AACR2 and are not found in modern catalogues. The main entry would be under Aitchison, Jean with an added entry under Gilchrist, Alan.

COLLECTIONS, AND WORKS PRODUCED UNDER THE DIRECTION OF AN EDITOR: 21.7 (26)

Editors of works consisting of contributions by different hands, and compilers of collections, are not regarded as having sufficient responsibility for their works to warrant main entry. In all cases, main entry is under title, with an added entry for the editor. If, however, a collection does not have a collective title, then main entry is made under the heading appropriate to the first contribution.

MIXED RESPONSIBILITY: 21.8–21.28 (27)

Notice the spread of rules; unusually, AACR2 takes a case-by-case approach in this section. Mixed responsibility covers works to which different persons or bodies have contributed different kinds of activity. Two types of mixed responsibility are distinguished: works that are modifications of other works (e.g., adaptations, revisions, and translations); and new works (e.g., collaborations between artist and writer, interviews, and – wondrously, but such works exist – communications 'presented as having been received from a spirit' through a medium). Principal responsibility is usually assigned to the person or body (or spirit!) named first. However, at 21.10A covering adaptations of texts, main entry is under the heading for the adapter, to the annoyance of children's librarians everywhere.

RELATED WORKS: 21.28 (28)

We now come to the sixth and last condition of authorship. Related works are separately catalogued works that have a relationship to another work. These include continuations and sequels, supplements, indexes, concordances, scenarios and screenplays, opera librettos, subseries, and special numbers from serials.

A related work is entered under its own appropriate heading, with an added entry under the work to which it is related. In some cases 'name-title' added entries are prescribed. These consist of the author and the title of the related work, for example,

Homer. Odyssey

for an adaptation that has a different main entry heading and title.

ADDED ENTRIES: 1.29–21.30 (29)

The rule for added entries consolidates and expands on all the above. 'Make an added entry under the heading for a person or corporate body or under a title if some users of the catalogue might look under that heading or title rather than under the main entry heading or title.' Added entries are to be applied judiciously and sparingly – the rules are almost as much concerned with when not to make an added entry as when to make one – there is though a splendid catch-all at

21.29D: 'If ... an added entry is required under a heading or title other than those prescribed in 21.30, make it.'

The specific rules at 21.30 cover:

- Two or more persons or corporate bodies involved. These include collaborators, editors, compilers, revisers, etc.; performers; and other related persons or bodies, such as the addressee of a collection of letters, or a museum where an exhibition is held. Corporate bodies warrant an added entry unless they function solely as distributor or manufacturer. Even so, an added entry is made for a publisher whose responsibility for the work extends beyond that of publishing.
- Two or more persons or bodies sharing a function. Entries are made under all of them if there are no more than three. If there are four or more, an added entry is made only under the first.
- Related works (which may need a name/title heading).
- Other relationships if needed, unless the relationship between the name and the work is that of a subject. The example given is that of an art collection from which reproductions of art works have been taken.
- Titles (with a few exceptions); today's automated catalogues will provide these automatically.
- And if thought appropriate: translators, illustrators, series title, and analytical added entries (entries for separate works contained within the item being catalogued: a collection of plays for example) guidance is given on this.

HEADINGS FOR PERSONS

Chapter 22 (31–43) is set out step by step. First, a choice may have to be made between different names by which the same person may be known. Second, once the name has been decided, the entry element must be decided. Finally, it may be necessary to make additions to names, to clarify the person's identity or to distinguish the name from other similar names.

CHOICE OF NAME: 22.1–22.3 (31–32)

Many people use more than one name. They may be a completely different names, as with authors who change their names on marriage, or who use pseudonyms, or are known to their friends and to posterity by a soubriquet or nickname, as with the Venetian painter Jacopo Robusti, whose father was a dyer and so was called Tintoretto. Or the names may be variants, as with Tony (for Anthony) Blair, or Ovid (Publius Ovidius Naso), or W(illiam) Somerset

Maugham. The general rule is to use 'the name by which a person is commonly known from the chief sources of information of works by that person issued in his or her language'; otherwise from reference sources in his or her language or country.

The principle that a person can appear under only one form of heading is broken only in the case of pseudonyms (22.2B). This complex rule tries to allow for the fact that nobody can be certain how many authors are lurking in catalogues under one or more pseudonyms (Stendhal is said to have used 71). Established writers may have two or more separate bibliographic identities, as with Charles Luttwidge Dodgson the mathematician and Lewis Carroll the author of *Alice in Wonderland*; AACR2 allows such writers to retain their separate identities. In the case of contemporary authors, the basis for the heading is the name appearing in each work, with connecting references where two or more names are known to belong to the same person.

ENTRY ELEMENT: 22.4–22.11 (33–39)

Once the name has been established, it is time to decide on the order of the components of the name in the heading. The general rule is to follow national usage, unless a person's preference is known to be different. In most cases the surname is the entry element. Problems occur with compound surnames (Lloyd George) and names with prefixes (if Van Gogh, why not Van Beethoven?). AACR2 lists the commoner national usages; the International Federation of Library Associations (IFLA, 1996) publication *Names of Persons* may be consulted for others.

The section tails off in an entertaining miscellany, including persons who are to be entered under a title of nobility (Lord Byron becomes Byron, George Gordon Byron, *baron*); under a given name (Leonardo, *da Vinci*); or under initials etc., or under a phrase: the lottery winner's friend Mystic Meg's name should surely have been inverted according to 22.11B; and the 1920s book *Memoirs of a Flapper/by One*, is solemnly entered under the heading One.

ADDITIONS TO NAMES: 22.12–22.20 (40–43)

In some instances AACR2 calls for additions to names. They may be needed for identification purposes (Francis, *of Assisi, Saint*; Moses, *Grandma*; Elizabeth I, *Queen of England*; or even Beethoven, Ludwig van *(Spirit)*). Often though they serve the collocative function, distinguishing names that would otherwise be identical (Smith, John, 1924– ; Smith, John, 1837–1896); Murray, Gilbert (Gilbert George Aimé); Murray, Gilbert (Gilbert John). There are also a number of special rules for names in certain languages, which cover a small number of Asiatic languages only. *Names of Persons* examines a wider range.

REFERENCES TO PERSONAL NAME HEADINGS

References generally are used to make different approaches to a heading. In this they differ from added entries, which make different approaches to a work. References are made from a form of name that might reasonably be sought to the form of name that has been chosen as a heading. References therefore should not be made to non-existent headings, and there must be a mechanism (normally a function of the authority file: see Chapter 13) to record under every heading which references have been made to it.

Chapter 22 gives some specific instances of the use of references. The conventional symbol x introduces the name from which reference is to be made, thus

Leonardo, *da Vinci*
  x Vinci, Leonardo da

is an instruction to make the reference

Vinci, Leonardo da *see* Leonardo, *da Vinci*.

References are treated in full in Chapter 26. *See* references are made as necessary from different names, from different forms of a name, and from different entry elements of a name. Two examples of each type follow:

Barrett, Elizabeth *see* Browning, Elizabeth Barrett
Konigsberg, Allen Stewart *see* Allen, Woody

Ovidius Naso, Publius *see* Ovid
Nanaponika, Thera *see* Nyanaponika, Thera

Dr Seuss *see* Seuss, *Dr*
James, Anne Scott- *see* Scott-James, Anne

In the case of pseudonyms, *see also* references are made to link the different headings used for the same person, for example:

Innes, Michael *see also* Stewart, J.I.M.
Stewart, J.I.M. *see also* Innes, Michael

A variant is the explanatory reference, typically for contemporary authors appearing under several pseudonyms:

Plaidy, Jean. *For this author under other names, see*
  Carr, Philippa, Ford, Elbur, Holt, Victoria, Kellow, Kathleen, Tate, Ellalice

CORPORATE BODIES

Before rules for headings for corporate bodies are given, AACR2 has a short chapter on geographic names. Geographic names are not used as such, but may constitute, or be added to, a heading for a corporate body. Specifically, they are used:

- as the names of governments and communities
- to distinguish between corporate bodies with the same name
- to add to some corporate names (particularly names of conferences).

They have their own chapter in AACR2 because of their pervasive nature. The chapter is, however, little more than an appendix to Chapter 24 (Corporate bodies) (45–47). The rules are uncomplicated (but note the international emphasis: country is almost always added to the names of places smaller than a country).

AACR2's definition of a corporate body was given earlier in this chapter: 'an organization or a group of persons that is identified by a particular name and that acts, or may act, as an entity'. From a cataloguer's viewpoint, the principal differences between a person and a corporate body are:

- Persons are unique and indivisible. A corporate body may have subordinate or related bodies whose names require the parent body's name for proper identification. (This can include government departments.)
- A person who changes their name remains the same person. Change of name in a corporate body normally denotes a change of purpose or scope, so that the body under its new name is a different body from the old.

ESTABLISHING THE NAME OF A CORPORATE BODY

Rule 24.1 (43), the General rule – 'Enter a corporate body directly under the name by which it is commonly identified' – was quite revolutionary when introduced in 1967. The examples are worth studying by anyone involved with manually searched indexes, since 'directly' is rigorously applied and often conflicts with telephone books and other everyday reference tools. Thus Colin Buchanan and Partners files under letter C, not at any inversion of the name under B; the University of Oxford is to be sought under U and not O; and so on.

The name by which a body is 'commonly identified' is to be determined if possible from items issued by the body in its language. When this condition does not apply, reference sources (including works written about the body) are to be used.

The rules for variant names broadly follow personal authors. For the most part they prescribe what most people would intuitively choose:

> Unesco
> not   United Nations Educational, Scientific and Cultural Organization
> Society of Friends
> not   Quakers, or Religious Society of Friends

Additions, in 24.4 (45), are prescribed for names which do not convey the idea of a corporate body. Study the examples: Bounty *(Ship)* and Apollo 11 *(Spacecraft)* help to illustrate the breadth of definition of a corporate body. Ships have a name and may act as an entity – the Bounty's logbook is a famous example. (Spacecraft, one assumes, qualify only if they are manned?) Rock groups and the like often require this kind of parenthetical qualifier, and one could endlessly argue the toss over whether Spice Girls conveys the idea of a corporate body as opposed to, say, Oasis.

The rule prescribing additions for bodies with identical or similar names takes us firmly into the field of the bibliographic catalogue. In the main, it is place names that are to be added. If the mind balks at some of the detail, such as the presumed documented existence of three different Red Lion Hotels in three different British towns all called Newport, it is as well to remember that much of the cataloguing envisaged by these rules can be quite specialized – the local studies departments of public libraries, for example.

Omissions, 24.5, do not require much attention; in the main, they codify common-sense omissions of initial articles, citations of honour, and terms indicating incorporation etc.

There are a number of special rules prescribing additions for specific types of body: governments and conferences are the most important of these. Additions for Governments, 24.6, are needed when governments at different levels share the same name, as with New York city and New York state. In the case of conferences, 24.7 (46), AACR2 comes very close to prescribing a 'structured' form of heading. We are instructed to omit from the name any indications of number, frequency or year(s). These are to be tacked on to the end of the heading, together with the date and location of the conference. The resulting headings take the following pattern:

> International Congress of Neurovegetative Research *(20th: 1990: Tokyo, Japan)*

How does one retrieve such a heading? With keyword access all is well; but in manually searched indexes, the slightest error in transcription ('Congress' misremembered as 'Conference', or even the substitution of 'on' for 'of') can make headings of this type well-nigh irretrievable. Experienced searchers faced with

261

this type of situation will have other search strategies to hand: a keyword search if one is available, or the subject approach, or better still access to *Boston Spa Conferences*.

SUBORDINATE AND RELATED BODIES

These are to be entered directly under their own name whenever possible, 24.12 (47): that is to say, when the name does not necessarily imply subordination. Thus the Bodleian Library belongs to the University of Oxford, but it is to be entered directly under its name, even though the format may be inconsistent with other university libraries.

Bodies to be entered subordinately, 24.13 (48) include:

- a body that is subordinate by definition: e.g., Department, Division, Committee: provided it cannot be identified without the name of the higher body
- a name that is so general that it requires the parent body for proper identification
- a name that does not convey the idea of a corporate body
- university faculties, institutes, etc., where the name simply denotes a field of study
- a name that includes the entire name of the higher or related body.

As always, AACR2R's examples should be studied carefully.

In many cases with subordinate bodies there is a hierarchy of subordination. Where there are three or more levels of subordination, cataloguers are instructed to omit intermediate elements in the hierarchy unless this might result in ambiguity. This rule had some purpose in manually compiled and searched indexes, in preventing headings from becoming unnecessarily long. However, it necessitates some complex references (as well as being difficult to apply consistently); and in the context of machine retrieval, it has been argued that it would be simpler either to use the subordinate body on its own as a heading, or to set down the complete hierarchy once and for all, allowing each searcher to home in on whichever part of it they wish.

GOVERNMENT BODIES AND OFFICIALS

Governments form one of the most important categories of corporate body. Governments operate at many levels: international, national, regional, local. Mostly, a government is entered under its conventional name, which is the geographic name of the area governed, 24. Essentially governments are treated in the same way as any other corporate body, and the Concise AACR2 does just that; but because of their complexity the full AACR2 devotes a section, 24.17–24.26, to them.

National governments have three traditional areas of responsibility: the legislature, for which the agency is the country's legislative body, e.g., Parliament, Congress; the executive, which consists of the government and its various departments, ministries, etc., and also its armed forces; and the judiciary, or courts of law. Governments also have ambassadors and other agencies to represent their interests abroad. Much of the complexity of headings for governments derives from the tendency of modern government to pervade and regulate more and more areas of everyday life. The range of government agencies today is such that AACR's general rule, 24.17, and default condition is that a body created or controlled by a government is to be entered directly under its name, with a reference from the agency as a subheading of the name of the government, thus:

Heading: Arts Council of Great Britain
Reference: Great Britain. Arts Council *see* Arts Council of Great Britain

The agencies performing the central functions of government are entered as a subheading of the name of the government according to rule 24.18, which somewhat paradoxically forms an exception to the general rules for governments. The proliferation of government agencies today is such that an official publication is to be assumed *not* to be concerned with one of the central functions of government. Rule 24.18 lists 11 types of government agencies to be entered subordinately. As a further exception, there are special rules for government officials, legislative bodies, constitutional conventions, courts, the armed forces, embassies and consulates, and delegations to international or intergovernmental bodies – all of which are entered subordinately. Where there are degrees of subordination, the general rules – 24.14, elaborated at 24.19 – apply. The special rules have some exceptions, however: the heading for the US Senate is United States. *Congress. Senate* and not simply United States. *Senate*; a similar construction is prescribed for other legislative bodies, and for armed forces.

AACR2 also devotes three pages to special rules for religious bodies and officials – 24.27.

REFERENCES TO HEADINGS FOR CORPORATE BODIES

The principles for making references to corporate bodies are similar to those for personal names. The following are some typical instances, covering different names, different forms of a name, and different entry elements:

263

Deutschland (Bundesrepublik) *see* Germany (Federal Republic)
Friends, Society of *see* Society of Friends
International Business Machines Corporation *see* IBM
Quakers *see* Society of Friends
Religious Society of Friends see Society of Friends
Roman Catholic Church *see* Catholic Church
RSPB *see* Royal Society for the Protection of Birds
United Nations Educational, Scientific and Cultural Organization *see*
  Unesco

Subordinate bodies lead to complications not found with personal names:

University of Oxford. *Bodleian Library see* Bodleian Library

and for more than one degree of subordination:

Great Britain. *Department of Energy. Energy Efficiency Office*
  see Great Britain. *Energy Efficiency Office*

Change of name in corporate bodies can give rise to more insidious complications:

Great Britain. *Board of Education*
  see also
Great Britain. *Ministry of Education*
Great Britain. *Department of Education and Science*
Great Britain. *Department for Education and Employment*

with similar references under the three other bodies. In such cases an explanatory reference is often recommended, giving the dates between which each name applied. Rule 26.3C has some even more complex examples.

UNIFORM TITLES: 25 (51–55)

Uniform titles are filing titles supplied by the cataloguer, and are used optionally. They have two functions:

1. To bring together entries for different editions, translations etc. of the same work, appearing under different titles.
2. To provide identification for a work when the title by which it is known differs from the title of the item in hand.

Function (1) is typical of collocative catalogues. It belonged originally to manually searched files: a uniform title such as

Dickens, Charles
[Martin Chuzzlewit] The life and adventures of Martin Chuzzlewit

could be retrieved electronically by keyword access even without the uniform title. Function (2) however is a finding-list function and is valid irrespective of the mode of searching. A person searching for an edition of Swift's *Gulliver's Travels* could conceivably have problems retrieving this without its uniform title:

Swift, Jonathan
[Gulliver's travels] Travels into several remote nations of the world / by Lemuel Gulliver

and a work such as this:

[Arabian nights] The book of the thousand and one nights

could be completely irretrievable.

There are a number of special categories of works that might carry a uniform title. They include:

- *Collections*: a uniform title may be used to collocate complete or partial collections of an author's works, where these appear under different titles; for example:

Maugham, W. Somerset
[Selections] The Somerset Maugham pocket book

Specific uniform titles are prescribed for use as appropriate, for example: [Works], [Poems], [Short stories], [Poems. Selections], [Short stories. Spanish. Selections].

- *Sacred scriptures*. Uniform titles for the more logical arrangement and retrieval of the Bible and other sacred scriptures are well established. The method is reminiscent of subject retrieval with its fixed citation order:

Bible. Testament. Book or group of books. Language. Version. Year.
For example:
Bible. N.T. Corinthians. English. Authorized.
Bible. English. Revised Standard. 1959.

- *Music*. Music, especially classical works, often requires a uniform title as the international nature of music publishing often results in editions of works having title pages in a variety of languages. They are best explained by examples:

Handel, George Frideric
[Messiah. Vocal score]
Rossini, Gioacchino
[Barbiere di Siviglia. Largo al factotum]
Schubert, Franz
[Quintets, violins (2), viola, violoncelli (2), D. 956, C major]

DISCUSSION

CITATIONS, CATALOGUE ENTRIES AND METADATA

This chapter opened by referring to earlier chapters where document representation was described. AACR2 is unusual in its careful separation of representation (description) and access. While Chapter 3 did not discuss document access as such, it did discuss citations, where the document representation has its own built-in access point. Also, in Chapter 2 we looked at metadata, a mechanism for both representing and accessing networked electronic resources. Citations, catalogues and metadata have evolved through quite different traditions. Figure 9.6 summarizes some points of similarity and contrast.

DIRECT VERSUS COLLOCATIVE IN AACR2

Showing the relationship of an item with others is complex and in some respects controversial in the context of cataloguing. A catalogue in its basic finding list function focuses on the individual item. Two works by the same author are clearly related to the extent that they are products of the same brain. Queen Victoria, after meeting the author of *Alice in Wonderland*, expressed the desire to be given a copy of his next book, and was presented to her disappointment with a mathematical treatise. AACR2 has relaxed the bibliographic unit of authorship to the extent of allowing both Carroll, Lewis and Dodgson, Charles Luttwidge as headings. Within the description, relationships may be shown in many ways. One kind of relationship that must be shown is one that the author considers important enough to incorporate into the title or statement of responsibility: this covers many works of mixed responsibility, 21.8–21.27, as well as those falling under the rule for related works, 21.28. Any edition statement implies a relationship with another edition; any series statement is a clear indication that the item has siblings. The Notes area is a catch-all for relationships which cannot be expressed within the body of the description – that is, which do not appear in the chief source of information. Rule 1.7 has several examples of notes indicating continuations, translations, adaptations, and the like. The

Citations	Catalogue entries	Metadata
Based on tradition of scholarly acknowledgement of predecessors' work.	Strongly influenced by tradition of historical bibliography: the identification of individual copies of hand-printed books. Often based on information used in compiling national bibliographies.	Recently developed from first principles.
Single entry only, under author or author substitute.	Multiple entries for responsible persons, corporate bodies, titles; one of these being designated the *main entry* and the rest *added entries*. In an OPAC these produce a range of access points. Also include *references* from different approaches to names.	One record with embedded keys to provide multiple access points
May include both monographs and papers that form part of a larger unit (journal articles, conference papers, etc.)	Items forming part of a larger unit are excluded (with few exceptions)	Indexer defines unit or document
Form short, single-purpose lists in both manual and machine-held files	In manual files, form long, multi-purpose lists.	Access is via search keys.
Do not normally give physical locations, but should include enough information to enable an item to be traced or a resource to be accessed.	Give locations (shelfmark)	Give location based on URL.
Good quality control. Inclined towards academic publications, often reports of research by individuals or small teams.	Quality mediated by considerations of commercial publishing and acquisition by libraries.	Material accepted on 'common carrier' basis. Some validated material, but no systematic quality control. Includes promotional material and worse.
Representation and access combined. Give sufficient information for identification purposes only	Representation and access separated. Identify and may often additionally characterize, as an aid to selection	Representation and access combined. Direct access to resource

Figure 9.6 Citations, catalogue entries and metadata

danger of this is the implied invitation for cataloguers to turn themselves into literary detectives, and the question to be asked is, does this information add anything to the usefulness of the catalogue? Is the fact that *The Second Sex* is a translation of *Le deuxième sexe* something that a person needs to be told in the catalogue, or can they be left to discover it for themselves? If the cataloguer can find the information within the item, then so can the reader.

AACR2 maintains an uneasy compromise between the direct and bibliographic functions of catalogues. The various rules that point to either function are as follows.

Rules pointing to a direct catalogue

- Access points are to be determined from the chief source of information (21.0B).
- The heading for a person is based on the name by which he or she is commonly known, as determined by the chief source of information (22.1).
- Persons who have established two or more bibliographic entities under different names may be entered under different names (22.2B).
- The heading for a corporate body is based on the name by which it is commonly identified (24.1).

Rules pointing to a collocative catalogue

- Parts of a full Description, such as Series (1.6) and edition and history notes (1.7B7) link the description to related works.
- Persons known by more than one name (other than a pseudonym) are to be entered under a single uniform heading, which may differ from that appearing in the chief source of information (22.2).
- Additions are prescribed to headings for persons in order to distinguish identical names: these may be dates (22.17), fuller forms of the name (22.18) or distinguishing terms (22.19).
- Where variant names of a corporate body are found, one of them is chosen as the basis for the heading (24.2–24.3).
- Additions are prescribed to names of corporate bodies to distinguish two or more bodies having the same name (24.4[en24.11).
- Uniform titles provide 'the means for bringing together all catalogue entries for a work when various manifestations (e.g. editions, translations) have appeared under various titles' (25.1).

In practice, there is a greater polarization than is immediately apparent. On the one hand, some national bibliographic agencies routinely make additions to names (dates of birth, expansion of forenames), even where these are not immediately required to distinguish identical headings. (It is cheaper to do this than to amend an existing heading when a conflict does arise.) On the other hand, the accuracy of any given catalogue is only as good as its authority file, and in particular the diligence with which this is applied. Failure to recognize an existing heading, the addition or omission of a distinguishing date, or the slightest variation in spacing or punctuation, will in most retrieval systems result in the same person appearing under more than one heading. Not surprisingly, there is a well-established lobby against the application of any kind of rules to names. While this is mainly to be found among the abstracting houses, it has also been suggested, with increasing plausibility as the technology improves, that it is possible to create working catalogues based on records derived directly from optically scanned title pages – the ultimate negation of the collocative function. In 1953 Lubetzky asked the question, Is this rule necessary? The question of the future may well be, Are any rules necessary?

THE OUT-OF-DATENESS OF CATALOGUING RULES

A set of cataloguing rules, like any other code of practice, depends on there being a well-established set of procedures that can be codified with general agreement. Codes are thus inevitably backward-looking, and liable to be over-taken by events the moment they are published. AA1908 was implicitly designed with printed book catalogues in mind, and was published just at the time when card catalogues were taking over. Both editions of AACR have been similarly afflicted. The MARC record format is built round cataloguing rules governing the production of card catalogues, and was first implemented in 1968, the year after the publication of AACR1. AACR2 and MARC are virtually two sides of the same coin, and AACR2 is essentially a code designed for manually searched indexes with their immensely long, static lists – and was published just as the first OPACs were coming into use. Twenty years on, not only do we still lack a set of rules designed explicitly for machine searchable bibliographic databases, but there is no consensus on the desirability or otherwise of developing AACR2 in that direction. The awful contemplation of having to restructure MARC and amend millions of existing MARC records is a powerful deterrent to radical revision.

There is movement for change, however, and already much groundwork has been done in redefining the principles of AACR according to the entity-relation-ship model. Other themes can be identified: for example the need to resolve the 'content versus carrier' question: whether cataloguing should be based on the item in hand (or on screen), or on the more generalized concept of the work. Whatever the future may hold, AACR2 has without doubt been highly successful both as a set of rules and as an instrument of universal bibliographic control. It is based on clear principles: treating all media equally; the separation of document representation (description) from document access; and Lubetzky's conditions approach. It is clearly set out, and lucidly written. It is the first truly international code, accepted and applied throughout the world, having been translated into 18 languages and forming the basis for other codes in use today. It is the first code to be hospitable to all types of communication media. It is easy, when censuring it for what it does not do – perhaps may never do – to forget its massive achievement.

SUMMARY

Headings in catalogues are in essence controlled vocabularies applied to classes of one. Even more than the general classification schemes, catalogues are encumbered with the detritus of well over a century of practice, and their rules remain in many respects Byzantine. In understanding the complexities of catalogue rules, an analytical approach, taking each problem a step at a time, yields the best results. The tension between the direct and collocative functions remains as strong as ever, and an understanding of these functions is fundamental to the appreciation of the role of catalogues and of the author approach generally.

REFERENCES AND FURTHER READING

Baughman, B. and Svenonius, E. (1984) AACR2: main entry free? *Cataloging and Classification Quarterly*, **5** (1), 1–15.

Boll, J. (1990) The future of AACR2 (in the OPAC environment). *Cataloging and Classification Quarterly*, **12** (1), 3–34.

Bryant, P. (1980) Progress in documentation: the catalogue. *Journal of Documentation*, **36** (2), 133–63.

Buckland, M. K. (1988) Bibliography, library records, and the redefinition of the library catalog. *Library Resources and Technical Services*, **32** (4), 299–311.

Carpenter, M. and Svenonius, E. (eds) (1986) *Foundations of Cataloging: A Sourcebook.* Littleton, CO: Libraries Unlimited.

Cutter, C. A. (1904) *Rules for a Dictionary Catalog*, 4th edn. Washington, DC: Government Printing Office (and later reprints).

Fattahi, R. (1995) Anglo-American Cataloguing Rules in the online environment: a literature review. *Cataloging and Classification Quarterly*, **20** (2), 25–50.

Gorman, M. (1978) The Anglo-American Cataloging Rules, second edition. *Library Resources and Technical Services*, **22** (3), 209–26.

IFLA (1996) *Names of Persons: National Usages for Entry in Catalogues*, 4th edn. Munich and London: K. G. Saur.

Lubtezky, S. (1953) *Cataloging Rules and Principles.* Washington, DC: Library of Congress.

Madison, O. M. A. (1992) The role of the name main-entry heading in the online environment. *Serials Librarian*, **22** (3/4), 371–91.

Maxwell, R. with Maxwell, M.(1997) *Maxwell's Handbook for AACR2R: Explaining and Illustrating the Anglo-American Cataloguing Rules and 1993 Amendments.* Chicago: American Library Association.

Oddy, P. (1996) *Future Libraries, Future Catalogues.* London: Library Association.

Piggott, M. (1988) *A Topography of Cataloguing: Showing the Most Important Landmarks, Communications and Perilous Places.* London: Library Association.

Piggott, M. (1990) *The Cataloguer's Way through AACR2: From Document Receipt to Document Retrieval.* London: Library Association.

Shoham, S. and Lazinger, S. S. (1991) The no-main-entry principle and the automated catalog. *Cataloging and Classification Quarterly*, **12** (3/4), 51–67.

Smiraglia, R. P. (ed.) (1992) *Origins, Content, and Future of AACR2 Revised.* Chicago: American Library Association. (Particularly: Gorman, M. After AACR2R: the future of the Anglo-American Cataloguing Rules, pp. 89–94; also responses, pp. 95–131).

Swanson, E. (1990) Choice and form of access points according to AACR2. *Cataloging and Classification Quarterly*, **11** (3/4), 35–6

Weihs, J. (ed.) (1998) *The Principles and Future of AACR: Proceedings of the International Conference on the Principles and Future Development of AACR2, Toronto, Ontario, Canada, October 23–25, 1997.* Ottawa: Canadian Library Association. For later developments, see the Joint Steering Committee's Web site: <http://www.nlc-bnc.ca/jsc/index.htm>.

Winke, R. C. (1993) Discarding the main entry in an online cataloging environment. *Cataloging and Classification Quarterly*, **16** (1), 53–70.

Part IV
Systems

10 System contexts for knowledge organization

INTRODUCTION

This chapter introduces the range of different types of systems or technologies in which the approaches to knowledge organization, which have been explored in the previous few chapters, are employed. All such systems offer access to databases. Some of these databases are bibliographic, while others are document databases. Systems, such as the online search services, the Internet and online public access catalogues offer access to a range of documents and databases of different types. At the end of this chapter you will:

- be familiar with the wide range of different contexts in which knowledge organization and information retrieval is important
- understand the nature of and the facilities offered by the online search services
- be aware of the role that CD-ROM plays in access to information
- understand the nature and role of online public access catalogues.

PUBLIC ACCESS SYSTEMS

This chapter reviews a number of types of systems that are available to support users in accessing information. All of these systems can be described as public access systems. Online search services offer access to a collection of databases and documents. CD-ROM is essentially a different type of distribution media for information products. Databases and documents can be distributed to consumer markets on CD-ROM, or alternatively, CD-ROM databases can be networked within an organization or library. Online public access catalogues are a unique type of system, which developed from the library catalogue function of providing access to the resources in a library, but have subsequently taken on a range of other functions. Another increasingly important public access system is the Internet and the World Wide Web. This provides access to a Pandora's box of information, and is becoming a main means of access to other systems, such as those of the online search services. The Internet is explored more fully in the next chapter. There are also other contexts in which public access systems provide access to information or the ability to complete transactions. All of these systems can be viewed as public access systems, and as such they must be designed to accommodate the differing needs of user segments, and the information seeking tasks that such users may seek to perform. Figure 10.1 briefly compares some of the features of such systems.

In general, public access systems exhibit challenges in respect of both the user profile and the task. The user profile has two aspects, which contribute to make system design more demanding:

● Users have a wide range of different educational backgrounds and levels of experience with the system. Users range from being subject domain novices and computer novices all the way to subject experts and computer experts. The degree of knowledge of the computer user and the domain experience should be reflected in the design of the user interface prompts, alerts and help facilities. Developers must also consider the needs of the system manager as user.

● A large proportion of the population are naïve and new users who need to be able to adapt quickly to different systems. Many users are also subject novices and their system use is constrained by their inability to appreciate what the system can be expected to contain.

The task is ill defined and there is an element of uncertainty in both:

● what the user is likely to retrieve and accept as output from the process
● the search strategies which will prove the most effective.

In the Internet environment, which will be considered further in the next chapter, the remoteness between information provider and information user is especially acute. Here, for example:

● the designer does not know who the user will be
● the user often does not understand how the search engines which they use to assist them with their search are conducting the search process.

	User Characteristics	Environment	Tasks	Technology
Online search services	Expert users and information managers	Office, academic library, corporate information centre	Retrieve information, download information and integrate into other documents	Range of different workstations. Earlier configurations with direct link to service. More state of the art applications links through Internet.
CD-ROM	Depends on database – can include children, general public, library users, professional users and others	Library, airport, home, office	Retrieve information, download information and integrate information into other documents	Often multimedia, GUI, mouse
Internet	Internet surfers – preponderance of academics, students and males	Study/work place, home	E-mail communication, shopping, file transfer	Desktop and portable PCs – with keyboard, screen and mouse
OPACs	Library users – profile depends on type of library.	In library In office/at home In other public venues	Narrowly defined – identify book availability – searching for information	Sometimes large screen, touch screen, special purpose keyboard, but also accessed through standard office equipment. Remote and local access may use different workstations.
Other Public Access Systems	General public	Public venues, such as the street, shopping malls, railway stations and airports	Perform transactions, collect information about range of goods or services available	Multimedia kiosks, ATMs etc. Keypads and touch screens.

Figure 10.1 Different types of systems contexts for knowledge organization

ONLINE SEARCH SERVICES

What is an online search service? Online search services offer access to a wide range of databases. The online search services that we are primarily concerned with in this section are what might be described as the traditional online search services or search services. In the last few years these have been joined by consumer online services such as America Online, CompuServe and Prodigy, and a wide range of other organizations that mount databases on servers on the Internet. The online search services that we are concerned with here mount a range of databases upon a large computer system and offer users access to these databases, usually in exchange for a fee. Some search services have an international market and encourage and support users from all over the world (or, more accurately, the developed world). Other search services, while they may have some users in other countries, operate more as national services. The early search services were established in the late 1960s and the early 1970s. There are now well over 10 000 databases available via such search services and mounted on computers based at various locations throughout the world.

The intending user of such an online search service must be able to access the search service computer. This may be achieved with the use of a terminal or workstation that can be linked through a telecommunications network to the search service computer. This is usually a personal computer (PC) with communication software and a modem, or a PC linked to a server that has appropriate communications software mounted. A wide range of different networks can be used, but increasingly the search services are accessed through the Internet. Internet access to online search services that were previously accessed through other telecommunications networks can make it difficult to differentiate between an Internet server and an online search service. Both offer access to databases. The diversification of the roles of online search services also adds to the complexity. Here we define an online search service as a special category of Internet service that can be described thus:

> An online search service seeks to mount a range of databases designed to meet the needs of a specific audience. It acts as an intermediary between the database producer and the end-user.

Online search services that provide access to a large number of databases convert the databases into a uniform format with some standardization in element names so that the basic commands and search techniques apply across all of the databases that are offered by a given vendor. The intending searcher needs some awareness of the range of search services that are available. Increasingly any one database may be available from several search services. Access to that database may be considerably cheaper, especially once telecommunications charges have been taken into account, via one search service than others. Alternatively, one search service may offer search facilities that support much more effective searching for a given topic than might be possible via another search service. Search services can no longer differentiate themselves on the availability of specific databases, but must offer customers other benefits, such as ease of searching, processing speed and competitive pricing. There are a number of different types of search service:

1. The traditional *supermarket online search services* that offer a range of 50 to 300-plus databases on behalf of database producers. Examples include: Dialog, DataStar and Questel Orbit. Although these online search services may offer many databases and may hope to be seen as a major presence in the information industry, continued commercial success depends on their ability to segment their market and to develop specialisms to match those segments. They are increasingly offering tailored services, such as KR ScienceBase, and Web-based services that support access to a range of services, such as Dialog Web.

2. *Specialist online search services*, such as DBE-Link, which offers German language and other European databases, and the search services offering access to business and financial databases, such as ICC. ICC deliver data online (with a Windows interface), offline, or via CD-ROM. Alternatively data can be delivered in bulk for integration into a company's own database or Intranet, via either magnetic tape or electronic data delivery (EDD). Some search services, such as Information Access Company, started with a database catalogue that was focused on one subject but have now started to diversify.

3. *Publishers as search services*. A number of major publishers have entered the market-place as search services. Some of these will have gained experience of electronic publishing through CD-ROM publishing, whilst others have formed alliances with other online service suppliers, to be able to offer an integrated information solution, which embraces both bibliographic data-bases for locating information and full-text databases for document delivery. Examples are EBSCOsearch service, Information Access Search bank and UMI's ProQuest Direct.

4. *Platform independent search services*, which provide access to databases on CD-ROM, the Web and client server platforms, possibly through a common user interface. Ovid Technologies are a good example of this type of search service. SilverPlatter is moving in this direction.

5. *Bibliographic utilities* that offer to specific communities access to a select

range of databases, often at special rates. Examples are OCLC First Search and BIDS.

In general, online service suppliers are beginning to be able to respond to the long-standing need for common interfaces to tools, such as bibliographic databases and directories (including directories of Web sites) which indicate the location of information, and the full text of the document which contains information. The identification of a document and its delivery are much closer to being integrated into a seamless service. The more sophisticated offerings also offer access to other information channels, such as the databases mounted by other services, the contents of other Web sites, information collections such as libraries, and people as information channels. This could be described as an

---

Dialog Web

Dialog Web is a WWW service which features:

- a database directory that works like a Web-based search engine to support database location
- access to over 450 Dialog databases
- Web Bluesheets to provide access to up-to-the-minute Dialog content, capabilities and prices
- Electronic Redistribution and Archiving (ERA), which allows distribution by e-mail or through the local Intranet
- Web interface to Alert (a current awareness service)
- a link to KR SourceOne, the document delivery service
- e-mail feedback for comments and suggestions.

Ei Village

Ei Village is an Internet-based virtual community that is designed as a packaged solution to all engineering information needs. The services offered with Ei include:

- Ei Village Directory, which provides quick access to relevant Web sites
- Ei Tech Alert – natural language concept searching for new developments
- Filtered News – access to bulletins on special disciplines
- Ei Corporate Gallery
- Ei Spotlights – weekly updates on topics
- Ei Annotation – guides to Web sites
- Articles on Call – ready to access, selected, pre-scanned articles
- EiDDS – e-mail document delivery
- Ei Connexion – an easy interface and gateway to 150 Dialog databases
- Ei Compendex*Web – unlimited fixed price access
- Ask a Librarian/ Ask an Engineer – advice on information searching
- Ask your peers – listservs and newsgroups selected.

Ei Village with Ei Compendex*Web can be purchased as a package, or, alternatively, either may be purchased separately. Ei also publish a number of their databases on CD-ROM and Engineering Index Monthly and Engineering Index Annual in print format.

Figure 10.2 Some examples of integrated information solutions

integrated information solution. Figure 10.2 describes two examples that seek to generate this integrated information solution. Such solutions need to be targeted to meet the needs of specific groups, and the service supplier must understand those needs, both in terms of the type of database to be accessed, and also in terms of specific features of interfaces and the most acceptable pricing strategies.

Figure 10.3 lists some of the major search services, shows the total number of their databases that may be accessed and gives some indication of the scope of the databases on offer. In addition to the range of databases available, many search services offer other services. These include current awareness services, access to web resources, Web directories, document delivery and databases on CD-ROM.

SEARCHING VIA ONLINE SEARCH SERVICES

The first steps in an online search are the choice of search service and database. For most searches only a few databases might be appropriate, and having, for instance, identified the databases that cover the required subject area, further choice may be between only two or three databases. In general it is not sufficient simply to know the subject coverage of a database. An experienced searcher will, for example, also be familiar with the style of the indexing language, the time span of the database, and how items are selected for inclusion in the database. Often there may be no one database that will provide an exhaustive search and it may be necessary to consult two or more databases before a search is complete. The checklist below lists some of the factors that the experienced searcher will weigh in the selection of a database.

HOW TO GUIDE: THE EVALUATION OF ONLINE SEARCH SERVICES

- Databases, including the number, subject coverage, time span and language.
- *Search facilities.* The elements of records that can be searched may differ from one search service to another. Certainly the field formats may vary and the field names may be different. Some systems offer more extensive facilities with regard to contextual or proximity searching and truncation. For source and full-text databases various special facilities may be required.
- *Interface options* – these should include options to support both novice and expert searching. GUI and Web-based interfaces are common.
- *Formats for records and documents.* Various formats are available for viewing the details of retrieved records. Sometimes it is possible for the searcher to select the elements that they require, but in searching other search services only a few standard formats are available.
- *Additional facilities.* Many search services offer other facilities in addition to

Search service	Base	Number of databases
Dialog Information Retrieval Services	Palo Alto, California	Over 450
Scope of databases	Science and technology, bibliography, reference, business, news, social sciences and humanities.	
European Space Agency's Information Retrieval Service (ESA-IRS)	Frascati, Italy	Over 130
Scope of databases	Science and technology, business and finance, corporate intelligence, health and safety, patents, news.	
DATA-STAR	Switzerland, but part of Dialog	Over 350
Scope of databases	Business and finance, chemical, engineering, news and media, medicine, food and agriculture, law and government, energy and the environment, science and technology, social sciences	
FT Information	London	Over 400 business sources
Scope of databases	Full-text information, including major newspapers, other international news services, international business magazines, companies, industries, markets, countries	
STN International		Around 200
Scope of databases	Agriculture, bioscience and technology, chemistry, medicine, patents, physics and science in general	
QUESTEL-ORBIT	France	Around 300
Scope of databases	Business, chemical information energy and earth science, engineering, health, safety and the environment, humanities and social sciences, materials science, news, patents, science and technology, trade marks.	
DIMDI	Germany	
Scope of databases	Biomedical, with some emphasis on German-language databases.	
BLAISE-LINE	London	Around 20
Scope of databases	Bibliographic records, catalogue databases	
ICC	Hampton, United Kingdom	
Scope of databases	Financial and industry analysis on all British companies.	
Information Access	Various	Around 30
Scope of databases	Many full-text databases, including areas such as academic, business and industry, computer technology, and general reference.	
LEXIS-NEXIS	London	11 000 sources
Scope of databases	News, financial reports, company and market reports.	
Dow Jones	United States	
Scope of databases	Business, investment support.	

Figure 10.3 Range of databases offered by some of the major search services

Search service	Base	Number of databases
WilsonWeb	New York	36 databases
Scope of databases	Full text, abstracts and indexes.	
Ovid Technologies	London	80 databases
	Health, biomedical, business, general reference, science and technology, humanities and social sciences	

Figure 10.3 *Concluded*

the basic online search facility. Often Selective Dissemination of Information (SDI) or document delivery services are available.

- *Support services.* Most search services offer some support and training services. Help desks, training courses, manuals, newsletters and other search aids can influence the effectiveness of a searcher
- *Cost.* Different search services have different pricing strategies. Some services are available on a subscription basis, whilst others are priced on a transaction basis. Some services allow a mixed of these two approaches, with customers, such as libraries, taking out a subscription for frequently used databases, and a transaction arrangement for less frequently used databases. There will also be special rates for additional services such as SDI or document delivery. The cost of telecommunications should also be considered, and this may vary between and within countries.
- *Experience.* The searcher's experience with a specific search service may be an important factor in determining his/her search effectiveness. Thus, from the searcher's point of view it is important not only to assess the specific features of the search service, but also to examine his or her own skills.

CD-ROMS

INTRODUCTION

Optical discs, and those specifically in the form of CD-ROMs, have become increasingly important as a medium for the storage and dissemination of information during the 1990s. CD-ROMs can be purchased by users and consulted at their own workstation. The price of many discs is currently such that many disc users would not buy them for personal use, but organizations and libraries buy discs on behalf of end-users. In this context, CD-ROMs represent a means of access to information alternative to online access to external databases via telecommunications networks, including the WWW. When the database recorded on the CD-ROM is the full text of a document such as a directory or an encyclopaedia, CD-ROMs may challenge the market position of the printed book. All three media are likely to continue to coexist, with each finding its market niche.

PROVIDING ACCESS TO CD-ROMS AND NETWORK CONFIGURATIONS

Network configurations have a significant impact on the way in which CD-ROMs can be exploited, especially in a multi-user environment. The basic stand-alone CD-ROM workstation provides a single user with access to a single disc. Clearly this configuration is incompatible with a networked environment where users are accustomed to access shared databases via their own workstations. The ideal CD-ROM configuration offers multi-user access to many databases in a way that allows the integration of databases on CD-ROM with other databases used by the information-seeker. First, we consider the basic stand-alone configuration.

CD-ROM drive linked to a stand-alone PC

The basic components of the stand-alone configuration are:

- a stand-alone PC
- a CD-ROM drive and appropriate software
- if required, a printer.

Most PCs have an integral CD-ROM drive, but if this is not available, the PC needs a spare expansion slot via which the drive can be linked, together with device-driver software, which tells the PC that a CD-ROM drive is connected. If hard-copy printouts of the results of a CD-ROM search are required, then a printer is essential. The choice of printer depends upon the environment and the relative priorities associated with noise, print quality and price.

In the early days of CD-ROM, compatibility was a very significant problem. There is much more standardization now, but it is still wise to check that all of the hardware and software components work with one another. The software situation is a little complex. In addition to the operating system of the micro-computer it is also necessary to have:

- retrieval software, which supports the searching of the CD-ROM database. This will be supplied by the producer of the CD-ROM product
- installation software, which controls the installation of the product on the user's equipment, and supports the setting of configuration options, such as user-defined passwords, and equipment specification.

Networking internal CD-ROM drives

There are two ways to network stand-alone drives:

1. Place the machines with their internal drives attached on a network. Users need to place the disc in their drive before they can use it.
2. Peer-to-peer networking, where one computer acts a the host machine, with the CD-ROM drive on that machine, and other PCs able to request access to the database This approach is easily implemented through Windows for Workgroups, but may be less easy to implement on other platforms; further, the performance depends on what the host is doing.

Using file servers and jukeboxes

The file server on a network can be used to provide access to the discs and software, rather than installing the software on individual machines. This file server can be the standard network file server, or may be a dedicated CD-ROM server or optical file server. This can either be directly plugged into the server, or logically connected across the network to the server. A dedicated server is preferable. The load on the network server may be too great, and not all CD-ROM titles will work off the server if they are not network aware. With a CD-ROM server it is easier to have all the discs and their software in one place for updating and general maintenance, and the configuration is expandable, and offers support for higher capacity jukebox systems.

A jukebox is a device that offers access to a large number of CD-ROM discs. Unlike CD-ROM drives, jukeboxes do not have a read head available for each individual disc. When a user wants to access a particular title it will be loaded by the jukebox and returned to its position after use in the same way as in audio jukeboxes. However, if there is simultaneous demand for more discs than there are drives the need to swap discs can slow down system performance.

Pre-caching

Pre-caching is the most recent approach to offering more speedy access to CD-ROM. Some publishers allow the user to copy the data from the CD-ROM disc directly on to a large magnetic hard drive. Pre-caching reduces the requirement for multiple CD-ROM drives, and more users can access the database at any one time. There are, however, a number of disadvantages:

- The permission (from database producers and publishers) to pre-cache can be expensive.
- Not all publishers offer pre-caching.

285

- The databases have to be updated. When using CD-ROM discs this is achieved by simply replacing the old disc; with a pre-cached system the disc has to be copied across.

Internet access

Another type of pre-caching can be achieved through Internet access; ultimately this has very little to do with CD-ROM, since the data is not being held on CD-ROM. Instead it is held on a remote site, either belonging to the publisher or one of their appointed agents. The software to access the databases is held locally, with a pointer to where on the Internet the retrieval interface should be looking. This option is being offered by a limited number of CD-ROM publishers but is likely to become a more significant option. This solution has many of the same advantages as pre-caching, and in addition the publisher's technical support department is charged with the task of keeping the system up and running on a 24-hours, 7-days-a-week basis. Updating of databases is the responsibility of the publisher, and can be done much quicker and, if appropriate more frequently, since the publisher can simply upload the data. The only drawback is that access to the data is subject to any Internet problems.

Applications where CD-ROM is best	Applications where use of an Online Search Service is best
Multimedia, such as books, games and reference materials	Bibliographic databases that are large and frequently used and updated
Stand-alone titles, such as single books	Directories, especially those with frequent updates
CD book collections	ASCII full text, especially large databases
When content, interface, and search techniques are tied to one another	Image collections or static texts such as journal articles, where only a few items in a journal collection will be used
When learning and not simply answering facts is part of the experience	Large databases
When you serve a relatively homogeneous population such as in a school library	Large numbers of simultaneous users
Where publishers do not publish elsewhere for reasons of security and copyright	Where sophisticated cross file searching is required
	Where a heterogeneous population requires a great variety in types of sources, subjects or topics, as for instance in public and university libraries.

Figure 10.4 Comparing CD-ROM and online search services

Figure 10.4 compares CD-ROM and online services.

CD-ROM PUBLISHERS AND PUBLISHING

Nearly all new PCs come equipped with CD-ROM drives; this provides an enormous installed base of CD-ROM drives. The bulk of the retail CD-ROM sales are multimedia with games and children's titles, followed by adult reference, being the most popular sellers. Libraries supplement this personal ownership by offering access to multiple titles. All projections anticipate a significant continued growth in the market for CD-ROM.

CD-ROM publishing is a relatively easy to market to enter, and consequently there are a large number of CD-ROM publishers. Most publishers are not prolific, and many have only a single product. Publishers may be engaged in various other aspects of the information industry. CD-ROM suppliers can be broadly divided into the following categories:

- *Supermarket CD publishers*, with a very significant catalogue of databases, which are produced by other organizations. Examples are Information Technology Supply Ltd and SilverPlatter. Another group is the online service services, such as Dialog with their KR OnDisc.
- *Database producers*, who will probably also be making their databases available via online and WWW media. Examples are CA (Chemical Abstracts) on CD, Wilson Business Abstracts, Mintel CD and Biosis GenRef on Compact Disc.
- *Publishers*. For example, Chadwyck Healey who started by publishing their own databases on CD-ROM but have added other HMSO and related documents, Blackwells and Wiley
- *Document Supply Centres* (such as the British Library) who make serials, books and conferences available on CD-ROM.

The market is still volatile, with new products entering the market as others leave. Nevertheless the number of titles and associated publishers continues to grow.

CONDUCTING A CD-ROM SEARCH

CD-ROM products have been specifically designed for ease of use and to facilitate end-user searching. Many offer both novice and expert mode interfaces. Retrieval facilities are similar to those that might be expected in any information retrieval product. For example, Boolean logic, truncation, field-specific searching, phrase searching and other facilities are featured in most of the

287

software used for retrieval in CD-ROM databases. An example was given in Figure 4.6. The unique feature of CD-ROM is the interface and dialogue design.

Some databases and user groups demand special information retrieval facilities. For example, Disclosure's Global Researcher has features that support the searching and analysis task that a company researcher might need to perform, including those that:

- identify companies by name, ticker symbol, geographic location, line of business or financial criteria
- rank companies based on financial performance
- perform instant point-and-click peer group comparisons
- analyse financial data using an Excel add-in
- create user-defined reports and ratios
- view real-time electronic filings.

HOW TO GUIDE: EVALUATING INFORMATION RETRIEVAL FEATURES ON CD-ROM

The availability of the following features should be sought:

- *Index*
  - Browse index
  - Number of postings
  - Cross references
  - Thesaurus
- *Search structure*
  - Term selection from index
  - Term selection from record
  - Case sensitivity
  - Search types
  - Combine searches
- *Search features*
  - Boolean
  - Truncation
  - Adjacency/proximity
  - Positional
  - Arithmetic
- *Search profile management*
  - Speed of performance
  - Save searches
  - Purge old searches
  - Search status

- Set and query management
- Number of search sets
- Search history display
- Search modification
- Search selection
- Statistics gathering.

Interface/dialogue design

CD-ROMs were one of the first media that were designed with the expectation that the end-user would perform searches without the intervention or support of an intermediary. When CD-ROMs first entered the market-place, online search services were operating primarily through command-based interfaces. Even early CD-ROM interfaces made extensive use of colour, graphics and menus. Most CD-ROMs today use GUIs. Although the Web-based interfaces, which use HTML, are a significant improvement on command-based interfaces, GUIs of CD-ROMs are becoming ever more sophisticated. Animation, sophisticated graphics, multimedia capability such as is used in embedded video clips, and help systems that talk to the user, are some of the options that are available on some CD-ROMs.

Multi-tasking is another feature of GUIs. In CD-ROM applications this could, for instance, be used to access an online database, while still connected to the CD-ROM database, and possibly to compare the results of the two searches.

The future for CD-ROMs

The number of publishers and products in the CD-ROM market-place is continuing to increase. A major issue for the future of the medium is the continued development of a consumer market. Figure 10.4 has already summarized the strengths of competing technologies. In addition to the Internet, CD-ROM may be overtaken by other technologies, such as digital versatile disc (DVD).

Specific developments that are already under way and that can be expected to continue include:

- Continuing growth in the number of CD-ROM titles. There has been significant recent growth in both the business and professional market-place and the consumer market-place.
- Price strategies are likely to consolidate in such a way that they recognize the different market sectors for different products. This will be partly content dependent with, for example, encyclopaedias and dictionaries priced as

289

consumer products, and bibliographic databases priced for library and corporate purchase. Greater transparency and simplicity of pricing strategies for networked use of CD-ROM will be demanded by customers.

- Further integration of technologies, with CD-ROM being used for core information delivery, and online access, often via the Web, being used for more current or real-time information to update the data available on the CD-ROM. Consumers will pay for immediacy for information that is only required occasionally. Frequently required material will be already paid for, and available on disc. Also the high capacity of DVD may be attractive for some applications

- Increasing sophistication of search interfaces, with tailoring to the requirements of specific user groups and types of databases. SilverPlatter's Search Advisor, which works with a GUI may be a model for the future. An intelligent retrieval client, the Search Advisor offers the tools used by professional searchers to develop search strategies, and supports novice searchers in their use of these tools. CD-ROM multimedia databases should be at the leading edge of the enhancement of interface design.

- Increased sophistication customer support from suppliers. KR, has, for instance recently launched Crossroads, a Web-based service that provides a forum for users to share their expertise and knowledge, and Learning Center which links visitors to a range of training options. These include web training sessions that are webcast live to participants, and prepared instructional modules.

- The use of Intranet technology to provide access to networked CD-ROMs. For example, KRSite offers access to the Knight Ridder collection of CD-ROMs via corporate intranets.

ONLINE PUBLIC ACCESS CATALOGUES

INTRODUCTION

Online public access catalogues have become a popular option for access to the resources of the collections of libraries, library consortia and other remote collections of information resources. They are one type of information retrieval system, but are distinct from other services in that the focus is on access to:

- collections of library resources and community information
- books, as opposed to, say, journal articles or Web-based resources.

Early OPACs provided access only to the documents in individual library collections, but as the options for networking have become more advanced the range of different collections to which users can gain access through a library OPAC has developed. Other developments have taken place in respect of the interfaces and search facilities offered by those interfaces, as discussed below. In addition, the range of different locations in which OPACs can be used has expanded. In academic libraries, for example, OPACs are frequently available in staff offices over the university network. Some public libraries are experimenting with public access kiosks in public areas such as shopping centres and community centres. Online public access catalogues are now an important shop window on library resources.

LIBRARY MANAGEMENT SYSTEMS

Online public access catalogues are created and maintained through library management systems. Such systems have a catalogue maintenance module and an OPAC module. There may also be a separate community information module, with an interface that is linked to that of the OPAC. Other modules in library management systems (LMSs) support the management and control of the library stock and its delivery to users; typical modules are those to cover circulation control, ordering and acquisition, serials control and management information.

There are a wide range of different library management systems in the market-place, designed for different types and sizes of library collections. Figures 2.3 to 2.6 show a search on an OPAC in one of these systems. Almost all large academic libraries have adopted a computer-based system. Most public libraries have also computerized, although a number of smaller authorities have been slower to take the plunge. In the large-systems market there is an increasing concentration on vendors maintaining existing customers, and continuing to upgrade their product so that existing customers do not switch systems. Clearly any library may review systems and choose to upgrade them by switching to another supplier from time to time. The mid-range and smaller-systems market is the area in which there is still growth. Smaller colleges, and special libraries in various sectors, are still entering the market-place, and there is more vola-tility in systems vendors. A number of the smaller systems are specifically marketed in the school library sector. However, even here, the established players are consolidating both their product and their market position.

All systems suppliers continue to upgrade their systems, and enhancement of the OPAC function has been central to the changes between the different gener-ations of library systems. Figure 10.5 is a useful summary of the differences between the four generations of library systems. The latest releases of systems generally fall somewhere between the third- and fourth-generation systems,

291

Feature	1st generation	2nd generation	3rd generation	4th generation
Programming language	Proprietary	C, Assembler	4GL	Object-orientated languages
Operating system	Proprietary	Vendor-specific	UNIX, DOS	UNIX, Windows
Database management systems	Proprietary	Proprietary	Entity relational	Object orientated
Communication	Limited	Some interfaces	Standards and increased interface opportunities	Full connectivity across the Internet
Import/Export	None	Limited	Onboard	Fully integrated; records added with one click
Hardware platforms	Locked	Vendor family	Multi-vendor	Multi-vendor
Reports	Fixed format	Fixed format	User-defined	User-defined. Also EIS facilities
Colour	None	None	Yes	Full multimedia
Capacity	Limited	Improved	Unlimited	Seamless
Module integration	None	Bridges	Seamless	Seamless
Architecture	Shared	Shared	Distributed	Client/Server
Interface	Command-based	Menu-based	Unlimited	Choice of interface, including Web, and GUI, incorporating multimedia.

Figure 10.5   Library management systems by generation

depending on the sophistication of their facilities for integration and interconnectivity. To some extent the fourth generation has yet to be realized. This profile of the four generations of LMS is a useful summary of the way in which systems have developed over the past 20 years.

The first generation of library management systems were developed on a module-by-module basis. There was very limited integration between modules, with systems either developing circulation control or cataloguing as a priority. Thus, the first edition of this text was able to divide systems according to their major function. Gradually suppliers developed a set of modules and, as they did so, started to recognize the benefits of linking these modules. Systems grew from an initial focus on, say, circulation control. Database structures differed, and might be described as proprietary. It was difficult to make any generalizations about database structure. Third- and fourth-generation systems are integrated systems based upon relational database structures.

In other respects also, first-generation systems demonstrated their lineage. They were developed to run on specific hardware platforms, and used proprietary software languages and operating systems. Some systems were specifically designed to be sold as part of an integrated hardware and software package as a turnkey system. Second-generation systems ran on a wider range of hardware platforms, but it took the introduction of UNIX- and disc operating system (DOS)-based systems for systems to become much more portable, between platforms. Fourth-generation systems are generally UNIX or Windows based.

Communication between systems was also generally non-existent in earlier systems. Links between systems for specific functions were a feature of second-generation systems. It was possible to import or export data to specific systems, but not generally. Third-generation systems embodied a range of standards that were a significant step towards open system interconnection, but a number of issues associated with end-user access and interfaces required resolution. Also implementation of systems that employed all of the appropriate standards was only gradual. Fourth-generation systems feature client/server architecture and modules that facilitate access to other servers over the Internet.

The user's interaction with the system has also become more fruitful and straightforward as systems have moved through the generations. For library managers, reports from early systems were very limited and there was little opportunity for users to define their own reports. The range of standard reports available in third-generation systems is wide, and users may, in addition, define their own reports. The latest executive information system (EIS) modules will allow managers to manipulate data and investigate various scenarios, and thereby have the potential to be a full decision support tool.

The user interface has also improved beyond recognition. Colour became standard in third-generation systems. Graphical user interface features, such as windows, icons, menus and direct manipulation, have become the norm. This is in stark contrast with the crude command-based interfaces of the early online systems, or the need to wrestle with batch processing and printed reports. Fourth-generation systems allow access to multiple sources from one multimedia interface. This very much enhanced user interface is symbolic of the change in user or customer focus in systems over the generations. Early systems were designed primarily for staff access. Online public access catalogues started to emerge in second-generation systems. Third-generation systems saw much more sophisticated GUI-based user interfaces. The fourth-generation OPAC can be accessed through a range of interfaces depending upon the client workstation

293

and the user. This range embraces public access terminals with limited functionality to sophisticated GUIs with a powerful range of search facilities.

CATALOGUE DATABASE CREATION

Online public access catalogues depend on the quality of the underlying database. One of the early advantages of the use of computer-based cataloguing was the opportunity to reduce the resources dedicated to the creation of catalogue records. There were two main ways in which this effort could be reduced: by the sharing of catalogue records, so that each individual library did not create its own records; and, because there was no longer a need to engage in the time-consuming task of filing of catalogue cards. The first of these, the sharing of catalogue records, was facilitated by the work of a number of library cooperatives and centralized cataloguing services. These cooperatives and cataloguing services took responsibility for the creation of records that could be used by subscriber or member libraries. Major agents in this were the Library of Congress and the British Library (BL). Other networks whose contributions have also been considerable include OCLC, Research Libraries Group (RLG), Birmingham Libraries Co-operative Mechanization Service (BLCMP) and London and South East Region (LASER). In order for these ventures to be successful, it was important that standards were adopted to support the creation of shared catalogue records. These standards have been discussed in earlier chapters of this book; they include AACR and MARC, and the Dewey Decimal Classification Scheme. This need to spread the work in the creation of catalogue records has, in fact, been responsible for the extent of standardization in library cataloguing, and has a major impact on the quality and nature of the databases to which OPACs provide access.

Key features in a cataloguing module are:

- data entry
- downloading
- authority control.

Easy data entry for local creation of records is important. It is usual for systems to use the same record for the ordering and acquisitions function as is used in the cataloguing module. Entry is via formatted screens with word processing-type facilities. Field labels and other areas of the screen should be protected, and data entry in some fields, such as the ISBN field, should be validated to ensure that the data entered are in the correct format.

As regards the record format, the MARC record format is a central consideration. External records from the bibliographic utilities are generally in one of the MARC record formats. Local systems must at least be able to handle the

MARC record format. Some systems are totally MARC based, others can accept records in the MARC format and convert them into an internal format. Where alternative formats are available, systems usually allow libraries to define fields for the bibliographic record. Most systems automatically update index files as soon as the record has been added to the file, so that retrieval is possible immediately. A wide range of different types of indexing may be possible.

Records from external databases may be added from tape, or via downloading direct from the files of the bibliographic utilities. A further option is to acquire records on CD-ROM and to download records from CD-ROM databases.

Authority control is important where the form of index terms or headings, such as author headings, or subject index terms, need to be controlled. Libraries maintain an authority file in order to improve consistency in indexing. Records in this file may be created locally or drawn from externally available files such as the Name and Subject Authority files of the Library of Congress. The authority file can usually be consulted during indexing and cataloguing, possibly by display in a separate window, and new headings are immediately added to the authority file, with an opportunity to review or authorize recently added headings at a later date. Sometimes it is also possible to add cross-references or related terms to the authority file, and these may be displayed in the OPAC. The subject authority file may take the form of a thesaurus that displays the full range of uses for related, narrower and broader terms.

Facilities to support catalogue database creation continue to improve, and these should lead to continuing increases in the efficiency of catalogue creation and updating, and the quality of the database. Two areas in which such improvements have focused recently relate to connectivity and authority control:

- Improved connectivity and interfaces support faster execution of library management operations in a number of functions. For catalogue creation this leads to improved capture of MARC records. For example, a database of such records on CD-ROM may be accessed. On the entry of an ISBN, either through scanning a bar code, or through keying, the MARC record is instantly displayed for any necessary editing. It is then automatically added to the database. The streamlining of this process is a particular asset for any library and resource collection that has yet to convert their catalogue records into a MARC format.

- Improved authority control. Amid the continuing debate concerning whether, with the availability of natural-language searching, it is necessary to control index terms and headings, a number of systems have enhanced their facilities for the control of index terms or headings. Authority control may be exercised in relation to subject index terms or headings, titles and author headings or access points. Authority control systems have been added by some vendors and enhanced by others. For example, some now allow a greater range of relationships to be used in the thesaurus. Where thesauri are available, and this is mainly in the systems marketed to the special library sector, these are often now displayed in sections via windows, and may thus be consulted during either indexing or searching much more easily than previously. More sophisticated authority control, with, in the most advanced systems, multiple authority files, and validation of a range of different types of heading on entry is also available. Thesauri may also be used to provide SEE and SEE ALSO cross references.

Cataloguing consistency can be improved further through spell checkers and style checkers, and de-duplications tools. If records are to be shared it will be necessary to know which spell checker has been used. Catalogue tidying and global amendment software will improve the quality of catalogue databases. The cataloguing of electronic documents still presents a number of challenges, but also opportunities. Free-text searching on the text of electronic documents offers access routes not traditionally available in catalogue records of print documents. Also there is scope for further enhancement of links between citation records and multi-media document types, and for further work on indexing of, for example, images or video clips.

INTERFACES AND SEARCH FACILITIES

Online public access catalogue interfaces need to offer facilities for both the searching of the catalogue database and the display of records.

Online public access catalogues have been available in some systems, for approximately ten years. During that period OPACs have passed through three generations. First-generation OPACs were derived from traditional catalogues or computerized circulation systems. Access was via author, or title (as a phrase), classmark and possibly subject heading (as a phrase), and acronym key such as author-title acronyms. First-generation OPACs expected exact matching of terms and were intolerant of user mistakes. These OPACs were acceptable for known-item searching and offered menu-based access, but this access was based on limited search facilities.

Second-generation OPACs began to rectify some of the limitations of the first systems. Systems designers started to incorporate some of the facilities to be found in other text information management systems and the software used by the search services. Second-generation OPACs offered much better search facilities based upon keyword searching and post-coordination of keywords. Usually these OPACs could be operated with a command language as well as through a menu-based interface. Although second-generation OPACs were a great improvement, two problems still needed to be addressed. Browsing through records remained difficult and it was necessary to work through different menu screens, while the large size and wide coverage of catalogue databases often led to many false drops.

Third-generation OPACs use a natural-language interface, so that the users may input their search strategy as a natural-language phrase. Interfaces and search facilities began to improve with the entry of the early GUI-based OPACs. The latest OPACs offer both touch screen for public access and full GUI for full functionality for more experienced users who wish to pursue complex search strategies across a number of different sources. A wide range of search facilities such as truncation, and proximity searching is becoming common; access to and prompts for the use of these are embedded in the interface.

Once records have been identified there are a number of ways in which they may be displayed. Some systems display the index or a listing of brief records before a full record is displayed; others, if there is only one match, will show the record directly. Usually the full record display includes holdings information relating to individual copies, as well as the basic bibliographic data. Where such data are available to the public, it is often necessary to consult another window to discover the loan status of the document. Record displays may be library defined. Security procedures may mask confidential information. For non-matches, some systems show the index. Since non-match will be relatively frequent, browsing of the index and/or a list of brief records is common.

Graphical user interfaces offer point and click, icons, pull-down menus, cut, copy and paste, and multi-tasking. So, as explained in Chapter 4, users can develop a search strategy in one window, call up a thesaurus display in another window, and consult help, or view the results of their search in yet a further window. When a successful search has been completed, components of documents may be integrated into other documents through a word-processing package or, alternatively, documents may be ordered through a document ordering service. Web interfaces are widely available so remote users can access the library OPAC through the Web.

Online public access catalogues can be further enhanced by offering multimedia interfaces and access to multimedia information. This can be achieved through multimedia objects linked to bibliographic citations, in such a way that the multimedia objects can be called by clicking on a button in this citation.

Multiple client options, which means that the client can be anything from a dumb terminal, a lower specification PC or network computer to a fully configured high-specification PC with client software, will facilitate access from a greater range of networked workstations. The interface displays differently on each client, but the client may access a number of applications through the same interface, thus making it easier for the user to develop familiarity with the interface that is available through their specific client. On the other hand, where users move between workstations to obtain access to the same database, this variation may be confusing.

Access to a range of other self-service functions, such as self-issue and self-renewal, and community information is often offered through the same interface as the OPAC. There has been considerable debate about the effect that self-service may have on customer perceptions of the quality of the library service, and the effect that remote renewal may have on control of library stock, but potential savings in staff time are attractive. Some of these applications are concerned with public access terminals in a kiosk format, and links to the Internet. Public access terminals are often based on touch screens. These interfaces are generally heavily reliant on menus in which the user selects an option by touching the screen. The range of search facilities is more limited than with terminals that include keyboard access. Kiosks are designed for use in any location in which there is significant footfall, including public libraries, shopping centres and railway stations.

Community information may be one of the first categories of information that libraries wish to make accessible over the Internet, or via public access kiosks. The core of this service is, often, lists of names and addresses of contacts such as local organizations. Such files may extend to many types of other information, including information about local leisure facilities, employment opportunities, children's activities and citizens' information. A community information module allows a library to develop its own database of whatever information it might like to offer its public.

Figure 10.6 shows features available in BLBMP TALIS in respect of public access modules and community information modules.

Public access
- Choice of user interface, including the Web
- MARC-based bibliographic file
- Z39.50
- Self-service facilities including reservations and renewal
- Subject searching including keyword and Boolean facilities, as well as author, title etc.
- Borrower enquiry and public reservations
- Related work searching
- Advanced OPAC facilities including relevance ranking and set manipulation

Community information (Talis Inform)
- Web based
- Full-text searching with relevance ranking
- Online editing of records by information providers
- Record dated and reminder letters generated

Figure 10.6 Features available in BLCMP TALIS

THE FUTURE FOR OPACS

Libraries are moving into a position where they will be able to encourage the use of electronic resource by large numbers of remote users for payment, or will be able to limit access to specific users. Online public access catalogues are a shop window in such an environment. External users must be able to access the library's OPAC but, in addition, library users may use the OPAC to access a wide range of other Internet resources. The OPAC can act as a window on the world of information resources. Each user will have one or more personal logins, allowing preferences, rights and activities to be stored for reuse. Search statements might be shared among users. Web browser concepts such as structured bookmarks, and back-tracking will become widespread. Users will use the OPAC as one of a number of methods to maintain personal files without rekeying data. Users need to be able to store and reuse search statements and results. Personal documents can be linked directly to library citations or electronic documents (e-documents), and can be submitted as a potential library acquisition or supplied in response to a library document request. Client/server computing will allow users to select a search interface for a task, rather than accept a standard set of options.

Online public access catalogue interfaces need to be designed for different types of users. Dynix's 'Kids Catalogue' is an early example. Facilities for disabled people, and particularly the visually impaired need to be incorporated into library OPACs. In all of this, users need the ability to choose their OPAC interface.

Most libraries now provide community information on Web pages, rather than via a library management system. Increasingly this may involve the publication of web documents, and even web journals. This may necessitate converting documents to HTML format or the use of a document management system. The same machine must be able to access these pages and the LMS, other applications on the local area network (LAN), such as CD-ROMs, the intranet and the Internet. It is important that the look, feel and functionality of interfaces to these different resources be consistent.

Systems may also facilitate user access to commercial databases, other library resources and document collections. Metainformation about WWW resources needs to be available. The systems must tackle issues concerning liability, control of copyright, licensing and collecting of appropriate payments. Asset trading agreements must be forged across the information chain. Such systems may also need to accommodate the assessment and evaluation of resources by those seeking to acquire them. Systems will need to be able to manage who is allowed access to what, when, for how long or to what maximum charge, the payment strategy and associated rights. They will need to manage copyright issues as an integral function, and will need to be linked to the systems of publishers, editors, indexers, picture libraries and authors.

The other side of access is security. Security must be built in, and be based on a comprehensive system of access rights, permissions, rules and parameters. Security also includes comprehensive, efficient and fast system backup and restoration of lost data. Security will increasingly be linked to charging. Proving access to the wealth of Internet resources is expensive; Smartcards that record customers transactions are likely to be increasingly used to support charging, and may also be used as the security device for access to a range of organizational and external information resources. They could also be used with self-issue kiosks.

In conclusion, the future offers a number of options, but there are unlikely to be generic solutions that will accommodate every library and information management function and task. Users will continue to choose information sources on the basis of convenience of use and access, and cost. Although future systems may offer users many opportunities to participate in systems design and to tailor interfaces and the collection of resources to which they have access, locating good, reliable and validated information is in some sense becoming more time-consuming and difficult, not easier, and there will remain a role for an information guide. Library management systems will be an important tool in the armoury of the information guide.

SUMMARY

This chapter has reviewed a number of systems contexts in which the principles of the organization of knowledge are to be encountered. Online search services offer access to a range of databases, often over the Internet. These resources include both source and reference databases. Some of these databases can alternatively be acquired on CD-ROM so that an organization or individual consumer can license the complete database. Organizations and libraries often network these databases, sometimes using Internet or intranet technology. Most libraries also use the OPAC modules of a library management system to provide online access to their catalogue databases. This access may be provided in the library but, often, catalogue databases can be accessed remotely, either through a local area network or over the Internet or Web. The issues associated with the organization of knowledge and, correspondingly, the search facilities offered in all of these different types of applications have many common features.

FURTHER READING

CD-ROM

Adkins, S. L. (1993) CD-ROM: a review of the 1992 literature. *Computers in Libraries*, **13** (8), 20–53.

Armstrong, C. J. and Hartley, R. J. (1997) *Keyguide to Information Sources in Online and CD-ROM Database Searching*. London: Mansell.

Batterbee, C. (1995) Open access CD-ROM in public libraries. *Aslib Proceedings*, **47** (3), 63–72.

Batterbee, C. and Nicholas, D. (1995) CD-ROMs in public libraries: a survey. *Aslib Proceedings*, **47** (3), March, 63–72.

Beheshti, J. (1991) Retrieval interfaces for CD-ROM bibliographic databases. *CD-ROM Professional*, **4** (1), 50–53.

Bevan, N. (1994) Transient technology? The future of CD-ROM in libraries. *Program*, **28** (1), 271–331.

Biddiscombe, R. (1992) Networking CD-ROMs in an academic library environment. *British Journal of Academic Librarianship*, **6** (3), 175–83.

Black, K (1992) CD-ROM networking: the Leicester Polytechnic experience. *Aslib Information*, **20** (7–8), 288–90.

Bosch, V. M. and Hancock-Beaulieu, M. (1995) CDROM user interface evaluation: the appropriateness of GUIs. *Online and CDROM Review*, **19** (5), 255–70.

Brackel, P. A. (1994) Implications of networking CD-ROM databases in a research environment. *South African Journal of Library and Information Science*, **61** (1), 26–34.

Bradley, P. (1996) *UKOLUG Quick Guide to CD-ROM Networking*. London: UK Online User Group.

Bradley, P. (1997) *Going Online, CD-ROM and the Internet*, 10th edn. London: Aslib.

Bryant, G. (1993) Combining online and disc. *Online and CD-ROM Review*, **17** (6), 396–8.

Budd, J. M. and Williams, K. A. (1993) CD-ROMs in academic libraries: a survey. *College and Research Libraries*, **54** (6), 529–35.

Carlton, T. (1995) CD-R on the cheap? *CD-ROM Professional*, **8** (4), 20–27.

Cawkell, T. (1996) *The Multimedia Handbook*. London: Routledge

CD-ROM Consistent Interface Committee (1992) CD-ROM consistent interface guidelines: a final report. *CD-ROM Librarian*, **7** (2), 18–29.

Clarke, K. (1993) New OVID software from CD PLUS Technologies. *CD-ROM Professional*, **6** (6), 230–32.

Clausen, H. (1997) Oneline, CD-ROM and Web: is the same difference. *Aslib Proceedings*, **19** (7), 177–83.

Diamond, S. (1993) Creating text and image CD-ROMs: getting it right the first time. *CD-ROM Professional*, **6** (6), 128, 130–31.

Falk, H. (1994) CD-ROM recording in every library *Electronic Library*, **12** (5), 304–7.

Fecko, M. B. (1997) *Electronic Resources: Access and Issues*. London: Bowker-Saur.

Guenette, D. (1996) The CD-ROM online connection. *CD-ROM Professional*, **9** (3), 30–44.

Hanson, T. and Day, J. (eds) (1994) *CD-ROM in Libraries: Management Issues*. London: Bowker-Saur.

Jasco, P. (1996) The Internet as a CD-ROM Alternative. *Information Today*, **13** (3), 29–31.

Kirby, H. G. (1994) Public library case study: CD-ROM at Croydon Central Library. In T. Hanson and J. Day (eds), *CD-ROM in Libraries: Management Issues*. London: Bowker-Saur.

Knight, N. H. (1997) Information metering: issues and implications. *Information Services and Use*, **17** (1), 1–4.

Koster, D. D. (1993) CD-ROMs: stand alone or networked. *Library Media Quarterly*, **21** (2), Winter, 127–8.

Lambert, J. (1994) Managing CD-ROM services in academic libraries. *Journal of Library and Information Science*, **26** (1), 23–8.

Large, J. A. (1989) Evaluating online and CD-ROM reference sources. *Journal of Librarianship*, **21** (2), 87–108.

Lopez, N. K. (1997) *Gale Directory of Databases.* Vol. 1 *Online Databases* and Vol. 2 *CD-ROM, Diskette, Magnetic Tape, Handheld and Batch Access Database Products.* Detroit, MI: Gale Research Inc.

Ma, W. (1998) The near future trend: combining Web access and local CD Networks; experience and a few suggestions. *Electronic Library*, **16** (1), 49–54.

Machovec, G. S. (1997) Electronic journal market overview. *Serials Review*, **23** (2), 31–44.

McBride, J. (1994) CD-ROM authoring and mastering: searching for the tools to bring it all together. *CD-ROM World*, **9** (1), 53–5.

O'Leary, M. (1997) Online comes of age. *Online*, **21** (91), 10–20.

Richards, T. (1995) Proliferation of CD-ROM retrieval software: stability at last. *Computers in Libraries*, **15** (10), 61–2.

Ronen, E. (1994) Internet CD-ROM survey. *Electronic Library*, **12** (6), 372–3.

Rowley, J. (1995) Issues in multiple use and network pricing for CD-ROMs. *Electronic Library*, **13** (5), 483–7.

Saffady, W. (1996) The availability and cost of online search services. *Library Technology Reports*, **32** (3), 337–456.

Stratton, B. (1994) The transiency of CD-ROM? A reappraisal for the 1990's. *Journal of Librarianship and Information Science*, **26** (3), 157–64.

Tenopir, C. (1996) Has online made CD-ROM obsolete? *Library Journal*, **12** (16), 33–4.

Wiedemer, J. D. and Boelio, D. B. (1995) CD-ROM versus online: an economic analysis for publishers. *CD-ROM Professional*, **8** (4), 36–42.

Worley, J. (1996) The CD-word: reflections on user behaviours and user service. *Electronic Library*, **14** (5), 411–13.

Yeardon, J. (1995) Experiences with SilverPlatter Electronic Reference Library at Imperial College. *Program*, **29** (2), 169–75.

ONLINE SEARCH SERVICES

Amor, L. (1996) *The Online Manual: A Practical Guide to Business Databases*, 5th edn. Oxford: Learned Information.

Amor, L. (1997) *Online Company Information 1997: The Directory of Financial and Corporate Databases Worldwide.* Oxford: Learned Information.

Armstrong, C. J. and Hartley, R. J. (1997) *Key Guide to Information Sources in Online and CD-ROM Database Searching*, 2nd edn. London and Washington, DC: Mansell.

Armstrong, C. J. and Madawar, K. (1996) *Investigation into the Quality of Databases in General Use in the UK.* British Library Research and Innovation Reports No. 11.

Basch, R. (1993) Annual review of database development. *Database*, **16** (6), December, 29–41.

Bates, M. J. (1996) The Getty end-user online searching project in the humanities: report No. 6: overview and conclusions. *College and Research Libraries*, **57** (6), November, 514–23.

Bjorner, S. (1994) Get ready, get SET, go for more control on Dialog. *Online*, **18** (1), January, 103–8.

Chishti, S. H. (1993) CD-ROM vs online: a comparison of PsycLIT (CD-ROM) and PsycINFO (DIALOG). *Reference Librarian*, **40**, 131–55.

Foote, J. B., Harrison, M. M. and Watson, M. (1997) Electronic Library resources: managing the maze. *Resource Sharing and Information Networks*, **12** (2), 5–17.

Galt, J. S. (1997) Does the future of online industry lie in individually customised services? How online hosts are adapting to the future. In D. I. Raitt et al. (eds), *Online Information 97: Proceedings of the International Online Information Meeting, London 9–11 December 1997*, pp. 13–18. Oxford: Learned Information.

Head, A. J. (1997) A question of interface design: how do online search service GUI's measure up? *Online*, **21** (3), May–June, 20–29.

Jeffcoate, J. (1993) Multimedia in the business market: is there a multi-media market? *Information Management and Technology*, **26** (5), September, 222–5, 228.

Online company information (1997). Oxford: Learned Information.

Online Information (1993, 1994, 1995, 1996) Proceedings of the 17th–20th International Online Information meeting. London, December 1993, 1994, 1995 and 1996. Oxford: Learned Information.

Poynder, R. (1996) STN International: the scientific and technical search service. *Business Information Review*, **13** (2), September, 183–90.

Rehkop, B. L. (1994) Cypress: a GUI interface to Dow Jones News/Retrieval. *Online*, 18 (1), January, 72–5.

Scott, J. (1996) Online access to international newspapers and wires: a status report. *Database*, **19** (4), August–September, 42–9.

Storey, T. and Dalrymple, T. (1996) On the Web with OCLC First Search and NetFirst. *OCLC Newsletter*, (220), March–April, 34–5.

Tenopir, C. and Bergland, S. (1993) Full text searching on major supermarket systems: DIALOG, DATA-STAR and NEXIS. *Database*, 16 (5), October, 32–42.

Tenopir, C. (1996a) Moving to the information village. *Library Journal*, **121** (4), March, 29–30.

Tenopir, C. (1996b) Generations of online searching. *Library Journal*, **121** (14), 128, 130.

Vickery, B. and Vickery, A. (1993) Online search interface design. *Journal of Documentation*, **49** (2), June, 103–87.

Webber, S., Baile, C. Cameron, A. and Eaton, J. (1994) *UKOLUG Quick Guide to Online Commands*. 4th edn. London: UK Online User Group.

ONLINE PUBLIC ACCESS CATALOGUES

Alper, H. (1993) Selecting Heritage/Bookshelf-PC for the District Library, Queen Mary's University Hospital, Roehampton. *Program*, 27 (2), 173–82.

Batt, C. (1994) *Information Technology in Public Libraries*, 5th edn. London: Library Association.

Batt, C. (1995) The last migration *Public Library Journal*, **10** (6), 159–61.

Cherry, J. M., Williamson, N. J. Jones-Simmons, C. R. and Xin Gu (1994) OPACS in twelve Canadian academic libraries: an evaluation of functional capabilities and interface features. *Information Technology and Libraries*, **13** (3), 174–95.

Cibbarelli, P. (1996) Library automation alternatives in 1996 and user satisfaction ratings of library users by operating system. *Computers in Libraries*, **16** (2), 26–35.

Collier, M. W. (1997) A model for the electronic university library In A. H. Helal and J. W. Weiss (eds), *Toward a Worldwide Library: A Ten Year Forecast*. Essen: Essen University Library.

Cousins, S. (1997) COPAC: new research library union catalogue. *Electronic Library*, **15** (3), 185–8.

Dempsey. L., Russell, R. and Kirriemuir, J. (1996) Towards distributed library systems: Z39.50 in a European context. *Program*, **30** (1), 1–22.

Electronic public information/one-stop shops/kiosks (1996) *Vine*, special issue (102).

Fletcher, M. (1996) The CATRIONA project: feasibility study and outcomes. *Program*, **30** (2), 99–107.

Furness, K. L. and Graham, M. E. (1996) The use of information technology in special libraries in the UK. *Program*, 30 (1), 23–37.

Griffiths, J.-M. and Kertis, K. (1994) Automated system marketplace. *Library Journal*, **119** (6), 50–59.

Grosch, A. N. (1995) *Library Information Technologies and Networks*. New York: Marcel Dekker.

Hanson, T. and Day, J. (1998) *Managing the Electronic Library: A Practical Guide for Information Professionals*. London : Bowker-Saur.

Keen, M. (1997) The OKAPI projects. *Journal of Documentation*, **53** (1), 84–7.

Lancaster, F. W. and Sandore, B. (1997) *Technology and Management in Library and Information Services*. London: Library Association.

Leeves, J. (1995) Library systems then and now. *Vine* (100), September, 19–23.

Leeves, J. and Russell, R. (1995) *Libsys.uk: a Directory of Library Systems in the United Kingdom.* London: LITC, South Bank University.

Matthews, J. (1995) Moving to the next generation: Aston University's selection and implementation of Galaxy 2000. *Vine* (101), December, 42–9.

Murray, I. R. (1997) Assessing the effect of new generation library management systems. *Program,* 31 (1–4), 313–27.

Robertson, S. E. (1997) Overview of Okapi projects. *Journal of Documentation,* **53** (1), 3–7.

Rowley, J. E. (1994) GENESIS: a new beginning or a new generation. *Electronic Library,* **12** (5), 277–83.

Stafford, J. (1996) Self issue the management implications. The introduction of self service at the University of Sunderland. *Program,* **30** (4), 375–83.

Tedd, L. A. (1995) An introduction to sharing resources via the Internet in academic library and information centres in Europe. *Program,* 29 (1), 43–61.

Wilson, M. (1994) Talis at Nene: an experience in migration in a college library. *Program,* 28 (3), 239–51.

Yeates, R. (1996) Library automation: the way forward? *Program,* **30** (3), 239–53.

11 The Internet and its applications

INTRODUCTION

Many of the online search services, and online public access catalogues described in the previous chapter may be accessed through the Internet, the WWW or intranets. This chapter focuses on the wide range of other information sources that may be accessed through the Internet, and considers the ways in which documents that are available over the Internet may be created and accessed. At the end of this chapter you will:

- understand the nature of the Internet, the WWW and the information resources to which they provide access
- be aware of the tools for searching such resources
- understand the basics of creating and maintaining a Web site
- appreciate the need for structuring of information in the context of subject gateways
- be aware of the processes associated with document creation and publication across the WWW
- appreciate the challenges for further development and effective exploitation of this type of networked 'tower of Babel'.

THE INTERNET

The Internet is a collection of interlinked computer networks, or a network of networks. It can connect millions of different computers and the rate of increase in use and in new subscribers is growing on a month-by-month basis. Historically, the Internet was essentially an academic network, but business use is growing, so that it is no longer an élite network for communication between eminent research centres, but also is accessible to small colleges, small businesses and libraries throughout the world. The Internet offers a gateway to a myriad of online databases, library catalogues and collections and software and document archives, in addition to frequently used store-and-forward services, such as UserNet News and e-mail. In addition, the commercial applications of the Internet are becoming significant. Electronic commerce (e-commerce) is of increasing concern to businesses. The main products sold through the Internet are books, CDs and music and software, but the potential is much greater. Sainsbury and Tesco and other leading supermarkets are in the process of major trials of Internet-based home delivery services. Most businesses regard it as important to have a presence on the Internet, in the form of a Web site, since the Internet is becoming an increasingly important means of promotion and visibility.

The terms Internet and World Wide Web tend to be used interchangeably. Strictly they are not the same thing. The Internet is a world-wide network of interlinked computer networks. The Internet provides global connectivity via a mesh of networks based on the transmission control protocol/Internet protocol (TCP/IP) and open systems interconnection (OSI) protocol. Documents are transferred between these networks using one of a variety of Internet transfer protocols, such as file transfer protocol (FTP) or hypertext transfer protocol (HTTP).

The Web comprises those servers linked to the Internet that use HTTP. This means that documents are linked to one another through hyperlinks that are embedded in each document. Users move from one document to the next using hyperlinks links, which are created through a combination of:

- an addressing system that allows the location of any object stored on a networked computer to be uniquely identified by a *uniform resource locator*
- *mark-up language* (*HTML*) that allows the authors of documents to identify a particular location within their document as the source of links, and to specify the location of the target of those links
- a *transfer protocol* (*HTTP*) that allows copies of target documents stored on remote servers to be retrieved and displayed
- a client program, or *Web browser* such as Netscape Navigator or Internet Explorer that provides the user with control over the retrieval process and over the links to be activated.

People and organizations create home pages to present their own information or service. A collection of home pages, located on the same server is called a *Web site*. Access to these pages is via the URL using a browser. These addresses link the user to the host computer and their individual files; these are then displayed on the user's personal workstation. With the appropriate software, users can read documents, view pictures, listen to sound and retrieve information.

From an indexing perspective, the hyperlinks on the WWW that form the basis of the browsing network are uncontrolled, but humanly assigned index terms (or on occasions other objects, such as images). They are normally terms in the body of the text of the Web page. There is no general control over which terms should be used as hyperlinks, but each hyperlink is individually coded by the creator of the HTML Web page that contains the hyperlink.

A Web browser add-on to a Web client program is an external program that can run individually without the help of the Web client software. Many Web clients allow a link to other software in order to represent the contents of a file for which the Web client software has no built in functionally. A plug-in to a Web client program is almost the same as an add-on, except that this plug-in cannot run on its own. Examples of add-ons are Adobe Acrobat and the portable document format; PDF is often used to distribute documents in computer readable form, giving a high-quality document that is very similar to the original hard copy.

Another concept often encountered in the Internet world is that of the intranet. An intranet is an organization's internal communication system that uses Internet technology. Intranets use Web browsers and graphical user interfaces. While the Internet provides largely unrestricted access to its contents to almost any member of the public, intranets have strict access controls, often described as firewalls. These firewalls protect corporate Web pages, document databases and other information from external access.

Many of the online search services, and on-line public access catalogues described in the previous chapter may be accessed through the Internet, the WWW or intranets. In addition the Internet offers access to a plethora of other resources. These resources are controlled by their providers and there is no inherent evaluation or validation embedded in their distribution or publication process. In addition, the resources can be volatile. Figure 11.1 summarizes the differences between general Internet resources, and more traditional databases, and the means of accessing such resources. This chapter explores the range of search tools that are available for locating Internet resources, and explores issues associated with the creation and maintenance of a Web site. The creation of subject gateways requires the use of metadata standards, name authority lists, thesauri and classification schemes. The final section on document publication and creation explains the tools that are used in the creation of documents that can be accessed over the Internet.

Feature	Internet-based databases	Traditional online and CD-ROM databases
Database coverage	Includes HTTP, FTP, newsgroup, and image, video and graphics data. Issued freely, with little validation or organization	From authoritative academic, governmental or professional journals – subjected to refereeing, filtering, selection and organization
Indexed fields	Located and indexed by automatic searching software	Indexed according to controlled vocabularies and thesauri-indexed fields are subject, keyword, author, title, organization
Abstracting and summarizing methods	Different approaches are used. Some search engines use automatic abstracting techniques to produce a paragraph of summary; others use primarily data on the home page, such as header, title, links, and a few words of the key paragraph	Uses author abstracts, or professional abstractors
Searching software	Search engines and directories. Search engines need to select sites for inclusion, either on the basis of evaluation and recommendation, or through the use of an algorithm. These processes must also be used for updating	Document management software or information retrieval software, which operates on predefined databases. These databases are updated in accordance with selection criteria that relate to the type of source, such as given journal title
Search interface	Often simple and advanced options available. Often includes key word search and search by subject category, but precise facilities vary between search engines. Uses Boolean search and other options such as proximity searching	Normally offer simple and advanced options, with a wide range of search facilities, including Boolean search, proximity, search on specified fields, truncation etc.
Output options	Search engine may allow user to limit number of hits, or use a preset number, or perform no limiting. Output is ranked in accordance with relevance calculated on the basis of word frequencies. Different algorithms are used in this ranking process, and this can have a significant effect on the effectiveness of the search engine. Users can sometime choose the metadata that is displayed for each source. Clicking on a URL will take the user straight to the resource.	Complete search set is shown for users to consider. This may be ranked in relevance or date order. Users may have options in relation to the fields in the record that are displayed. If full-text databases are being searched these will be displayed on request, but with bibliographic databases, the user needs to initiate a document delivery process.

Figure 11.1 Comparing Internet resources and traditional online and CD-ROM databases

Feature	Internet-based databases	Traditional on-line and CD-ROM databases
Downloading data	Data comes in a variety of different formats, and specifically is not normally in ASCII format, and Web pages often include graphics. Integration with local databases can present difficulties	Records are normally in ASCII and, subject to appropriate licensing arrangements, can be downloaded into local databases and integrated with records from other sources
Other services	Help pages, and FAQ pages to answer basic questions. Opportunities for users to suggest new URLs for inclusion in the database. Hyperlinks to associated documents.	Help windows. News on new facilities. Current awareness options. Document delivery.

Figure 11.1 *Concluded*

SEARCHING THE INTERNET

With the vast array of databases and other services available via the Internet it has been important to design interfaces that help users search the information sources and services available on the Internet. Retrieval is recognized to be a significant problem on the Internet, with databases in a wide variety of different formats and numerous different search and retrieval software packages mounted on the different computers and providing access via different interfaces to subsets of the databases. Various print-based similes have been used to describe the situation, one of which is that the current state of the Internet can be likened to a library in which everyone in the community has donated a book and tossed it into the middle of the library floor. Accordingly, a range of tools have been created which help users to locate Internet resources. Some of these rely entirely, or almost entirely, on automatic search and retrieval techniques, while others use human intervention in selection, evaluation and indexing.

Tools that are used for searching the Internet often operate in client/server mode. Server software that allows the user to search the database in a more intuitive way has been set up on many computers on the Internet. The user's local system runs the equivalent client software that communicates with the server software and gives a homogeneous interface to the data.

Browsers, described above, allow users to navigate between linked documents, but browsing is not an effective means of identifying specific information; this requires a search engine.

SEARCH ENGINES

A *search engine* is a retrieval mechanism that performs the basic retrieval task, the acceptance of a query, a comparison of the query with each of the records in a database, and the production of a retrieval set as output. The primary application of such search engines is to provide access to the resources that are available on the WWW, and stored on many different servers. A related area of application that is likely to grow in the next few years is the use of search engines as retrieval mechanisms in intranet environments for retrieval of documents from one organization's collection. Most search services are free, with their financial support coming from advertising revenue and through sales of the underlying technology. They can be located on a remote server on the Web, or located on a local PC or internal network. Increasingly search engines are becoming more than a Web index, and are adding content to their sites, in the form of additional services. Some believe that they are fast becoming information providers or 'hosts' in their own right.

Since search engines need to provide access to a large and distributed document collection the retrieval process must be efficient. This efficiency is achieved by the search engines using metadata to represent Web sites. Typical metadata includes URL, titles, headers, words and first lines. Some search engines also use abstracts and full text.

Each of the records contained in the database maintained by a global Web search service is created automatically by a program called a spider, robot, Web wanderer or Web crawler. Each time a spider is run, it is initially issued with the URLs of a small seed set of target Web pages. It retrieves and downloads copies of the targets of those links and then activates every link contained in those pages, and so on, until it has downloaded copies of every single page that it can find. Typical target Web pages are server lists, What's new pages, and the most popular sites. The main functions of a spider are the indexing of Web documents, HTML validation, link validation (do links still exist?), what's new monitoring and mirroring of Web sites.

The content of each page is stored in a record which also contains other fields containing basic metadata such as the title of the document, the date on which it was last modified, its size in megabytes and its URL. The values of these attributes are determined automatically from the document. Searching on these records is facilitated by the creation of an inverted index. The nature of this index depends on whether searching is by Boolean search or best-match searching (see Chapter 5). The inverted index is stored using compression techniques that reduce to a significant extent the storage capacity that it requires.

The *user interface* supports the interaction between the user and the system. For query formulation, the Web page presented to the user of a Web search engine typically contains a 'form' made up of a text entry box in which the user is invited to enter search terms. Check boxes or menu boxes to allow field limitations or the use of operators may also be featured on the form. Once the query has been formulated, the depression of a button labelled 'Submit' or some related term triggers a standard HTTP request to GET a document of a particular URL from the search service's Web server. The data entered by the user is appended to the URL in the form of a string of characters representing certain parameters and their values, together with a specification of the search program which is to be run, and to which those values should be passed, before the GET request is fulfilled.

Most Web search services use a best-match search process and present search output in order ranked by relevance. Relevance is calculated by the search engine and is based on:

- how many of the search terms were found in the document
- how often the search terms were found in the document
- where in the document the search terms were found (e.g. URL, metatags etc.)
- proximity of the terms to one another
- rarity of the terms.

Different search engines give different weightings to each of the above elements.

The assumption here is that the more similar a record is to a query, the more likely the document that it represents will be relevant to the user's information need. It is not unusual to find a very large number of hits; if this is the case, a rule of thumb is to scan the first 50 hits and, if these do not provide useful information, to consider redesigning the search strategy. On occasions it is possible with some search engines to get a completely different set of results on the basis of the same search strategy. This idiosyncrasy arises because some search engines, Alta Vista being a prime example, allocate a set amount of time to each search, and with complex or long searches the results displayed are those found when time has run out, and are not a complete set.

Once the search has been run, the Web server responds to the GET request by sending to the user a Web page for display in place of the original search form, whose content includes the output of the search program. The displays of the retrieval set typically take the form of a list of Web pages representing the records retrieved, ranked in order of their potential relevance to the query and presented a certain number, say, ten at a time; each of these incorporates a hypertext link to the source document presented by the record, and clicking on it will call up the source document This may be accompanied by a statement of how often each of the search terms were found in the whole database.

The information that is displayed for each entry in the results list derives from the data that is used to describe the site in the search engine database and typically includes:

- the title of the page
- the URL of the page
- a description taken from the metatag at the start of the Web page
- the relevance ranking of the site as calculated by the search engine
- the size of the page or file
- a date, which is usually the date that the page was loaded on to the server.

There are a number of different types of search engines. These include directories, subject gateways, meta search tools, and search bots and intelligent agents.

- *Basic search engines*, such as Alta Vista, collect data by sending out programs, known as spiders or robots, on to the Internet to look for new and updated Web pages. Information is brought back to the database. The whole process is automated.
- *Directories*, such as Yahoo! add value through human intervention in the assignment of subject headings to records in databases. In addition, all sites are visited and evaluated prior to inclusion. Web site creators may submit their page for consideration, but inclusion is subject to an evaluation process. Searching is via menus of the added subject headings, or through keyword searching. The maintenance of such directories is a labour-intensive process, which means that the search service is selective in the sites that are included. However, selection reduces the amount of garbage that can often present real problems in searching the Internet. Experiments are under way in the areas of semantic knowledge bases and the use of thesauri to improve search effectiveness. In addition, the users' ability to assess the relevance of a document depends critically upon the metadata that is displayed about the document in the displays of the retrieved set. Accordingly this is another area of current interest.
- *Subject gateways*, are similar to directories except that they have a specific subject focus. All resources are evaluated prior to inclusion. Some examples are listed in Figure 11.2. Most of those listed in Figure 11.2 are funded through the UK eLib initiative and, in general, represent the work of a group of academic libraries. There are also a number of more specialized gateways produced by libraries or individuals. Subject listings maintain an up-to-date list of these gateways, and can be useful in locating a gateway in a specific subject area. The creation and maintenance of subject gateways is explored in more detail below.

Type of tool	Name
Directories	Yahoo! YELL UK Yellow Pages
Basic search engines	AltaVista Hotbot Excite Infoseek Northern Light Lycos WebCrawler Euroferret EuroSeek SearchUK
Meta search tools	Metacrawler Debriefing
Searchbots	WebFerret WebCompass WebSeeker
Subject gateways	ADAM, the Art, Design, Architecture and Media Gateway SOSIG, the Social Science Information Gateway OMNI, the Organising Medical Networked Information project EEVL, the Edinburgh Engineering Virtual Library IHR-info, the Institute of Historical Research gateway HUMBUL Humanities Gateway
Subject source listings	BUBL NISS Directory of Networked Resources W3 Virtual Library List

Figure 11.2 Some examples of Internet search tools

- *Meta search and all-in-one tools* search for words and phrases across a number of search engines at the same time. They then amalgamate results, remove duplicate entries and present a single listing. They are a quick way of searching across several search tools, although they may not support some of the more sophisticated search facilities.
- *Search bots* act like meta search tools, and search many Internet search engines in parallel. They differ from meta search tools, in that they are loaded on the local workstation, rather than operating in client server mode.
- *Intelligent agents* can be used to collect relevant items on the basis of a search profile. Once a search has been performed, the user needs to assign relevance rankings to the items retrieved. The intelligent agent uses this information to modify its search process in its next iteration. Such tools are

313

particularly useful in current awareness searching and other contexts in which the same search needs to be rerun.

Search engines differ from one another in the following important respects:

- *Coverage of the database.* Some engines only provide access to WWW resources, whereas others provide access to a wide range of Internet resources. Other constraints may relate to the section of the site that is indexed. Yahoo!, for example, indexes only the home page of a site that is listed and not every page.
- *Search facilities and process.* Search engines search different parts of HTML documents. Some search only titles and headers, and not the full text of the HTML document. The range of search facilities also varies. Some search engines offer only basic keyword searching, but others offer Boolean searching and, even, proximity searching. Figures 11.3, 11.4 and 11.5 give some examples of the search facilities offered by search engines.
- *Results list.* Some engines display a simple list of resources, while others include the context of the hit, weighted results and options to link to similar pages.
- *Versions of search tool.* Many search tools have different versions for different countries. Yahoo!, for example, has a common main database, but the interface and headings are in the local language, and the results listings are displayed with sites based in that country region at the top. Current news stories and events also reflect local interests.

An awareness of the strengths and weaknesses of the different search engines is important in searching the Internet for resources (Figure 11.6). If a library is designing a Web site, it is important to be aware of the search engines that users may use in accessing that Web site.

CREATING AND MAINTAINING A WEB SITE

Most businesses and other organizations will use a Web site to increase their visibility in cyberspace. The Web is increasingly being seen as an opportunity for communication with customers and potential customers, suppliers and staff. The range of applications of a Web site for a typical organization may include:

- *Providing basic information about the organization,* such as product and services available, hours of availability, contact people, addresses and policies. There is an opportunity to make such information more interesting than through other media, through the inclusion of pictures of staff, a short sound file or direct e-mail links which allow users to send messages.

New Yahoo! Pager
Get My Yahoo!

Internet access

Win a trip to Florida
– with Disney

classification

Search Options

Search: ● All sites ○ UK & Ireland sites only

News - Finance - Sport - Weather - Cars - People Search - Free Email for UK & Ireland - My Yahoo!
Shopping - Horoscopes - Accommodation - **Yahoo! Online** - Business Finder - **Yahoo! Pager** - more
features

Arts & Humanities
Literature, Photography...

Business & Economy
Companies, Investments, Taxes...

Computers & Internet
Internet, WWW, Software, Games .

Education
UK, Ireland, Universities..

Entertainment
Humour, Movies, Music, Cool Links...

Government
UK, Ireland, Europe, Politics...

Health
Medicine, Drugs, Diseases, Fitness...

News & Media
Full Coverage, Newspapers, TV. .

Recreation & Sport
Sport, Outdoors, Travel, Motoring...

Reference
Libraries, Dictionaries, Phone Numbers...

Regional
UK, Ireland, Countries, Regions...

Science
CS, Biology, Astronomy, Engineering..

Social Science
Anthropology, Sociology, Economics...

Society & Culture
People, Environment, Royalty, Religion...

In The News

· **Kosovo:** Attacks to
continue

· **Pinochet:** Straw must
decide after Lord's ruling

· Take That! Robbie loses
court battle

· Seven million adults
struggle to read or count

· Major millennium bug
problems expected in July

[headlines...]

Inside Yahoo!

· **Yahoo! Pager:** Real time
instant messaging

· **Get the most out of
Yahoo!** with our site
directory

· **New to Yahoo!?** - For
help click here

[more features .]

**World
Yahoo!s**

Europe: Denmark - France - Germany - Italy - Norway - Spain - Sweden
Asia Pacific: Asia - Australia & NZ - Chinese - Hong Kong - Japan - Korea - Singapore -
Taiwan
Americas Yahoo! - Canada - Spanish

Other Guides
Yahooligans! - My Yahoo! - Full Coverage - Yahoo! Internet Life - Picks of the Week
Irish Picks - Scottish Picks - UK Net Events - News Ticker

Smart Shopping with **VISA**

Company Info - Advertise on Yahoo! - Privacy Policy - Get some Yahoo! - Adding a Web Site - Jobs @ Yahoo!

Figure 11.3 Yahoo! search page: search specification

315

 Search Help - Personalise Quotes - Football - People Search - News - Weathe

Search Result Found **7** categories and **156** sites for **classification**

Categories	Web Sites	Web Pages	News Stones

Yahoo! UK & Ireland Category Matches (1 - 7 of 7)

Buy It Here!

Computers and Internet > Internet > World Wide Web > Searching the Web > Indices to Web Documents > Dewey Decimal **Classification**

Buy Books
amazon.co.uk
Find books fast!
Up to +0% off

Reference > Libraries > Professional Resources > Technical Services > Cataloging > LC **Classification**

Science > Biology > Molecular Biology > Protein Research > SCOP: Structural **Classification** of Proteins

Reference > Libraries > Professional Resources > Library **Classification** on the Web

Reference > Standards > North American Industry **Classification** System (NAICS)

Computers and Internet > Internet > World Wide Web > Searching the Web > Indices to Web Documents > Universal Decimal **Classification**

Computers and Internet > Internet > World Wide Web > Searching the Web > Indices to Web Documents > Library of Congress **Classification**

Yahoo! UK & Ireland Site Matches (1 - 13 of 156)

Reference > Libraries > Library and Information Science > Organisations

- **Classification** Society of North America (CSNA) - promotes the scientific study of **classification** and clustering (including systematic methods of creating **classifications** from data)

Science > Biology > Systematics and Taxonomy

- **Classification** of Living Things - learn about the Linnaean system of **classification** used in the biological sciences to describe and categorize all living things, with a focus on finding out how humans fit within this system
- Nuts and Bolts of Taxonomy and **Classification** - exercise illustrating the creativity involved in taxonomy and the roles form and function, ancestral traits, and derived characters play in generating **classification** schemes

Science > Biology > Systematics and Taxonomy > Organisations

Figure 11.4 Yahoo! search page: search results

316

LYC S
Your Personal Internet Guide

Search for: [   ] (**Find**)

All Search Options

Help
Service

	and/or	and/or	
Company Name	Business Type	Town or County	

Lycos Homepage > Search > Results

News
Pictures of the Day
Weather

Advertise on Lycos
Add Your Site
Contact Lycos
Home On The Net
Jobs@Lycos
Link to Lycos
Legal Infos
Lycos Explorer
Safe Search

Classifieds
UK Businesses
Jobs
Search Options
Translation
Pictures&Sound

Help
Search
Search Options
Relevancy
Boolean
Pics&Sounds
Add a Site

You searched webpages worldwide for "**classification**".

CD NOW
Music Store

Check These Out

Buy Books about **classification** from The Internet Bookshop
Pages in UK/Ireland: **classification**
Pictures: **classification**
Sounds: **classification**
To Find UK businesses search the **Thomson Directory**

Results 1-10

<< . **1** . 2 . 3 . 4 . 5 . 6 . 7 . 8 . 9 . 10 . >>

members.tripod.com
 Atlnatic Basin Tropical Cyclone Classification
 Continue with hurricane classification figures.: This will
 take you back to my home page.:
 http://members.tripod.com/~chaos53/hurclass2.html (1k)
 More like this

 Trivial Knowledge - Natural History - Classification of Li
   Categories Classification of Living Organisms
 Foreword Classification of the Human Species The Five
 Kingdoms Back to Natural History
 http://members.tripod.com/~Theroux/trivia/nathist01.html (3k)
 More like this

 sci\classification
 FANCYSKI CLASSIFICATIONS General Classification
 Pos.NameSurnamePoints 1° Stefano Guagnetti 991 2°
 Carlo Castello 958 3° Luca Barlassina 920 4° Mauro
 Busnelli 908 5° Roberto Castell
 http://members.tripod.com/~ccastel/sci/ingcla.htm (1k)
 More like this

 Internet: Classification de l'Information
 Internet: Classification de l'information Recension de
 l'information automatisée sans discrimination automatisée
 et discriminée classification plutôt humaine Type de
 classement mot ou groupe de mots a
 http://members.tripod.com/~Delisle2/pres2/tsld008.htm (1k)
 More like this

Figure 11.5 Search results from Lycos

317

Facility	Yahoo!	AltaVista	Lycos
Web	750 000	140 m	30 m
Usenet search	Yes, via Options	Yes – 2 weeks	No
Case sensitive	Sometimes	Yes, if required	No
Wildcard/Truncation	*	*	No
Phrases	" ...... "	" ...... "	" ...... "
Must include word	+	+	+
Exclude (NOT)	–	–	–
Default search options	Any of your words	Any of your words	Any of your words
Word in URL	u:word	url:word	Lycos pro
Word in title	t:word	Title:word	Lycos pro
Links to specificed URL	No	Link:url	No
Specify part of domain	No	Domain:	No
Specify Web site	No	Host:	No
Limit by date	Yes – via Options	Yes, Advanced	No
Limit by language	No	Yes	Lycos pro
Limit by geography	Yes (Country Yahoo!)	Yes e.g. +domain:uk	Yes in country versions
Search operators	AND, OR	AND (&), OR ( ), AND NOT (!), NEAR (~)	AND, OR, NOT, ADJ, NEAR, FAR, BEFORE
Refine search	No	Yes	Yes

Figure 11.6 Comparing search facilities in search tools

- *New ways through which customers can access organizational facilities and services.* Examples for libraries include:
  - book request forms that can be completed by users, and then converted into catalogue data
  - remote access to catalogues
  - improved OPAC search interfaces
  - showcase to library resources, such as library tours, or a video of story-time
  - new information services, such as a home page linked to a collection of electronic texts, databases and other Internet resources; such access can be designed for specific user groups, such as children, or the housebound
  - access to the resources of the online search services.
- *Interactive home pages,* offering facilities such as:
  - fill in forms used for feedback and services

- requests for purchases
- questions concerning services.
- *Linking customers to remote information*, and connecting to information resources around the world. These resources may be other sites that the organization thinks might be useful or, alternatively, the sites of related organizations whose products and services they may wish to promote. Hot lists and bookmark files of frequently used resources for support in answering frequently asked questions, may be provided.
- *Staff development*. Offering a WWW service allows staff the opportunity to keep involved in developments in this field, and to be aware of what related organizations are doing in the areas of e-commerce, and e-communication.
- *Communication with suppliers* – The Internet can provide access catalogues of suppliers' products, and mechanisms for placing orders.
- *Policy and practice documents, and other internal documents* can be distributed to geographically scattered sites in order to keep the various members of staff in an organization aware of developments.
- *Document delivery.* Electronic documents are one of the main products that can be provided digitally. The use of the networked pubic access catalogues of other libraries, and the online search services, coupled with document delivery services is an increasingly important avenue for document delivery.

The creation and maintenance of a Web site needs continuing commitment. Web sites need to be professionally designed and regularly updated if they are to portray a positive message about the organization. A Web site is a shop window for an organization and its services. A Web site needs to be managed in much the same way as any other promotional venture or service. Clear objectives need to be identified at the beginning of a project to create a Web site; these will determine the content and design of the site. In a burst of enthusiasm it is easy to view a Web site as a one-off project. For continued effectiveness the resources need to be available for updating, evaluation and maintenance. Some of the issues that need to be considered include:

- *Objective*: the creation of a Web site must start with the identification of the objectives of that Web site. Standard promotional questions need to be asked and answered: Who is the audience? What is the message? Which is the most appropriate form in which to convey the message? How can the likelihood that the message will be seen or heard be maximized? If the Web site also has a purpose in supplying services, or in offering access to other information, the nature and scope of these facilities need to be determined and agreed. In large organizations it may be necessary to coordinate the creation of a number of Web sites, and to agree the distinct objectives of each.
- *Staff ownership*: staff should identify with and be aware of the site and its

intended objectives. This can most effectively be achieved by keeping staff involved in the development of the site, and encouraging them to visit the site from time to time. Staff involvement is essential because they need to be aware of the messages that are being conveyed to others and, in particular to customers, and also, if they are in contact with customers, when to refer customers to the Web site services. In addition, staff input of a variety of different types will be needed in order to be confident that the information provided on the Web site is current. Staff may be involved in updating basic information about the organization's activities, or alternatively they may be responsible for other aspects of the content of the Web site, such as the maintenance of links to other related Web sites.

- *Content*: information may need to be drawn from sources across the organiz- ation; these sources must be identified. Any new content will need to be designed. Remote content needs to be located, and evaluated prior to selec- tion. Further discussion of the evaluation of content for inclusion in Web sites follows in the section on setting up a gateway.

- *Presentation* is concerned with structure and style of the Web site. This includes the design of the individual pages, but also the underlying template and design that provides a standard for all pages. Consistency in this area can be a particular challenge for large multinational organizations, where there may be a number of different Web sites loaded by different parts of the organization. A corporate image needs to be established and used throughout. In this context it is important to remember that the Web facili- tates global communication. The Web space structure, which is determined by the way in which pages are linked together, is also an important element in design.

- *Promotion* is concerned with attracting visitors to the site. As with any other product or service, the work does not stop when the product is completed. A Web site needs promotion. This can be achieved through workshops, posters and over the WWW. Links with other sites, and inclusion in search engines are much coveted for promotional purposes.

- *Evaluation* is concerned with monitoring whether the Web site is achieving its objectives. The number of visits to the site is one measure of success, but more searching evaluation can be achieved through user evaluation, and whether interest or business is being generated as a result of the visit. Regular communication with users through electronic suggestion boxes and other interactive devices provides useful information for evaluation.

- *Maintenance* can be a major task. Information needs to be updated, and, as the information is updated, links between pages must be reviewed. A new corporate image or design requires a complete overhaul of the design of all pages in the Web site.

ESTABLISHING A SUBJECT GATEWAY

A number of organizations, including groups of academic libraries, have sought to establish gateways to Internet resources, or to embed some guidance on appropriate resources in a home page. Some examples of such gateways are listed in Figure 11.2. These projects are a recognition that, although there is a wealth of information available through the Internet, browsers and search engines are not always effective in identifying the most important sources. This is largely because such tools are, at best, limited in the extent to which they seek to evaluate sources. Internet resources:

- include a large amount of junk
- have grown rapidly, which leads to significant changes in the resources available on a daily basis.
- include resources which disappear, or cease to be of use because they are not updated.

A key issue for users, and for the creators of gateways that are intended to help users in navigating Internet resources, is quality assurance and, specifically, quality assurance in a shifting morass of resources. There is no standard or authority associated with publishing on the Web. Publishing standards that have been well tested and established in print publishing do not yet apply to the Internet. Internet resources are not subject to the type of evaluation, refereeing, reviewing and editing processes associated with print publishing. In other words, some of the stages in the 7 Rs model (Figure 1.1) are bypassed. The onus for evaluation lies with the user, or with the information professional who seeks to create a subject gateway. The key issues in quality assurance are authority, accuracy, appropriateness and accessibility:

- *Authority* is often evaluated on the basis of the author, the publisher, or the originating institution for a given resource. Problems arise when one of these cannot be identified, or when it is difficult to assess the authority of the agent in this context. This assessment of authority requires subject knowledge and an awareness of the authority and reputation of originators of information.
- *Accuracy* is more difficult to assess in the absence of reviewing, assessing and editing. It is possible to check superficial factors, such as spelling, typography and grammatical errors. Evaluation of the accuracy of the content depends on the evaluator's subject knowledge.
- *Appropriateness*, or the interests of the anticipated audience. Key aspects in determining appropriateness are subject and currency. A gateway may define its boundaries in terms of subject coverage, or may be seeking to provide a service for, say, a specific academic community with relatively wide subject

multiple approaches to one source. The internationally recognized standards, such as DDC, UDC and LCC are not always appropriate in gateways with a specific subject orientation. Again, special classification schemes may assist in some applications, but many gateway developers may need to design and maintain a classification scheme that meets their particular purposes.

- *Search facilities and interfaces* are determined by the search software that is used to create the gateway. It is desirable for there to be both simple and advanced interfaces. A useful range of search facilities includes: Boolean logic, searching on specific fields, stemming or truncation, proximity searching and relevance ranking. The integration of thesauri supports the expansion of searches. Other useful facilities are the ability to handle natural-language enquiries, duplicate checking and report-generating tools.
- *Evaluation and updating.* The effectiveness of the gateway needs to be evaluated, with feedback from users. In addition, the sources that are included in the gateway, as well as, from time to time, the design of the gateway will need revision.

HOW TO GUIDE: QUESTIONS FOR USE IN THE EVALUATION OF INTERNET RESOURCES

- What is the intended audience? Is this academic, business, professional or popular?
- What is the frequency of update? Is there any information on updating?
- What is the affiliated institution?
- What is the resource developer's expertise? Is there an 'about' section that describes the author/creator?
- What is the relationship between resources and other resources on the same topic? Are there any links or references to these related resources?
- Are there any reviews or evaluations of the site? What do these say?
- Is any permission needed for access, and are any charges made for access?

DOCUMENT PUBLISHING ON THE WEB

Document publishing systems are systems that support the creation, storage and subsequent retrieval and dissemination of documents and/or document representations or metadata. They are widely used in information retrieval applications and, in particular, are important in supporting the publication of documents on CD-ROM or the Web. The documents that such systems manage may be in any medium, including text, graphics, sound, still or moving images, video, or any mixture of these, in the form of a multimedia document. Although there are increasing opportunities for multimedia document creation, the volume of text-based information is increasing at an alarming rate, with a great diversity of form. This ranges from the relatively unstructured memo, letter or journal article, to the more formally structured report, directory or book. Such text-based documents were previously managed through the earlier generations of document publishing and management systems, then described as text management systems, or text retrieval systems. Text management systems were distinguished from other database management software by a set of characteristics that supported the effective management of text-based applications. These characteristics are still applicable to document publishing and management systems:

- the ability to handle variable-length fields and the expectation that many of the fields in the records will be of variable length
- access to records is usually through an inverted file of index keys or words from the text of the records on the database
- a range of retrieval facilities that support retrieval based on words in records; these are necessary to accommodate the fact that there is limited control over the form in which the search key might appear in the record
- emphasis on the management of one or more distinct databases, since the ability to draw data from a number of related databases is not central to the application
- relatively fixed applications which require limited programming or systems development facilities.

Large publishers make use of such software in the distribution of a wide range of electronic documents, such as electronic journals and books. In addition, corporate publishing across a corporate intranet is an important application of such systems.

What is the difference between Internet document publishing products and Internet search engines such as Yahoo! and Lycos? The major issue is that Yahoo! and Lycos work on repositories of HTML documents. This gives rise to two problems. First, HTML indexing and retrieval tools have limitations. Second, in many organizations considerable information exists in documents that are not HTML structured, such as word-processed documents and spreadsheets. If these repositories are large it may not be feasible to convert them to HTML documents or, if they are changing, it may not be desirable to manage an ongoing conversion process. In such cases, Yahoo! and Lycos cannot index or search the documents. Internet document publishing products support the indexing of unstructured documents, and provide users with the full-text searching capabilities of those indices. The original document format can be directly searched and made available on the Internet through an HTML search form. These capabilities facilitate publishing internally generated documents for either Internet or intranet use.

THE PUBLICATION PROCESS

In order to appreciate the features that are necessary in a document publishing system, it is useful to review the nature of and steps in the electronic publication process. The stages in the process that is associated with making documents available in electronic form, via the Internet or intranet, are represented in Figure 11.7. The stages in the first column of Figure 11.7 are also applicable to publication on CD-ROM. In such applications, the fourth stage becomes publication on CD-ROM. This then needs to be followed by a stage in which the CD-ROM is mounted in a workstation or, for multiple users, a server.

The stages in Figure 11.7 can be divided into two groups:

- those executed by the systems designer and document creator
- those executed by the document user.

The first four stages are associated with the creation and preparation of the electronic document, or document publishing. The final three stages are concerned with document retrieval. Each of these stages is described briefly.

First, the systems creator will design an appropriate database environment and set up dynamic search and index support tools such as thesauri. Next, documents are entered and tagged, and converted into appropriate formats, often described as populating the database. Such database creation includes indexing. The database or document will then be uncompressed and mastered for delivery in whichever format is appropriate. This may include Internet, CD-ROM, LAN or WAN. Next the user takes over and submits search requests, which are then processed by the software. This results in the display of a results list, from which the user selects one or more documents to view and/or download.

The key issues that a document publishing system needs to address to support effective publication and retrieval are:

- the integration of mixed computing platforms in order to avoid disenfranchisement of some users
- data entry and document creation
- control over documents once they have been published, including issues associated with security (including control of access) and updating
- effective access and retrieval whenever documents are required.

Figure 11.8 lists some document management and publishing systems, together with their suppliers. Contact addresses are not given, since all of these suppliers

Phase	Description	Initiated By
Identify content	Identify a subset of documents to be indexed and made available on the Internet	System administrator
Database set-up	Define a database template or framework for the text database, which will store the indices of the processed documents	System administrator
Populate database	Performs indexing and populate database with the indices of the processed documents	Systems administrator
Internet enable/publish	Once the documents are processed and appropriate Internet connections are made (i.e. TCP/IP), an HTML input form is created as an interface through which users can enter their search requests	User/client
Process search requests	When search criteria are provided to the HTML form, the text retrieval engine performs a search on the repository. This typically includes building the logic for the search and translating it (if SQL) into a native programming language.	User/client
Present results	Displays the search results in the form of a hit list. Users can make selections from the hit list in order to view a particular document	User/client
View/download original	When the user selects an item from the hit list, the retrieval engine transmits the required document from its original location and presents it to the client in a viewable format. If the user wants to download the document, request is made to the server, which assists the client Internet browser downloading of the file	User/client

Figure 11.7 Phases of the Internet document management and publishing process

can be accessed through the Web, using the name of the system supplier as a search key.

Document publishing systems need a range of document creation features, such as:

- visual desktops in which documents can be easily arranged for chapter ordering
- book catalogues which manage groups of documents
- ease of access to creation formats, such as word processing, tables, charts and graphics
- advanced tools to support the creation of graphics and images

System	Supplier
askSam	AskSam Systems
BASIS	Information Dimensions Inc.
CAIRS	CAIRS Text and Library Systems
DB/TextWorks	Soutron
Clearview and Clearnet Authoring and Retrieval	Clarinet Systems Ltd
Insight	Enigma-Sumitomo UK
TINlib	EOS International
AIRS	Euritis S A
FOLIO	FOLIO
OLIB	FretwellDowning Informatics Ltd
HEADFAST	Head Software International
ODARS	Infoware Gmbh
Recall Plus	Insoft Ltd
Muscat	Muscat Ltd
PLWeb	Systematic Datasearch Ltd
ZyIMAGE	ZyLAB
WebVISION	Abacus Software Ltd
Reference Manager	Research Information Systems

Figure 11.8 Some document management and publishing systems

- version control – to manage document versions throughout the life cycle
- access control – to allow different types of access to documents, as well as to implement information security policies for secure document access
- tracking – to track document access and change, creating its history to support audit requirements
- templates – for defining standard document types, and behaviour and establishing consistent application properties.

The most sophisticated of these packages have an object-oriented architecture. Group-working is supported by view-only facilities, coupled with annotation. Support for multiple languages may also be available, and special features that support the creation of SGML documents. Some of these manage document objects, rather than complete documents. The really large systems need to be capable of operating on multiple servers to serve vast user communities and store vast databases. This requires very large database (VLDB) capability to allow an index to be split physically across several files.

Once the document has been created, questions of *use and retrieval* arise. In this context the range of information retrieval facilities is important. The retrieval facilities associated with a document publishing system are central to the effective operation of the system. With increasing connectivity, many more users need sophisticated search facilities as they seek to navigate their way through vast quantities of knowledge. Accordingly, more and more of the search facilities that were once unique to *document or text management* systems are now to be found in the search engines on the Internet, and on library public access systems. Indexing facilities that are especially appropriate in document publishing applications include:

- indexing on any field or part of a structured or unstructured document
- combinations of automatic indexing, tagged indexing (terms manually selected from text), manual keyword indexing and relational indexing.

Thesaurus construction and maintenance facilities are important and may, for instance, allow the automatic posting of preferred and macro (generic group) terms. Hyperlinks are useful in moving between documents. In a multimedia database, these hypertext links may be pictures, images, spreadsheets and word-processed documents. Other new facilities include 'note search' which allows the user to collect selected terms from the output and to use these as a basis for another search if required.

Interface design is also important in effective searching. Most document publishing systems offer GUIs. The use of GUIs has facilitated search strategy editing, recall of earlier search sets, browsing, and the selection and highlighting of relevant documents for later printing or downloading to a personal database. Some systems offer different interfaces for different categories of user, such as expert or novice modes. Multilingual interfaces are a feature of a few systems.

Security is important in any multi-user database environment. The first level of security is concerned with database security. Features such as automatic recovery subsequent to a system failure are important in maintaining the integrity of the database. Access to the database is another aspect of data security. The better systems offer selected access, according to user group, to specified databases, specified documents or records or specified fields. Thus the early definition of document types and attributes is an important device in determining the document views that individual users have of the database. Some users may have read-only access whereas others may be allowed to change the data. Important categories of user might be producer, consumer and administrator. The consumer may only have access to the author and title, the producer may have access also to date, category and abstract, and the administrator may also have access to version and security. The chief security measures offered are passwords and user identification numbers. Security login is useful to report any attempts to breach security. Data encryption is a feature in some document publishing systems.

Special issues that need to be considered when publishing databases over the Internet include:

1. *Access* – ensuring that access to the database is stable, but also that users

only have access to the files on the server to which they should have access; security must be available for confidential information such as staffing or financial records. Search speed is also crucial; this requires a sufficiently powerful file server.

2. *Database quality and maintenance*, including appropriate indexing, needs just as much attention in the Internet environment as in other contexts.

3. *Support* – often in the form of online help, but possibly also accompanied by printed documentation. A telephone or e-mail contact point for when things go wrong is often necessary. Also communication with users about new developments is important.

4. *Marketing* – databases need to be promoted. Channels include electronic mailing lists and bulletin boards. Other channels such as press releases and receptions still remain important, as are any other contacts with key user groups, such as those at exhibitions. The database also needs to be included in database directories and Internet resources guides. Demonstration discs are valuable.

FURTHER DEVELOPMENTS

As more and more organizations recognize the value of effective management of their electronic document collections, the role of document publishing systems will become ever more significant. It is likely that a significant number of these applications will be supported by intranet technology, because this offers the immense attraction of platform independence. Issues that are likely to be significant in the future for document publishing include:

- *Workgroup publishing* – suppliers are beginning to revisit the document creation aspect of document management and to incorporate features that support team-based document creation. As the demand to create more documents in multimedia format grows, so the facilities for group work publishing will need to become more sophisticated.

- Increased use of *hybrid publication*, including the use of CD-ROM/Web. Features necessary to support integration of access to data in different formats will need to be further developed. This includes indexing facilities that can provide access to data stored in these different formats.

- Increasing *globalization*, with applications supporting organizations operating across several countries. The need to manage documents in multiple languages is becoming more pressing.

- Closer *integration of document publishing and document management* facilities in order to create a seamless process of document assembly, management, retrieval, distribution and publication. For some products this will be linked to increased sophistication in their facilities for data entry and document creation.

● Closer *integration with Web server technology* in order to provide Web opportunities that offer seamless access to information. For example, the BASIS Web server gateway is fully integrated with Microsoft Internet Server (IIS) and Netscape Enterprise Server.

Internet and intranet technology offer platforms for document publishing. Document publishing systems already offer important opportunities for electronic publication; it is likely that the number and type of applications supported by these systems will escalate over the next few years.

CHALLENGES FOR THE INTERNET

Projections of the growth in the number of Internet servers and users accessing Internet resources are available from numerous sources, and change too rapidly to be encapsulated in a book; accordingly, none of these are reproduced here! Nevertheless, the Internet has the potential to realize the final stage of the exponential curve that was embedded in the speculations of writers on the information explosion earlier in the twentieth century. This in itself will pose yet more problems for information management but, in the mean time, there are a number of other problems associated with the exchange of information over the Internet that need to be addressed. Some of these are less pressing if the Internet is viewed largely as a tool for a community of IT enthusiasts and as a means for communication between individuals, but now that commercial applications are becoming significant they will need to be addressed. The issues are:

● *The 'World Wide Wait'.* One of the most annoying features of the Internet is the speed with which Web pages are delivered to a screen. The graphics embedded in many pages are demanding of transmission capacity and there are a number of servers and clients that suffer from relatively slow telecommunications links. Delays can be further aggravated by high traffic on some sections of the Internet. This will get worse rather than better as the volume of traffic increases, unless higher capacity telecommunications links are available across more elements of the networks that comprise the Internet, and/or improved data compression algorithms allow more data to be transmitted through the same bandwidth.

● *Security and ownership.* Issues of copyright and intellectual property are of particular concern to the information industry, since issues of ownership are at the heart of rights, responsibilities and who has the authority to make commercial arrangements associated with information. These must be addressed through a mixture of legislation that is relevant across an international network (and this is a true challenge in itself), practice, licences and the agreements. However, in addition, to be able to conduct commerce on the Internet, the ability to keep monetary and other propriety information (such as order information) secure as it passes across the Internet, and the need to authenticate the status and identity of the sender, is crucial for effective commercial transactions.

- *Structure.* Users cannot locate the information or the site that they want on the Internet unless they are searching with a specific address, and addresses change. Even the most hardened of technocrats, have been heard to rehearse the wonders of Dewey and other classification schemes. As discussed above, some of the search engines offer evaluation, classification and indexing of Internet resources. The role that search engines play in providing access to Internet resources will evolve over the next few years. Search engines will be viewed as increasingly central in determining which sites users visit; as consumer guides they have the potential to be very powerful. In addition, a greater number of search engines will be necessary to meet the needs of different client groups. An important element in the professional development of information managers will be current awareness in respect of the scope and features of the search engines.

SUMMARY

The Internet and the World Wide Web have changed the landscape of information retrieval. Many of the online search services can be accessed through the Web, and a plethora of other information resources are available through this channel. Although browsers are useful in allowing users to move between documents in searching, search engines are necessary if searchers are to locate specific information There are a number of different types of search engines, including basic search engines, directories, subject gateways, meta search tools and search bots. Search results differ between different search engines. Many organizations create their own Web site in order to enhance their visibility in cyberspace. Other organizations, including groups of academic libraries, have sought to establish gateways to Internet resources. Information managers will not only be involved with the identification of information on the Web, but may also have responsibility for document publishing. Document publishing systems support the creation, storage, and subsequent retrieval and dissemination of documents and document representations or metadata.. Key challenges for the future of the Internet concern the 'World Wide Wait', security and ownership, and the structuring of knowledge.

FURTHER READING

There are a wide range of sources on the Internet and intranet, in both print and electronic form. This is a small sample of such resources that either offer practical advice, or describe case study experiences that might also offer guidance to others embarking on similar projects.

Anon (1996) CD-ROM indexing/authoring systems *Digital Publishing Techniques*, **1** (12), 12–16.

Ashford, J. A. and Willet, P. (1989) *Text Retrieval and Document Databases*, Bromley, Chartwell Bratt.

Biddiscombe, R., Knowles, K, Upton, J. and Wilson, K. (1997) Developing a Web library guide for an academic library: problems, solutions and future possibilities. *Program*, 31 (1), 59–74.

Blakeman, K. (1997) Intelligent search agents: search tools of the future? *Business Information Searcher*, **7** (1), 16–18.

Blakeman, K. (1998) *Search Strategies for the Internet: How to Identify Essential Resources More Effectively.* Caversham: RBA Information Services.

Blinko, B. B. (1996) Academic staff, students and the Internet: the experience at the University of Westminster. *Electronic Library*, **14** (2), 111–16.

Boyle, J. (1997) A blueprint for managing documents. *Byte*, **22** (5), May, 75–6, 78, 80.

Bradley, P. (1997) Going online, CD-ROM and the Internet, 10th edn. London: Aslib.

Bradshaw, R. (1997) Introducing ADAM: a gateway to Internet resources in Art, Design, Architecture and Media. *Program*, **31** (3), July, 251–67.

Branse, Y. et al. (1996) Libraries on the Web. *Electronic Library*, **14** (2), 117–21.

Chowdhury, G. G. (1999) The Internet and information retrieval research: a brief review. *Journal of Documentation*, **55** (2), 209–25.

Clarke, S. J. and Willett, P. (1997) Estimating the recall performance of Web search engines. *Aslib Proceedings*, **49** (7), 184–9.

Cox, J. (1995) Publishing databases on the Internet. *Managing Information*, **2** (4), April, 30–32.

Cunningham, S. (1995) Electronic publishing on CD-ROM. In *International Conference on Digital Media and Electronic Publishing*, Weetwood Hall Conference Centre, Leeds, December 1994. London: British Computer Society.

Curle, D. (1997) Downloading data from the Web: you are not in ASCII any more. *Online*, 21 (4), 51–8.

Davenport, E., Proctor, R. and Goldenberg, (1997) A distributed expertise: remote reference service on a metropolitan area network. *Electronic Library*, **15** (4) August, 271–8.

Davies, R. (1996) The Internet as a tool for Asian libraries. *Asian Libraries*, **5** (1), 43–52.

Dawson, A. (1997) *The Internet for Library and Information Professionals*, 2nd edn. London: Library Association.

Dong, X. and Su, L. T. (1997) Search engines on the World Wide Web and information retrieval from the Internet: a review and evaluation. *On-line and CD-ROM Review*, **21** (2), 67–81.

Ellis, D., Ford, N. and Furner, J. (1998) In search of the unknown user: indexing, hypertext and the World Wide Web. *Journal of Documentation*, **54** (1), 28–47.

Falk, H. (1996) Working the Web. *Electronic Library*, **14** (5), October, 453–69.

Falk, H. (1997) World Wide Web search and retrieval. *Electronic Library*, **15** (1), 49–55.

Garlock, K. L. and Piontek, S. (1996) *Building the Service Based Library Website; a Step-by-Step Guide to Design and Options.* Chicago and London: ALA.

Hamilton, F. J. (1998) Document management: getting better or just complicated? *Information Management Report*, April, 13–16 .

Harrison, S. (1997) NHSWeb: a health intranet. *Aslib Proceedings*, **49** (2) February, 36–7.

Heery, R. (1996) Review of metadata formats. *Program*, **30** (4), 345–73.

Helm, P. (1997) Hewlett Packard and the intranet – case study and alliances. *Aslib Proceedings*, **49** (2), February, 32–5.

Hitchcock, S., Carr, L. and Hall, W. (1997) Web journals publishing: a UK perspective. *Serials*, **10** (3), 285–99.

Jasco, P. (1996) The Internet as a CD-ROM alternative. *Information Today*, **13** (3), 29–31.

Jasco, P. (1996) Who's doing what in the CD-ROM publishing realm. *Computers in Libraries*, **16** (9), 55–6.

Jeffcoate, G. (1996) Gabriel: gateway to European national libraries. *Program*, **30** (3), 229–38.

Kalin, S. and Wright, C. (1994) Internexus: a partnership for Internet instruction. In R. Kinder (ed), *Libraries on the Internet: Impact on Reference Services*, pp. 29–41. New York: Haworth Press.

Kimberley, R. (1986) *Integrating Text with Non-Text [En] a Picture Is Worth 1K Words: Proceedings of the Institute of Information Scientists Text Retrieval '85 Conference*, London, Taylor-Graham.

Kimberley, R. (ed.) (1990) *Text Retrieval: A Directory of Software*, 3rd edn. Aldershot: Gower.

Kimberley, R., Hamilton, C. D. and Smith, C. H. (eds) (1985) *Text Retrieval in Context: Proceedings of the Institute of Information Scientists Text Retrieval '84 Conference*, London, Taylor-Graham.

MacLeod, R. and Kerr, L. (1997) EEVL: past, present and future. *Electronic Library*, **15** (4), August, 279–86.

Marcoux, Y. and Sevigny, M. (1997) Why SGML? Why Now? *Journal of the American Society for Information Science*, **48** (7), 584–92.

McMahon, K. (1995) Using the BUBL information service as an Internet reference resource. *Managing Information*, **2** (4), 33–5.

McMurdo, G. (1995) How the Internet was indexed. *Journal of Information Science*, **21** (6), 479–89.

Merchant, B. and Winters, N. (1997) Small libraries on the Internet. *Library Technology*, **2** (4), August, 78–9.

Morrel, P. (1997) Building intranet-based information systems for international companies etc. *Aslib Proceedings*, **49** (2), February, 27–31.

Nieuwenhuysen, P. and Vanouplines, P. (1997) Libraries and the World Wide Web. *Electronic Library*, **15** (2), April, 79–81.

Notess, G. R. (1997) Internet search techniques and strategies. *Online*, 21 (4), 63–6.

Pal, A., Ring, K. and Downes, V. (1996) *Intranets for Business Applications*. London: Ovum Reports.

Poutler, A. (1997) The design of the World Wide Web search engines: a critical review. *Program*, **31** (2) 131–45.

Pritchard, J. A. T. (1998) Developments in document management systems. *Information Management Report*, March, 15–18.

Rowlands, I. (ed.) (1987) *Text Retrieval: An Introduction*. London: Taylor-Graham.

Rowley, J. (1996) Retailing and shopping on the Internet, *Internet Research: Electronic Networking Applications and Policy*, **6** (1), 81–91.

Rusch-Feja, D. (1997) Subject oriented collection of information resources from the Internet, *Libri*, **47** (1), 1–24.

Still, J. (ed.) (1994) *The Internet Library: Case Studies of Library Internet Management and Use*. Westport, CT: Mecklermedia.

Storey, T. and Dalrymple, T. (1996) One the Web with OCLC FirstSearch and NetFirst. *OCLC Newsletter*, (220), 26–9.

Tedd, L. A. (1995) An introduction to sharing resources via the Internet in academic libraries and information centres in Europe. *Program*, **29** (1), January, 43–61.

Tegenbos, J. and Nieuwenhuysen, P. (1997) My kingdom for an agent? Evaluation of Autonomy, an intelligent search agent for the Internet. *Online and CD-ROM Review*, **21** (3), 139–48.

Tseng, G., Poulter, A. and Sargent, G. (1997) *The Library and Information Professional's Guide to the World Wide Web*. London: Library Association

Watson, J. (1996) Evaluating Internet text retrieval products. *Document World*, May–June, 3.

Willet, P. (ed.) (1988), *Document Retrieval Systems*. London: Taylor-Graham for IIS (The Foundations of Information Science, Vol. 3).

Winship, I. and McNab, A. (1996) *The Student's Guide to the Internet*. London: Library Association.

333

Woodward, J. (1996) Cataloguing and classifying information resources on the Internet. *Annual Review of Information Science and Technology,* **31**, 189–220.

Yip, K. F. (1997) Selecting internet resources: experience at the Hong Kong University of Science an Technology (HKUST) Library. *Electronic Library,* **15** (2) April, 91–8.

12 Manual information retrieval systems

INTRODUCTION

This chapter draws together a number of information retrieval topics, many of which are of particular interest in printed and card-based indexes. Although electronic indexes have taken on a central significance, there remain many applications in which it is necessary to arrange printed documents, or to create and use printed indexes. Most kinds of index today are computer-produced. They are nevertheless discussed here, as the mode of searching concerns us even more than the means of production. At the end of this chapter you will:

- understand the principles associated with document arrangement for effective browsing and document location
- know the points of similarity and contrast between manual and machine-searchable indexes
- understand the components of printed catalogues and indexes
- be aware of the main approaches to the creation of printed indexes
- understand some techniques for the effective searching of printed indexes
- be acquainted with the key principles of book indexing
- appreciate the significance of filing sequences and some of the problems associated with establishing effective filing sequences.

DOCUMENT ARRANGEMENT

GENERAL PRINCIPLES

Documents in libraries or resource centres must be physically stored. With closed access collections, storage may be by factors that are not significant for retrieval, for example by size or by date added. Access is by means of indexes, and the information professional will act as an intermediary between the stock and the user. Open access environments are different. Documents must be arranged or physically stored in an order which requires a minimum of explanation, and which matches as far as possible the search patterns of users.

The open access principle helps both management and users. Self-service was commonly available in libraries for many years before it was taken up by the retail trade. Managerially it is clearly cheaper to allow users to carry their own books off the shelves than to have to request them from a librarian and have them fetched from a stack. The self-service principle also respects the privacy of the user. Users may not have clearly articulated their requirements in their own minds, and a library whose shelf arrangement and physical environment encourage browsing is one of the simple pleasures of civilization.

In some environments document arrangement may be the only retrieval device available to, or used by, users. Examples of such environments are bookshops, music shops, small public libraries and document filing systems. In larger document collections browsing the whole collection is not an option, but subsets of the collection may be examined by browsing. Various document characteristics that are rarely reflected in catalogues, such as the precise scope of the work and its level of difficulty, as well as its physical format, the quality of production and the design of the cover, can be identified. Hence, despite its relative lack of sophistication, document arrangement is an important and frequently used retrieval device.

APPROACHES TO DOCUMENT ARRANGEMENT

The arrangement in a collection is unlikely to follow one sequence for all types of material. As always, a balance must be struck between managerial priorities and user convenience. In this section, the various types of shelf arrangement that encourage browsing will be discussed, followed by the factors which may lead to sequences being modified or broken.

- *Detailed classified subject arrangement.* Detailed, or 'close', classification is the commonest arrangement for the majority of open access stock in all but the smallest collections. Long sequences of books sharing the same classmark but having heterogeneous but related subjects are an irritation to purposeful browsing, and a detailed classified arrangement minimizes this.

  This arrangement is subject to the problems of classified order generally, whereby complex relationships have to be accommodated within a one-dimensional linear order, so only one relationship can be shown, and other related material is inevitably separated. Occasionally libraries try to improve the collocation of DDC's main classes by rearranging their physical sequence in what is known as *broken order*. Class 400 (Languages) may be located adjacent to 800 Literature, for example.

- *Broad classified subject arrangement.* The principal drawback of detailed classification specifically is that shelfmarks can become unmanageably long. Smaller libraries may opt for a less detailed version of a published classification – often DDC, which publishes an official abridged edition; there are abridged versions of UDC and BC1 also. This reduces the length of classmarks (though they may still have seven or more digits in the Abridged DDC). Where segmented DDC classmarks are available on MARC records, abridged DDC classmarks can be obtained by programme, by cutting off the classmark at the first segmentation point. Otherwise classifiers have either to classify from scratch or apply their own abridgement. The *Dewey Decimal Classification for School Libraries* offers even broader arrangements designed for secondary and (with even less detail) primary schools. As an example, 690 Building and related activities has just three divisions, and the recommendation for primary schools is to class everything at 690.

  Some public branch libraries have adopted 'reader interest' arrangement. This name is given to a whole group of single-facet classifications, mostly devised in-house. Reader interest arrangement is born out of exasperation: the exasperation of readers trying to find their way round DDC's unhelpful collocations and overlong notations, and of readers' advisory staff trying to explain to them that d-i-y is classed at 643.7, except that carpentry is at 694, but not woodworking which is 684, unless it's marquetry and similar handicrafts, for which you will need 745.51. And so on. These arrangements are often intuitive and very broad, 30–40 classes sufficing for the whole collection, with simple, sometimes iconic, notations.

- *Verbal subject arrangement* may be considered if a collection is small enough, and the range of topics restricted enough, for the whole collection to be comprehended together. This warning is offered because of the inevitable limitation of verbal subject arrangement. It is quite indifferent to relationships, and gives an arbitrary sequence. The distinction between a verbal arrangement and a very broad classified arrangement is a fine one: some reader interest arrangements do not attempt to show relationships between subjects, and might be better considered as verbal subject arrangements. This is the kind of arrangement commonly found in bookshops. It also has its uses for the arrangement of small, specialist collections, for example, files of community information material or of photographs in a local collection.

- *Title arrangement* for direct retrieval is found mainly in the specialized context of periodicals, often within broad subject categories corresponding to the library's physical organization.

- *Author arrangement* is traditionally found in the fiction section of public libraries, though even here it is increasingly common to find genre fiction grouped or labelled separately. Within a classified sequence, items are commonly subarranged by author, and the shelfmark will indicate this.

Parallel sequences

Very few libraries arrange their classified stock in a single sequence. A variety of parallel sequences is almost universally found. Some situations that lead to sections of stock being shelved in a separate classified sequence are as follows:

- *Physical form.* While improvements in packaging have made it possible to box up many videos, audio cassettes and other audiovisual materials in a way that makes them suitable for interfiling with books, many libraries prefer for security or other reasons to house such materials separately. This applies particularly if equipment – video cassette recorders (VCRs), PCs, fiche readers, slide viewers and the like – is needed to use such material within the library. Some items, such as graphic materials and portfolios, are simply too large or awkwardly shaped to be shelved with books.

  Books themselves often have one or more separate sequences for oversize items. Pamphlets, reports and similar items that are too slim to have a spine may be placed in separate sequences.
- *Nature of use.* Separate sequences may be established for items where special conditions are imposed on their use, for example short-loan collections in academic libraries. Lending and reference stock are commonly segregated, and there is often a separate quick reference sequence for yearbooks, directories and other materials that are designed for rapid consultation.
- *Readership level.* Separate undergraduate collections may be found in academic libraries. School and public libraries often split the stock into categories reflecting the child's level of reading and emotional development.

GUIDING

Library guiding is essentially the system/user interface as described in Chapter 4, but writ large, and static rather than interactive. The range of sequences that are likely to be found even in quite small libraries underlines the need for users to be given clear information about the whereabouts of every item of stock. Such guidance may take forms that are specific to individual environments, but may include:

- group or individual instruction in the layout and use of the collection

- within the catalogue, shelfmarks must clearly indicate the sequence within which an item is housed
- users of the catalogue should have easy access to information guiding them to each sequence
- clear and explicit guidance that is visible within the library
- guidance as necessary on book presses and shelves.

LIMITATIONS OF DOCUMENT ARRANGEMENT

Document arrangement is a crude retrieval device that normally needs to be supported by other approaches. Specifically its limitations are that:

- documents can be arranged in only one order, and grouped according to one characteristic
- any given document can only be located in one place in any given sequence
- the document arrangement adopted is often broken; parallel sequences are common, and additional complexity may be introduced by the need to accommodate large collections on several different floors of a library building.
- only part of the library collection will normally be visible on shelves, or in filing cabinets. Documents that may be available through a library, but which will not be evident through browsing include: documents on loan, documents which might be obtained by interlibrary loan, and any collections that are maintained on closed access.

While document arrangement has some significant limitations for the retrieval of both documents and the information contained within those documents, it is important to remember that document arrangement is used widely in documents, archive collections and paper-based filing systems, and, overall has an important impact on information retrieval.

MANUAL AND COMPUTERIZED CATALOGUES AND INDEXES COMPARED

A conscious effort of imagination is often needed when changing from a manual to a machine method of searching or vice versa. This section discusses manual and machine techniques generally. It has to be borne in mind that the capabilities of mechanized searching vary enormously according to system and that some systems, particularly older OPACs, offer relatively few enhancements over manual searching.

AVAILABILITY AND ACCESSIBILITY

There will continue to be some demand for printed indexes for manual searching for the foreseeable future, on account of their familiarity, instant availability, portability and freedom from mechanical or electrical failure. Manual indexes are normally purchased, singly or on subscription, by libraries and other information organizations, and made available freely to authorized users. Some printed indexes may be locally produced, for example, printed catalogues, and copies may be available for sale. Card indexes are usually assembled on site.

Microforms require readers, but they are subject to mechanical breakdown. These, and card indexes, are not portable. Other manual systems are always accessible and their use does not require machinery. Printed indexes are portable, and may be carried around and used with other materials: for example, printed abstracting and indexing services may be used alongside the journals that they index. This is not usually possible with mechanized formats. Computerized systems are also subject to downtime and networked systems can suffer from slow transfer rates or connection failure.

Manual indexes have a long life span and are usable for as long as needed. The contrast here is with WAN-based systems, where access time is limited by expense. In-house mechanized systems, such OPACs and CD-ROMs, are usable for as long as needed.

While the range and date span of machine searchable databases have improved dramatically over the past generation, some search services are still only available in manual formats. There are also many defunct manual indexes that are still of value, especially in the arts and the humanities, as well as the pre-computerized back files of machine-searchable databases in all subjects. Nor must it be forgotten that developing areas of the world may not have the resources – or even a reliable electricity supply – to support automated systems.

CURRENCY

The currency of manual indexes of all types is usually inferior to that of machine systems, as time is taken up for physical production and for the distribution of published indexes. Even locally maintained card indexes often have a backlog of entries for filing, as the work involved is slow and tedious and at the same time requires great accuracy and a knowledge of complex filing procedures. The updating of machine systems is usually instant – though the release of updates of publicly available systems is done on a regular-interval basis. CD-ROMs share with manual systems the feature of requiring physical production and distribution.

340

STATIC AND DYNAMIC LISTS

One of the two most important points of contrast between manual and mechanized systems is that the former depend on static lists. A static list is any index that has a physical substrate – printed page, card, microform or the physical arrangement of library materials. The list is permanent, or nearly so, and is not altered by use. These lists are costly to compile and (where applicable) to distribute, and take up physical space. Access is by consulting relevant sections of the list. A search is only able to retrieve what is on the list, so queries have to be tailored to what the list can offer.

With machine systems the physical ordering of records is hidden from the user. Interrogation of the system produces dynamic lists. These are the records that have been retrieved from the system in response to a specific query. Each list is tailored to its query. Depending on the sophistication of system and user, it may be possible to fine-tune a list in respect of record format and file arrangement.

ACCESS POINTS

These considerations lead to the second most important point of contrast. Because of the cost in space and time of producing and maintaining static lists, information organizations make them as simple as they can, by limiting both the amount of data in the individual record and the number of access points available. Access points in manual systems typically consist of: the first word of the title, the author and one or more subject access points – rarely exceeding four or five, and often fewer.

In machine systems the number of access points depends on the size of the record, the number of indexed fields and on whether a keyword facility is available. The number of access points is normally far higher than in machine systems.

SEARCHING

Because of the limited number of subject access points in manual systems, each one may carry a heavy freight of information. This means that manual systems are often pre-coordinate systems, where a single access point may carry two or more elements of information, the subordinate elements being picked up by means of references. The searcher has to scan through static lists, therefore it is laborious to modify a manual search. However, because the exhaustivity of indexing is limited and pre-coordinate systems are commonly used, false coordinations are uncommon, and the precision of a search can be high.

341

Scanning and browsing can be easy or difficult, depending on layout and typography. Manual systems can be accessed with a minimum of preliminary training. Written instructions should be available, however, and training may be useful in situations where more complex search patterns are available – as for example in some scientific abstracting services. At best, the 'browsability' of manual indexes encourages serendipity. A combination of machine searches supplemented by manual indexes and citations is an effective and absorbing way to conduct a literature search and build up a personal bibliography.

Machine systems normally operate in post-coordinate mode, where it is easy to modify a search by adding or discarding search terms. While great strides have been made in improving the user-friendliness of user interfaces, there are still many situations where much training and practice are needed to exploit systems to the full. Scanning and browsing capabilities depend on the interface; in the case of the WWW they are seductively easy.

SEARCH OUTPUT

Output from a manual search has to be memorized or copied: by manual copying in most cases, otherwise by photocopying or electronic scanning. All are laborious. However, the portability of most systems makes it easy to compare different sources. Output from machine systems can usually be printed or down-loaded to file – though institutions may impose restrictions.

PRINTED CATALOGUES (INCLUDING CARD AND MICROFORMS)

Any catalogue comprises a number of entries, each entry representing or acting as a surrogate for a document (see Chapter 3). There may be several entries per document, or just one. Each entry comprises three sections: the heading, the description and the location.

Headings determine the order of a catalogue sequence. The entries in an author catalogue will have authors' names as headings, and the catalogue will be organized alphabetically according to the author's name.

The common types of catalogue are:

- Author catalogues, which contain entries with authors' names as access point. Authors may be persons or corporate bodies; the term 'author' is normally extended to include illustrators, performers, producers and others with intellectual or artistic responsibility for a work. A variant sometimes found is the *name catalogue*, which includes in addition personal names as subjects and, sometimes, corporate bodies.

- Title catalogues, which contain entries with titles as access points.
- Author/title catalogues contain a mixture of author entries and titles entries; since both are alphabetical these can be interfiled into one sequence.
- Subject catalogues use subject terms as access points.
- Alphabetical subject catalogues use verbal subject headings as headings.

Classified subject catalogues use notation from a classification scheme as a heading. As this order is not self-evident, classified catalogues require a subject index, an alphabetical list of subjects and their classmarks.

Normally a combination of these catalogue sequences will be used. There are two different approaches:

- classified catalogue, which has the following sequences: an author/title catalogue or index (or separate author and title catalogues), a classified subject catalogue and a subject index to the classified subject catalogue
- dictionary catalogue, which has only one sequence (like a dictionary) with author, title and alphabetical subject entries interfiled.

PRINTED INDEXES

Two basic types of indexes are common: author indexes and subject indexes. A subject index has alphabetical terms or words as headings. Entries are arranged in alphabetical order according to the letters of the heading. An author index may be created; here entries are arranged alphabetically by authors' names. The descriptive part of an entry in an index depends upon the information or document being indexed. Three important contexts in which printed indexes are encountered are:

- *Book indexes.* A book index is an alphabetically arranged list of words or terms leading the reader to the numbers of pages on which specific topics are considered, or on which specific names appear. Many non-fiction books and directories include an index; this is often a subject index. The section below explores some of the principles of the creation of book indexes in greater detail.
- *Periodical indexes.* A periodical index is an index to a specific periodical titles (for example *Proceedings of the London Mathematical Society,* or *Managing Information*) Usually indexes are generated at intervals to cover several issues; annual indexes are common. Periodicals may have subject, author and/or title indexes.
- *Indexing journals* and the indexes to printed abstracting journals are alphabetical indexes to the literature of a subject area. Usually many of the entries relate to the periodical literature, but monographs, conference proceedings

and reports may also be covered. The indexing journal normally comprises an alphabetical subject index, possibly also supported with an author index. The 'description' is the bibliographical citation that gives details of the document that is being indexed. Different approaches to generating these indexes in printed form are discussed in the next section.

ENTRIES AND REFERENCES

In catalogues or indexes there are two possible approaches to the provision of multiple entries for one work. One of these is to use main and added entries. The main entry includes the complete catalogue record of the document. In a classified catalogue the main entry will be the subject entry in the classified sequence. In a dictionary catalogue the main entry will be as determined by AACR or whichever catalogue rules are in use – normally the principal author. Added entries will be made for additional access points or headings. For example, in an author catalogue added entries might be expected for collaborating authors, writers, editors, compilers and illustrators (see Chapter 9). Typically, added entries do not include all of the components of the description that are used in the main entry, but only the minimum needed for identification. The second approach is the use of unit entries; in a unit entry catalogue all entries are equivalent and contain the same descriptive detail. This approach is commonly found in card catalogues. Printed catalogues and indexes tend to prefer the main and added entry format, which uses less space.

Entries are usually supplemented by references. A reference provides no direct information about a document but, rather, refers the user to another location or entry. References take less space than added entries in a printed index, and require less detail to be printed on a card. There are two types of reference: *see* and *see also*. These operate in a similar way whether they are used to link authors' names or subject headings.

A *see* reference directs the user from a name, title, subject or other term which has not been used as an entry heading to an alternative term at which words occur as a heading or descriptor. *See* references may link two subjects with similar meanings (for example, Currency *see* Money) or variant author names (for example, Council for the Education and Training of Health Visitors *see* Great Britain. *Council for the Education and Training of Health Visitors*). Some bibliographies use references in situations where AACR would require an added entry, as with second authors. For example, the added entry:

Frink, Elisabeth Frink / Edward Lucie-Smith and Elisabeth Frink. – Bloomsbury, 1994. – 138p. – ISBN 0-7475-1572-7

from Figure 3.7 would be replaced with the reference

Frink, Elisabeth *see* Lucie-Smith, Edward *and* Frink, Elisabeth

A *see also* reference connects subject headings or index terms which have a hierarchical or associative relationship (Chapter 5). For example, the following *see also* reference links two headings under which entries may be found:

Monasteries *see also* Abbeys

The searcher is recommended to examine entries under both index terms if it is likely that documents might prove to be relevant. *See also* references between personal names, corporate bodies and uniform titles are prescribed also by AACR in a very limited number of circumstances, for example, where the same person's works are listed under different pseudonyms or where a corporate body has changed its name.

Explanatory references may be either *see* or *see also* references that give a little more detail than merely the direction to look elsewhere. An example might be:

Devon, Sarah
   For works of this author published under other names see
Murray, Jill; Treves, Kathleen.

Association of Assistant Librarians
   See also the later name:
Library Association. *Career Development Group*

CREATING AND SEARCHING PRINTED INDEXES

One of the first applications of computers in information retrieval was in the production of printed indexes. Computers were used for in-house indexes to reports lists, local abstracting and indexing bulletins, patents lists, etc. and for the production of published indexes to many of the major abstracting journals. Particularly for the large abstracting and indexing organizations, computerization of indexes and indexing yielded considerable savings in the production and cumulating of indexes. Originally index production was an isolated operation. Now, many indexes are merely one of a range of database products.

In spite of the growth of online searching, for some time yet there will be searches in which reference to a printed index is cheaper and simpler. Several different access points may be used in printed indexes. The most important of these are subject and author; but chemical formulae, trade names, company names and patent numbers are all possible access points.

All indexes consist of a series of lead terms, arranged usually in alphabetical

345

order. Each lead term may be qualified and must have a link that leads the user to other lists or documents. Computer-generated indexes may rely on automatically assigned index terms or intellectually assigned terms. Each of these possibilities will now be considered.

KEYWORD INDEXES

A KWIC index is the most basic of natural-language indexes. KWIC or keyword in title (KWIT) indexes are popular because they are straightforward and relatively cheap to create. In the most basic of KWIC indexes, words in a title are compared with a stoplist, in order to suppress the generation of useless index entries. The stoplist or stopword list contains words under which entries are not required, such as: them, his, her, and. Each word in the title is compared with those in the stoplist and if a match occurs it is rejected; but if no match is found, the term is designated a keyword. These keywords are used as entry words, with one entry relating to the document for each word. The word is printed in context with the remainder of the title (including stopwords). Entry words are arranged alphabetically and aligned in the centre or left column. A single line entry, including title and source reference, is produced for each significant word in the title. The source reference frequently amounts to no more than a document or abstract number, but may extend to an abbreviated journal citation. Alternatively, a full bibliographic description, with or without abstract, can be located in a separate listing. Entries under one word are arranged alphabetically by title. Figure 12.1 presents an example of a KWIC index layout.

From *Biological abstracts*. This index is more user-friendly than some, making good use of white space. Even so, many titles are drastically truncated on any given index line. The index uses title enrichment: subject terms are added to the title to enhance or clarify it. The slash (/) appears at the end of the title and separates it from the added subject terms.

Subject context	Keyword	Subject context	Ref. No.
CONTROL WEED CONTROL/	ALTITUDINAL	DISTRIBUTION OF THE LANT	205
LIMIT TEMPERATURE/ ECOLO		OWNSTREAM REPLACEMENT	3128
ZONATION SYNONYMY/ A SU		RA-SPLENDENS VEGETATION	1458
. . .			
ED CONTROL/ ALTITUDINAL	DISTRIBUTION	OF THE LANTANA LACE BUG	205
IVORY COAST CAMEROON/		OF THE MATING TYPE ALLE	9684
URE BRAIN DEVELOPMENT/		OF THE NOVEL DEVELOPME	7907
. . .			
ANCE BIOLOGICAL CONTROL	WEED	CONTROL/ ALTITUDINAL DIST	205
ING AND FREQUENCY SEED		CONTROL/ COTTON GOSSYPI	172
HUS-RETROFLEXUS GROWTH		CONTROL/ PETROLEUM OIL A	9759

Figure 12.1 KWIC index

The merits of title indexes derive mainly from the low human intervention. Since a simple KWIC index is entirely computer generated, a large number of titles can be processed quickly and cheaply. The elimination of personal interpretation enhances consistency and predictability. Indexing based on words in titles reflects current terminology, automatically evolving with the use of the terminology. Also, the creation of cumulative indexes (to, say, cover five-yearly annual volumes) is easier and does not demand any added intellectual effort, only an extra computer run.

However, for all their convenience, title indexes are open to criticism on several counts:

- Titles do not accurately mirror the content of a document. Titles can always be found which are misleading or eye-catching rather than informative, e.g. 'The black/white divide' (politics or graphics?).
- Basic KWIC indexes are unattractive and uncomfortable to read, due to their physical arrangement and typeface.
- Many KWIC indexes display only part of a title.
- Subarrangement at entry terms would also improve the scannability and searchability of KWIC indexes, by breaking down long sequences of entries under the same keyword.
- The remainder of the criticisms of title indexes is concerned with the absence of terminology control. Irrelevant and redundant entries are inevitable. The mere appearance of a term in a title does not necessarily herald the treatment of a topic at any length in the body of the text. Further, even when the term assigned is relevant, with no terminology control, all the problems, which a controlled language aims to counter, re-emerge. Subjects will be scattered under a variety of terms with similar meanings. No directions are inserted between related subjects.

The more sophisticated KWIC-type programs attempt to negotiate these limitations. Readability can be improved by simply altering the printed format. A KWOC index, for instance, extracts the keyword from the title; the keyword is used as a separate heading, with titles and accession numbers listed beneath it. An asterisk sometimes replaces the keyword in the printed title. Indexes where the keyword appears both as heading and in the title are strictly keyword and context (KWAC) indexes, but this distinction is rarely made, and KWOC is the generic term used. Subarrangement at entry terms further enhances scannability. The index user is released from the necessity of scanning every entry associated with an index term and can select relevant entries by the alphabetical arrangement of qualifying terms. Both Permuterm and double-KWIC indexes provide a solution.

The Permuterm index (as used in Science and Social Sciences Citation

347

Indexes) is based on pairs of significant words extracted from the title. All pairs of significant terms in a title are used as the basis of index entries; such pairs are arranged alphabetically with respect to each other. An accession number accompanies each pair but no title. Accession numbers, titles and other information are printed in a separate listing. Similar paired listings can also be used in searching the electronic database associated with Science and other Citation Indexes.

Double-KWIC indexes also give subarrangement at entry terms, but are fuller than a Permuterm index in that the title is displayed as part of the entries in the index. Their extreme bulkiness prevented them from gaining any significant popularity.

More refined computer-indexing packages instil a degree of control into the selection of index terms. By widening the indexing field, terms from free or controlled vocabularies may be added to the title and treated in the same way as terms in the title. Alternatively, specific terms in the remainder of the record in, say, the abstract, may be marked by the indexer to be used as terms to augment the index terms in the title. Further control may be exercised in such a way that all of the keywords under which index entries are to be found can be designated manually, prior to input. Exerting this amount of control tends to undermine most of the advantages of title indexing, but does provide for terms being assigned in accordance with the document being indexed and its content, rather than arbitrarily assigning a term as an index term merely because it appears in a record. Also, with control, terms may be signalled as comprising more than one word, e.g. international economics, since two words can be signalled as being linked.

INDEXES BASED ON STRING MANIPULATION

Controlled indexing languages (such as may be recorded in thesauri and lists of subject headings, see Chapters 5 and 6) are still preferred by many index producers including, for example, *Index Medicus, Science Abstracts, Engineering Index* and the *British National Bibliography.* Nevertheless, the computer still has a role in the production of indexes based on intellectually assigned index terms, by formatting and printing such indexes, and particularly in making cumulations. In addition, the computer has a hand in the generation of indexes based on string manipulation. Here, the human indexer selects a string of index terms from which the computer, under appropriate instructions, prints a series of entries for the document to which the string of index terms relate. The techniques of pre-coordinated subject headings have been described in Chapter 6.

CITATION INDEXES

Citation indexing is a means of producing an effective index by exploiting the computer's capacity for arranging and reformatting entries. Input to the indexing system comprises the references of recent articles in relatively few core journals and, for each article, the list of works that it refers to. A citation index then lists cited documents together with a list of those items that have cited them (citing articles). This is an effective way of covering a fairly wide subject field with almost no human intervention. The prime examples of citation indexes are those produced by the Institute for Scientific Information (ISI), i.e., Social sciences, Arts and humanities, and Science citation indexes. Thus, given one document in a field, the searcher should be able to trace other related documents. However, the many inconsistencies in citation standards cause problems, and the reasons for citing a document are not always to do with shared subject content. While citation indexes started life as printed products, most users now encounter citation in databases, such as those produced by ISI, that include citation links. In this context, citation links can provide a valuable additional approach to the identification of related documents.

SEARCHING PRINTED INDEXES

Many of us today are so accustomed to conducting all our searches via the terminal that the techniques specific to printed indexes are apt to be forgotten. This brief checklist of practical factors to be aware of supplements the more generalized account in 'Manual and computerized catalogues and indexes compared' above.

- *Coverage.* Check – either by examining any prefatory material or by direct inspection – how the subject (or other) field has been defined, and what range of material is included. If the coverage appears marginal to the information need, then *either* bear this in mind when searching *or* check literature guides and other secondary sources for more appropriate indexes. Is retrospective coverage adequate? Be aware that a long retrospective search through annual cumulations will be slow, repetitive and often heavy work.
- *Depth of treatment.* Are there indexes only, or are there abstracts also? How exhaustive is the indexing? If there are abstracts, are they informative or merely indicative? In many cases, where there are print and electronic formats of the same database, the printed index will offer far fewer search keys, even within the same field – for example, by not making minor descriptors available for searching.
- *Up-to-dateness.* Some abstracting journals have a time-lag of several months or even a year or two. Verify by spot-checking. If unacceptably dilatory, then

349

see if more up-to-date hard-copy alternatives are available: for example, the *Current Contents* series of indexes. Otherwise, networked electronic files are usually more up to date than hard copy.

- *Arrangement*: Indexes are basically either one-stage or two-stage.
  - A one-stage, or dictionary, index has all approaches interfiled in a single A–Z sequence. A variant has a single A–Z subject sequence with a separate author index.
  - A two-stage index has (1) a bibliography (citations with or without abstracts), often in a broadly classified subject grouping to permit browsing. For specific searching the bibliography is accessible via (2) author and subject indexes; occasionally other indexes also. Author indexes may give a full citation; more usually just a reference. Depending on the nature of the subject, other specialist indexes may be found, e.g., the Biosystematic index in *Biological Abstracts*.
- *Subject approaches*. These are often very limited, certainly compared with electronic versions. There is a great variety of styles, of which this is a very crude typology:
  - Keyword indexes, usually based on titles. At their best, the title will appear in full at each access point, perhaps with title enrichment; at their most basic, there will be a simple keyword index.
  - Heading consisting of a word or phrase expressing a single concept, e.g., CLUMSY CHILDREN. Indexes of this type are primarily intended for machine searching, the printed versions being a by-product and nothing more. Examples: *British Education Index, Information Science Abstracts*.
  - Heading + single subheading, e.g., FOOTBALL – INJURIES. Examples: *Index Medicus*; *Engineering Index*.
  - Heading + a variable number of subheadings, but rarely exceeding three facets in all. Examples: any catalogue or index based on the Library of Congress Subject Headings; subject indexes based on the Dewey Decimal Classification; also most H. W. Wilson indexes, e.g., *Cumulative Book Index, Library Literature*.
  - Fully faceted systems, allowing complete flexibility to express complex subjects. Examples: the PRECIS system, used to index *BNB* between 1971 and 1990; *Abstracts in New Technologies and Engineering* (*ASSIA* uses the same system).
- *Scatter in subject indexes*. A limitation of rotated indexes of all kinds is that the citation order used for indexing may not match the search pattern. For example, if a searcher has in mind: 'Football in Scotland', an index may or may not have entries at, say,

Football. Scotland

and at

Football. Management. Clubs. Scotland.

It is easy to overlook the second entry, particularly if it is surrounded with a mass of similar-looking entries in close print.

OTHER POINTS TO CHECK

- Use library catalogues and guides, literature guides etc. to ascertain what is available in the subject area. Check both hard copy and electronic sources.
- Instructions for using indexes are often found at the front of the index. Sometimes there are separate guides, from the publisher or produced by the library, or even video tutorials for the more complex indexes.
- Layout and arrangement of bound volumes and unbound issues. How do the issues cumulate? Are the indexes in separate volumes? Current (uncumulated) issues of many abstracting journals may lack some or all indexes.
- Be aware of the filing rules in use.
- For subject searches, start with the most recent issue and work systematically back.
- If there is an accompanying thesaurus, use it to suggest alternative approaches.
- Do not expect too much of printed indexes. Many are less exhaustively indexed than their electronic versions, and increasingly printed indexes may not be designed for easy use.
- Know when to stop. The Law of Diminishing Returns applies. At what point do citations become so old as to cease to be useful?

BOOK INDEXING

Book indexes are one type of printed index. They are important in assisting the user to locate concepts within the text of a book. Since book indexes can be compiled by authors, or by professional indexers, the quality of such indexes varies considerably. A small extract from an index in a book (a book on indexing) was given in Figure 5.2. Entries may be the names of persons, corporate bodes or places, or alphabetical index terms to represent subjects, followed by number of those pages on which the information is to be located.

The purposes of an index are, according to the relevant British Standard (BS 3700:1988), to:

- identify and locate relevant information within the material being indexed
- discriminate between information on a subject and passing mention of a subject
- exclude passing mention of subjects that offers nothing significant to the potential user
- analyse concepts treated in the document so as to produce a series of headings based on its terminology
- indicate relationships between concepts
- group together information on subjects that is scattered by the arrangement of the document
- synthesize headings and subheadings into entries
- direct the user seeking information under terms not chosen for the index entries to the headings that have been chosen, by means of cross-references
- arrange entries into a systematic and helpful order.

The same principles can be used to guide the creation of entries in book indexes, as are outlined elsewhere in this book. The indexer creates an informal controlled vocabulary, one that is based on the language used by the author. Headings for person, places and corporate bodies can follow the model offered by AACR in matters such as the identification of best known names and the use of abbreviations of names. For subject entries, the problems associated with the variability of language and the indication of relationships between subjects still need to be addressed. Figure 5.2 shows clearly how the index groups together subjects that the document scatters. In this particular index the grouping is assisted by the frequent use of *see also* references (not shown in Figure 5.2), for example:

alphabetization *see also* filing order; sorting.

See references are also found, as:

audience *see* readers.

Where subentries have been used, the indexer should provide appropriate access points. For example, the index used in Figure 5.2 also has such entries as:

alphabetization
    of abbreviations, 130

and

double-posting
    of abbreviations, 130

Indexes should subdivide entries rather than offer long lists of page numbers.

Any main heading with more than five or six reference locators should be considered for subentries, as long undifferentiated lists of page or section numbers are a hindrance to the user.

Many word-processing packages support an indexing function, but they are relatively unsophisticated. Index entries are made either by applying a markup code to keywords in the text, or by embedding in the text words or phrases that will appear as index entries only. Dedicated indexing software is available in a variety of packages (CINDEX, Indexer's Assistant, MACREX, among others), and is recommended for all but the simplest indexes. The features found in dedicated software include:

- Editing and display features: copying a previous entry; transposing (flipping) main heading and subheading; searching and find-and-replace entries; creating a subset of the index for the indexer to work on; verifying cross-references; onscreen editing.
- Sorting features: word-by-word or letter-by-letter alphabetizing, immediate sorting of entries, page number sort, merging of index files.
- Formatting and printing features: removal of duplicate entries or page references; automatic formatting and printing of the index in a range of styles, including user-selected formats; creation of user-defined style sheets.

EXHAUSTIVITY OF INDEXING AND SPECIFICITY

The indexer is required to judge which items of information are relevant and which are to be passed over. The depth of indexing required will be affected by the nature and length of the book. An average ratio of index pages to text pages is 3 per cent, but for reference books this may be much higher. A well-structured book may be easier to index than a less well-structured one. Specificity of index headings can also be guided by the content of the book.

FILING ORDER AND SEQUENCES

Earlier sections have considered in some detail the headings and search keys to be used in catalogues and indexes. In any situation where a number of such headings or terms are to be displayed one after another in a static list, some well-recognized filing order must be adopted. Thus in printed and card catalogues and indexes, the filing order is important in assisting the user in the location of a specific heading or term. In computer-based systems, lists of index terms or search keys are sometimes encountered, and here it is also useful to work with a defined filing order, especially where a large collection or database is being

353

indexed. If no filing order is adopted, the only way in which appropriate headings and their associated records can be retrieved is by scanning the entire file.

Since most headings in catalogues and indexes comprise primarily Arabic numbers and letters of the roman and other alphabets, it is these characters that must be organized and for which a filing order must be defined. While the letters of the alphabet do have a canonical order, letters, unlike numbers, are not primarily handled for their ordinal values. The larger the file, the slower and more complex the consultation process, and some users will have difficulty finding their way through large, complex files. As much help and assistance should be given, both within and outside the catalogue or index, as is reasonably possible.

Maintaining a coherent sequence requires, first, a set of filing rules. It also requires that these rules be followed accurately and consistently. In many printed indexes filing is done by program, which does ensure absolute consistency once the program has been instructed on the desired filing order. Such programs must take account of human expectations, which may conflict with unmediated machine procedures. For example, most character sets give upper case letters a lower numeric value than lower case, which would make *Great Britain* file before *Great apes* if there were no machine instruction to ignore case. Modern software mostly takes care of problems at this level; but other problems may be encountered at higher levels. A very common one is to try to manipulate numbers within an alphanumeric character set, which produces the sequence 1, 10, 100, . . . 11, . . . 12, . . . 2, . . . 3 etc. Machine filing also requires accurate data: the accidental omission of a space or a comma from a heading at the time of data entry can result in a record being filed way out of sequence.

Where filing is done manually, which is slow and expensive, the need for accuracy is critical. Nowhere is this more so than in the card index, where only one record is visible at a time, and a single misfiled card seems to acquire a magnetic attraction for other cards, causing it to grow into a substantial double sequence which may lurk undetected for years. Card indexes, and the physical location of documents, are the places where manual filing is most likely to be encountered.

Modern filing rules take into account the requirements of machine filing. There has been a welcome tendency to simplify procedures: rules such as the *ALA Rules for Filing Catalog Cards* (2nd edn, 1968) had grown pedantically complex.

PROBLEMS AND PRINCIPLES IN ALPHABETICAL FILING SEQUENCES

Filing value of spaces and punctuation symbols

If spaces between words are given a filing value, word-by-word filing results; if not, the order is letter-by-letter. These give:

Word-by-word	Letter-by-letter
Leg at each corner	Legal writing
Leg ulcers	Leg at each corner
Legal writing	Legends of King Arthur
Legends of King Arthur	Leg ulcers

Word-by-word order is the more common, at least in the English language, but letter-by-letter filing is by no means dead. Hyphenated words are a related problem: where would *Leg-irons* file within either of the above sequences? And dashes also, which are not the same as hyphens: how would *Leg – bibliographies* file?

Acronyms fall within this category, as their filing value may be affected by whether they incorporate full stops and possibly spaces. Does *A.L.A.* file near the head of the sequence of As or somewhere between *Al Capone* and *Alabama*? What if it is written *A. L. A.*? Or *A L A*? Or *ALA*?

Subject headings beginning with the same word may be interfiled in different ways according to the filing value given to inverted headings, phrase headings and subdivided headings. Frequently the filing value accorded to a subdivided heading (where the punctuation is a dash) may be different from that for inverted headings (which use commas), which may lead to deviations form the strict and most obvious alphabetical sequence. Where certain symbols have a filing value, they introduce a classified element into an alphabetical file (Figure 12.2).

'As if' and 'File as is' filing

Some kinds of character string may file otherwise than as given. Filing rules designed with automated filing in mind tend to minimize the amount of 'as if' filing, and to file as given in most cases. Examples include:

- abbreviations, particularly of terms of address: for example, *Dr* and *St* filing as *Doctor* and *Saint*
- ampersands (&) may file as they stand – ampersand generally files before numbers and letters. 'As if' filing would have to translate & as *and, et, und* etc., according to the language of the document
- diacriticals: should *Müller* file as *Muller* or *Mueller*? Ligatures also: does

355

This and the following two figures have been adapted from the National Library of Australia's *ABN Cataloguing Manual*, September 1990 (URL: widow.nla.gov.au/2/abn/catman.html)

COOKERY	*Word(s) alone*
COOKERY, AFRICAN	*Word(s) followed by a comma and qualifying word*
COOKERY, CHINESE	
COOKERY (APPLES)	*Word(s) followed by parenthetical qualifier*
COOKERY (MEAT)	
COOKERY FOR ALLERGICS	*Word phrases*

In any subject heading, subdivisions (subordinate elements following a double or em dash) are grouped in the following order:

ART—19th CENTURY	*Period subdivision*
ART—20th CENTURY	
ART—BIBLIOGRAPHY	*Form and topical subdivision*
ART—PHILOSOPHY	
ART—AFRICA, WEST	*Geographical subdivision*
ART—NEW YORK (CITY)	

The following example provides a comprehensive illustration of filing:

COOKERY	*Word(s) alone*
COOKERY—1965	*Word(s) alone, period subdivision*
COOKERY—BIBLIOGRAPHY	*Word(s) alone, form/topical subdivision*
COOKERY—HISTORY	
COOKERY, AMERICAN—BIBLIOGRAPHY	*Word(s) comma word and word with form/topical subdivision*
COOKERY, AMERICAN—MARYLAND	*Word(s) comma word and geographical subdivision*
COOKERY, INTERNATIONAL	*Word(s) followed by a comma and word*
COOKERY (BABY FOODS)	*Word(s) followed by parenthetical qualifier*
COOKERY (MEAT)	
COOKERY FOR ALLERGICS	*Phrase beginning with word in above subject heading*

Figure 12.2 Filing values of subject headings

Æthelred file under E or A? 'As if' filing uses the first, 'As is' the second, in each case

- numbers: should Arabic numbers file as numbers, in a sequence preceding letters? In an ordinal sequence, or as characters? Should roman numbers file as numbers or as letters? And if as letters, how will this affect the filing of headings like Pius VIII, *pope* and Pius IX, *pope*? How should more complicated numbers, or strings containing numbers and other characters (e.g., $50, 1/10, 3rd, πr^2, 0.5), file?

- Scottish and Irish names beginning with Mac and variants: filing rules of British origin often interfile Scottish and Irish names beginning with Mac, Mc, M^c, and M'.

Czolowski, Ted
D., H.   (D is a word)
Da Costa, Beverly   (Da is a word)
Da Ponte, Lorenzo, 1749–1838
Dabbs, James McBridge, 1896–1970
De George, Richard T.
De Young Memorial Museum
De, Kay L.
DeArmond, Frederick Francis, 1893–
Maass, John, 1918–
MacArthur, Robert H.
Madden, David, 1933–
Mazzeo, Henry
McAllester, Susan
McWilliams, Margaret
Mead, Cary Hoge, 1897–
Segal, Lore Groszmann
Segal (Martin E.) (*Firm*) *see* Martin E. Segal and Company, Inc.
Segal, Sydney
Washington, Jim
Washington.
Washington (*State*). *Attorney General's Office*
Washington (*Territory*). *Governor*
Washington/Alaska Regional Medical Program
Washington and Lee University
Washington Association of Soil and Water Conservation Districts
Washington Metcalfe, Thomas
Washington Sea Grant Program
Washington State Association of Counties

Figure 12.3 Comprehensive punctuation and filing in the author index

Non-filing elements

Many headings include an additional non-filing element. Most commonly, definite and indefinite articles (*The*, *A*, *An*) at the beginning of titles are ignored. Some text management systems incorporate in their sort procedures a routine for automatically ignoring initial articles – or more precisely, title strings beginning with A An or The. This is satisfactory provided all the titles are in the same language, though even here there could be the occasional misfit of the type *A Apple pie*. Another non-filing element commonly met is *Sir* etc. in British titles of honour of the type: Reynolds, *Sir* Joshua.

Many of the problems touched on here are illustrated in Figures 12.3 and 12.4.

357

1, one dancing drum	(*1 is a word and files before all titles beginning with the letter A*)
2rabbit, 7wind	
1100 words you need to know	
The 1971 deer population	
8,000 stones	
The AAAS science book list for children	(*AAAS is a word*)
The abacus	
ABCs of tape recording	
Able seaman, deckhandscowman	
The advertising man	(*The at the beginning of a title is disregarded for filing purposes*)
AEIHover policy studies	(*AEI is a word*)
The Aeneid of Virgil	
Cyrano de Bergerac	
D. B. Kabalevsky's Joey the clown	(*D. B. files as D B, where D and B are separate words*)
D. W. Griffith: his life and work	
Daddyji	
Do you remember England?	
Doctor Spock	
Doctoral students in schools of social work	
Down's syndrome	(*Down's files as Downs*)
Dr. Sam: an American tragedy	(*Dr. files as Dr*)
Dracula	
Encyclopedia directory of ethnic newspapers and periodicals in the United States	
An end and a beginning	(*An at the beginning of a title is disregarded for filing purposes*)
The end of nowhere	
Enemies	
Epidemiology as medical ecology	
EQMM annual	(*EQMM is a word*)
Equal justice	
I, Pig	
I. Q. in the meritocracy	(*I. Q. files as I Q where I and Q are separate words*)
I remember it well	
II VI semiconducting	(*II files as alphabet letters*)
The IQ cult	(*IQ is a word*)
Ira sleeps over	
Once upon a Christmas	
One acre and security	(*One files alphabetically*)
The two worlds of Jim Yoshida	
The U.N. Convention on the elimination ...	(*U.N. files as U N, where U and N are separate words*)
U.S.A. and the Soviet Myth	
U.S. Foreign economic policy and the domestic economy	
The UFO experience	(*UFO is a word*)
The underwater war	
UNESCO collection of representative works	
The unforgotten	
United Nations peacekeeping operations	
The United States, 1492–1877	

Figure 12.4 Comprehensive punctuation and filing in the title index

358

Different types of headings beginning with the same word

Headings may arise as author, title and subject, and all types of headings may commence with the same word. 'Black', 'Rose', 'London' are all words that could be part of author, title or subject headings. The problem is whether to adopt a strict alphabetical sequence or whether the user would find it helpful to have entries of the same type grouped together.

Arrangement of entries under the same heading

A prolific author may be responsible for a number of books, or a subject heading may be assigned to several books that discuss the same subject. The preferred sequence for multiple entries under the same heading or term needs to be established. First, it is normal to distinguish between references and added entries, and then to group references at the beginning of the sequence associated with a given term or heading. Next, it is necessary to order the works for which entries are made under a specific subject or author heading. Often the title is used for this purpose but, sometimes, chronological order may be preferred.

SUMMARY

It is a measure of the growth of machine searching that for this edition we have seen fit to relegate manual searching to a single chapter near the end of the book. In particular, the rapid growth of the World Wide Web into a single platform for services that until very recently had to be consulted by using OPACs, CD-ROMs, command-based online search services or bound volumes, has introduced an element of one-stop shopping into our information needs and has led to a growing attitude that any information that cannot be located electronically is not worth searching for at all.

This is an unsound attitude, for a number of reasons. First, there are many parts of the world where the infrastructure to support machine-based systems is inadequate or lacking. Even in developed areas there may be power failures or system downtime. Second, many information resources are still only available in hard copy. Many of these are very specialized, either because they appeal to a small clientele or because they extend a long way back in time (which amounts to much the same thing). Next, the permanence and browsability of hard-copy sources aid serendipity and creativity. Finally, only printed sources are fully portable and lend themselves to continuous consultation. To that extent, this chapter does not relegate manual searching, but serves to draw attention to it.

REFERENCES AND FURTHER READING

American Library Association (1980) *ALA Filing Rules*. Chicago: ALA.

British Standard Institution. (1985) *British Standard Recommendation for Alphabetical Arrangement and the Filing Order of Numbers and Symbols*. BS 1749:1985. London: British Standard Institution.

British Standard Institution. (1988) *British Standard Recommendation for Preparing Indexes to Books, Periodicals and Other Documents*. BS 3700:1988. London: British Standard Institution.

Cleveland, D. B. and Cleveland, A. (1990) *Introduction to Indexing and Abstracting*, 2nd edn. Littleton, CO: Libraries Unlimited.

Knight, G. N. (1979) *Indexing, the Art of*. London: Allen and Unwin.

Mulvany, N. C. (1994) *Indexing Books*. Chicago: University of Chicago Press.

Wellisch, H. (1991) *Indexing from A to Z*. New York: H. W. Wilson.

Management of systems for the organization of knowledge

13

INTRODUCTION

The infrastructure for systems for the organization of knowledge has three components: databases, hardware and software. All of these three components need to be designed and maintained. Business organizations will take responsibility for performing these activities in relation to the transaction and management information systems that underpin the effective operation of the organization. Commercial software developers and information providers are concerned to develop the quality of their product and to maintain their competitive position. Public sector organizations and businesses play roles in designing and maintaining systems that support the organization of public and published knowledge. They make a national and international contribution to the development of systems that ensure the preservation of, and access to, the knowledge and information that forms our cultural heritage and economic wealth. This chapter considers the following aspects of the design and maintenance of systems:

- evaluation of systems for the organization of knowledge and information retrieval
- maintaining databases and authority control
- managing systems
- evolving and migrating systems
- organizations in the organization of knowledge.

Some of these issues will be considered in greater detail in texts on information systems. They are briefly listed here lest in enthusiasm for the richness of knowledge we forget the platforms that facilitate organization and access to knowledge. The most important message embedded in this chapter is that systems for the organization of knowledge are dynamic. Users, information professionals and others involved with the design and maintenance of such systems need to manage that change.

EVALUATION OF SYSTEMS FOR THE ORGANIZATION OF KNOWLEDGE AND INFORMATION RETRIEVAL

An important aspect of the management of systems for the organization of knowledge is the evaluation of those systems. Both researchers and systems producers participate in the evaluation of systems. This section explores some of the key measures that can be used in the evaluation of the success of information retrieval, and then briefly identifies the approaches available to performing evaluation.

Recall and precision have been traditional measures in the evaluation of information retrieval systems. While they are still important, as discussed below, they are not the only measures that can be used. Accordingly, the approaches for the evaluation of information retrieval systems are often concerned to gather a more general perspective on the user's reaction to the system, rather than simply considering recall and precision. In addition, it is important to remember that there are two perspectives on the evaluation of information retrieval systems, characterized by the two distinct questions:

- How can we design the best system?

or

- Given a specific system, how can that system be searched most effectively?

EVALUATION MEASURES: RECALL AND PRECISION

Recall and precision, the classic measures of the effectiveness of a retrieval system, have been mentioned in a number of places in the course of this book. It is now time to discuss them more fully. *Recall* relates to the system's ability to retrieve wanted items in a subject (as opposed to a known-item) search. *Precision* relates to the system's ability to filter out unwanted items. The two are capable of being measured under controlled conditions, and it is usual therefore to express them as ratios. A search for documents in a database has four possible outcomes:

1. Some relevant items are successfully retrieved. These we call *Hits*.

2. Some items that are not relevant are retrieved. This is known as *Noise*.
3. The search fails to retrieve some relevant items. These are *Misses*.
4. Some irrelevant items are not retrieved. These have been successfully *Dodged*.

The *recall ratio* is the number of hits (relevant documents that have been retrieved) as a percentage of the total number of relevant documents in the system or database. The *precision ratio* is the number of hits (relevant and retrieved documents) as a percentage of the total number of documents retrieved, whether relevant or not (Figure 13.1).

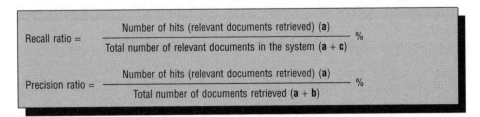

$$\text{Recall ratio} = \frac{\text{Number of hits (relevant documents retrieved) } (a)}{\text{Total number of relevant documents in the system } (a+c)} \%$$

$$\text{Precision ratio} = \frac{\text{Number of hits (relevant documents retrieved) } (a)}{\text{Total number of documents retrieved } (a+b)} \%$$

Figure 13.1 Recall and precision ratios

Indexing systems and search software should be designed to maximize both recall and precision: that is, to minimize Noise (2) and Misses (3). However, in a given search, recall and precision are usually held to be *inversely* related: to improve the one, the other tends to be reduced. Suppose a person is searching for items about asbestos roofing. The topic is represented in the collection, but only in a limited quantity. It is, however, possible to broaden the search and find additional information on asbestos roofing by retrieving general documents on roofing and extracting pertinent sections. This will trace more information on asbestos roofing, but only by considering all the documents listed under the much broader category of roofing. The search will have retrieved a number of non-relevant documents (noise). By broadening the search we have improved the recall but at the cost of lower precision.

It is thus unlikely to be possible to achieve a system that gives 100 per cent recall at the same time as 100 per cent precision. Thus anyone designing a retrieval system must choose an appropriate blend of recall and precision for each individual application. Quite frequently a user will be satisfied with a few items on a topic as long as they are relevant and meet other criteria such as language, date and level. Here, high precision and low recall are satisfactory. On other occasions, as, for example, when planning a research project, a user may want every document or piece of information on a topic traced, and then high recall must be sought to the detriment of precision.

- *Entry vocabulary:* is there a good range of lead-in terms to guide the user from specific concepts to the terms used in the index to represent them?
- *Control of word form:* (number, grammatical form, word order, etc.), to prevent the loss of relevant documents through the scatter of different word forms.
- *Control of synonyms and quasi-synonyms:* to prevent their scattering under more than one heading.
- *Hierarchical and associative relationships* widen the search by suggesting closely related terms.
- *Structural display of relationships:* a classified or other systematic form of display gives the user a conspectus of closely related terms.
- *Exhaustivity of indexing* in computer-searchable databases is effectively a function of record length. The greater the number of terms used to index a document the greater the likelihood of a document being retrieved.
- *Truncation and wildcards:* are features of most computer searching systems.
- *Relevance-ranking* of output, available in some computer searching systems.

Figure 13.2 Index language devices influencing recall

The first two (specificity and coordination) are by far the most important.

- *Specificity of the indexing language:* the greater the specificity the larger the number of terms and the more precise the subject specification.
- *Coordination of terms:* concepts required are described more accurately, and unwanted documents eliminated, by increasing the number of index terms in combination. This is done by the searcher in post-coordinate systems, and by the indexer in pre-coordinate systems.
- *Pre-coordination level:* multi-term concepts (e.g. COAL MININGS) are introduced to ensure that subjects may be minutely identified. (A search on COAL AND MINING could lead to some false relationships.)
- *Links, roles, and relational indicators:* devices which label groups of associated controlled descriptors, or indicate the roles of terms, in order to avoid false relationships.
- *Weighting:* for differentiating between major and minor concepts within a record.
- *Exhaustivity of indexing* is a two-edged sword, influencing both recall and precision. The greater the number of terms available for searching, the greater the likelihood both of marginally relevant documents being retrieved and of false relationships (false drops).
- *Word proximity operators* are found in many interactive search systems to reduce the number of false relationships.

Figure 13.3 Index language devices influencing precision

An indexing language has a number of devices that improve recall (Figure 13.2), balanced by devices for improving precision (Figure 13.3).

Controversy has always surrounded recall and precision. Some of the problems may already have suggested themselves in the course of reading this account. The more important ones are summarized as follows:

- What is a relevant document? Relevance is not a black and white concept. Retrieved documents may be highly suitable to a particular information need, or marginally so. It has already been suggested that users look at other criteria besides pure subject relevance when deciding whether a retrieved document is suitable to their needs. Other measures, including *novelty* and *accuracy*, have been proposed to refine the concept of relevance.

- Recall and precision originally assumed delegated, as opposed to end-user conducted, searching. In the latter the searcher is able to reject irrelevant material heuristically during the course of the search. Hence precision is, indirectly, a measure of user time and effort.
- The concept of retrieval assumed that a document is either retrieved or it is not. The results of many search systems are now relevance ranked. In end-user conducted searches recall is also an indirect measure of user time and effort.
- Under working conditions it is impossible without scanning the entire database to know the total number of relevant documents in the system. *Relative recall* tries to get round this problem by comparing the numbers of documents retrieved by different indexing systems applied to the same database.
- The concept of the database is no longer clear-cut. Many external online systems permit searching on a range of databases simultaneously. The World Wide Web is a 'bottomless pit', the extent of which can only be estimated. If the size of the database is not known for certain, then it is impossible to know how many relevant documents it contains.

For all the difficulties surrounding recall and precision, they remain invaluable as rule-of-thumb evaluation measures, especially when reviewing search results. Figures 13.4 and 13.5 list some of the practicalities for improving searches that deliver low recall and low precision respectively.

OTHER MEASURES

Recall and precision are measures of index effectiveness, indicating the extent to which relevant documents are retrieved. A good information retrieval system must also be efficient and cost-effective. Other measures that are used to evaluate the efficiency of the system might include the following:

The *time* that it takes to perform a search. This is an important parameter for the individual user but, unfortunately, general measures are likely to prove elusive. The time that it takes to perform a search in a system is a function of a number of factors, including the user's previous experience with the system, aspects of system design and the nature of the search. In an experimental situation some of these variables could be controlled, and average search times could be computed for different systems. The time taken to perform a search is not only a function of the indexing language and the system, but may also be affected by system response times, available search facilities and interface features.

If a search gives *low recall*, some questions that may be asked are:

- Am I in the correct database?
- Is the search problem over-specified?
- Is there, in fact, a literature on the search problem?
- Have sufficient search terms been used to properly represent the concepts?
- Are the proximity operators too restrictive?
- Was Boolean logic used correctly?
- Did I make a technical error?
- Should natural language be used rather than controlled descriptors?
- Should truncation be used to capture all word forms of search terms?

The heuristics for increasing recall most often suggested are:

- Use additional synonyms combined with Boolean OR to represent search concepts.
- Use more generic terms in addition to specific terms.
- Use natural language (for richness in the variety of ways ideas can be expressed) as well as controlled vocabulary.
- Search additional subject fields.
- Delete AND and NOT facets from the formulation.
- Increase term truncation.
- Use less restrictive proximity operators.
- Remove restrictions, such as publication date or type from the formulation.

Figure 13.4 Low recall in search results

If the output is *low precision*, these are some questions that may be asked:

- Am I in the correct database?
- Is the search problem under-specified, or do the concepts have an unintended relationship (false drops)?
- Is Boolean logic used correctly?
- Are terms too vague, ambiguous or generic?
- Should terms be restricted to elements of a controlled vocabulary?
- Are the proximity operators too loose?
- Are search terms truncated too severely?

The heuristics for increasing precision most often suggested include:

- Delete near synonyms or ambiguous terms.
- Use more specific terms to represent concepts.
- Use controlled vocabulary if it describes a concept precisely.
- Use natural language if it represents a concept precisely and does not appear to cause multi-meaning problems (it is highly specific or captures subtle nuances of meaning).
- If the above do not apply, search fewer subject fields (e.g., do not search full-text or abstract fields)
- Use additional facets with AND or NOT.
- Decrease term truncation.
- Use more restrictive proximity operators.
- Add restrictions such as publication type, date, language etc.

Figure 13.5 Low precision in search results

Cost is a further measure of system effectiveness. Clearly, it is desirable to minimize search costs that include any expense associated with the acquisition of the source or access to it, as well as the searcher's time. The economics of accessing data through different media, such as networked CD-ROM and Web access, vary considerably. For external databases, these costs depend upon the pricing strategy for access to the database through different routes. For internal databases, it may be difficult to separate search cost from data input and system maintenance costs. Another factor in cost is that natural-language indexing tends to shift the intellectual effort necessary for effective retrieval to the end-user. This collection of factors makes it difficult to calculate the cost of a search, but, nevertheless, cost remains an important factor.

Usability is another key factor in system evaluation. This concept was introduced in Chapter 5. Usability needs to take into account both interface design and the nature of the indexing language. Usability may affect the cost of searching, and the speed with which retrieval can be achieved. It will also impact upon training requirements.

EVALUATION: PROCESSES

There are a number of different approaches to the evaluation of information retrieval systems. Early tests sought to explore in some depth the effectiveness of different indexing languages, often in a card-based retrieval environment. This work on indexing languages has continued, but most of the more recent work has focused on the search behaviour of searchers in specific environments, such as using search engines on the Web, CD-ROM and OPACs. These studies recognize that, while the indexing language is a factor which contributes to search success, a number of other factors are also important, including:

- the searching style of the searcher
- subject area, and the precision associated with terminology in a subject area
- the number of databases used in a search.

System evaluation needs to embrace all aspects of the system, including specifically the interface, the indexing language, the nature of the databases being searched and other aspects of the context in which the system is being used. Typically, it is also important to take into account the characteristics of intended user groups. There are two arenas for evaluation:

- Evaluation by the producer of the information product during the design process and subsequent to the design process, in order to gain user feedback that will influence the design of upgrades and subsequent versions of the system. Evaluation is the gathering of data about the usability of a product for a specific activity within a specific environment. In general, the objective of evaluation is to find out what the users want, and what problems they experience, with a view to improving product design.

- Evaluation conducted by researchers who are interested in establishing general principles about systems, possibly in relation to user needs and behaviours, or the effectiveness of specific system features. Recently this research has focused on the following issues: search engines; retrieval evaluation; the reliability of information on the Web; user interfaces; user search behaviour; information organization on the Web; vocabulary control; intelligent search agents; and, analyses of the relative performance of the Web, online and CD-ROM.

Possible approaches to system evaluation include:

- *Observing and monitoring users' interaction*, in either a laboratory setting, or the environment in which a search would normally be performed. The most popular approaches are those which involve some kind of indirect observation. Examples of such approaches are those in which a video recording of the user is made, or where the keystrokes that the user performs are logged through data logging or transaction logging.
- *Eliciting users' opinions*, which can offer a greater insight into why users perform particular actions, or pursue specific search strategies and can identify the problems that users might have with a system. Approaches which may be helpful in this context include individual interviews, focus groups (group interviews), questionnaires and surveys.
- *Experiments or benchmark tests* in which the experimenter seeks to control some of the variables, while examining the effect of varying others. Typically such tests are conducted in a laboratory environment and work focuses on usability objectives and measures. Typical usability objectives might be suitability for the task, learnability and error tolerance.
- *Prototyping*, in which the user and the designer work together to evolve the system. This may be performed in a laboratory setting, or in a real-life setting. The designer creates a prototype; the user tests the prototypes, and identifies any weaknesses in the prototype; the designer produces a further prototype, and so on until the designer is satisfied that the prototype meets the user requirements.
- *Predictive evaluation*, is concerned with predicting the usability of a product without direct feedback on users' opinions. Prediction is typically based on expert reviews and usage simulations. These simulations may be more or less structured. One way of structuring such simulations is to use walkthroughs. Walkthroughs require experts to simulate the actions that a user might take

in using the system. Experts are asked to report on their experience with the system.

MAINTAINING DATABASES AND AUTHORITY CONTROL

Chapter 5 discusses the various different types of databases, and notes that a range of print or electronic products may be produced from one database, and packaged to meet the particular needs of a specific groups of users. All databases or other knowledge repositories need to be kept up to date, in other words, new information needs to be added. There are three different kinds of amendments that can be made to a database:

- addition of new records
- amendment of existing records
- deletion of existing records.

Bibliographic databases are updated primarily by adding new records to the established collection of records. Catalogue databases may be updated by adding new records to correspond to additions to stock but, also, amendments may be made to existing records to accommodate, for example, the relocation of a document or the removal of documents from the collection. Other databases, such as directory databases, are primarily updated with corrections to existing records, such as changes of address, or amendments to an entry to reflect the latest social or technological developments.

AUTHORITY CONTROL

A key issue in updating bibliographic records is authority control. Authority control is concerned with the maintenance and application of standard access points or index terms. Authority control consists of the creation of authority records for established headings, the linking of authority and bibliographic records, and the maintenance and evaluation of an authority system. Authority control can be exercised locally or within a regional or international network. Three kinds of authority control can be maintained: for names, for subjects, and for classification.

Name authority control has three purposes:

- to ensure that works by an author are entered under a uniform heading
- to ensure that each heading is unique – i.e., to prevent works by more than one author from being entered under the same heading (i.e., to manage the collocative function of the catalogue)

- to save having to establish the heading every time a work is catalogued.

When a personal or corporate name is used for the first time, a *name authority record* is made. This contains:

- the heading, usually based on AACR
- the sources used in establishing the heading
- tracings for references to the heading.

If a heading changes, the name authority record is updated and all existing catalogue entries under that heading are altered. Cataloguers of the old school used to await in eager anticipation the publication of the Queen's new year and birthday honours lists in order to discharge this function. Today, the first use of a name is more likely to be within the offices of a national bibliographic agency. Bibliographic agencies may contact authors whose names are not represented on their authority files, to verify their full and preferred form of name, any other names they may have used and their date of birth. The Library of Congress and the British Library are cooperating in setting up a joint name authority file, which is made available to other bibliographic utilities and to individual subscribers, to be used as the basis for their own authority files.

Where authority control is automated, it is feasible to link the name authority file to the bibliographic file. The catalogue maintenance modules of many automated library systems check headings as they are entered, warn if a heading is not on file and display close matches. They may also allow authority control on other fields of the record, e.g., names of publishers.

Subject authority control exists to ensure that subject headings, and their references, are applied uniformly and consistently. A *subject authority record* is made whenever a new subject heading is established. It contains:

- the heading
- a scope note, if required
- sources used in establishing the heading
- details of references to and from the heading.

This comes very close to the contents of a thesaurus record and, indeed, many a published thesaurus began life in this way. A thesaurus that has been developed for in-house use may act as its own authority file.

Many LCSH headings are synthesized by the use of subdivisions that do not specifically appear in the list, or may be personal, corporate or geographic names which are excluded from the list. These headings are published by the Library of Congress and are available in a variety of formats, including CD-ROM as *CDMARC Subjects*.

Shelfmark control is carried out by means of a *shelflist*: a set of records, one for each physical bibliographic unit, arranged in the order in which they are shelved. This is used primarily as an inventory list, for stock control. It may hold acquisition details or other management information relating to the specific item. In libraries where a unique shelfmark is assigned to each item, it is used in assigning individual book numbers. In libraries with dictionary catalogues, it may be accessible to readers as a classified list. The shelflist is typically held on cards. Many libraries with automated catalogues no longer maintain a shelflist.

The *USMARC format for classification data* has been developed by the Library of Congress, who maintain an authority record for DDC and LCC classmarks as applied. Like LCSH headings, many classmarks are formed by synthesis or, in the case of LCC, by alphabetical subarrangement.

DATABASE MAINTENANCE

Thesauri, classification schemes and lists of subject headings need to be kept up to date. New subjects emerge and need to be represented within the scheme. The key issues in the maintenance of such lists are:

- the identification of new subjects, as they arise in the literature to be indexed
- a process for agreeing on the notation or terms that are to be used to represent those new subjects
- the identification of relationships between new subjects and existing subjects
- processes for recording both new subjects and their relationships with other terms
- processes for notifying all indexers using the scheme of the modification
- processes for ensuring that searchers have access to an up-to-date version of the controlled indexing language.

When a controlled indexing language is used only to index one database or document, it is relatively straightforward, especially with the aid of special software for thesaurus maintenance, to maintain a current version of a thesaurus, to which all indexers may have access. On the other hand, for the large classification schemes, such as the Dewey Decimal Classification, or subject headings lists such as the Library of Congress Subject Headings list, agreement on new terms may require elaborate and extensive consultation. Indexers all around the world may need to be notified of changes, and changes could have a potential impact on many libraries, search intermediaries and end-users.

In the context of subject terms and classification codes two issues cause complexities:

1. As well as the addition of a term, it is necessary to ensure that all relationships between that term and earlier and related terms have been adequately

371

indicated. Significant new areas of knowledge may require new sections in classification schemes, or a collection of new related terms in a subject headings list or thesaurus.

2. Many subject terms and classification codes are drawn from published lists or schemes, and revision requires agreement on the introduction of such terms. This agreement may inject a delay in the updating of the lists or schemes. The issue of revision for classification schemes has been explored more fully in Chapter 8.

Reclassification may involve a once and for all migration to a different classification scheme, or the routine updating of the existing scheme. Changes affecting the physical distribution of stock in a library may involve significant effort and disruption to the library's normal operation. The components of this exercise are:

- Retrieve documents.
- Retrieve records.
- Amend classmark on document and record.
- Re-file documents.
- Re-file records.

Measures which may be taken to reduce the disruption include:

- Rolling reclassification: separate classes are reclassified consecutively.
- Reclassification by osmosis: new accessions only are classified by the new system. Existing stock is gradually weeded out, leaving only a small nucleus of old stock to be reclassified.

MANAGING SYSTEMS FOR KNOWLEDGE ORGANIZATION

The hardware and software platforms that support access to knowledge need to be managed and users need to be supported in their access to such systems. Typically, this involves attention to day-to-day maintenance issues and system integrity, security and user support.

SYSTEM MAINTENANCE

System maintenance is concerned with keeping the hardware and software working. This involves:

- monitoring the quality and integrity of databases, from a more technical perspective than outlined above. In other words, it is important that all of the most recent version of the database is available to those users who are authorized for access

- dealing with any hardware or software malfunctions, such as faulty workstations or software bugs
- making sure adequate backups of databases are taken
- troubleshooting any situations where the system does not work as it might and, in general, having and being able to implement contingency plans in a crisis
- implementing upgrades of software and hardware, to existing systems. This might include the installation of new workstations or further developments to an existing network. Upgrades to software may offer new features and facilities; users need to be informed of any changes that affect their interaction with the system
- liaison with hardware and software suppliers, in relation to both new and future developments.

SECURITY

The other side of access to information is security. Proper attention to security ensures that:

1. All users have access to the databases and functions for which they are authorized.
2. No users have access to databases and function for which they are not authorized.

Loss of security occurs from both accidental and deliberate threats. Accidental threats arise from poor system features such as overloaded networks or software bugs. Deliberate threats arise from human intent, and include theft, computer fraud, vandalism and other attempts to break the system. Typically such threats may lead to:

- the interruption of data preparation and data input
- the destruction or corruption of stored data
- the destruction or corruption of software
- the disclosure of personal proprietary information
- injury to personnel
- removal of equipment or information.

Security is a particular challenge in systems where the users are not members of the staff of a specific organization. Libraries, online search services and publishers will want to implement security that is linked to the licensing arrangements that have been contracted with organizations or individual users. Security issues in this context cover everything from the security of items in the library's collections, to privacy concerning user information. As a quick checklist, some of the issues are:

- authentication of the user, so that users can only access their own accounts
- security of hardware, to avoid theft or vandalism
- prevention of hacking into networks, leading to access to other databases that should not be publicly accessible
- data privacy, concerning user information
- item identifiers, and ensuring that these are unique
- buildings' design, to increase hardware and user security.

Increasingly systems will facilitate user access to commercial databases, library resources in a number of libraries and document collections. The systems must tackle issues concerning liability, control of copyright, licensing and collecting of appropriate payments. Asset trading agreements will increasingly be forged across the information chain. Such systems may also need to accommodate the assessment and evaluation of resources by those seeking to acquire them. Systems will need to be able to manage who is allowed access to what, when, for how long or to what maximum charge, payment strategy and associated rights. They will need to manage copyright issues as an integral function, and will need to be linked to the systems of publishers, editors, indexers, picture libraries and authors.

Security will increasingly be linked to charging. Providing access to the wealth of Internet resources is expensive; Smartcards that record customers' transactions are likely to be used increasingly to support charging, and may also be used as the security device for access to a range of organizational and external information resources. They could also be used with self-help kiosks.

USER SUPPORT

User support is concerned with ensuring that all potential users of a system can make effective use of that system. Chapter 6 has reviewed the different categories of users. Another significant group of users is information professionals, who may use a system on behalf of other users. Support will be offered through a combination of:

- *Documentation*, in both online and printed form. Lists of key operations, commands and menu options are particularly helpful in print format. Many systems now have extensive help systems available on screen, but these may not be attractive when remote communication implies costly additional time online. In addition, with some help systems, help is needed in navigating the help system!

- *Training* through courses, seminars and one-to-one hands-on sessions. Users of library systems fall into two categories: staff and library users. User training for staff can proceed as with many other systems, although, due to the exigencies of the issue desk, much training may need to be conducted on a one-to-one basis. Training for library users is much more difficult to achieve in many libraries. The position is better in academic and organizational libraries than in public libraries, but there is always some fluidity of clientele and, generally, a lack of interest in systematic training. The immediate focus for library users is often on the OPAC and associated CD-ROM products.

- *Interface design* – with sophisticated GUIs, implicit support can often be integrated into the interface design. Appropriate labels in menus, and good icon design, coupled with different interfaces for quick search and advanced search can do much to make the search process intuitive.

- *Help desks*, and other in-person support, available either remotely or at the location where the user is likely to perform the search. These are particularly valuable for problem-solving, troubleshooting and supporting the new user.

EVOLVING AND MIGRATING SYSTEMS

Over the past 20 years technological developments have led to many changes in the systems platforms. Changing the platform on which a database is mounted, or which provides user access to information or knowledge, is a significant project which will affect both operations as conducted by information professional staff and the services available to, and accessed by, users. It is therefore important that the transition from one system to another be managed effectively and efficiently. There are three perspectives on such a transition; those offered by:

- information-systems methodologies
- strategies for the management of change
- strategic information systems planning.

INFORMATION SYSTEMS METHODOLOGIES

An information systems methodology is a methodical approach to information systems planning, analysis and design. A methodology involves recommendations about phases, subphases and tasks; when to use which and their sequence;

what sort of people should perform each task; what documents, products, reports should result from each phase; management, control, evaluation and planning of developments. Information system methodologies have been developed by systems developers and designers as tools to aid in modelling information systems and designing a computer-based system that meets the requirements of the user of the information. The adoption of a systematic approach to information-systems development offers a number of advantages. Broadly the advantages for the manager include:

- control over planning, since progress can be charted, and financial allocations can be predicted
- standardized documentation which assists in communication throughout the systems planning and life
- continuity provided as a contingency against key members of staff leaving the systems staff.

Although information systems methodologies vary, the following five main stages are common:

- definition of objectives
- definition of systems requirements
- design
- implementation
- evaluation.

Figure 13.6 gives a more complete summary of some of the typical elements of such stages.

MANAGING CHANGE

The literature on the management of change recognizes that change will only be successful if people as well as systems change. Information systems have been one of the main levers for change within organizations as we move towards

---

- *Definition of objectives:* Terms of reference developed; initial needs analysis as a study proposal, leads to feasibility study, including evaluation of options and analysis of existing systems.
- *Definition of systems requirements:* Specification of systems requirements.
- *Design phase:* Logical systems model; physical systems model; choice and ordering of hardware and software configuration.
- *Implementation phase:* Planning and preparation; education and training; database creation; system installation; switch-over.
- *Evaluation phase:* Initial evaluation, ongoing monitoring, maintenance, evolution.

Figure 13.6 Summary of stages in systems analysis and design

a knowledge-based society. For many systems users change is one of gradual evolution punctuated by occasional incremental change. Employees, and other users of systems, must feel able to adjust to systems change if they are to continue to create and use the databases upon which the organization of knowledge depends. Users will often have an opportunity to participate in systems changes. In order to allow staff and users to make a positive contribution in a change situation a manager must adopt an appropriate change strategy. Possible change strategies are:

- Directive, where the manager makes a decision and indicates the direction in which he expects change to take place.
- Normative, where the manager seeks to win the 'hearts and minds' of staff and to persuade them to share their vision of the positive value of change.
- Negotiating, where bargaining in the form of: 'if you do this, I will do that', is employed.
- Action centred, where change is tried and experimented with, and introduced on a step-by-step basis without necessarily defining the ultimate outcome in advance.
- Analytical, where the best changes are identified by an expert, say, a consultant, and their advice is taken in selecting the changes.

These strategies have not been discussed extensively in the context of information systems, despite the fact that information systems either within the organization or outside have been responsible for much of the recent change in organizational structure, culture and market-place. This may be because, with information-systems implementation, it is always possible to resort to taking away someone's old systems and presenting them with new systems so that they have no option but to use the new system. In this context it is relatively easy to adopt a focus on the Directive and Analytical strategies. However, without some application of Normative and Negotiating strategies there is not much chance that the user will use the system effectively, and enjoy the experience.

STRATEGIC INFORMATION SYSTEMS PLANNING

Information systems methodologies are a useful tool at the individual project level. In recent years there has been a growing awareness that information systems planning within organizations should be integral to the organization's strategic plan. This has led to developments in the approach to the management of information systems. This approach can be described as strategic information systems planning (SISP). Strategic information systems planning is the process of establishing a programme for the implementation and use of information systems in such a way that it will optimize the effectiveness of the organization's information resources and use them to support the objectives of the whole enterprise as much as possible. The outcomes of an SISP are typically a short-term plan for the next 12 to 18 months, as well as a longer-term plan for the next three to five years. Strategic information systems planning has been evolving over the last ten years, fuelled by the recognition that the hardware/software approach to information systems planning was not producing results either for the information systems department or for the organization as a whole. Put very simply, it has become clear that information systems are so integral to effective management, that managers at all levels, including the very top, need to participate in information systems planning.

The central focus of SISP is the matching of computer applications with the objectives of the organization, so as to maximize the return on investment in information systems. Strategic information systems planning has a dual nature. It covers both detailed planning and budgeting for information systems at one level, and strategic issues and formulation at another. One of the characteristics of SISP is that in some cases it leads management to reassess the appropriateness of the enterprise's objectives and strategies, and it has occasionally been known to lead to major strategic reformulation.

ORGANIZATIONS IN KNOWLEDGE ORGANIZATION AND DELIVERY

The organization of knowledge is achieved through the activities of various information professionals, such as cataloguers, indexers, knowledge workers and others. These individuals are usually employed by organizations, such as libraries, library consortia, abstracting and indexing services, publishers, and Internet search engine providers. Libraries in particular have a long history of collaboration in their efforts to organize knowledge in order to preserve and develop the cultural heritage of our society. In Chapter 11 a number of the organizations that are involved in the organization of knowledge as database producers, publishers and online search services have been discussed. In general, the Internet offers an infrastructure, which supports a wide range of different types of document and information exchange. While these exchanges could be performed on an *ad hoc* basis, they are usually facilitated by the development of a range of relationships, otherwise described as a network. Such networks may comprise users, libraries, national libraries, publishers and a range of other agencies in the information industry. These relationships may be the basis for exchange of, or provision of access to, a range of databases and document types. Figure 13.7 summarizes the key relationship types and Figure 13.8 lists some categories of databases and documents that may be made available through the such networks.

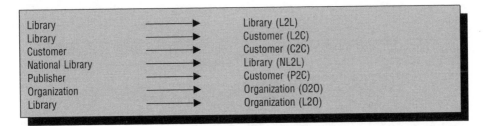

Library	⟶	Library (L2L)
Library	⟶	Customer (L2C)
Customer	⟶	Customer (C2C)
National Library	⟶	Library (NL2L)
Publisher	⟶	Customer (P2C)
Organization	⟶	Organization (O2O)
Library	⟶	Organization (L2O)

Figure 13.7   Relationship types in knowledge networks

Electronic
  E-journals
  CD–ROM documents
  Bibliographic databases
  Reference databases
  Document databases
  Multi-media

Print
  Journals
  Journal articles
  Books
  Indexing and abstracting services

Figure 13.8   Document types covered by knowledge networks

The ultimate aim of most networking is to make documents, information or knowledge accessible to the end-user. However, there may be a number of other relationships in the supply chain, which supports this end-user delivery, including in particular those roles concerned with document creation. Figure 13.9, for example, is a summary of the roles in document creation and delivery, and identifies some of the organizations and individuals that might adopt these roles in the electronic information market-place. It is perhaps particularly significant that some organizations and professional groups may be involved in a number of these stages or, to put it another way, may control several stages in the supply chain.

Librarians have long engaged in cooperative ventures, or networks and consortia. The early objectives of these networks were associated with exchange of catalogue records and print-based document delivery or interlibrary loan. These functions still remain important, but they are now facilitated by electronic exchange of records, and record keeping. Often, print document delivery has been supplemented by electronic document delivery.

Groups of libraries have maintained union catalogues for many years. The

Role	Example
Producers of intellectual content	Authors, illustrators, multimedia creation teams.
Controllers of intellectual content, with reference to quality standards and suitability	Editors, referees, reviewers
Publisher – establishes a corporate brand image and acts as an interface between producers of intellectual content and distributor	Publisher, printer, database producer
Distributor – ensures that the document/ information reaches the potential customers, and engages in appropriate promotion	Library supply agents, booksellers, Web sites, online hosts, Videotex services, Audiotex services, distributors of CD-ROM
Archivers – maintain archival copy for later retrieval	Libraries, private collectors
Re-distributors – make documents or information available to others	Libraries, educational institutions through copying for students, information consultants
Users	Corporate and individual users

Figure 13.9 Stakeholder roles in the electronic information market-place

earliest union catalogues were large card catalogues whose creation was a labour of love and which were very difficult to keep up to date. Similarly, interlibrary loan arrangements existed between libraries long before the latest computer-based systems and data networks. However, under these arrangements, inter-library loan was often a slow process. Cooperation is generally seen as a means of sharing resources or containing cataloguing costs. In recent years, networks have increasingly become dependent upon telecommunication networks and computer systems. The first computer-based cooperative ventures, while ambitious for their time, would seem very basic now. Batch systems, with too much paper, little connectivity between processors and limited online access, predated the much more streamlined systems that it is easy to take for granted today. Systems have undergone major development since the late 1960s and early 1970s. Nevertheless, the central objectives of networking remain constant. These are to:

- reveal the contents of a large number of libraries or a large number of publications especially through accessibility of catalogue databases, using OPAC interfaces
- make the resources shown in these catalogue databases available to individual libraries and users when and where they need them
- share the expense and work involved in creating catalogue databases through the exchange of records and associated activities.

Ancillary functions that might also be fulfilled by networks include:

- distribution and publication of electronic journals and other electronic documents
- end-user access to other databases, such as those available on the online search services and CD-ROM;
- value-added services such as electronic mail, directory services and file transfer
- exchange of bibliographic and authority records, usually in MARC format.

In the beginning networks were established with limited and well-defined objectives. As the use of networking has become more pervasive, and as the infrastructure has become available which makes data transfer more common, consortia and participants in consortia are likely to be linked to other consortia or members in consortia. The end-user can choose more than one route through the maze of networks in order to locate a given document. Barriers are already less defined by the physical limitations of networks than by licensing and access arrangements. Technology imposes few constraints, but politics and economics are beginning to define the boundaries.

The key agencies in library networking fall into two main categories:

1. Large national libraries or centralized cataloguing services which create large bibliographic databases and, in some instances, provide leadership in document delivery.
2. Cooperatives set up by groups of libraries who feel that they and their users can profit by resource-sharing, such as might be associated with interlibrary loans and document delivery, and sharing in the creation of a union catalogue database.

DEVELOPMENTS IN THE USA

The USA is internationally significant in library networking, developments there will be reviewed first. Among the front-runners in US networking and responsible for much of the success of networking is the Library of Congress. The Library of Congress first contributed to networking by acting as a centralized cataloguing service, and distributing printed catalogue cards, commencing in 1901. Experimentation with computer-based systems started in the 1960s with the MARC Project and led to the MARC Distribution Service. The LCMARC database is central to the Library of Congress's cataloguing services. The database is based on the Library of Congress's cataloguing of its own collections, with additional records from cooperating libraries. The database can be accessed online via a number of online search services. The Library of Congress has also played a major part in coordinating networking and has been involved in a number of projects that demonstrate its commitment to cooperation. Two major projects that merit mention are Cooperative Online Serials (CONSER) and the Linked Systems Project (LSP). The CONSER was a cooperative venture, which sought to build a machine-readable database of serials cataloguing information. The LSP, started in 1980, aimed to establish a national network of services and utilities linked by a standard interface.

Another agency in US networking that has made a very major contribution is OCLC, founded in 1971 by a group of college libraries in Ohio. The OCLC has played a major role, both in the USA and beyond, in record supply, research and the sharing of experience. Its original acronym stood for Ohio College Library Center; it is now the Online Computer Library Center. Currently over 33 000 libraries in 65 countries use OCLC services. The OCLC database is the largest catalogue records database in the world. Various services are related to the database; these are summarized in Figure 13.10.

Other networks in the USA and Canada include:

- WLN, known previously as the Western Library Network, and earlier as the Washington Library Network
- RLG, or the Research Libraries Group
- UTLAS International, formerly University of Toronto Library Automation System, is an important Canadian initiative.

As in the USA, the first networking activities in the UK were associated with the centralized cataloguing service. The *British National Bibliography*, which is now the responsibility of the British Library Bibliographic Services Division, was established in 1950. Initially *BNB* was a printed product that listed books received on legal deposit; since 1991 the main classified section contains two sections, a list of forthcoming titles and a list of titles recently received on legal deposit. A MARC distribution service began in 1969, initially based on machine-readable versions of the records in *BNB*, referred to as the BNBMARC database. The BLMARC database now includes many other records generated by other sections of the British Library. The British Library Automated Information Service (BLAISE), is a major avenue through which BLMARC records may be accessed. Alongside these developments, the British Library Document Supply Centre has established itself as one of the leading document delivery agents. The BLDSC supplies 4 million documents a year. Requesting is electronically through the BLDSC's proprietary ART system, although requesting by e-mail is increasing. Requests by every route are stored in the Automated Request Processing, which streams them to the relevant document storage area. Journal articles are then picked from the shelves to be copied or scanned, or selected from the ADONIS electronic journal archive. The British Library's Digital

Reference services:

- OCLC FirstSearch service provides access to more than 75 databases, many of them full-text, with access to more than 1800 electronic journal titles and links to EconLit, MEDLINE, PsycFIRST, PsycINFO, and Social Sciences Abstracts.
- OCLC SiteSearch manages distributed library information resources in the World Wide Web environment.

Collections and technical services:

- OCLC Cataloging and Database Services: a wide range of cataloguing services and options for using WorldCat (the OCLC Online Union Catalog), the world's largest bibliographic database.

OCLC authority control services:

- OCLC Dewey Cutter Macro provides an automatic Cuttering function for Dewey Decimal Classification numbers.
- OCLC Cataloging Label Program allows OCLC Cataloging users to import, display, create, edit, and print labels.
- OCLC Selection Service provides access to multiple resource files, including the Books In Print database and WorldCat, for ordering and acquisitions.
- OCLC TechPro Service provides off-site contract cataloguing and physical processing.
- OCLC Record Transfer Services.
- OCLC CJK Services: access to one of the largest library automation databases of Chinese, Japanese, and Korean (CJK) bibliographic records in the world. Services include: OCLC CJK software, OCLC TechPro, the OCLC AsiaLink service (pre-selected collections of adult and juvenile books), and the OCLC RetroCon® service.
- Cooperative Online Serials Program (CONSER)
- OCLC RetroCon® Services for retrospective conversion.

Resource sharing services: for interlibrary loans, including a Union List Service.

Access services: offer Internet access to OCLC online services, with a range of hardware and software options.

OCLC International: divided into Asia Pacific Services, OCLC Europe, the Middle East and Africa, based in Birmingham, OCLC Latin America and the Caribbean, and OCLC Canada.

OCLC Forest Press Division: publishes the Dewey Decimal Classification and market-related products.

Preservation resources: services to meet the preservation and access needs of libraries, archives, and other institutions.

Figure 13.10 Summary of OCLC services

Library Programme has a priority article alerting service and improved request and delivery from digital store.

Inside Science Plus and Inside Social Sciences and Humanities Plus jointly offer access to the contents of 20 000 journals. Electronic ordering of any articles retrieved from the database is possible. Delivery options include two-hour fax, courier and post.

The British Library's Automated Information Service provides access to over

British National Bibliography 1950–
Library of Congress 1968–
Whitaker (British Books in Print) 1965–
The Stationery Office (formerly HMSO) 1976–
ISSN UK Centre for Serials 1974–

BLAISE also mounts a comprehensive range of British Library catalogues including the complete online holdings of the Document Supply Centre, as well as some specialist databases.

Figure 13.11 BLAISE Bibliographic Files

22 databases containing over 17.5 million bibliographic records. As an online search service access is available either using a command language, or using a GUI on the WWW. A direct link to the British Library Document Supply Centre means that customers can place orders for documents very easily. Figure 13.11 shows the bibliographic files that are available through BLAISE. These can be used for subject searching, bibliographic checking, acquisition, compiling booklists or record supply. The British Library's Automated Information Service also offers access to a number of specialist databases, and the catalogues of the British Library collections.

There are also a number of library networks in the UK. Two long-standing organizations are: BLCMP and LASER.

Formerly known as Birmingham Libraries Co-operative Mechanization Project, BLCMP is a cooperative venture that embraces a range of services that are used by a large number of libraries. The BLCMP maintains extensive MARC databases, which include records for books, audiovisual items, music and serials. An extensive authority file is also maintained. TALIS is BLMCP's library management system. In 1999 BLCMP Library Services Ltd ceased to be a cooperative and was renamed Talis Information Ltd.

The London and South East Region started life with a focus on interlending and resource sharing, rather than on cataloguing. Nevertheless, in order to achieve its objectives it built a large union catalogue, and later a bibliographic database. This is at the heart of LASER's V3.Online service, which provides access to this database and an electronic interlending system. A significant recent development led by LASER has been Electronic Access to Resources in Libraries (EARL). The EARL consortium of UK public libraries was established in 1995 to develop the role of public libraries in providing library and information services over the network. Its membership includes more than 50 per cent of UK public libraries. Examples of EARL initiatives include EARLWeb, a network of public library information resources, and a consortium purchase deal to OCLC's Firstsearch service.

Exchange of expertise and plans for further UK networking have also been fostered by a number of other groups, agencies and activities. The Consortium of University Research Libraries (CURL), for example, succeeded in creating a major machine-readable catalogue database, covering the catalogue records of the UK's seven largest university libraries. The records are available for shared cataloguing and are distributed on tape, using file transfer and capturing session logs. The database is available to other libraries via JANET and via the more recently developed COPAC interface.

The Joint Academic Network (JANET) is not a library network, but a telecom-munication network that provides communication links between users of computing facilities in over 100 universities, research establishments and other institutions. The JANET has been widely exploited by libraries for mutual access to library OPACs, and for file transfer and electronic mail. Gateways are avail-able to other networks such as EARN (European Academic Research Network), Internet (US) and to public data networks.

Bath Information and Data Services (BIDS) is a service offered by the UK Office for Library Networking (UKOLN) which was established in 1989 with funding from the British Library; it is based at the University of Bath. The function of UKOLN is to support the development of networking activities among UK libraries by representing the needs of libraries to the computing and telecom-munication industry, and promoting effective use of existing and developing networking infrastructures in the UK and abroad. The BIDS has played an important role in making electronic databases available at competitive rates within the UK academic community. Key databases are: BIDS ISI Service, BIDS EMBASE Service, BIDS COMPENDEX service, BIDS UnCover service and BIDS Inside Information Service. BIDS is unique in being one of the first national services to offer access to bibliographic databases free at the point of delivery.

The UK Pilot Site Licence Initiative, was instigated by the Joint Information Systems Committee of the Higher Education Funding Councils (JISC). Pub-lishers make their journals available to all universities and colleges throughout the UK, through their own servers. Access to the servers is provided by the JournalsOnLine service hosted by BIDS. JournalsOnLine provides Web access to a search form on which the user selects the publisher and enters the search strategy. The search is made against a headings file at BIDS, which is compiled from publishers' data. On discovering useful documents, the user has the option of requesting them online and taking delivery online. The publishers store their electronic journals in PDF, which preserves the look of the printed counterpart when delivered to the desktop. This project finished in 1998 and is replaced by the National Electronic Site Licence Initiative (NESLI), which is seeking to establish a range of consortium licence arrangement with publishers which will provide access to electronic journals and other documents for UK academic libraries and their users.

Libraries have formed library cooperatives and networks for many decades. Such networks have played a major role in resource sharing and in the development of computerized library management systems. Networks in Europe and the USA, such as BLCMP, LASER, OCLC and WLIN have now been well established since the late 1960s.

Many established library network ventures were early participants in the investigation of potential for computerization and have been major proponents in the development and implementation of library management systems. Cooperation in recent years has been fuelled by the increase in volume of publications, expenses involved in obtaining them and new forms of publication.

Such networks have always been concerned with document delivery. Recently there have been a number of initiatives and projects associated with electronic document delivery. One example of this is the Ariel software, which was developed by RLG. Ariel is a document scanning and transmission system. The software resides on a PC running TCP/IP networking protocol and Windows GUI. It controls a locally attached scanner and printer and can sense and receive scanned documents via FTP. Records for interlending and document request are not dealt with by the system, and need to be separately managed. Ariel has been widely used between libraries within consortia. In the UK it was used in the LAMDA project, which involved four libraries from the M25 Consortium and five from the CALIM consortium. Version 2 of the software, released in 1997, included the option of transmitting documents as Multimedia Internet Mail Extensions (MIME) attachments to Internet mail. The work with Ariel has provided a platform for more ambitious projects that seek to integrate the whole process of information access, from discovery to delivery. Such projects place library consortia in direct competition with online search services. EDIL for example, identified the available mechanism for electronic document delivery, and informed the growing view that Internet standards and electronic mail are the most appropriate approaches to electronic document delivery. The EDDIS developed this further. This project developed an operational system in which users log into a local server, and the server manages access to remote databases and suppliers. Remote systems could be other EDDIS systems or any system that is EDDIS compliant, in the sense that it is implementing the same standards. The EDDIS is designed as an end-user service that integrates document discovery, location, request and receipt available through a WWW interface. In addition, it allows the librarian to control end-user activities transparently by configuring the system with library business policy decisions and by offering varying levels of mediation as part of the service. The local OPAC remains external to the server, along with remote OPAC's and other bibliographic databases. The system might provide access to books and periodical articles in print and digitized form. Projects such as EDDIS have demonstrated that electronic document delivery is possible, but implementation depends upon an acceptance of standards and a critical mass of users. They also illustrate the centrality of the role of major libraries, special collections and library consortia in information access and document delivery.

OTHER COUNTRIES

Similar roles are adopted by national libraries and consortia in other countries in the world. Figure 13.12, for example, summarizes some of the services offered by the National Library of Australia and the Australian Bibliographic Network (ABN).

In conclusion, many of these consortia have made significant contributions to the realization of the electronic library, both through the continuing evolution of library management systems, and through the creation of large shared bibliographic databases which have contributed significantly to the reduction in original cataloguing. Currently such networks are serving as important focal points for developments associated with electronic document delivery, electronic journals and a variety of Web-based facilities which provide access to a wide range of other databases and information resources.

SUMMARY

This chapter has explored a number of issues associated with the management of systems for the organization of knowledge and information retrieval. Evaluation is a key issue for the effective and efficient use of systems and systems development. Key evaluation measures are recall and precision. Evaluation has been conducted by systems developers, in respect of specific systems, and by researchers, in search of general principles that should guide system design. The databases to be searched need to be maintained and updated. Authority control over the form of names and subject terms helps to instil consistency into the database, and thereby assists with database quality. Other issues in the management of systems include maintenance, security and user support. Systems are dynamic; the evolution of systems needs to be managed. Information systems methodologies and other approaches to the management of change can assist in this context. There are many organizations that are involved in the organization of knowledge. Significant among these organizations are the national libraries and the library consortia or networks. These organizations make a significant contribution to the sharing of resources, and the sharing of

The Australian Bibliographic Network provides a range of catalogue, reference and interlibrary loan services to Australian libraries. It has been in operation for 15 years. Its aim is to promote cooperation and resource sharing within the Australian library community.

National Bibliographic Database (NBD): contains over 12 million bibliographic records and 25 million locations. Activities that are supported by ABN are:

- *Copy Cataloguing:* Libraries are able to find between 75% and 90% of their cataloguing on ABN. MARC Records can be received by downline loading through Internet file transfer (MARC*LINK) tapes, diskettes or cartridges (Holdings File Service), or by off screen capture.
- *Catalogue products,* including microfiche catalogues, printed book catalogues, catalogue cards and new title lists.
- *ABN Authorities* can be purchased in their entirety, or as subsets, such as name authorities or authorities relating to library's holding records.
- *Adding and Maintaining Holdings:* Libraries are encouraged to add their holdings to ABN; they receive a credit to be used against subsequent copy cataloguing charges. Libraries can also then use ABN to produce listings of their special collections or other subsets of their collections. This holdings information is central to effective resource sharing. Libraries are also expected to update their holdings statements.
- *Original Cataloguing on ABN:* Libraries are encouraged to contribute to original cataloguing on ABN
- *RLIN Gateway Service* ABN provides a gateway to the Research Libraries Information Network (RLIN). If a record is not available from ABN, a search can be performed on the RLIN database. The record will then be posted to the ABN database.
- *Retrospective Conversions Service,* supports the acquisitions of MARC records for retrospective conversion.
- *ABN Supersearch,* a command driven information retrieval interface, for reference searching and the production of bibliographies.
- *Interlibrary Loan Subsystems:* all incoming requests are filtered through the ABN database, and automatically routed through a list of eight libraries.

Document Delivery services, having 4 components:

- *Interlibrary Loans Subsystem,* as described above.
- *Document Supply Service* (DocSS) drawing on NLA's extensive research collection. Three services are available: the standard service, the fast-track service, and fast track plus. Options for document delivery include photocopy, fax delivery and loans (for monographs and microfilms).
- *Supply 1* is designed for small to medium-sized libraries and businesses and individuals. It draws on world-wide resources, including:
  - NLA's resources
  - UnCover
  - Medline
  - CISTI (Canadian Institute of Scientific and Technical Information), and
  - BLDSC (British Library Document Supply Centre)
- *UnCover Australia* supports the searching of the UnCover multidisciplinary database.

Figure 13.12 Australian Bibliographic Network and the National Library of Australia

the work associated with the compilation of databases that are an essential prerequisite to full access to the resources which can be accessed through a number of different libraries and other information providers.

FURTHER READING

ORGANIZATIONS

Arnold, S. E. (1990) Marketing electronic information: theory, practice and challenges 1980–1990. *Annual Review of Information Science and Technology*, **25**, 87–144.

Barker, P. (1994) Electronic libraries – visions of the future. *Electronic Library*, **12** (4), 221–29.

Barwick, M. (1997) Interlending and document supply: a review of recent literature – XXXII. *Interlending and Document Supply*, **25** (3), 126–32.

Basch, R. (1995) *Electronic Information Delivery: Ensuring Quality and Value.* Aldershot: Gower.

Batt, C. (1997) *Information Technology in Public Libraries*, 6th edn. London: Library Association.

Blunden-Ellis, J. (1997) LAMDA – a project investigating new opportunities in document delivery. *Program*, **30** (4), 385–90.

Boss, R. W. (1990) Linked systems and the online catalog: the role of OSI. *Library Resources and Technical Services*, **34** (2), 217–28.

Boyd, N. (1997) Towards access services: supply times, quality control and performance related services. *Interlending and Document Supply*, **25** (3), 118–23.

Bradley, P. (1997) The information mix: Internet, online or CD-ROM. *Managing Information*, **4** (9), 35–7.

Braid, A. (1996) Standardisation in electronic document delivery: a practical example *Interlending and Document Supply*, **24** (2), 12–18.

Brown, D. J. (1996) *Electronic Publishing and Libraries: Planning for the Impact and Growth to 2003.* London: Bowker-Saur.

Buckland, M. K. and Lynch, C. A. (1988). National and international implications of the Linked Systems Protocol for online bibliographic systems. *Cataloging and Classification Quarterly*, **8** (3/4), 15–33.

Castells, M. (1996) *The Rise of the Network Society.* Oxford: Blackwell.

Cawkell, A. E. (1991) Electronic document supply systems. *Journal of Documentation*, **47** (1), 41–73.

Cousins, S. A. (1997) COPAC: the new national OPAC service based on the CURL database. *Program*, **31** (1), 1–21.

Dempsey, L. (1991) *Libraries Networks and OSI: A Review with a Report on North American Developments.* Bath: UK Office for Library Networking.

Greenaway, J. (1997) Interlending and document supply in Australia: the way forward. *Interlending and Document Supply*, **25** (3), 103–7.

Grosch, A. N. (1995) *Library Information Technologies and Networks.* New York: Marcel Dekker.

King, H. (1995) Walls round the electronic library. *Electronic Library*, **11** (3), 165–74.

Landes, S. (1997) ARIEL document delivery: a cost effective alternative to fax. *Interlending and Document Supply*, **25** (3), 113–17.

Larbey, D. (1997a) Project EDDIS: an approach to integrating document discovery, location, request and supply. *Interlending and Document Supply*, **25** (3), 96–102.

Larbey, D. (1997b) *Electronic Document Delivery.* London: Library and information Technology Centre (Library and Information Briefing 77/78).

Lynch, C. F. (1997) Building the infrastrucutre of resource sharing: union catalogs, distributed search, and cross-database linkage. *Library Trends*, **45** (3), 448–61.

Morrow, T. (1997) BIDS and electronic publishing. *Information Services and Use*, **17** (1), 53–60.

Moulto, R. and Tuck, B. (1994) Document delivery using X.400 electronic mail. *Journals of Information Networking*, 1 (3), 191–203.

Report on Phase 1 of the Evaluation of the UK Pilot Site Licence Initiative. Bristol: Commonwealth Higher Education Management Service, April 1997.

Rowland, F., McKnight, C. and Meadows, J. (eds) (1995) *Project EVLYN*. London: Bowker-Saur.

Rowley, J. E. and Slack, F. S. (1998) New approaches in library networking: reflections on experiences in South Africa. *Journal of Librarianship and Information Science*, 31 (91), March, 33–8.

Smith, P., Stone, P., Campbell, C., Marks, H. and Copeman, H. (1997) EARL: collaboration in networked information and resource sharing services for public libraries in the UK. *Program*, 31 (4), 347–63.

Stone, P. (1990) *JANET: A Report on its Use for Libraries.* London: British Library Research and Development Department (British Library Research Paper 77).

Tuck, B. (1997) Document delivery in an electronic world. *Interlending and Document Supply*, 25 (1), 11–17.

Turner, F. (1995) Document ordering standards: the ILL protocol and Z39.50 item order. *Library Hi-Tech*, 13 (3), 25–38.

Wiesner, M. (1997) EDI between libraries and their suppliers: requirements and first experience based on the EDILIBE project. *Program*, 31 (2), 115–29.

SYSTEMS

Crinnion, J. E. (1992) *Evolutionary Systems Development.* London: Pitman.

Cutts, G. (1991) *Structured Systems Analysis and Design Methodology,* 2nd edn. Oxford: Blackwell.

Harbour, R. T. (1994) *Managing Library Automation.* London: Aslib.

Hughes, M. J. (1992) *A Practical Introduction to Systems Analysis and Design: An Active Learning Approach.* London: DP Publications.

Lester, G. (1992) *Business Information Systems,* Vol. 2, *Systems Analysis and Design.* London: Pitman.

Mason, D. and Willcocks, L. (1994) *Systems Analysis, Systems Design.* Henley-on-Thames: Alfred Waller.

Pachent, G. (1996) Network '95: choosing a third generation automated information system for Suffolk Libraries and Heritage. *Program*, 30 (3), 213–28.

Remenyi, D. S. J. (1991) *Introducing Strategic Information Systems Planning.* Oxford: Blackwell.

Rowley, J. (1990) *Basics of Systems Analysis and Design.* London: Library Association.

Schuyler, M. (ed.) (1991) *The Systems Librarian's Guide to Computers.* Westport, CT: Meckler.

Skidmore, S. (1994) *Introducing Systems Analysis,* 2nd edn. Manchester: NCC/Blackwell.

Vaughan, T. (1994) *Multi-Media; Making it Work,* 2nd edn. Berkeley, CA and London: Osborne McGraw-Hill.

EVALUATION

Basch, R. (1991) My most difficult search. *Database*, 14 (3), June, 65–76.

Bates, M. J. (1988) How to use controlled vocabularies more effectively in online searching. *Online*, 12 (6), November, 45–56.

Bawden, D. (1990) *User-Oriented Evaluation of Information Systems and Services.* Aldershot: Gower.

Borgman, C. L., Hirsh, S. G., Walter, V. A. and Gallagher, A. L. (1995) Children's searching behaviour in browsing and keyword searching online catalogs: the Science Library Catalog Project. *Journal of the American Society for Information Science*, 46 (9), 663–84.

Buckland, M. and Gey, F. (1994) The relationship between recall and precision. *Journal of the American Society for Information Science*, 45 (1), 12–19.

Clarke, S. J. and Willet, P. (1997) Estimating the recall performance of Web search engines. *Aslib Proceedings*, 49 (7), 184–9.

Cleverdon, C. W. (1967) The Cranfield tests on index languages devices. *Aslib Proceedings*, **19** (6), 173–94.

Cousins, S. A. (1992) Enhancing subject access to OPACs: controlled vocabulary versus natural language. *Journal of Documentation*, **48** (3), 291–309.

Felix, D., Graf, W. and Kreuger, H. (1991) User interfaces for public information systems. In H. Bullinge (ed.), *Human Aspects of Computing*. New York: Elsevier.

Fugmann, R. (1982) The complementarity of natural language and indexing languages. *International Classification*, 9 (3), 140–44.

Garzotto, F., Mainetti, L. and Padini, P. (1995) Hypermedia design, analysis, and evaluation issues. *Communications of the ACM*, **38** (8), 74–86.

Gordon, M. D. (1989) Evaluating the effectiveness of information retrieval systems using simulated queries. *Journal of the American Society for Information Science*, **41** (5), 313–23.

Hancock-Beaulieu, M., Fieldhouse, M. and Do, T. (1995) An evaluation of interactive query expansion in an online catalogue with a graphical user interface. *Journal of Documentation*, **51** (3), 225–43.

Hill, S. (1995) *A Practical Introduction to the Human-Computer Interface*. London: DP Publications.

Hix, D. and Hartson, H. R. (1993) *Developing User Interfaces: Ensuring Usability through Product and Process*. New York: Wiley.

Karat, C. M., Campbell, R. and Fiegel, T. (1992) Comparison of the empirical testing and walkthrough methods in user interface evaluation. In P. Bauersfield, J. Bennett and G. Lynch (eds), *Proceedings of ACM HCI '92 Conference of Human Factors in Computing Systems*, pp. 397–404. Monterey, CA: ACM.

Kearsley, G. and Heller, R. S. (1995) Multimedia in public access settings: evaluation issues. *Journal of Educational Multimedia and Hypermedia*, **4** (1), 3–24.

Keen, E. M. and Digger, J. A. (1972) *Report of an Information Science Index Languages Test*. Aberystwyth: Department of Information Retrieval Studies, CLW.

Keen, M. (1997) The OKAPI projects *Journal of Documentation*, **53** (1), 84–7.

Lancaster, F. W. (1969) MEDLARS: report of the evaluation of operating efficiency. *American Documentation*, **20** (2), 119–42.

Mizzaro, S. (1997) Televance: the whole history. *Journal of the American Society for Information Science*, **48** (9), 810–32.

Morley, E. T. (1995) The SilverPlatter experience. *CD-ROM Professional*, **8** (3), March, 111–18.

Robertson, S. E. and Beaulieu, M. (1997) Research and evaluation in information retrieval. *Journal of Documentation* **53** (1), 51–7.

Schamber, L. (1994) Relevance and information behavior. *Annual Review of Information Science*, **29**, 3–48.

Su, L. T. (1992) Evaluation measures for interactive information retrieval. *Information Processing and Management*, **28** (4), 503–16.

Shneiderman, B., Brethauer, D., Plaisant, C. and Potter, R. (1989) Evaluating three museum installations of a hypertext system. *Journal of the American Society for Information Science*, **40** (3), 172–82.

Slack, F. E. (1996) End user searches and search path maps: a discussion. *Library Review*, **45** (2), 41–51.

Index